LANGUAGE MATTERS

Language Matters: Communication, Identity, and Culture is a remarkable collection of timely essays written to emphasize the centrality of language and the social uses of language in all parts of human experience. Perhaps, at no time in human history, has the study of language and the intersection of communication, identity, and culture had a greater impact on the way we pursue our daily routines. The differences we manage across generations, within families, between those with and without power, and in our basic cultural interactions are not only discussed in this text but are placed into the forefront of scholarly debate. I recommend all serious social scholars give this text a serious read.

Jon NUSSBAUM
Professor and Head
Department of Communication Arts & Sciences
Penn State University

An excellent multi-cultural collection emphasizing the pervasive relevance of the cultural to functioning of social identities in face-to-face interaction.

W. Peter ROBINSON
Professor of Social Psychology
University of Bristol

This is a unique and highly informative book. It is unique not only because it specifically highlights the indispensable and crucial role of language in understanding the interactions and relationships between communication, identity, and culture, but also because both Western and Eastern perspectives meet to illuminate those interactions and relationships. It is informative because it is full of creative constructions of new theories and concepts, novel applications and extension of previously formulated ones, and succinct presentations of significant empirical findings. All these make the book a "must" for readers in humanities and social and behavioral sciences.

Kuo-shu YANG
Professor of Psychology
National Taiwan University

This book is an excellent account of the inter-relationships of language, culture and social identity, richly illustrated by real-life examples. Can you imagine that "time is space" is a typical Chinese saying whereas "time is a moving object" is a typical English saying? Why and how do Rap songs draw their support from young people? When you give directions to a foreigner unfamiliar with the city, do you notice that your interpersonal communication is in fact intergroup? These and many other intriguing questions on the communication-culture-identity nexus are addressed by over thirty authors who have contributed to this volume, which will be of great interest to scholars in China as well as around the world.

Ying ZHU
Professor of Psychology
Peking University

Language Matters
Communication,
Identity, and Culture

Edited by

Sik Hung NG
City University of Hong Kong

Christopher N. CANDLIN
Macquarie University

Chi Yue CHIU
University of Illinois, Urbana-Champaign

City University of Hong Kong Press

First published 2004
Printed in Hong Kong

ISBN: 962-937-107-3

Published by
City University of Hong Kong Press
Tat Chee Avenue, Kowloon, Hong Kong

Website: www.cityu.edu.hk/upress
E-mail: upress@cityu.edu.hk

Table of Contents

Section I
Communication

Section II
Cultural Processes

5. Making Sense of Differences:
Language, Culture, and Social Reality
Terry Kit-Fong AU **139**

6. Symbols and Interactions:
Application of the CCC Model
to Culture, Language, and Social Identity
Chi Yue CHIU and Jing CHEN **155**

Section III
Social Identity

Section IV
Communicating Culture and Identity
in Natural Social Settings

17. Improving the Evaluation of Mentoring Programs

18. Discursive Construction of Knowledge and Narratives about Gangster Youth:
A Critical Discourse Analysis of Social Work Research Interviews

19. Rap Lyrics and Antisocial Effects on Young People in Hong Kong

Language Matters:

Communication, Identity, and Culture

Communication, Culture, and Identity: Overview and Synthesis

Sik Hung NG
Chi Yue CHIU
Christopher N. CANDLIN

This volume is both a record and extension of the interflow of ideas at the 8th International Conference on Language and Social Psychology held in Hong Kong in 2002. Most of the twenty chapters herein are selected from papers presented at the Conference. In this sense, the present volume is a record of the Conference, which, like its predecessors since 1979, was dedicated to enriching the "diversity of perspectives focusing on the intersection of language and social behavior and experience."

The papers so selected have since been revised, extensively in some cases, to take note of comments made during the Conference as well as from reviewers. As a means of extending and broadening the scope of the Conference, a few additional chapters have been solicited by the editors to complement and strengthen the discussion of those themes that now serve to structure the contents of this volume.

The book as a whole is about language use, that *language matters* greatly in almost every aspect of human behavior and experience. Biologically and culturally, humans are powerfully equipped to acquire language and to use it for a variety of cognitive and social purposes. It is, however, with the social uses to which language is put, and not so much with its cognitive counterpart, that the present volume is centrally concerned. It goes without saying, of course, that the cognitive and the social are interwoven, and hence the present stress on the social is only relative and does not preclude cognitive consideration. Indeed, several chapters take such a cognitive position.

This central focus on language will be elaborated along the themes of *communication, culture* and *identity,* each based on four chapters. The three themes interact to a certain extent, and hence are not rigidly exclusive of one another, although the chapters are grouped under only one heading for presentation purposes.

A conspicuous feature of the Conference was the large number of paper presentations that provided many real-life illustrations of the ways in which communication, culture and identity interact. This interaction itself constituted an important additional theme, voiced by a number of presentations, and to this end we have identified the communication of culture and identity in real-life contexts explicitly as a fourth theme in the book.

In what follows we provide an overview of the chapters and from this suggest a theoretical framework within which one may approach the complex inter-relationship of communication, culture and identity.

Overview

Communication

Seemingly interpersonal communication may turn out to be intergroup encounters. For example, giving directions to a foreigner who is unfamiliar with the city, or to a fellow citizen in wheelchair, may be on the surface a straightforward interpersonal encounter. Yet on the closer scrutiny offered by linguistic and discourse analyses, such communicative exchanges are often scripted in the format of "secondary baby talk," a typical mode of group-based communication triggered by social stereotypes that override individuality.

Extending this intergroup communication approach, Abrams and Giles (Chapter 1) develop a model for understanding how heterosexuals can exclude gays and lesbians at various language and communicative levels. In a similar vein, Palmores, Reid and Bradac (Chapter 2) offer an account of gender-linked communicative behavior based on self-categorization and the concept of gender identity salience. Watson and Gallois (Chapter 3), working from communication accommodation theory (CAT), extend the proposition of an optimal balance of intergroup and interpersonal salience to communicative exchanges in a medical setting and further argue that a combination of high intergroup and high interpersonal salience is conducive to positive medical talk. Also working from CAT, Williams, Garrett and Tenant (Chapter 4) report results showing, among other things, that young adults (aged 18 to 25 years old) view interaction with (younger) teenagers in intergroup terms.

As a whole, the four chapters attest to the prominence of an intergroup approach to communication, most notably CAT, and cognate theories such as self-categorization theory. It is refreshing to see a number of examples here of cross-fertilization. For example, linkages are made with terror management theory (Chapter 1), as well as gender-as-culture and dominance theories (Chapter 2). The role of emotional expression as a sociolinguistic strategy in CAT has been elaborated to an extent greater than in previous accounts (Chapter 3), while lifespan developmental communication, itself an important topic in intergenerational communication, is juxtaposed alongside CAT for a fuller interpretation of young adults' perception and satisfaction of communication with teenagers (Chapter 4).

Cultural Processes

Human culture, in contrast to anima cultures, is so intimately embedded in language, and language in culture, that much about language use can be learnt from cross-cultural differences, and *vice versa*. Au (Chapter 5) makes the point that as more and more cross-cultural differences are found, to take stock and make sense of them is no longer just a matter of fun or curiosity, but is a serious scholarly pursuit in itself. She narrates examples from the field of language acquisition to infer insights on how cross-cultural (and cross-linguistic) differences might be approached. Following on from this, in Chapter 6 Chiu and Chen propose a culture-carrier-context (CCC) model to explicate the complex yet orderly inter-relationship of language, culture and social identity. Whilst CCC harks back to George Herbert Mead's symbolic interactionism (Mead, 1934), much of it is based on cultural dynamical research that has been conducted in recent years.

Authors of two follow-on chapters each deals with a specific aspect of culture in the culture-communication-identity nexus. Ota (Chapter 7) argues, on the basis of recent cross-cultural studies on intergenerational communication in Pacific Rim nations, that similarities and differences in communication experiences are cross-cutting among the nations in ways more complex than can be accommodated by some simple East-West dichotomy. Sources of such cross-age and cross-national communication differences include culture-based norms of respect for elders, and a number of intergroup variables relating to the vitalities, identities and stereotypes of different age groups. Zhou (Chapter 8) looks at the metaphorical representation of time in China and England. Both cultures have similar structural dimensions, eleven in all, of time metaphors. Their prototypical metaphors, however, differ. For example, it is claimed that "Time is space" is more characteristic of Chinese whereas "Time is a moving object" is more characteristic of English culture.

Identity

The social identity perspective (Tajfel, 1974), best known for its seminal influence on the study of intergroup relations, has also inspired the development of an intergroup approach to language and communication most clearly represented by communication accommodation theory (e.g., Chapters 1 to 4). In recent years, as Hogg (Chapter 9) has noted, there appears to have been a "drifting apart" of the social identity perspective on the one hand and the study of language and communication on the other. In part this is due to a deepening of the social cognitive emphasis in contemporary social identity research, but also because of the rapid expansion of language and communication studies towards a more discursive direction. Whatever the historical reasons, the potential for integration or cross-fertilization remains. After reviewing some of the historical reasons, Hogg focuses on recent social identity analysis of deviance and of leadership to illustrate the potential benefits that a closer engagement with research on language and communication would bring.

Noels, Clément and Gaudet (Chapter 10) discuss aspects of a ten-year research programme on the relations between language and ethnic identity, to show how the expression of different patterns of identity is contextually grounded in ethnolinguistic vitality of the language group and the intimacy of the immediate interpersonal situation. For example, although the heritage ethnic identity is likely to be sheltered in more intimate settings, such a sheltering effect is limited in the case of minority group members.

The next two chapters are concerned with the formation or emergence of new identities. In their ethnographic study of social support in a multigenerational community of women, Pitts and Kundrat (Chapter 11) identify seven perceived functions of social support (e.g., encouraging communication, sustaining independence). These functions are related to the formation of the "Montrose Women" social identity and the concomitant transformation of a collection of women into a cohesive community that functions as an effective social support network. A different kind of new identity, one that emerges in the globalization of tourism, is proposed by Jaworski and Thurlow (Chapter 12). The authors look at language use in tourist-host interaction and in tourism discourse (inflight magazines, TV holiday programmes, and so forth) to analyse the role of language and other semiotic resources in packaging tourism as a global cultural industry while promoting the emergency of more parochial identities of tourists-travellers.

Communicating Culture and Identity in Natural Social Settings

A particular strength of this book is that it provides many real-life illustrations of the interaction of communication, culture and identity. Examples already noted are the analysis of tourist experience (Chapters 12), the formation of a women's group for social support (Chapter 11), and the application of CAT in gender, medical and peer communication (Chapters 1 to 4). There are many more, and we bring these together under the heading of natural social settings to highlight their emphasis on real-life situations and issues.

Ill health and caregiver identity are the foci of two chapters by Savundranayagam and Hummert (Chapter 13) and by Gallois (Chapter 14), respectively. The former explores how language deterioration associated with dementia makes it difficult for family caregivers to maintain their spousal or filial identities, and as a result, makes caregiving a stressful experience for many caregivers. Gallois' chapter, on the other hand, is directed toward the management of disability, which has become an increasingly widespread problem for older adults in the context of individual longevity and population ageing. Existing literature shows that stereotypes about disability reproduces itself in communication that healthcare providers and the general public have with patients. Such stereotype-based communication evokes reciprocal communication by patients, thus validating those stereotypes. The vicious cycle of communication predicament may then aggravate health outcomes, and inculcate a negative stereotype in the patient's social identity.

The next group of chapters deal with mentoring and mentor-mentee communication. As Kalbfleisch (Chapter 15) has noted, although mentors and protégés may have different linguistic referents in different cultures, the concept of someone helping another to succeed is part of being human. Three specific forms of mentoring relationship are explored in as many chapters. On the basis of her theory of communication in mentoring relationships, Kalbfleisch argues that the success of initiating mentoring relationships depends on the kind of language used. By first couching requests for help in terms of task-specific requests, protégés will be more likely to succeed in developing a mentoring relationship in stages rather than abruptly. Preliminary results from students in a multi-ethnic university indicate that most protégés used the language of specific requests, but the eventual success of this strategy remains to be seen.

Pawson and Gibbes (Chapter 16) investigate the potential role of mentoring in reducing recidivism among youth offenders. Their results highlight, among others, the need for a model wherein social psychological and criminological evidence is integrated for evaluating processes and outcomes of mentor-based interventions. The challenge of assessing the effectiveness of mentoring programmes for youths who are at-risk is further discussed by Renger (Chapter 17). He proposes a three-step approach to address, first, antecedent conditions contributing to youths' problem behavior; second, activities targeting the antecedent conditions; and third, measurable changes in the antecedent conditions (rather than endpoints).

The strong focus on youths in Chapters 16 and 17 continues in the next two chapters. Lin and Lo (Chapter 18) report interviews of young gang members conducted by social work researchers to show how negative knowledge and narratives about youths are constructed through interviewers' discursive control of the interviews and, interestingly, how some youngsters contest those discursive constructions. From lessons based on their critical discourse analysis, Lin and Lo highlight the need for social work to adopt a critical, reflexive stance toward its role as a discipline and a helping profession.

Rap songs, as part of a youth subculture, draw their support from young people in various ways. One such way, Cheung (Chapter 19) infers from terror management theory, is that young people who are conscious of death would endorse anti-social lyrics in rap songs for self-defence and tension-reduction. By manipulating terror or death awareness in an experiment, Cheung obtains results that support the prediction above whilst revealing complex relations among death awareness, liking of rap songs and anti-social lyrics in rap songs.

Thus far, the theme of communicating culture and identity in natural social settings has centred on issues of health and disability, mentoring, and youths. The final chapter by Noller and Feenay (Chapter 20) draws attention to families. Of concern to the authors are families with adolescents wherein patterns of social and communicative relationship are no longer confined to spousal (marital) relationship, but also include those between parent-child and between siblings. To understand how the mosaic of relationships is interwoven, and how components thereof mutually affect each other, is a tall order for research. Noller and Feenay approach the task from family systems theory and provide an integrative review of a large number of studies on family conflict. A strong theme emerging from the review is the bi-directional, or even circular, pattern of influence from parents to children to siblings and to parents. Another theme concerns the role of social comparison among adolescents and negative emotions arising from unfavourable comparisons with a sibling on an activity central to their identities. The rich array of findings demonstrates, once again and to varying degrees, the subtle contextual influence of communication and identity on family culture.

A Theoretical Model
of Communication, Culture, and Identity

In the past three decades, inspired by the seminal works of Nobel laureate Kahneman and other psychologists, many social psychologists have invested their psychological imagination in the search for distinctive and novel phenomena. With a new surge of energy, the discipline has been able to produce a range of excellent outcomes. The recent edition of the *Handbook of Social Psychology* (Gilbert, Fiske, & Lindzey, 1998), for example, is replete with numerous newly discovered social psychological phenomena to which corresponding mini theories have been associated. Unfortunately, such mini theories that have been proposed with their attendant phenomena are also limited by a restricted focus on the phenomena themselves, and, in consequence seldom manage to achieve the status of a comprehensive theory. Reflecting this, much recent social psychology presents itself as a discipline rich in phenomena yet wanting in integration. A similar situation applies to research at the intersection of language and social behavior. The new edition of the *Handbook of Language and Social Psychology* (Robinson & Giles, 2001), one of the benchmarks in the field of language and social psychology, is remarkably similar to the *Handbook of Social Psychology* for its richness in the presentation of language behavior phenomena running ahead of theoretical integration.

As we review the ideas and research findings presented in this volume, we are struck by their richness and tempted by the challenge they present for such integration. In the final part of this introduction, we take up the challenge to construct some broad integrated principles of social action. In doing so, we make use of theories already cited or elaborated by the contributors, such as communication accommodation theory, system justification theory, self-categorization theory and others, and also introduce ideas of our own.

The Basic Model

Contributors to the present volume are from diverse intellectual traditions. Nonetheless, they share several assumptions about the nature of human sociality that inform the theoretical model to be developed below. A basic assumption is that people live in a collectively constructed social environment, which in our view consists of at least two components: (a) shared knowledge of social practices and their meanings, and (b) structures of social actions (e.g., distribution of power and status, level of formality, structure of interdependency). The first component is often referred to as symbolic or interpretive culture. The second component evolves from the collective material (e.g., subsistence strategies, economic system) and institutional-social cultures (e.g., kinship system, social class).

Within the collectively constructed social environment, people interact and communicate with each other, and align themselves as members of various social practices. Through their social experiences, people define their selves in terms of who they are in relation to others (personal identity), and which groups they belong or do not belong to (social identity). Both personal identity and social identity are socially constructed, mediated by language, and embedded in culture.

Social groups and their histories, statuses, and other structural properties define to a large extent the structure of social actions in society. By categorizing the self as a member of certain social groups, individuals acquire a sense of their group-based position in society and cognitively represent it relative to that of others. Thus, membership in privileged groups is a source of collective self-esteem that confers tangible and intangible benefits on its members. In addition, group norms and patterns of intergroup relation provide structure and order in one's social life, as well as behavioral guidelines for navigating social situations. In short, participation in social groups is a social process whereby people fulfill some basic psychological needs, such as uncertainty reduction, self-verification, and self-enhancement (see here Hogg's chapter).

Besides identity-related activities, people negotiate and discursively construct shared meanings in their interactions with others. Meanings arise from categorization. Thus, people respond to their own and others' social categories, as they do to the meanings of other people's communicative actions.

Social identities, shared knowledge, and structures of social actions are collective phenomena that cannot be reduced to individual psychology. Together, they constitute a person's socially based reality. Individuals may mentally represent the social reality as (a) internalized personal beliefs and values, (b) beliefs, values, and practices characteristic of another person or a collection of people, or (c) beliefs, values, and practices characteristic of the generalized other. When these cognitive representations are accessed and have become salient in the behavioral context, the corresponding social reality exercises its influence on individual behavior, and becomes validated and reproduced as people engage in interpersonal and intergroup communication. However, the maintenance and reproduction of shared reality is not unproblematic. More often than not, it involves negotiation as different individuals and groups contest or change the meanings of current practices or social arrangements.

The social reality, social actions, and individual's psychological experiences in social interactions are interconnected. Causal influences are typically bidirectional or reciprocal in nature. Figure 1 depicts a sketchy outline of what an integrated theoretical model of social actions might be represented. Language (or more specifically, discourse), as a primary medium for representing, communicating, and negotiating meanings in social interactions, is implicated in every aspect and connection point in the model. In short, language ties social identity, culture, and social actions together within a framework of human communication.

The shaded cross in the middle of Figure 1 represents language, broadly defined as a system of signs or symbols used to convey meanings. Here, we are concerned primarily with human languages, which involve all human-made mimetic, phonetic, and external symbols. To that extent language might be better formulated as discourse or even as semiotics since it is not restricted to the formal linguistic codes of verbal texts. Mimetic symbols emerged at speciation of *Homo erectus*, when early hominoids used their entire body to communicate meanings. Phonetic signs started to emerge at the speciation of *Homo sapiens*, and external symbols (e.g., painting, written languages) began to surface at the early Stone Age when external memory devices began to appear.

To emphasize that communication always involves the use of language, we embed the box representing communicative actions in the shaded cross. There are substantial overlaps in the shaded cross

Figure 1
Language matters: Dynamic interactions of communication, identity, and culture

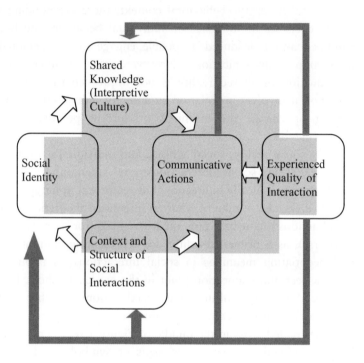

and boxes representing social identity, shared knowledge, structure of social interactions, and interactional experience, signifying that language is used or implicated in all these processes. Much shared knowledge in an ethnolinguistic group is encoded and carried in the language of the group. In her chapter, Zhou shows that in the English language, the most coherent group of metaphors of time represents time as bounded objects that travel speedily in space (e.g., whirligig, winged chariot, ship). Such metaphorical representations render the perception of time as something that is meant to be caught and yet is difficult to catch. In the Chinese language, the most coherent group of metaphors of time represents time as a boundless bearer of undefined or ill-defined objects, memories and emotions. These metaphors render the perception of time as a boundless container that extends in space, with an unlimited capacity for carrying human memories, experiences, and emotions.

The fact that language is a carrier of shared knowledge does not imply that language stands in any isomorphic relation to shared knowledge (or culture). Further, as Au maintains in her chapter, any attempt to achieve understanding of language or culture by describing static language or cultural differences is bound to fail. Language is dynamic, and so is culture. As people use language and shared knowledge in social interactions to construct their social life, shared knowledge will evolve, and the meanings encoded in language will be reconstituted (see chapter by Chiu and Chen).

In the Basic Model shown in Figure 1, the arrows represent the reciprocal causal relationships among the depicted theoretical constructs. To foreshadow the untangling of the reciprocal relationships for analytical purposes, Figure 1 distinguishes notched arrows and bidirectional arrows from bent arrows. Notched arrows and bidirectional arrows represent micro processes whereby the interaction context embedded in a preformed structure of social interaction, together with the individual's identity and shared knowledge, jointly influence communicative actions and the experienced quality of interactions. Conversely, bent arrows represent the constitutive and reconstituting roles of communicative actions and experienced quality of interactions in social identity, shared knowledge, and structure of social interactions. In the next two sections, we first attempt to explain communication actions and experiences of social interactions (in terms of social identity and other variables), and then, by reversing the causal direction, attempt to make use of communication actions and experiences of social interactions for explaining social identity and other variables in the model.

Explaining Communicative Actions

As shown in Figure 2, social identity, shared knowledge, and the context and structure of social interactions are key variables in the model for explaining communicative actions. The roles of these variables will be elaborated below, followed by a separate section on the experienced quality of interactions.

Figure 2
Explaining communicative actions and experiences of social interactions

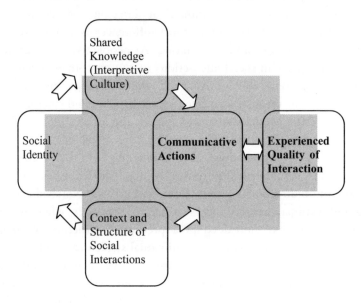

Roles of Social Identity and Shared Knowledge

Social identity evokes relevant shared knowledge including shared beliefs that people hold about attributes characteristic of a social group. Such beliefs may be organized into group stereotypes (chapter by Gallois). A group stereotype consists of a complex of over-generalized positive and/or negative attributes. Social stigmas can be regarded as shared representations of groups attached with strong negative evaluations (chapter by Abrams and Giles). When a person is treated as a member of a particular group, the person's group identity takes precedence over her/his personal identity in defining the person in the behavioral context, and stereotypic qualities are attributed to the person. The shared stereotype, once activated, may be drawn upon to guide communication with the person. The present volume contains many concrete illustrations of this process. For instance, Abrams and Giles describe how the gay and lesbian identities evoke stigmatized representations of these groups. When heterosexuals interact with a gay man or a lesbian woman, they may regard their interlocutor as a member of a stigmatized group and, as a consequence, may be inclined to adopt a divergent communication strategy.

Much shared knowledge about a social category is highly contextualized. For example, as pointed out by Palmores, Reid and Bradac in their chapter, men are expected to dominate in some contexts and be submissive in other contexts, and the same can be said about women. In addition, men and women are expected to cooperate with each other in some situations and compete with each other in different situations.

Every society is situated in a unique social historical context. The same social identity may be given different meanings in different societies, and in different institutions within a given society. For instance, as Ota points out, in Asian countries, younger people are expected to show deference to older adults. This expectation is not as strong in Western countries. Such cultural differences may account for some East-West differences in the way intergenerational communication is conducted and experienced. In a multicultural society, the meeting of knowledge from different cultures may highlight cultural contrasts and trigger a meaning negotiation process that fuels cultural change.

Roles of Context

Communicative actions invariably take place within a social context. Social identities influence communicative actions only in contexts where social identities are salient (see the chapter by Chiu and Chen). For example, gender differences in communication emerge in contexts where gender identity is salient and disappear when it is not (see the chapter by Palmores, Reid and Bradac).

Environmental cueing can increase the accessibility of certain items of shared knowledge. However, as pointed out by Chiu and Chen, knowledge that is accessed will direct communication only when it is currently applicable. Thus, when men and women communicate, a particular context may render a cooperative communication strategy accessible or applicable, while another may call for a competitive strategy (see the chapter by Palmores, Reid and Bradac).

The context may also render a psychological motive salient. People are particularly likely to rely on their social identity when they face uncertainty (see the chapter by Hogg) or existential anxiety. Research has shown that reminding people of their mortality increases their reliance on shared knowledge or established worldviews. They also become particularly intolerant of deviant practices. For instance, as shown in Cheung's study, mortality awareness may diminish university students' liking of rap music as a counter subculture.

Psychological Responses to Communication: Experienced Quality of Interactions

Interpersonal relationships are constructed and negotiated in the process of communication. This negotiation is particularly intense when individuals from different social categories communicate with each other. In an intergroup context, as Williams, Garrett, and Tennant have pointed out, an individual may be treated as a member of her/his social category (as when young adults communicate with an adolescent), and/or an individual person (as when young adults communicate with their peers). In addition, communication can be characterized by positive interdependence (cooperation, mutual support) or negative interdependence (hostile competition). When an individual is treated as a member of a social category, speech accommodation communicates an orientation towards positive interdependence, whereas non-accommodation such as speech divergence communicates an orientation towards negative interdependence. When an individual is treated as an individual, expressed interest in and concern for the individual communicate an intention to foster positive interdependence and to avoid negative interdependence (see the chapter by Watsons and Gallois).

Individuals may respond to a particular communication strategy in different ways. In general, Deutsch's (1985) simple law of social interaction holds: the psychological orientation brought into a social interaction is reinforced as the result of the interaction. Noller and Feeney's in-depth studies of family interactions offer many illustrations of this law. Similarly, Williams, Garrett, and Tennant found that young adults experience a higher level of satisfaction in their interaction when their interaction partners display more frequently speech accommodation and positive emotions. This is the case regardless of whether the interaction partner is a peer or a younger adolescent. In short, positive feelings ensue from communication that fosters positive interdependence, whereas negative feelings result from communication that promotes negative interdependence.

The above generalization applies to communication in helping relationships. In the Watson and Gallois studies, patients reported more satisfactory relationships with healthcare providers who expressed interest in and concern for them as individuals. Watson and Gallois also found that in a medical setting, patients expect from health providers professional service congruent with their professional identities. Thus, an optimal balance of interpersonal and intergroup salience in communication may be most advantageous to the construction of congenial healthcare provider-patient relationships. Similarly, in the mentor-protégé relationship, protégés who can identify specific rather than diffused contributions from prospective mentoring are better able to individuate the role relation (see the chapter by Kalbfleisch). The mentor-protégé relationship established on this basis provides valuable support and resources, particularly for buffering developmental risks of socially disadvantaged youths (see the chapter by Pawson and Gibbes), although evaluating the effectiveness of mentorship programs could be a tricky business (see the chapter by Renger).

Explaining the Structure of Social Interactions, Social Identity, and Shared Knowledge

To complete the picture, we now constitute the structure of social interactions, social identity, and shared knowledge as objects of explanation.

Figure 3
Explaining structure of social interactions, social identity, and shared knowledge

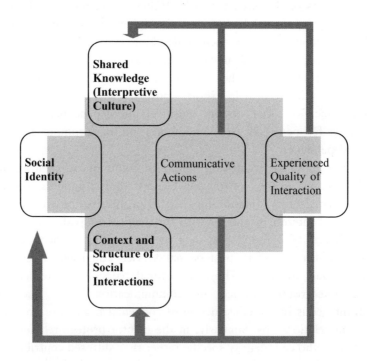

Explaining the Structure of Social Interactions

Structures of actions and intergroup relations are useful for self-verification, uncertainty reduction, and for various other social purposes. Yet, these structures are useful only when they are relatively stable and legitimate. Thus, both dominant and dominated groups, especially the former, have a vested interest in maintaining current social arrangements through conscious or unconscious engagement in system justification behavior. As pointed out by various authors, members of dominant groups are driven by self-enhancement (see the chapter by Hogg) and ingroup enhancement (see the chapter by Abrams and Giles) motives to maintain a divergent strategy in their interactions with subordinate groups. More often than not, members of stigmatized groups may internalize the same (negative) intergroup attitudes expressed in the dominant group's divergent communication strategy (see chapters by Abrams and Giles, and by Lin and Lo). In this way intergroup communication may preserve and reinforce intergroup distinctions directly, and through this, contribute indirectly to the maintenance of existing social stratification and power/status distribution.

There are other forces acting to preserve the status quo, one of which is communication disadvantage. For stigmatized and minority groups, their disadvantage in public communication through lack of access to mass media deprives them of a voice that may otherwise effect changes to the status quo (see chapter by Abrams & Giles). This raises the important question of psycho-social change and how it may be effected.

Psycho-social change has important psychological implications at both societal and personal levels. At the societal level, psycho-social change involves redistribution of normative structures and/or shared meanings in formal and informal institutions and life practices, as well as alignment of old social and life practices with the redistributed norms and shared meanings. At the personal level, psycho-social change may result in the modification of a person's cultural frame, the development of alternative cultural frames, and just as important, the redefinition of identities. It is the latter, more personal level of change that will concern us here.

Many routes lead to psycho-social change. From the perspective of the present model, change is initiated when new normative structures and/or shared meanings are brought into contact with established ones in society. This admittedly narrow view of change allows us to explore the roles of communication in initiating personal change, a task that we shall attempt exploring in the remaining sections of this introduction.

Explaining Social Identity

To a large extent, social identity is a discursive construction. In their chapter, Jaworski and Thurlow describe how the new "international citizen" identity is constructed and romanticized in tourism discourse. As tourists participate in international travel, they are socialized into the reality represented in inflight magazines, newspaper travelogues, and television holiday programs. The language and rhetoric used provide the semiotic materials for constructing a global identity while simultaneously shaping and bolstering a relatively parochial identity.

Pitts and Kundrat's study of Montrose women illustrates the sequence of collaborative events comprising communicative and other social actions that have led to the emergence of a new social identity. The Montrose women live in a multigenerational community that provides positive communication and social support to each other. The positive feelings ensued foster the development of a sense of community and shared identity. In short, as people communicate with a new group, they develop a new identity.

Paradoxically, the link between communication and identity is most obvious when communication breaks down. As the mental condition of a demented person deteriorates, the patient's family members will find it increasingly difficult to maintain meaningful communication with the patient, which is vital to safegurading their familial identities. In response to the patient's communication disorder, some family members may start to construct a new caregiver identity that does not require direct communication with the patient (see the chapter by Savundranayagam and Hummert).

Identity change also occurs in immigrant populations and minority groups, in part mediated by the tendency to accommodate one's identity to that of the interaction partner, whereby validating one's own (see the chapter by Noels, Clement, and Gaudet). When immigrant or minority groups are surrounded by members of the mainstream group at work or in other public domains, they gradually strengthen their identification with the latter. In other contexts (e.g., family) where they interact primarily with members of their own ethnolinguistic groups, they may be able to retain their ethnolinguistic identity. This is exactly what Noels, Clement, and Gaudet have discovered in their study of ethnocultural identification among international students and minority groups in Canada.

Explaining Shared Knowledge

Through communication, shared meanings are negotiated, reproduced, and transformed. In their chapter, Chiu and Chen maintain that when people interact with each other, more widely shared knowledge has a greater probability of being evoked in communication and reproduced in social interactions, a greater persuasive force, and greater influence on how people define social reality.

Communication also serves to perpetuate group norms and shared knowledge about a group. Through communication, members of a group collaborate to establish prototypical group roles. For example, prototypical representations of leaders and deviants define the shared values and norms central to the group's identity (see Hogg's chapter).

However, communication also provides a mechanism for changing shared knowledge in society. On some occasions, members of a stigmatized group may contest the meanings mainstream people attribute to them, as Lin and Lo have observed in their analysis of conversations between gangster youths and social workers. Gallois offers another example of how members of disadvantaged groups (people with disabilities) contest the meanings assigned to their group. They may do so by developing communicative strategies intended to induce treatment of them as individuals rather than as members of a disabled group. Alternatively, they may develop communicative strategies to change popular assumptions of the disabled.

Final Remarks

Henri Tajfel (1981) once wrote, "the aim of a theory of intergroup behaviour is to help us understand certain selected uniformities of social behaviour. In order to do this, we must know (i) something about the ways in which groups are constructed in a particular system; (ii) what are the psychological effects of these constructions; and (iii) how the constructions and their effects depend upon, and relate to, forms of social reality." (p. 46). In a similar vein, we believe social actions must be understood with reference to their structure and the social reality within which they are situated. We further propose that through the use of language as discourse, the interactive consequences of structures of social actions and social reality are expressed in communicative actions. As the construction of shared meanings is a collaborative process as well as a collective project, here too language, or semiotics more broadly, provides a set of shared symbols for constructing shared meanings, the collective consciousness, and group identities. Finally, language plays a pivotal role in constituting and reproducing the existing structures of social actions and social reality. In all these, *language matters*, a theme that we believe has been richly illustrated by authors who have contributed generously to this book.

As editors, our own contribution is no more than to overview and outline some social psychological and communication principles to integrate the diverse ideas and findings presented by the contributing authors. In doing so, we have been reminded once again of the need for a theory that explains not only stability and the status quo, important though they are, but also allows for, and accounts for psycho-social change. The latter, as Serge Moscovici (1976) has argued so passionately, should be taken seriously. To explain how language matters in effecting change as well as maintaining stability is an ideal to which we aspire, but one that still remains somewhat remote from the theoretical model that we have developed here. Hopefully, the model will stimulate further attempts to construct comprehensive theories that will bring the fascinating phenomena of communication, culture and identity under a unified conceptual framework.

Acknowledgments

Many colleagues have helped to review the chapters right from the very beginning of screening and selecting papers for presentation at the 8th International Conference on Language and Social Psychology. For this we thank Pamela Kalbfleisch, Rodrigue Landry, Susan McKay, Jon Nussbaum, Jeff Pittam, Itesch Sachdev, Crispin Thurlow, and Angie Williams. The final production of this book has benefited greatly from the encouragement and editorial assistance given by Patrick Kwong, Vivian Lee, Christine Lam and Betty So, as well as from the financial support of the City University of Hong Kong (Grant 9380024).

References

Deutsch, M. (1985). *Distributive justice: A social-psychological perspective.* New Haven, CT: Yale University Press

Gilbert, D. Y., Fiske, S.T., & Lindzey, G. (Eds.) (1998). *The handbook of social psychology.* New York: McGraw-Hill.

Mead, G. H. (1934). *On social psychology.* Chicago, IL: University of Chicago Press.

Moscovici, S. (1976). *Social influence and social change.* London, UK: Academic Press.

Robinson, W. P., & Giles, H. (Eds.) (2001). *The new handbook of language and social psychology.* Chichester, UK: John Wiley.

Tajfel, H. (1974). Social identity and intergroup behavior. *Social Sciences Information, 13*, April, 65–93.

Tajfel, H. (1981). *Human groups and social categories: Studies in social psychology.* Cambridge, UK: Cambridge University Press.

Section I

Communication

1

An Intergroup Approach to Communicating Stigma: Gays and Lesbians

Jessica R. ABRAMS
Howard GILES

Over the years, social psychologists have devoted effort to studying stigma. However, endeavors to uncover how stigma is *communicated* have been slow (see, however, Cox & Gallois, 1996; Pittam & Gallois, 2000). The goal of the present paper is both to critically analyze as well as invigorate the available (admittedly American) literature from a language and intergroup communication perspective. Although Crocker, Major, and Steele (1998) claim there is no defining set of features that exclusively indicate a social group is stigmatized, they suggest the stigmatized share some common features. Some prototypical features include "being the target of negative stereotypes, being rejected interpersonally, and being discriminated against" (p. 505). From our perspective, these "features" are inherently communicative. Similarly, pejorative names, media messages, institutional practices, and so forth all are instrumental in communicating and languaging stigma.

Crocker *et al.* (1998) offer four theoretical approaches (self-enhancement, terror management, ingroup enhancement, and system justification) to explain the value stigmatizing serves for the individual who stigmatizes. We explore and analyze each of these approaches. Consistent with our contention that communication occurs on many different levels, the theories also explain the value of stigma on the interpersonal, intergroup, or system/societal level. Because little to no effort has been made to examine critically which of these theoretical approaches offers researchers the most explanatory power, we argue that since the self-concept is inextricably linked to one's social group membership, an intergroup communication approach (e.g., Tajfel & Turner, 1986; Harwood & Giles, in press) to studying stigma yields the most comprehensive perspective for understanding the functional value stigmatizing serves. As a case study, we focus on gays and lesbians as a stigmatized group[1].

Gays and Lesbians as a Stigmatized Group

Scholars contend that social stigma is ubiquitous and that despite variations of what blemishes constitute stigma status, all societies have stigmatized individuals (Crocker *et al.*, 1998). The term stigma originates from the Greeks, where it referred to bodily signs intended to expose something unusual and bad about the *moral* status of the possessor (Goffman, 1963). In his seminal work, Goffman borrowed the term to refer to an "attribute that is deeply discrediting" that functions to reduce the individual ". . . in our minds from a whole and usual person to a tainted, discounted one" (p. 3). Put another way, the stigmatized possess a "mark" that defines "him or her as deviant, flawed, limited, spoiled, or generally undesirable" (Jones *et al.*, 1984, p. 6).

While the definition of stigma is fairly robust, less lucid is who determines whether a group possesses an attribute that conveys a negative social identity. Goffman (1963) clearly links stigma to the construction of social identity by explaining that social norms of identity lead to conformity, as well as perceived deviation. Similarly, Jones *et al.* (1984) reason that because identity is socially constructed, rules about the stigmatized are defined by society. As a group, gays and lesbians have long been "marked" or considered "deviant." In Goffman's (1963) classic delineation of stigma, homosexuality falls under "stigma of blemishes of individual character" and individuals who possess these are perceived as "weak will, domineering or unnatural passions, treacherous and rigid beliefs, and dishonesty" (p. 4).

Prior to the 1960's, homosexuality was assumed, primarily, to be a form of psychopathology. After lobbying, political activism, and scientific literature challenged the psychopathological viewpoint of homosexuality, the American Psychiatric Association (APA) removed homosexuality from its *Diagnostic and Statistical Manual* as a form of mental illness in 1974 (Herek, 1984). While homosexuality is no longer construed as a form of psychopathology by most professional psychological and sociological associations, and opinions and attitudes toward homosexuals have improved (Hugick, 1992; Jorgansen, 1986), the literature supports the claim that gays and lesbians remain a stigmatized group (e.g., Herek, 1998; Kite & Deaux, 1986; Whitley, 1990).

Homosexuality is defined as feeling sexually attracted only to people of the same sex as oneself. However, because many heterosexuals may interpret the term homosexual as referring exclusively to gay males (Black & Stevenson, 1984; Kite & Whitley, 1998), hereafter, the term gay will be used to refer to males and lesbian to refer to women. Relatedly, despite the fact that homosexuals are examined as a group, meta-analyses on heterosexuals' attitudes toward homosexuality indicate that heterosexual men and women react differently to homosexuality (Kite & Whitely, 1996). The literature strongly suggests that heterosexual men generally have more negative attitudes toward gays and lesbians than heterosexual women (Childers, 2000). The difference results mainly from heterosexual men's attitudes toward gay men, which are consistently more negative than both their attitudes toward lesbians and heterosexual women's attitudes toward either lesbians or gay men (e.g., Herek & Capitanio, 1999; Kite, 1984). Despite this, attitudes held by many heterosexuals toward gays and lesbians are, in general, largely negative (Haddock, Zanna, & Esses, 1993) and often manifested in behavior. As Unks

(1995) argues, "picking on persons because of their ethnicity, class, religion, gender, or race is essentially taboo behavior, but adults and children alike are given license to torment and harm people because of their sexuality" (p. 3).

Homophobia is perhaps the most apparent communicator of the group's stigmatized status. Homophobia was originally coined to refer to the dread of being in close quarters with homosexuals (Weinberg, 1972). However, as the term spread through professional and non-professional circles, it became loosely defined as "any negative attitude, belief, or action directed against homosexual persons" (Hudson & Ricketts, 1980, p. 357). Today, the term is now used widely in mainstream society. When someone refuses to sit next to, speak with, or befriend another person who is homosexual, few hesitate to label the person as homophobic. Over the years, numerous investigators have examined some of the correlates of homophobia (e.g., Kite, 1984; Madon, 1997; Young, Gallagher, Marriott, & Kelly, 1993). While heuristic, the research remains primarily descriptive, and several theoretical approaches (critiqued below) addressing the value stigmatizing serves for the stigmatizer have more explanatory value.

Terror Management

Crocker *et al.* (1998) contend that stigmatizing may serve to maintain and validate an individual's worldview. Relying on terror management theory (TMT), they suggest that stigmatizing serves an anxiety-buffering or terror management function. Based on the work of Becker (1973, 1975), terror management proposes that mortality salience – or bringing individuals to think about their own death – "increases the negativity of their reactions to those who hold different beliefs and values" (Greenberg, Simon, Pyszczynski, Solomon, & Chatel, 1992, p. 212). Theorists argue that mortality salience reminds individuals of their vulnerability which, in turn, creates an overwhelming and paralyzing anxiety, or terror

(Greenberg *et al.*, 1990; Solomon, Greenberg, & Pyszczynski, 1991). In an effort to manage their anxiety, people subscribe to a highly rigid worldview where stability, coherence, and predictability are valued and maintained (Greenberg *et al.*, 1992). Thus, according to TMT, "people's beliefs about reality provide a buffer against the anxiety that results from living in a largely uncontrollable, perilous universe, where the only certainty is death" (Greenberg *et al.*, 1990, p. 308). Derogating individuals who threaten one's cultural worldview is assumed to neutralize, or buffer, the threat posed to one's values (Rosenblatt, Greenberg, Solomon, Pyszczynski, & Lyon, 1989). Gays and lesbians are often viewed as violating cultural norms and can be construed as deviant (Page & Yee, 1985). Furthermore, rather than individuals contemplating their own worldviews, gays and lesbians are, instead, seen as threatening that worldview and, thereby, stigmatized.

Crocker *et al.* (1998) argue the more central the values being violated, the more severe the negative sanctions against the group. Principles and values used to assess *morality* seem to be particularly central to a culture. Furthermore, for many people, moral principles are heavily guided by a system of religious beliefs and values that seek to transcend death. From a TMT perspective, religious beliefs are a very important component of the anxiety-buffering worldview. As Solomon *et al.* (1991, p. 100) explain, "for most people, deities and associated religious and spiritual concepts play a central role" in one's sense of security. Because many highly religious people perceive homosexuality as challenging their fundamental values, it is not surprising that they reject gays and lesbians and do not endorse their human rights (Johnson, Brems, & Alford-Keating, 1997), nor that religious institutions prohibit gay and lesbian membership or clergy.

Sex roles and traditional attitudes of women and men are also related to negative attitudes toward gays and lesbians. Whitley and Egisdottir (2000) argue that "dislike of lesbians and gay men should be particularly strong among people who hold traditional gender-role attitudes because homosexuality poses an especially strong threat to their system of gender beliefs" (p. 949). Based on this same rationale, Shields and Harriman (1984) conducted an experiment to determine how attitudes toward gay men were related to fear responses. Their results demonstrated that heterosexual males who hold negative attitudes toward gay men often demonstrated defensive responses, or simultaneous heart rate acceleration and constriction of blood vessels in the scalp when exposed to slides of male partners, as opposed to a heart rate orienting response, which occurs in the presence of novel or interesting stimuli. This study illustrates that in addition to stigma being transmitted through physical communication, it may also be communicated *intra*-individually through physiological responses (see Blair, Park, and Bachelor [2003] regarding expressed anxiety).

Negative attitudes toward gays and lesbians have also been found in individuals who are considered highly authoritarian (see Whitley and Lee [2000] for a recent meta-analysis). Because high authoritarians maintain traditional values (viz., the tendency to endorse male superiority and female inferiority, and reject egalitarian gender-role relationships), it has been suggested that they perceive gays and lesbians as maintaining a value system markedly different than their own, and these perceived differences in values serve as the primary determinant of their negative attitude (Whitley & Egisdottir, 2000). Communicatively, because some religious and political leaders condemn lesbians and gays, people high in authoritarianism may see them as acceptable targets of prejudice and hostility. Consequently, because the authoritarian personality is a defensive way of coping with threats, it is not surprising that high authoritarians hold the negative attitudes they do (Greenberg *et al.*, 1990).

Taken together, research clearly illustrates a relationship between values and negative attitudes toward gays and lesbians. According to Herek (1984, 1986, 1988), these negative attitudes may serve a value-expressive function, whereby traditional standards of acceptable behavior are affirmed. Moreover, a TMT perspective would argue that homosexuals are perceived as not upholding basic values (i.e., morality) and their mere existence calls into question the validity of many heterosexuals' worldviews.

Because of the perceived threat and violation gays and lesbians poses to the latter, they should be punished and communicated toward negatively.

Self-Enhancement

A second theoretical approach, self-enhancement, also assists in the understanding of stigma from an individual's perspective. Some theorists contend that stigmatizing, or derogating another, can function to enhance one's self esteem (e.g., Crocker *et al.*, 1998; Katz & Braly, 1933). Based on Festinger's (1954) theory of social comparison which maintains that people need to have stable, accurate appraisals of themselves, Wills' (1981) downward comparison theory asserts that persons can enhance their own subjective well-being by comparing themselves with those less fortunate (see also, Hajek & Giles, 2002; Taylor & Lobel, 1989). In addition, Wills claims that individuals who experience a decrease in subjective well-being are more likely to engage in downward comparison. Derogation, discrimination, or even causing harm are examples of downward comparison that communicate stigma and, arguably, can bolster one's own self esteem. Although Wills originally contended that persons who are temporarily or chronically low in self-esteem would have greater motivation for self-enhancement and, thus, engage in more downward comparison processes, more recent evidence suggests the dynamic to be much more complex. That is, following a threat to the self-concept, individuals high in self-esteem can maintain their positive self-concept by engaging in self-enhancing social comparisons (Crocker, Thompson, McGraw, & Ingerman, 1987). Relatedly, Baumeister, Smart, and Boden (1996) argue that individuals with "inflated, unstable, or tentative beliefs" (p. 5) about the self's superiority are most likely to engage in downward comparison.

An arguably broader approach, self-affirmation theory (Steele, 1988) assumes that people have a fundamental desire to maintain an image of global self-integrity (Steele, Spencer, & Lynch, 1993). The theory assumes that if individuals experience a threat to their self-integrity, they initiate a so-called self-affirming image maintaining process (i.e., prejudice) in order to reaffirm the self. Attempts to restore the image may involve acts of downward comparison. According to Fein and Spencer (1997), these acts serve to reevaluate and reinterpret "experiences and events in ways that reaffirm the self's integrity and value" (p. 31). In a test of the theory, they investigated whether self-image maintenance processes contribute to derogating outgroup members. In Study 2, they manipulated sexual orientation to determine whether a self-image threat would exacerbate the effects of stereotyping and prejudice. Results suggest that when respondents are ego-threatened, they are more likely to derogate a homosexual target than a heterosexual target. Fein and Spencer concluded that their findings were supportive of the hypothesis that derogating a stereotyped target in response to a self-image threat mediates an increase in self-esteem.

Taken together, lesbians and gays are prime targets for outgroups to engage in downward comparisons. Various forms of prejudice help maintain an image of self-integrity and keep the group stigmatized. Furthermore, in light of recent literature, it appears that people who are high in self-esteem may be particularly prone to derogating gays and lesbians. Surprisingly, little research has examined how levels of self-esteem might be related to the communication of stigma of gays and lesbians. Interestingly, Agnew, Thompson, Smith, Gramzow, and Curry (1993) found physical self-esteem (the view of one's own body, state of health, physical appearance, skills, and sexuality) to be a significant predictor of homophobia, but not general self-esteem (the total of physical, moral, personal, family, and social subscores). The authors propose that heterosexuals with high physical self-esteem might be reacting to their perceived dissimilarity from lesbians and gays.

Despite a lacuna in the empirical literature regarding how levels of self-esteem are related to the stigmatization of gays and lesbians, admittedly selective true-life accounts indicate a relationship. For example, on September 22, 2000, 53-year-old Ronald Gay walked into the local gay bar, the Backstreet Café, in Roanoke, VA, pulled out a nine-millimeter handgun and fired at least eight rounds. The shots from his gun killed Danny Lee Overstreet and wounded six other patrons. When police inquired into the motive, Gay said he was angry about being teased because of his name and wanted to "waste some faggots" (Tate, 2000, p. 14). He also told police some of his children changed their last name to avoid jokes being made at their expense. Despite the fact that other motives such as sheer anger at being teased (irrespective of self-esteem threat) cannot be ruled out, true-life accounts such as this indicate a relationship between self-esteem and violence against gays and lesbians.

Jost and Banaji (1994, p. 4) note that self-enhancement or ego-justification "remains among the least studied of the functions" of discrimination (see, however, Herek, 1986, 1992). They also suggest that ego-justification, while appealing, fails to produce satisfactory empirical evidence. They note several deficiencies in the ego-justification approach. For example, the theory cannot sufficiently explain why many people subscribe to negative stereotypes of groups with whom they have never had contact and, therefore, would have no information to rationalize. They also point to the weakness of ego-justification being unable to elucidate why stereotypes of stigmatized groups are consensual. Gays and lesbians are not exempt from the consensual nature of stereotypes (Jackson & Sullivan, 1990). For example, stereotypes of gay men are: having a liking for art and literature, being concerned with appearance, effeminate, friendly, sensitive, individualistic, wearing an earring, and having high-pitched voices. Consensual stereotypes of lesbians include using harsh language, feeling comfortable in expressing aggression, being masculine, having short hair, and behaving positively toward females (e.g., Haddock *et al.*, 1993; Page & Yee, 1985).

A Critique

Terror management and self-enhancement explanations both emphasize how stigmatizing others functions to enhance an individual's self worth. While these two theoretical approaches are illuminating, neither is able to explain how stigmatizing functions to maintain one's worldview or boost self-esteem, or why one group would communicatively reject another group. That is, these two approaches do not address the fact that who we are as individuals is inextricably tied to our social group memberships.

According to intergroup theorists (e.g., Tajfel and Turner, 1986), part of our self-concept (or identity) is defined and formed on the basis of group affiliations. Relatedly, we classify others and ourselves according to these group memberships (i.e., African-American, man/woman, gay/lesbian) (Brown, 1995). Goffman (1963) also recognizes the ubiquity of categorizing others based on group membership. He remarks that "society establishes the means of categorizing persons and the complement of attributes felt to be ordinary and natural for members of each of these categories" (p. 2). Tajfel and Turner (1986) also suggest that people prefer to have a positive group identity rather than a negative one. With this in mind, people want to belong to the "good," rather than the "bad," groups. Based on the desire to belong to distinct groups, group members seek differentiation from outgroups (e.g., gays and lesbians). Relatedly, Pittam and Gallois (2000) contend that "the pressure to distance oneself from others through the positioning of self and others into ingroups and outgroups stems from the ubiquitous need to categorize people socially, particularly when the context involves threat or stigma" (p. 27). Thus, stigmatizing may function to differentiate one's own group in order to feel positive about the ingroup.

The failure of the self-enhancement perspective in acknowledging that one's self-concept is inherently linked to group memberships is perhaps why the explanation fails to yield empirical support. And, although TMT does not explicitly discuss the importance of groups to one's self-concept, there is room to filter the explanation from an intergroup perspective. The central assumption of TMT is mortality salience increases the negativity of individuals' reactions to others who are perceived to hold different values, beliefs, and worldviews (Solomon *et al.*, 1991). From an intergroup perspective, individuals can be "grouped" according to their beliefs, values, and worldviews (i.e., religious vs. non-religious). Since gays and lesbians often challenge and thus threaten outgroups' worldviews, they are stigmatized. Despite self-enhancement and TMT offering insightful explanations for the function stigmatizing serves, an intergroup approach is even more robust.

Goffman (1963) also recognized the value of a group approach to studying stigma. He contended that a "good portion of those who fall within a given stigma category may well refer to the total membership by the term 'group' or an equivalent, such as 'we,' or 'our people.' Those outside the category may similarly designate those within it in group terms" (p. 23). Because our identities are tied to group memberships and certain groups are considered to be better than others, we contend an intergroup approach provides the most robust explanation for the functional value stigmatizing serves (see also Molloy & Giles, 2002). Toward that end, the following two theoretical approaches, ingroup enhancement and system justification, examine stigma from an intergroup perspective.

Ingroup Enhancement

According to social identity theory (SIT), the dominant theory driving the ingroup-enhancement explanation, persons have a *social* identity as well as a personal identity (Tajfel & Turner, 1986). Personal identity refers to an individual's own unique characteristics, whereas social identity consists of those aspects of an individual's self-image that are derived from being a member of a group. The theory is concerned with the latter. Specifically, SIT proposes (as stated above) that people generally have preferences for seeing themselves positively rather than negatively. That is, because the groups in which we claim membership in part define our self-concept, individuals desire a positive, rather than a negative social identity. Accordingly, individuals can maintain or achieve a positive social identity by making favorable comparisons with relevant outgroups that function to positively distinguish one's ingroup from outgroup(s) (Brown, 1995). Derogating outgroups is one way to maintain and communicate a positive group identity. Although the self-enhancement and group-enhancement arguments are remarkably similar, self-enhancement and terror management focus on *personal* identity, whereas the latter seeks to maintain a positive *group* identity. Thus, according to an intergroup perspective, the search for ingroup superiority may explain the stigmatization of gays and lesbians.

Despite the fact that communication researchers have spent little time investigating stigma, existing theory in the social psychology of language provides a useful framework. Drawing in part upon SIT, Giles and colleagues developed communication accommodation theory (CAT) in an effort to understand the role of identity in language and communicative use (e.g., Giles, Mulac, Bradac, & Johnson, 1987). The theory maintains that communication is an important marker of identity. Specifically, we are motivated to accommodate, or adjust our speech, language, and nonverbal communication toward or away from others to achieve a desired level of social distance (Giles, Coupland, & Coupland, 1991). CAT theorists propose many types of accommodation. The broad strategies of convergence and divergence represent the core of the theory (see Shepard, Giles, and Le Poire [2001] for a more detailed discussion). Convergence, or adjusting communicative behavior to become more similar to one's communicative partner, indicates liking and approval for the other person. Conversely, divergence, or accentuating communicative differences between oneself and others, is used to show dislike and disapproval as well as a valued differential from others (Giles & Noels, 1998).

Anxiety, expressiveness, and touch are examples of how divergent nonverbal behavior can communicate gays and lesbians' stigmatized status (Karr, 1981; Roese, Olson, Borenstein, Martin, & Shores, 1992). Similarly, in their experimental field study of differential treatment by salespersons, Walters and Curran (1996) found that heterosexual couples were helped significantly quicker than gay and lesbian couples (confederates). Moreover, staff failed to assist one third of the homosexual couples, whereas all heterosexual couples were helped. Response time was not the only way in which gay and lesbian couples were treated differently. Gay and lesbian couples consistently reported, as did the observers, discourteous employee behavior, and being laughed and pointed at. In another investigation that demonstrates the nonverbal communication of stigma, Cuenot and Fugita (1982) found that some heterosexuals experience situational anxiety when interacting with a perceived homosexual. Specifically, they found that due to heightened anxiety, subjects engaged in more rapid speech when interacting with a perceived gay or lesbian than when they interacted with a heterosexual confederate.

Anti-gay and lesbian slurs, jokes and graffiti are examples of how divergent verbal behavior can communicate gays and lesbians stigmatized status (Herek, Gillis, Cogan, & Glunt, 1997; Louis Harris and Associates, 1993). In a classic case of verbal divergence, Thurlow (2001) examined homophobic pejoratives and the verbal abuse of lesbian, gay, and bisexual high-school students. He found that when he asked high school students to generate a list of pejoratives, of the 6,000 generated, 10 percent were homophobic. When students were asked to rank which items they considered the "worst," 28 percent of the homophobic items were rated. And, although there was a host of homophobic pejoratives reported, the most common was "gay" – the self-label many young homosexuals prefer to adopt for themselves. Interestingly, and more recently, the word "gay" also serves as a term used to loosely describe anything undesirable (Redman, 1994). As Thurlow explains, "it may well be that homophobic pejoratives are not always used with serious intent, but perhaps this is exactly where their vitriol lies: used with such carefreeness (or, rather, carelessness)" (p. 13). In the same vein, Valentine (1998) contends that name-calling is a frequent abusive practice reported by gays and lesbians. Importantly, he maintains that "naming" is central to questions of identity and power. According to Valentine, "abusive naming practices are indexical of social attitudes and mark delineations, whether latent or explicit, of ingroup and outgroup" (p. 3). With this mind, naming others is an obvious act of divergence for proclaiming identity and establishing who belongs to the community and who does not.

Anti-gay attitudes do not inevitably translate into divergent communication. Le Poire (1994) demonstrated that in some situations speakers can camouflage their negative inclinations (for a discussion of psychological divergence with linguistic convergence, see Thakerar, Giles, and Cheshire, 1982). More specifically, she found that individuals who reported less knowledge about and more fear toward gays communicated greater expressions of nonverbal involvement in face-to-face situations with them. Le Poire concluded that although some individuals are threatened by gays, individuals with negative attitudes may go out of their way to "meet the normative requirements of the situation and match the mostly pleasant behavior of the confederate" (p. 272). Clearly, stigma can be communicated in discriminatory behavior, however Le Poire's research demonstrates that it can also be masked or compensated for by over-pleasantness.

Lack, or the avoidance, of intergroup contact – another divergent strategy – can also communicate stigma. Not surprisingly, gays and lesbians are commonly confronted with rejection and isolation. One national survey found that only 12 percent of men aged 15- to 19-years reported that they felt confident they could befriend a gay person (Marsiglio, 1993). Even so, there is a substantial body of evidence that suggests that increased contact with gays and lesbians functions to reduce negative attitudes (e.g., Agnew *et al.*, 1993; Estrada & Weiss, 1999). In fact, Herek and Glunt (1993) found interpersonal contact predicted attitudes toward gay men better than did any other demographic or social psychological variable they measured. As they point out, this is consistent with the contact hypothesis, which predicts a reduction in prejudice against minority group members when equal status contact between minority and majority group members occurs in the pursuit of common goals (Allport, 1954).

SIT argues that ingroup members, in this case heterosexuals, may derogate outgroup members, gays and lesbians, in an effort to feel positive about their own group (Tajfel & Turner, 1986; see also Herek's symbolic function, 1984). While the above studies do indicate ingroup bias, the studies yield little support for the arguments that outgroup derogation actually enhance one's social identity. This lack of support is consistent with other literature (e.g., Hogg & Abrams, 1990). Crocker *et al.* (1998) contend that the evidence that ingroup bias enhances social identity remains equivocal. Even so, the group enhancement approach does compensate for much of what self-enhancement and terror management cannot explain. Specifically, according to Jost and Banaji (1994), ingroup enhancement can explain why it is possible for people to possess stereotypes of groups they have never encountered, but whom members of their ingroup have encountered. They also contend that the explanation can account for why disadvantaged groups would promote negative stereotypes of one another (for competition).

While SIT can explain why stereotypes are consensual within groups, the theory cannot explain why the same stereotypes of a particular group are held by several different outgroups, nor why people who hold negative attributions about a particular group (e.g., gays and lesbians) also often hold similarly unfavorable attitudes about other social minorities, including racial and gender outgroups (Agnew *et al.*, 1993; Haddock *et al.*, 1993). Furthermore, the many instances of disadvantaged group members subscribing to the stigmatizing stereotypes about their own group and about themselves can still not be accounted for. Jost and Banaji (1994) use these deficiencies regarding SIT as a rationale for their system justification approach. In line with social identity theory, system justification also explores stigma from an intergroup approach.

System Justification

System justification is defined as the "psychological process by which existing social arrangements are legitimized, even at the expense of personal and group interest" (Jost & Banaji, 1994, p. 2).

This approach borrows heavily from social dominance theory which contends that "societies minimize group conflict by creating consensus on ideologies that promote the superiority of one group over others" (Pratto, Sidanius, Stallworth, & Malle, 1994, p. 741; see also Herek's discussion of 'defensive attitude', 1984, 1986). Social dominance theory addresses many of the challenges classical and contemporary theories of social attitudes and intergroup relations have difficulty explaining.

The theory begins with the basic observation that all human societies tend to be structured as systems of group-based social hierarchies. Group-based social hierarchies refer to the social power, prestige, and privilege an individual possesses by virtue of his or her ascribed membership in a particular socially constructed group such as sexual orientation (Whitley & Egisdottir, 2000). Conceptually, system justification is intended to bring into prominence the degree to which the stigmatization of outgroups is used to justify or explain the state of affairs. As Crocker *et al.* (1998) contend, people of higher status groups may stigmatize lower status groups to justify the advantages they gain from society's current structure. Moreover, system-justification allows one to feel that one's group is more deserving and the system is, indeed, fair. According to social dominance theorists, social hierarchies are promoted and maintained through ideologies, or hierarchy-legitimating myths. It is through these myths (or, in our terms, the communicating of them) that discrimination is legitimized and maintained. As Pratto *et al.* (1994) comment, in order for these ideologies "to work smoothly, they must be widely accepted within a society, appearing as self-apparent truths" (p. 741). When ideologies are accepted in society, consensus is created and group inequality is maintained.

While sometimes being the forum for questioning them, the media is a prominent means by which system legitimating myths are transmitted (Abrams, Eveland, & Giles, 2003) and positive social identities sustained (Reid, Giles, & Abrams, in press). Because the media is a pervasive force in the United States, the attitudes and behaviors promoted in the media have the ability to permeate the fabric of society. Academics and advocacy groups have long recognized the powerful force of media content (e.g., Bronski, 1984, 1986; Myrick, 1998; Wolf & Kielwasser, 1991). Some argue that because lesbians and gays often grow up in isolation from each other and even from heterosexual peers, they turn to the mass media for information and ideas about themselves (Dyer, 1984). Unfortunately, they are confronted with a dearth of representation, although this is slowly changing (Abrams *et al.*, 2003). If depicted, the manner in which gays and lesbians are portrayed is critical. Because the topic of homosexuality is still a difficult subject, especially for adolescents, the media are often relied upon to supply information (Sprafkin & Silverman, 1982).

In light of this, media portrayals of gays and lesbians may be especially impressionable. Kielwasser and Wolf (1994) highlight the impact of mainstream media on adolescent sexuality: "Every evening, the adolescent inhabitants of television fall in and out of love, kiss, cuddle, and date; they occupy a substantial amount of prime time with their dramatic or comedic considerations of sexual intercourse, marriage, child-rearing and family-making . . . For lesbian and gay youth, the message – ubiquitous, consonant, cumulative – is that only heterosexual adolescents matter, only heterosexual 'coming of age' rituals are acceptable and communicable" (p. 73). When all is said and done, the mainstream mass media is a major cultural institution that serves to transmit and reinforce the stigmatization gays and lesbians (Kielwasser & Wolf, 1992).

Undeniably, homosexuals have experienced grievous injustices. In our present state of maintaining the discourse of political correctness (see Suhr & Johnson, 2003), it can still be seemingly legitimate to derogate gays and lesbians. The reason for the continued communicative divergence and acceptance of negative jokes and stereotypes, derogation and violent crimes against gays and lesbians may be a function of the system legitimating such discrimination. Jost and Banaji (1994) explain that people will develop ideas about the characteristics of the self and others on the basis of some social arrangement, like an outcome of a legal decision or victimization of assault.

Media aside, there is a litany of widespread societal practices that communicate the stigmatization of gays and lesbians. For example, basic civil liberties are routinely denied to homosexuals. Fueled by the claim that homosexuals are often denied the same rights as heterosexuals, there is continual debate over "special rights" (endorsed by conservative groups) versus "equal rights" (endorsed by gay and lesbian groups, human and human rights advocacy groups. Over the past few years, legislation attempting to prohibit discrimination on the basis of sexual orientation has been thwarted by conservative constituencies, and discriminatory polices have routinely been upheld by the courts (Walters & Curran, 1996). Some evidence also suggests that incidents of violence based on one's sexual orientation (or perceived sexual orientation) are increasing annually (Kielwasser & Wolf, 1994).

Gays and lesbians have long been victims of violence, the most extreme form of communicating stigma. Data indicate that many gays and lesbians in the U.S. have suffered physical violence, intimidation, and harassment because of their sexual orientation (e.g., Berrill, 1992; Otis & Skinner, 1996). For example, Herek *et al.* (1997) found that forty-one percent of their sample of gays, lesbians, and bisexuals reported experiencing a bias-related criminal victimization (e.g., assault, property crimes, attempted crimes, and witnessing the murder of a loved one) since the age of sixteen. These data corroborate the U.S. Justice Department's claim that the lesbian and gay community is the most frequent victim of hate crimes.

Gays and lesbians are not protected from discrimination under the law in almost every important aspect of their lives. For example and until recently, thirteen States still outlawed sodomy (Human Rights Campaign, 2003). States' rights to uphold such laws were enforced and mandated by the U.S. Supreme Court in 1986 (Bowers v. Hardwick, 1986). However, in a recent historic landmark decision (Lawrence v. Texas), the Supreme Court overturned Bowers v. Hardwick and struck down sodomy laws. The outcome of the decision is still unknown. Still, only in eleven States, and the District of Columbia is discrimination on the basis of sexual orientation prohibited in housing, public accommodations, and employment (Gay and Lesbian Defense Organization, 2001). Furthermore, although domestic partnership ordinances (a non-legal recognition of relationship status) often make the news, they remain rare and often go on to be challenged in most States or municipalities. Currently, twenty six States have passed "anti-gay" marriage (or same-sex marriage) acts. Moreover, gay and lesbian parents can lose legal custody of their children when their sexual orientation becomes known (Falk, 1989) and there are a few States that ban gays and lesbians from adopting children (Human Rights Campaign, 2001).

The military, the Boy Scouts of America, and public services (e.g., insurances and access to credit) still are other areas where gays and lesbians are not protected by law (e.g., Badgett, Donnelly, & Kibbe, 1992; Long, 1996). The educational arena brings no sign of relief either to gay and lesbian students or educators. For instance, references to homosexuality in curriculum remain invisible. Spotlighting the communication discipline, Heinz (2002) argues that the gay and lesbian community is largely excluded from communication textbooks, syllabi, and curricula. Gay and lesbian students and educators also experience taunts, threats, and potential dismissal because of their sexual orientation (e.g., Harbeck, 1991; Walters & Hayes, 1998). When the scope of legalization of gay and lesbian discrimination is examined, it is easy to see how institutionalized discrimination functions to justify the larger system. Whether the conditions are social, political, economic, sexual, or legal, the system appears to legitimate discrimination against gays and lesbians. Additionally, such system justification of discrimination of gays and lesbians might serve to support, and even facilitate, hate crimes.

The Impact of Being Stigmatized

Thus far, the diverse ways stigma is communicated has been illustrated. However, for every communicative act, there is a communicative reaction. Because identities are socially constructed through communication with others (e.g., Abrams, O'Connor, & Giles, 2003), there are likely to be outcomes from the communication of stigma. Jost and Banaji's (1994) concept of false consciousness, or "the holding of beliefs that are contrary to one's personal or group interest and which thereby contribute to the maintenance of the disadvantaged position of the self or the group" (p. 3) directly addresses how the communication of stigma affects gays and lesbians. Internalized homophobia is evidence that the communication of stigma has resulted in false consciousness among gays and lesbians. Internalized homophobia refers to gays and lesbians endorsing the negative attitudes and beliefs of homosexuals that pervade society (Smith, 1988). That is, through the process of heterosexist socialization, gays and lesbians come to incorporate the negative attitudes and beliefs about homosexuals in their own psyche.

Internalized homophobia, then, is the incorporation of negative attitudes about homosexuality into one's identity (Meyer & Dean, 1998; Wagner, Serafini, Rabkin, Remien, & Williams, 1994). With this in mind, it is not surprising that some gays and lesbians, as perpetual targets of stigma, have incorporated the stigma into their identity. Importantly, internalized homophobia may have implications for gays and lesbians. Specifically, levels of internalized homophobia may predict the extent to which an individual feels a sense of belonging to the group or identifies with the group. Gays and lesbians with high levels of internalized homophobia may experience low identification with other gays and lesbians, whereas individuals who feel proud to be gay or lesbian may experience high identification with other gays and lesbians. On the other hand, an individual may have high identification with being gay or lesbian, but still feel little attachment to the relevant culture (see Fortman & Giles, in press). For instance, an individual may have a strong sense of gay or lesbian identity, but does not want to be associated with the stigma surrounding the group. Despite lacking empirical data, there seems to be a strong case to suggest that the communication of stigma has real implications for gays and lesbians.

Troiden (1989) argues that the negativity surrounding

homosexuality impacts gays and lesbians who are "coming out." In his exploration of the formation of homosexual identity, he proposes that homosexuals often experience identity confusion. That is, gays and lesbians have difficulty accepting their sexual orientation. He reasons that because of the stigma and stereotypes surrounding homosexuality, adolescent (and some adult) homosexuals struggle with their sexuality. Acknowledging one's homosexuality may be especially difficult for those individuals who do not know any gays or lesbians. These individuals do not have the opportunity to learn what gays and lesbians are actually like or judge for themselves whether there are any perceived similarities between their own desires and behaviors and those of other gays and lesbians (Troiden, 1989). Instead, these individuals are already aware of the negative stereotypes surrounding homosexuality. Furthermore, the negative stereotypes about gays and lesbians may explain why people who are coming out often engage in denial (denying their homosexual feelings), repair (attempts to eradicate homosexual feelings), and avoidance (avoiding homosexual thoughts, behaviors, or fantasies) strategies (Troiden, 1989).

The communication of stigma also impacts gays and lesbians in other ways. For example, Otis and Skinner (1996) found a negative relationship between internalized homophobia and mental well being; and many lesbians believe that physician knowledge about their sexual orientation would hinder the quality of medical care received (e.g., Eliason & Schope, 2001; Stein & Bonuck, 2001). Moreover, Wagner *et al.* (1994) conclude the later in life a gay man experiences an ongoing gay relationship, accepts being gay, and has positive feelings related to being gay, the more likely he is to report he has suppressed his gay identity and has internalized society's negative attitudes toward homosexuals. They also found that gay men felt the necessity to join gay-identified organizations to help deal with internalized homophobia. Interestingly, a secondary benefit to joining gay and lesbian organizations may be the development of a sense of belonging to the gay and lesbian community.

Gay and lesbian youth may be particularly vulnerable to stigma, experiencing alcohol and substance abuse, prostitution, running away, and school problems (Grossman & Kerner, 1998). Perhaps the most severe outcome of stigma is that, in comparison to their non-gay and lesbian peers, gay and lesbian youth are not only more likely to consider suicide, but also to make serious suicide attempts (Hammelman, 1993; Savin-Williams, 2001). These outcomes are highly illustrative of the deleterious impact stigma has on gays and lesbians.

Epilogue

Future research examining stigma from an intergroup approach can yield significant understanding of the communication of stigma. With this in mind, there are several areas that seem particularly ripe for investigation. For example, in an effort to break the pernicious cycle of expressed discrimination, future research should consider how to reduce the stigmatized status of gays and lesbians. Intergroup contact theory, and in particular the contact hypothesis (see Hewstone & Brown, 1986), delineates conditions by which intergroup contact can function to reduce intergroup prejudice. Even so, researchers have been slow to examine what transpires communicatively during intergroup contact.

Research can illuminate how group boundaries may be drawn when there is a threat to ingroup identity during intergroup contact (see Pittam and Gallois, 2000). With respect to sexual orientation, there is much for social psychologists of language to gain in learning how social distance or intergroup boundaries are drawn when communicating with apparent outgroup members (i.e., homosexuals). From a communication accommodation perspective, we might expect heterosexuals to maximize differences when interacting with gays and lesbians, or in an effort not to appear prejudiced, heterosexuals may be overly pleasant (i.e., overaccommodate). Perhaps the same type of communicative behavior may come from gays and lesbians. As McMillan and Chavis (1986) lament, "while much sympathetic interest in and research on the deviant have been generated, groups members' legitimate needs for boundaries to protect their intimate social connections have often been overlooked" (p. 9). That is, in an effort to maintain their distinct identity as a group, gays and lesbians may also diverge in communicative interactions or communicate in an overly accommodative manner. Such intergroup communication is likely to have significant impact on important communication outcomes such as communication satisfaction. Sadly, communication dissatisfaction may be a routine consequence of intergroup contact. Because intergroup contact has the potential to reinforce existing intergroup prejudices, scholars should consider investigating communicative transactions during intergroup contact. Communication may well be the lynchpin to understanding why, or under which conditions, contact seems to decrease or reinforce intergroup prejudice. Only when members from different groups are brought together can we begin to understand how contact may help or hinder in reducing a group's stigmatized status.

In his investigation of the divergent ways identity is communicated, Thurlow (2001) found that boys rated homophobic pejoratives significantly more taboo than girls. Moreover, the vast majority of all the homophobic items reported referred to male homosexuality (see also Sutton, 1995). These findings are not surprising given the literature (as indicated above) clearly reports that males have more negative attitudes toward gays than lesbians. Thurlow suggests that the absence of pejoratives for lesbians is possibly related to broader issues of sex inequality, such as marginalization, or "silencing" of lesbians (see Jaworksi, 1992). Perhaps evidence of this silencing can be found in lesbians' attitudes toward gay men. Kristiansen (1990) found feminist lesbians (primarily involved in the women's movement), compared with gay-movement lesbians (primarily involved with the gay-movement), had less favorable attitudes toward gay men, associated with fewer gay men, perceived less common fate with gay men, wished to cooperate less with gay men, and perceived less similarity with gay men. Interestingly, rather than sharing an *intragroup* relationship, these findings suggest that feminist lesbians share an *intergroup* relationship with gay men. Kristiansen argues that because gay men are perceived to violate important values to feminist lesbians (e.g., freedom, happiness, and inner harmony) and feminist lesbians are striving for a positive social identity, they will negatively evaluate gay men. Thus, the data suggest that the communication of stigma may be different for gay men than for lesbians. As noted earlier, we have treated the gay and lesbian community as one group. However, within any community there are likely to be intragroup differences. Future research can elucidate the relationship between the degree of stigma communicated to gays and lesbians.

The current paper has only explored some of the ways in which the stigmatization of gays and lesbians is communicated, but clearly our understanding of social stigma can benefit from a consideration of other stigmatized communities such as elderly people and persons-with-disabilities (see Levy [2003] and Ryan, Bajorel, Beaman, & Anas [in press], respectively). For example, in their discussion of stigma, Crocker *et al.* (1998) argue that visibility (or concealability) and controllability are important dimensions when considering stigma. Moreover, they insist these two dimensions can have significant influence on communication. These scholars contend that those with concealable stigmas have a different set of communicative concerns than those who possess a visible stigma. Specifically, they assert that groups who possess a concealable stigma may alter their communication (e.g., speech) to avoid revealing their negative identity. For example, Crocker *et al.* (1998) contend that people with concealable stigmas can communicate with others "without their negative social identity filtering how everything about them is understood" (p. 507). With this in mind, as a way of managing their stigma, we might expect those groups who possess a conceable stigma (i.e., homosexuals or stigmatized religious affiliation) to converge to their partner during intergroup communication. Conversely, visible stigmas (i.e., race, disfiguring conditions, obesity) cannot be hidden from others. Knowing the visible stigma can provide the primary schema through which all communication is filtered (Crocker *et al.*, 1998); groups who possess visible stigmas may strategically use communication to infer their communicative partner's attitudes.

The controllability dimension refers to how the mark came to be, specifically whether the mark has congenital or noncongenital causes and whether it is perceived as being controllable. Jones *et al.* (1984) argue that perceptions of the individual's own role in engendering her or his mark may have more negative consequences than a mark that is perceived to be congenital. They contend that a marked individual is treated better when he or she is judged as not being responsible for the condition. Similarly, based on attribution theory, Weiner, Perry, and Magnusson (1988) argued, and found support for, their contention that causal perception, or whether the individual is seen as responsible or having caused their stigma, influences the negativity of people's responses to the stigmatized. Subsequent literature also supports this argument. For example, despite being unable to determine the actual origin of homosexuality, the literature indicates perceived controllability is a predictor of negative attitudes toward gays and lesbians (e.g., Ernulf, Innala, & Whitam, 1989; Whitley, 1990). Similarly, other stigmas that are perceived to be controllable, such as obesity (e.g., Crandall, 1994) and drug use (Weiner *et al.*, 1988), are also associated with negative attitudes. Regardless of the facts surrounding the controllability of a particular stigma, as long as people continue to think an identity is controllable, the stigma may remain. Moreover, we might expect communicative interactions for those groups who are perceived not to have caused their stigma (i.e., physical handicap) to be more positive than those who are perceived to cause their stigma (i.e., AIDS or obesity).

In closing, we have detailed the numerous ways being a member of a stigmatized group is communicated. As a case study, we explored gays and lesbians. We hope that social psychologists of language will assist in bridging the gap between stigma, traditionally a social psychological construct, to stigma, an important communication construct. Importantly, communication does not simply refer to language. Actions, rules, laws, behavior, discrimination, labels, physical attacks, personal rejection, negative stereotypes, and derogation all communicate the stigmatized status of gay and lesbians.

We have also examined the social psychological explanations for the value stigmatizing serves. While several theoretical explanations have been offered, efforts to critically analyze each of these approaches have largely been neglected. Because social categorization is fundamental to the human condition and our self-concepts are largely dependent on the social categories in which we belong, we advocate examining stigma from an intergroup approach. In support for this argument, Crocker and Major (1989) also note the prevalence of social categorization based on group membership (with respect to voice and sexual orientation, see Smyth, Jacobs, & Rogers, 2003) and, in their definition of stigma, they argue that stigmatization refers to "social categories about which others hold negative attitudes, stereotypes, and beliefs, or which, on average, receive disproportionately poor interpersonal or economic outcomes relative to members of the society at large because of discrimination against members of the social category" (p. 609). Clearly, group membership is at the heart of stigma. With this understanding in mind, we may begin to "extend our sense of 'we' to people whom we have previously thought of as 'they'" (Rorty, 1989, p. 192). Importantly, social identity, communication accommodation, and system justification theories offer valuable frameworks for learning about social stigma from an intergroup perspective.

Acknowledgments

We are grateful to Brenda Major, Dale Brashers, Dolly Mullin, Beth Le Poire, Nancy Collins and an anonymous reviewer for their incisive comments on earlier versions of this paper.

Note

1. Considering the purpose of the current analysis, we have treated gays and lesbians as a collective group. However, we acknowledge later that, in other contexts, gays and lesbians might have separate group identities with very different histories, ideologies, and so forth.

References

Abrams, J. R., Eveland, W. P., & Giles, H. (2003). The effects of television on group vitality: Can television empower non-dominant groups? In P. Kalbfleisch (Ed.), *Communication Yearbook 27*, 193–219. Thousand Oaks, CA: Sage.

Abrams, J. R., O'Connor, J., & Giles, H. (2002). Identity and intergroup communication. In W.B. Gudykunst (Ed.), *Cross-cultural and intercultural communication* (pp. 209–224). Thousand Oaks, CA: Sage.

Agnew, C. R., Thompson, V. D., Smith, V. A., Gramzow, R. H., & Curry, D. P. (1993). Proximal and distal predictors of homophobia: Framing the multivariate roots of outgroup rejection. *Journal of Applied Social Psychology, 23*, 2013–2042.

Allport, G. (1954). *The nature of prejudice*. New York: Addison-Wesley.

Badgett, L., Donnelly, C., & Kibbe, J. (1992). *Pervasive patterns of discrimination against lesbians and gay men: Evidence from surveys across the United States*. Washington D.C.: National Gay and Lesbian Task Force.

Baumeister, R. F., Smart, L., & Boden, J. M. (1996). Relation of threatened egotism to violence and aggression: The dark side of high self-esteem. *Psychological Review, 103*, 5–33.

Becker, E. (1973). *The denial of death*. New York: Free Press.

Becker, E. (1975). *Escape from evil*. New York: Free Press.

Berrill, K. T. (1992). Anti-gay violence and victimization in the United States: An overview. In G. M. Herek & K. T. Berrill (Eds.), *Hate crimes: Confronting violence against lesbians and gay men* (pp. 19–45). Newbury Park, CA: Sage Publications.

Black, K. N., & Stevenson, M. R. (1984). The relationship of self-reported sex-role characteristics and attitudes toward homosexuality. *Journal of Homosexuality, 10*, 83–93.

Blair, I. V., Park, B., & Bachelor, J. (2003). Understanding intergroup anxiety: Are some people more anxious than others? *Group Processes and Intergroup Relations, 6*, 151–169.

Bowers v. Hardwick, 106 S.Ct . 2841 (1986).

Bronski, M. (1984). *Culture clash: The making of gay sensibility*. Boston: South End Press.

Bronski, M. (1986). "Gay men and movies: Reel to real." In E. E. Rofes (Ed.), *Gay life: Leisure, love and living for the contemporary gay male* (pp. 226–235). Garden City, JY: Dolphin/Doubleday.

Brown, R. (1995). *Prejudice: Its social psychology.* Cambridge, MA: Blackwell Publishers.

Childers, K. (2000). Status characteristics theory and sexual orientation: Explaining gender differences in responses to sexual orientation. *Current Research in Social Psychology, 5,* 1–10.

Cox, S., & Gallois, C. (1996). Gay and lesbian identity development: A social identity perspective. *Journal of Homosexuality, 30,* 1–30.

Crandall, C. S. (1994). Prejudice against fat people: Ideology and self-interest. *Journal of Personality and Social Psychology, 66,* 882–894.

Crocker, J., & Major, B. (1989). Social stigma and self-esteem: The self-protective properties of stigma. *Psychological Review, 96,* 608–630.

Crocker, J., Major, B., & Steele, C. (1998). Social stigma. In D. Gilbert & S. Fiske (Eds.), *Handbook of social psychology* (pp. 504–553). Boston: McGraw-Hill.

Crocker, J., Thompson, L. L., McGraw, K. M., & Ingerman, C. (1987). Downward comparison, prejudice, and evaluations of others: Effects of self-esteem and threat. *Journal of Personality and Social Psychology, 52,* 907–916.

Cuenot, R. G., & Fugita, S. S. (1982). Perceived homosexuality: Measuring heterosexual attitudinal and nonverbal reactions. *Personality and Social Psychology Bulletin, 8,* 100–106.

Dyer, R. (Ed.). (1984). *Gays and film* (rev. ed). New York: New York Zoetrope.

Eliason, M. J., & Schope, R. (2001). Does "don't ask don't tell" apply to health care? Lesbian, gay, and bisexual people's disclosure to health care providers. *Journal of the Gay and Lesbian Medical Association, 5,* 125–134.

Ernulf, K., Innala, S., & Whitam. (1989). Biological explanation, psychological explanation, and tolerance of homosexuals: A cross-national analysis of beliefs and attitudes. *Psychological Reports, 65,* 1003–1010.

Estrada, A. X., & Weiss, D. J. (1999). Attitudes of military personnel toward homosexuals. *Journal of Homosexuality, 37,* 83–97.

Falk, P. (1989). Lesbian mothers: Psychosocial assumptions in family law. *American Psychologist, 44,* 941–947.

Fein S., & Spencer, S. J. (1997). Prejudice as self-image maintenance: Affirming the self through derogating others. *Journal of Personality and Social Psychology, 73.* 31–44.

Festinger, L. (1954). A theory of social comparison processes. *Human Relations, 7,* 117–140.

Fortman, J., & Giles, H. (in press). Communicating culture. In J. Baldwin, S.

Faulkner, M. Hecht (Eds.), *Culture [re]defined: Analyzing culture from diverse viewpoints.* New Jersey: Erlbaum.

Gay and Lesbian Defense Organization (http://www/glad.org)

Giles, H., Coupland, N., & Coupland, J. (1991). Accommodation theory: Communication, context, and consequence. In H. Giles, J. Coupland, & N. Coupland (Eds.), *Contexts of accommodation: Developments in applied sociolinguistics* (pp. 1–68). Cambridge: Cambridge University Press.

Giles, H., Mulac, A., Bradac, J. J., & Johnson, P. (1987). Speech accommodation theory: The next decade and beyond. In M. McLaughlin (Ed.), *Communication Yearbook 10* (pp. 13–48). Newbury Park, CA: Sage.

Giles, H., & Noels, K. A. (1998). Communication accommodation in intercultural encounters. In J. N. Martin, T. K. Nakayama, & L. A. Flores (Eds.), *Readings in cultural contexts* (pp. 139–149). Mountain View, CA: Mayfield Publishing Company.

Goffman, E. (1963). *Stigma: Notes on the management of spoiled identity.* Englewood Cliffs, NJ: Prentice Hall.

Greenberg, J., Pyszczynski, T., Solomon, S., Rosenblatt, A., Veeder, M., Kirkland, S., & Lyon, D. (1990). Evidence for terror management theory II: The effects of mortality salience on reactions to those who threaten or bolster the cultural worldview. *Journal of Personality and Social Psychology, 58*, 308–318.

Greenberg, J., Simon, L., Pyszczynski, T., Solomon, S., & Chatel, D. (1992). Terror management and tolerance: Does mortality salience always intensify negative reactions to others who threaten one's worldview? *Journal of Personality and Social Psychology, 63*, 212–220.

Grossman, A. H., & Kerner, M. S. (1998). Self-esteem and supportiveness as predictors of emotional distress in gay male and lesbian youth. *Journal of Homosexuality, 35*, 25–39.

Haddock, G., Zanna, M. P., & Esses, V. M. (1993). Assessing the structure of prejudicial attitudes: The case of attitudes toward homosexuals. *Journal of Personality and Social Psychology, 65*, 1105–1118.

Hajek, C., & Giles, H. (2002) The old man out: An intergroup analysis of intergenerational communication in gay culture. *Journal of Communication, 52*, 698–714.

Hammelman, T. (1993). Gay and lesbian youth: Contributing factors to serious attempts or considerations of suicide. *Journal of Gay and Lesbian Psychotherapy, 2*, 77–89.

Harbeck, K. M. (1991). Gay and lesbian educators: Past history/future prospects. *Journal of Homosexuality, 22*, 121–140.

Harwood, J., & Giles, H. (in press). *Intergroup communication: Multiple perspectives*. New York & Berlin: Peter Lang Publishers.

Heinz, B. (2002). Enga(y)ging the discipline: Sexual minorities and communication studies. *Communication Education, 51,* 95–104.

Herek, G. M. (1984). Beyond "homophobia": A social psychological perspective on attitudes toward lesbians and gay men. *Journal of Homosexuality, 10,* 1–21.

Herek, G. M. (1986). The instrumentality of attitudes: Toward a neofunctional theory. *Journal of Social Issues, 42,* 99–114.

Herek, G. M. (1988). Heterosexuals' attitudes toward lesbians and gay men: Correlates and gender differences. *The Journal of Sex Research, 25,* 451–477.

Herek, G. M. (1992). Psychological heterosexism and anti-gay violence: The social psychology of bigotry and bashing. In G. M. Herek & K. T. Berrill (Eds.), *Hate crimes* (pp. 149–169). Newbury Park, CA: Sage.

Herek, G. M. (1998). *Stigma and sexual orientation: Understanding prejudice against lesbians, gay men, and bisexuals*. Thousand Oaks: Sage.

Herek, G. M., & Capitanio, J. P. (1996). "Some of my best friends": Intergroup contact, concealable stigma, and heterosexuals' attitudes toward gay men and lesbians. *Personality and Social Psychological Bulletin, 22,* 412–424.

Herek, G. M., & Capitanio, J. P. (1999). Sex differences in how heterosexuals think about lesbians and gay men: Evidence from survey context effects. *The Journal of Sex Research, 36,* 348–360.

Herek, G. M., Gillis, J. R., Cogan, J. C., & Glunt, E. K. (1997). Hate crime victimization among lesbian, gay, and bisexual adults: Prevalence, psychological correlates, and methodological issues. *Journal of Interpersonal Violence, 12,* 195–215.

Herek, G. M., & Glunt, E. D. (1993). Interpersonal contact and heterosexuals' attitudes toward gay men: Results from a national survey. *Journal of Sex Research, 30,* 239–244.

Hewstone, M., & Brown, R. J. (1986). Contact is not enough: An intergroup perspective on the "contact hypothesis." In M. Hewstone & R. J. Brown (Eds.), *Contact and conflict in intergroup encounters* (pp. 1–44). Oxford: Blackwell.

Hogg, M., & Abrams, D. (1990). Social motivation, self-esteem, and social identity. In D. Abrams & M. Hogg (Eds.), *Social identity theory: Constructive and critical advances* (pp. 28–47). Hemel Hempstead: Harvester Wheatsheaf.

Hudson, W. W., & Rickets, W. A. (1980). A strategy for the measurement of homophobia. *Journal of Homosexuality, 5,* 357–372.

Hugick, L. (1992). Public opinion divided on gay rights. *Gallup Poll Monthly, 321*, 2–6.

Human Rights Campaign (http://www.hrc.org/newsreleases/2003/030626sodomy.asp)

Jackson, L. A., & Sullivan, L. A. (1990). Cognition and affect in evaluations of stereotyped group members. *The Journal of Social Psychology, 129*, 659–672.

Jaworksi, A. (1992). *The power of silence.* Thousand Oaks: Sage.

Johnson, M. E., Brems, C., & Alford-Keating, P. (1997). Personality correlates of homophobia. *Journal of Homosexuality, 34*, 57–69.

Jones, E. E., Farina, A., Hastorf, A. H., Markus, H., Miller, D. T., & Scott, R. (1984). *Social stigma: The psychology of marked relationships.* New York, NY: WH Freeman.

Jorgansen, X. (1986). *Marriage and the family: Development and change.* New York: Macmillan.

Jost, J. T., & Banaji, M. R. (1994). The role of stereotyping in system-justification and the production of false consciousness. *British Journal of Social Psychology, 33*, 1–27.

Karr, R. G. (1981). Homosexual labeling and the male role. In J. W. Cheseboro (Ed.), *Gayspeak: Gay and lesbian communication* (pp. 3–11). New York: The Pilgrim Press.

Katz, B., & Braly, K. (1933). Racial stereotypes of one hundred college students. *Journal of Abnormal and Social Psychology, 28*, 280–290.

Kielwasser, A. P., & Wolf, M. A. (1992). Mainstream television, adolescent homosexuality, and significant silence. *Critical Studies in Mass Communication, 9*, 350–373.

Kielwasser, A. P., & Wolf, M. A. (1994). Silence, differences, and annihilation: Understanding the impact of mediated heterosexism on high school students. *High School Journal, 77*, 58–79.

Kite, M. E. (1984). Sex differences in attitudes toward homosexuals: A meta-analytic review. *Journal of Homosexuality, 10*, 69–82.

Kite, M. E., & Deaux, K. (1986). Attitudes toward homosexuality: Assessment and behavioral consequences. *Basic and Applied Social Psychology, 7*, 137–162.

Kite, M. E., & Whitley, B. E., Jr. (1996). Sex differences in attitudes toward homosexual persons, behaviors, and civil rights: A meta-analysis. *Personality and Social Psychology Bulletin, 22*, 336–353.

Kite, M. E., & Whitley, B. E., Jr. (1998). Do heterosexual women and men differ in their attitudes toward homosexuality? A conceptual and methodological analysis. In G. M. Herek (Ed.), *Stigma and sexual* orientation: *Understanding prejudice against lesbians, gay men, and bisexuals* (pp. 39–61). Newbury Park, CA: Sage.

Kristiansen, C. M. (1990). The symbolic/value-expressive function of outgroup attitudes among homosexuals. *The Journal of Social Psychology, 130,* 61–69.

Le Poire, B. A. (1994). Attraction toward and nonverbal stigmatization of gay males and persons with AIDS: Evidence of symbolic over instrumental attribution structures. *Human Communication Research, 21,* 241–279.

Levy, B.R. (2003). Mind matters: Cognitive and physical effects of aging self-streotypes. *Journal of Gerontology: Psychological Sciences, 58B,* P203–211.

Long, C. D. (1996). For gays and lesbians, it's win some, lose some. *Academe, 82,* 10.

Louis Harris and Associates. (1993, June). *Hostile hallways: The AAUW survey on sexual harassment in America's schools* [Study number 923012]. Washington, DC: American Association of University Women Educational Foundation.

Madon, S. (1997). What do people believe about gay males? A study of stereotyped content and strength. *Sex Roles, 37,* 663–685.

Marsiglio, W. (1993). "Attitudes toward homosexual activity and gays as friends: A national survey of heterosexual 15- to 19-year-old males." *Journal of Sex Research, 30,* 12–17.

Martin, J. N., & Nakayama, T. K. (1997). *Intercultural communication in contexts.* Mountain View, CA: Mayfield Publishing Company.

McMillan, D. W., & Chavis, D. M. (1986). Sense of community: A definition and theory: *Journal of Community Psychology, 14,* 6–23.

Meyer, I. H., & Dean, L. (1998). Internalized homophobia, intimacy, and sexual behavior among gay and bisexual men. In G. M. Herek (Ed.), *Stigma and sexual orientation: Understanding prejudice against lesbians, gay men, and bisexuals* (pp. 160–186). Thousand Oaks, CA: Sage Publications.

Molloy, J., & Giles, H. (2002). Communication, language, and law enforcement: An intergroup communication approach. In Glenn, P., LeBaron, C., & Mandelbaum, J. (Eds.), *Excavating the taken-for-granted: Essays in social interaction* (pp. 327–340). Mahwah, NJ: Lawrence Erlbaum.

Myrick, R. (1998). AIDS Discourse: A critical reading of mainstream press surveillance of marginal identity. *Journal of Homosexuality, 35,* 75–93.

Otis, M. D., & Skinner, W. F. (1996). The prevalence of victimization and its effect on mental well-being among lesbian and gay people. *Journal of Homosexuality, 30,* 93–117.

Page, S., & Yee, M. (1985). Conception of male and female homosexual stereotypes among university undergraduates. *Journal of Homosexuality, 12,* 109–118.

Pittam, J., & Gallois, C. (2000). Malevolence, stigma, and social distance: Maximizing intergroup differences in HIV/AIDS discourse. *Journal of Applied Communication Research, 28,* 24–43.

Pratto, F., Sidanius, J., Stallworth, L. M., & Malle, B. F. (1994). Social dominance orientation: A personality variable predicting social and political attitudes. *Journal of Personality and Social Psychology, 67,* 741–763.

Redman, P. (1994). Shifting ground: Rethinking sexuality education. In D. Epstein (Ed.), *Challenging lesbian and gay inequalities in education* (pp. 131–151). Buckingham: Open University Press.

Reid, S., Giles, H., & Abrams, J. R. (in press). A social identity model of media effects. *Zeitschrift für Medienpsychologie.*

Roese, N. J., Olson, J. M., Borenstein, M. N., Martin, A., & Shores, A. L. (1992). Same-sex touching behavior: The moderating role of homophobic attitudes. *Journal of Nonverbal Behavior, 16,* 249–259.

Rorty, R. (1989). *Contingency, irony, and solidarity.* Cambridge: Cambridge University Press.

Rosenblatt, A., Greenberg, J., Solomon, S., Pyszczynski, T., & Lyon, D. (1989). Evidence for terror management theory: The effects of mortality salience on reactions to those who violate or uphold cultural values. *Journal of Personality and Social Psychology, 57,* 681–690.

Ryam. E.B., Bajorek, S., Beaman, A., & Anas, A. (in press). Intergroup perspectives on communication and disability. In J. Harwood & H. Giles (Eds.), *Intergroup communication: Multiple perspectives.* New York & Berlin: Peter Lang.

Savin-Williams, R. C. (2001). Suicide attempts among sexual-minority youths: Population and measurement issues. *Journal of Consulting and Clinical Psychology, 69,* 983–991.

Shepard, C. A., Giles, H., & Le Poire, B. A. (2001). Communication accommodation theory 25 years on. In W. P. Robinson & H. Giles (Eds.), *The new handbook of language and social psychology* (pp. 35–56). New York: Wiley.

Shields, S. A., & Harriman, R. E. (1984). Fear of male homosexuality: Cardiac responses of low and high homonegative males. *Journal of Homosexuality, 10,* 53–67.

Smith, J. (1988). Psychopathology, homosexuality, and homophobia. *Journal of Homosexuality, 15,* 59–73.

Smyth, R., Jacobs, G., & Rogers, H. (2003). Male voices and perceived sexual orientation: An experimental and theoretical approach. *Language in Society, 32,* 222–267.

Solomon, S., Greenberg, J., & Pyszczynski, T. (1991). A terror management theory of social behavior: The psychological functions of self-esteem and cultural worldviews. *Advances in Experimental Social Psychology, 24,* 93–159.

Sprafkin, J., & Silverman, L. T. (1982). "Sex on prime time." In M. Schwartz (Ed.), *TV and teens* (pp. 130–135). Reading, MA: Addison Wesley.

Steele, C. M. (1988). The psychology of self-affirmation: Sustaining the integrity of the self. *Advances in Experimental Social Psychology, 21,* 261–302.

Steele, C. R., Spencer, S. J., & Lynch, M. (1993). Self-image resilience and dissonance: The role of affirmational resources. *Journal of Personality and Social Psychology, 64,* 885–896.

Stein, G. L., & Bonuck, K. A. (2001). Physician-patient relationships among the lesbian and gay community. *Journal of the Gay and Lesbian Medical Association, 5,* 87–93.

Suhr, S., & Johnson, S. (Eds.) (2003). Special issue on "Political correctness". *Discourse and Society, 14,* 5–110.

Sutton, L. A. (1995). Bitches and skanky hobags: The place of women in contemporary slang. In K. Hall & M. Bucholtz (Eds.), *Gender articulated: Language and the socially constructed self* (pp. 279–296). New York: Routledge.

Tajfel, H., & Turner, H. (1986). The social identity theory of intergroup behavior. In S. Worchel & W. G. Austin (Eds.), *Psychology of intergroup relations* (pp. 7–24). Chicago: Nelson.

Tate, R. (2000, November 7). Two sides of a town. *Advocate,* 26–28.

Taylor, S. E., & Lobel, M. (1989). Social comparison activity under threat: Downward evaluation and upward contacts. *Psychological Review, 96,* 569–575.

Thakerar, J. N., Giles, H., & Cheshire, J. (1982). The psychological and linguistic parameters of speech accommodation theory. In C. Fraser and K.R. Scherer (Eds.), *Advances in the social psychology of language* (pp. 205–255). Cambridge, Cambridge University Press.

Thurlow, C. (2001). Naming the 'outsider within': Homophobic pejoratives and the verbal abuse of lesbian, gay and bisexual high-school pupils. *Journal of Adolescence, 24,* 25–38.

Troiden, R. R. (1989). The formation of homosexual identities. *Journal of Homosexuality, 17,* 43–73.

Unks, G. (1995). *The gay teen: educational practice and theory for lesbian, gay, and bisexual adolescents*. New York: Routledge.

Valentine, J. (1998). 'Naming the other: Power, politeness and the inflation of euphemisms.' *Sociological Research Online, 3*, 1–23.

Wagner, G., Serafini, J., Rabkin, J., Remien, R., & Williams, J. (1994). Integration of one's religion and homosexuality: A weapon against internalized homophobia? *Journal of Homosexuality, 26*, 91–110.

Walters, A. S., & Curran, M. C. (1996). "Excuse me, sir? May I help you and your boyfriend?": Salespersons' differential treatment of homosexual and straight customers. *Journal of Homosexuality, 31*, 135–152.

Walters, A. S., & Hayes, D. M. (1998). Homophobia within schools: Challenging the culturally sanctioned dismissal of gay students and colleagues. *Journal of Homosexuality, 35*, 1–21.

Weinberg, G. (1972). *Society and the healthy homosexual*. New York: St. Martins Press.

Weiner, B., Perry, R. P., & Magnusson, J. (1988). An attributional analysis of reactions to stigmas. *Journal of Personality and Social Psychology, 55*, 738–748.

Whitley, B. E., Jr. (1990). The relationship of heterosexuals' attributions for the causes of homosexuality to attitudes toward lesbians and gay men. *Personality and Social Psychology Bulletin, 16*, 369–377.

Whitley, B. E., Jr., & Egisdottir, S. (2000). The gender belief system, authoritarianism, social dominance orientation, and heterosexuals' attitudes toward lesbians and gay men. *Sex Roles, 42*, 947–967.

Whitley, B. E., Jr., & Lee, S. E. (2000). The relationship of authoritarianism and related constructs to attitudes toward homosexuality. *Journal of Applied Social Psychology, 30*, 144–170.

Wills, T. A. (1981). Downward comparison principles in social psychology. *Psychological Bulletin, 90*, 245–271.

Wolf, M. A., & Kielwasser, A. P. (1991). *Gay people, sex, and the media*. Binghamton, NY: The Harrington Park Press.

Young, R. K., Gallaher, P. E., Marriott, S., & Kelly, J. (1993). Reading about AIDS and cognitive coping style: Their effects on fear of AIDS and homophobia. *Journal of Applied Social Psychology, 23*, 911–924.

2

Emotional Expression as a Sociolinguistic Strategy: Its Importance in Medical Interactions

Bernadette WATSON
Cindy GALLOIS

Effective communication between health professionals and patients is an important topic for both providers and patients, and has been the focus of much interdisciplinary research over the past 20 years (e.g., Cegala, McGee & McNellis, 1996; Inui & Carter, 1985; Korsch & Negrete, 1972; Roter & Hall, 1991; Street, 1993; 2001, Thompson, 1994). In this chapter we focus on the patients' perspective of the interaction and we define effective communication as consultations rated by patients as being satisfying and positive experiences. We discuss findings from three studies in which we examined interactions between health professionals and patients from a communication accommodation theory (CAT) perspective. From these studies we make two observations. First, we suggest that the health professionals and patients perceive their interaction as effective when they achieve an optimal balance of intergroup and interpersonal salience. This observation is constructed from CAT and is discussed fully below. Second, we focus on relational needs in interactions between health professionals and patients. Our findings indicate that patients are more likely to view communication as effective when there is recognition of the relational dimension of the interaction. We explore the relational dimension of interactions between health professionals and patients by examining the role that emotional expression plays in these interactions.

Background
to Health Communication Research

Unfortunately, much of the research conducted in health communication has been atheoretical (e.g., Pendelton, 1983; Thompson, 1994). Research that is not theory driven does not provide clear explanations about the observed behaviors and has relatively poor predictive value. Within the past decade some researchers have addressed this lack of theory within health communication research. Researchers such as Cegala *et al.*, (1996) applied "communication competence" as a theoretical framework within which future research could be conducted. Roter and Hall (1991) adopted social exchange theory and the *reciprocity principle* to explain the dynamics of the interaction between health provider and patient (Hall, Roter & Katz, 1988; Roter & Hall, 1992). In addition, Hummert and Ryan (1996, 2001) developed a theoretical approach to their investigations of patronizing talk directed at older adults. Hummert and Ryan build on the work of Ryan and colleagues, who have taken a dynamic process approach to interactions and focus on the identity of each participant in relation to age as an intergroup marker (e.g., Harwood, Giles, Fox, Ryan & Williams, 1993; Ryan, Giles, Bartolucci & Henwood, 1986; Ryan, Hummert & Boich, 1995). Ryan and colleagues' perspective of the communication process, based on CAT, is strongly related to the framework adopted in this chapter. However, we examine health communication between patients and health professionals as it affects all types of patients and a range of health professionals.

The idea that one's social role (e.g., age, profession, gender) can be an intergroup marker during a medical interaction is focal to our research. Street (1991) observed that some interactions are characterized by role, power or other social differences and that the doctor-patient interaction is one of these. In these situations interactants respond according to their social role. Often the patient's reason for arranging the interaction is not social but rather business. For the health provider it is also a professional encounter even though the patient may discuss personal and possibly intimate matters. Thus we propose that medical interactions move through differing levels of intergroup and interpersonal salience. This proposition accords with those of other researchers (e.g., Gallois, Franklyn-Stokes, Giles, & Coupland, 1988; Gallois & Giles, 1998), who have proposed that intergroup and interpersonal salience operate as two correlated dimensions rather than as two ends of a continuum (Tajfel and Turner, 1979). Building on this notion of interactions between health professionals and patients as intergroup interactions that occur at the interpersonal level, we use CAT as our theoretical framework.

Communication Accommodation Theory and an Intergroup Perspective

CAT, which was first developed by Giles (1973) and Giles and Powesland (1975), forms the theoretical basis of our research. CAT is a general theory of communication that explains interactions through exploring the motivations and social cognitions of the interactants. CAT describes communication as a dynamic process between interactants and theorizes each interactant's beliefs and values about the encounter. These beliefs are influenced by a number of factors, including the context of the interaction, the role and status of each speech partner, and the importance or implications of the encounter. Because CAT is a broad theory of communication, it leads to a general set of principles for all communication encounters. However, the theory also takes into account the unique set of social norms and rules that define a given interaction. For a fuller discussion of CAT than we can provide here, see Gallois and Giles (1998) and Shepard, Giles and Le Poire (2001).

As noted above, CAT posits that all encounters contain both interpersonal and intergroup elements. In many interactions it is our social memberships that are paramount during conversations with others. This premise does not deny that at times we interact with a speech partner and focus on his or her personal characteristics, as well as our own. Rather, it recognizes that we move between highlighting ourselves and our speech partners as members of one or more social groups (high intergroup salience), and emphasizing the personal characteristics and traits of both the other person and oneself (high interpersonal salience). In any one interaction, CAT proposes that we can move through the dimensions of high or low interpersonal to high or low intergroup salience.

In the health context, CAT posits that during a medical encounter interactants are aware of their group membership – health professional or patient – and are motivated to interact in ways that reflect the beliefs and values they possess as group members. Other factors, such as the seriousness of the illness, the length of time each person has known the other, similarity in socio-economic status, age, and interests also influence the encounter for both interactants. According to CAT, these factors determine the levels of intergroup and interpersonal salience that unfold during the consultation. Much of the literature on health professional and patient relations assumes that the nature of the interaction is interpersonal. However, taking into account the differing memberships that individuals bring to medical encounters, each person is likely to be aware of his or her social role and to act accordingly.

CAT, as we have noted, opens the way to taking a genuinely intergroup perspective on health interactions and the language and communication that occur in them. It integrates the core concepts of social identity theory (Tajfel, 1978) and focuses directly on the impact of the intergroup and interpersonal history on communicative moves and their impact in interaction. Although it is not commonly adopted in health communication research, the intergroup perspective provides a rich source of understanding. CAT follows through the stages of an interaction in order to predict both the outcome of the interaction and the evaluations and attitudes that individuals will take with them to their next similar encounter.

It is not possible to describe the complete CAT model here. Rather, our aim in this chapter is to discuss what may constitute the optimal balance of intergroup and interpersonal salience in medical encounters and to examine in more depth one specific aspect of the theory: the strategies interactants use to achieve their interactional goals. Specifically we wish to draw attention to one particular strategy – emotional expression. Thus, the immediate context within which conversation occurs is our area of attention, and especially the sociolinguistic strategies interactants employ.

To date there have been four systematically theorized sociolinguistic strategies: *approximation, interpretability, discourse management*, and *interpersonal control*. Approximation strategies involve shifts in communicative behavior, such as changes in accent, speech rate, and pause length. The strategy of interpretability reflects a speaker's perception of the other's level of communication competence and comprehension. In a successful interaction, speakers appropriately adapt their speech, including vocabulary, to ensure that a speech partner fully comprehends the encounter. Discourse management strategies are reflected in a speaker's perception of the other's needs. Good discourse management results in mutual topic sharing, appropriate levels of floor holding, and showing interest in what the other says through behaviors such as back-channelling and questions. Finally, the strategy of interpersonal control is reflected in a speaker's perception of the importance of the role relations in the interaction. Accommodative behavior here involves each speaker having the freedom to choose her role (within the normative constraints of the context), and to move in or out of it as a choice. Overall, sociolinguistic strategies are used accommodatively when each interactant's behaviors are attuned and in synchrony with the behaviors and needs of the other interactant. Thus, for example, accommodation in discourse management would be reflected in behaviors such as a health professional allowing a patient adequate time to describe his or her situation and by showing interest in what the patient says. Accommodation in interpretability would be reflected in behaviors such as answering a patient's questions and providing clear information about medical procedures.

An important aspect of communication in many situations is the extent to which interactants provide reassurance and show concern when appropriate. In the medical context, strategies of *emotional expression* involve patients expressing their health anxieties and concerns, and health professionals providing appropriate reassurance and understanding. In this relationship, there are two important features: (1) the ability of health professionals to manage their own emotional expression appropriately, and (2) the ability of patients to meet their own needs in medical interactions (cf. Cegala, McNellis & McGee, 1995; Williams, Giles, Coupland, Dalby & Manasse 1990; Kreps, 1988; Thompson, 1994). Appropriate emotional expression occurs when the other person's individual needs for reassurance are met, his or her mood and anxiety levels are addressed, and the individual receives acknowledgment and support for concerns felt. While the importance of emotional expression as a strategy has been noted by CAT researchers (e.g., Giles, Coupland & Coupland, 1991; Williams *et al.*, 1990), there has not been a substantial attempt to theorize the role of emotional expression from a CAT perspective.

The Role of Emotional Expression in the Health Context

In the next section, we examine more closely how appropriate emotional expression facilitates interactions between patients and health professionals. To illustrate the ways in which this strategy is used, we draw on three studies (Watson & Gallois, 1998, 1999, 2002). These were part of a larger project, which focused on the patient's perspective and contained data and analyses that are not reported here. Here we focus on those parts of the studies that are directly relevant to emotional expression and meeting emotional and relationship needs. Taken together, they provide a strong incentive for CAT to incorporate emotional expression, as Giles *et al.* (1991) recommended. The studies also provide evidence that when patients and health professionals manage their interactions with an appropriate balance of intergroup and interpersonal salience, patients rate the interaction more positively than do patients who experience interactions which are high in only intergroup salience.

Study 1

In the first study reported here, we took a grounded theory approach to develop goal and strategy categories. From a CAT perspective, goals drive interactions. Individuals enter conversations with one or more goals which can alter as the interaction develops. Although, investigating the types and numbers of goals that occur during a conversation is not the aim of this chapter, it is important to acknowledge the role that goals play in influencing an interactant's communication behavior (c.f., Gallois and Giles [1998] and Shepard, Giles and Le Poire [2001]). The patient whose goal is to obtain information about their illness from the health professional may use different communication behaviors from that of the anxious patient who is seeking reassurance from the health professional. Of course, both goals can and often do co-exist. Thus when considering the communication strategies used by patients, we cannot ignore the possible goals that drive those behaviors.

The data in Study 1 were participants' written retrospective descriptions of satisfactory and unsatisfactory conversations they had experienced while they were hospital in-patients. There were 79 satisfactory and 69 unsatisfactory descriptions. We focused on three of the four communication strategies: discourse management, interpretability, and interpersonal control. Approximation was not examined because written descriptions do not easily lend themselves to approximation analysis. In addition, as Gardner and Jones (1999) noted, approximation may occur at the subconscious level and so is often not reported. However, we also included emotional expression as fifth communication strategy.

Differences in patient goals differentiated the two types of descriptions and provided an insight into the communication behavior reported by patients. In the descriptions of satisfactory conversations the key goals were to seek reassurance, develop relationships and to obtain information. In the descriptions of unsatisfactory conversations, patients reported that their goals were to assert themselves, request tasks, and, as in the satisfactory conversations, to obtain information. With these goals in mind, we found that in the satisfactory conversations the most frequently mentioned health professional strategies were positive interpretability (18 percent) and positive discourse management (18 percent). Positive emotional expression was the third most frequently reported strategy (9 percent). In fact, patient goals seemed to be complemented by the health professionals' communication strategies. A different pattern of results emerged in the descriptions of unsatisfactory interactions. There the most frequent strategies mentioned for health professionals were neutral and negative discourse management (8 percent and 9 percent, respectively), neutral interpretability, and negative interpersonal control (10 percent and 8 percent, respectively). Given that patient goals involved more functional aspects of an interaction, there does not appear to be the same match between the patients' goals and the health professionals communication strategies. The possible exception being the patients' goal of obtaining information and the health professionals' strategy of neutral interpretability (e.g., providing information). Patients did not report any incidents of positive emotional expression by health professionals.

From a CAT perspective, these results indicate that patients viewed positive emotional expression by health professionals as more appropriate, in that they occurred in interactions chosen as satisfactory. Further, these strategies were in general described using positive language, which also implicates accommodative behavior. There was plentiful evidence of behavior by health professionals described in negative language in the unsatisfactory descriptions, which suggested non-accommodative behavior by health professionals.

In addition with respect to optimal levels of intergroup and interpersonal salience, we identified a number of differences in behavior, attributions of behavior, and evaluations of the interaction and the health professional between descriptions of satisfactory and unsatisfactory conversations. These findings indicated higher interpersonal salience in the satisfactory conversations and higher intergroup salience in the unsatisfactory ones. These results support the assumption that consultations between health professionals and patients are better understood as interpersonal interactions that occur at varying levels of intergroup salience.

This study, however, was based on the self-reported experiences of the participants. Previous studies (e.g., Street, Mulac &Wiemann, 1988, Street & Wiemann, 1988) have examined how well outsiders' ratings concur with insiders' perceptions. To extend our understanding of how others rate these sociolinguistic strategies, we investigated outsider's rating of exemplars derived from the conversational descriptions obtained in Study 1.

Thus this study contains two parts (see Watson & Gallois, 1999, for full details). The first part provided the exemplars and in the second part of the study we obtained ratings of exemplars of the main themes. To obtain the exemplars we investigated the differences in thematic content between patients who described their experiences of satisfactory and unsatisfactory conversations with health professionals. This part of the study is reported here to highlight the importance of the strategy of emotional expression as it emerged from the themes.

Study 2, Part 1: Theme Identification

The descriptions of satisfactory and unsatisfactory conversations were subjected to a theme analysis, using an iterative reading process. Each theme identified a single type of behavior between the patient and the health professional. Initially 41 themes were identified, and then similar and overlapping themes were collapsed into single categories. For example, instances of health professionals

Table 1
Definitions of themes

Themes and Theme Definitions for Satisfactory Conversations	Number of Patients Who Used Theme	% of Patients Who Used Theme
Health Professional (HP) shows concern for patient The HP: – asks how the patient is feeling – checks any concerns the patient may have – is unable to fulfil the patient's request but tries to compromise	35	44
HP converses with and shows interest in patient The HP interacts with the patient about matters other than the patient's medical condition	31	39
Self-Disclosure HP or patient or both talks about herself or himself	27	34
HP provides information HP explains procedures or rules to the patient	19	24
HP reassures patient The patient states that he or she is reassured by the HP or the HP's behavior indicates reassurance	17	22
Patient mentions negative condition Patient mentions some form of pain or discomfort	12	15
Patient describes HP positively Patient provides a positive description of the HP	10	13

scolding or complaining to patients were subsumed under the theme "Health professional shows displeasure towards patient". Only themes that were reported by 10 percent or more of the participants were included. This process identified 13 main themes across the descriptions of satisfactory and unsatisfactory conversations. See Table 1 for the frequency with which themes were mentioned. There were seven themes for each conversational type, since one theme, "the patient explicitly mentioning being ill or in pain", occurred in both types of descriptions. In the descriptions of satisfactory conversations, four of the themes concerned positive interactions by

Table 1 (*continued*)
Definition of themes

Themes and Theme Definitions from Unsatisfactory Conversations	Number of Patients Who Used Theme	% of Patients Who Used Theme
HP shows displeasure towards the patient The HP: – scolds or complains to the patient – talks down to the patient (e.g., uses patronizing tone) – is unfriendly to the patient	28	41
HP does not show concern The HP seems not to care about the patient's well being (e.g., carrying out medical procedures in an uncaring or impersonal manner).	21	30
Patient mentions negative condition Patient mentions some form of pain or discomfort	17	25
Patient experiences negative emotions The patient states: – s/he is upset, scared or annoyed – the HP has made the patient feel ill at ease – the HP has not reassured the patient.	15	22
HP is not responsive to patient The HP: – does not listen to the patient or does not take the patient seriously – conducts a one-sided conversation with the patient, or conducts a conversation with the patient when the patient does not wish to talk – is not interested in the patient	15	22
HP provides poor quality information The HP does not provide sufficient information or the information provided is not presented in an appropriate way (e.g., too much medical jargon included).	12	17
Non-positive response to patient's request The patient requires the HP to carry out a task and the HP either complies but is surly or does not comply	11	16

Note: Seventy-nine participants wrote descriptions of satisfactory conversations, and 69 participants wrote descriptions of unsatisfactory ones.

health professionals: provides information, converses with and shows interest in patient, shows concern for patient, and reassures patient. A fifth theme, self disclosure, involved either one or both interactants contributing to the interaction. The sixth theme was about the patient's positive perception of the health professional. The most prevalent themes were the health professional showing concern and interest in the patient. The theme of self disclosure was also frequently mentioned. In the descriptions of unsatisfactory conversations, five themes focussed on the health professional: provides poor quality information, is not responsive to the patient, does not show concern, shows displeasure toward the patient, and provides a non-positive response to the patient's requests. The sixth theme, the patient experiences negative emotions, did not necessarily include the health professional as the cause of the dissatisfaction, although often it did. The seventh theme, as for the satisfactory conversations, referred to the patient's explicit mention of feeling ill or in pain. The most prevalent themes in the unsatisfactory conversations were health professionals showing displeasure or not showing concern for the patients.

The themes demonstrated the importance that health professionals need to place on the emotional and relationship needs of patients, which is consistent with CAT. There were three themes in the satisfactory conversations and three in the unsatisfactory ones that dealt with emotional and relationship needs. In the satisfactory conversations, these themes highlighted talking to patients, showing interest and concern for them (suggesting an addressee focus by the health professional on the relationship needs of the patient), and reassurance by the health professional (suggesting an addressee focus by the health professional on emotional needs). In addition, in the satisfactory conversations, there was a theme of mutual self-disclosure (suggesting a focus on both relationship needs and role relations). Conversely, the three themes in the unsatisfactory interactions that concerned the patient's relationship and emotional needs indicated that the health professional did not show concern and was not responsive, and that the patient experienced negative emotions.

These findings confirm the importance of examining affective processes in interactions between patients and health professionals (e.g., Cegala *et al.*, 1996; Street, 1991). However, it is clear that more research needs to be conducted which emphasizes the health professional's role in responding to the patient's relational and emotional needs.

Study 2, Part 2: Rating Emotional Expression

In the second part of the study we obtained ratings of exemplars of the 13 main themes. One hundred and thirty-four participants responded to items which tapped (1) the communication behaviors of the health professionals, and (2) evaluations of the interactions.

The satisfactory conversations received significantly more positive ratings than the unsatisfactory ones on all items. Participants rated health professionals as seeing the patients more as individuals, taking more notice of what the patients said, and allowing them to negotiate topic selection. With respect to the relational dimension of the interactions, participants rated the health professionals in the satisfactory conversations as higher in emotional expression than those in the unsatisfactory ones. The scores for the three items that represented interpersonal control indicated that health professionals in the satisfactory conversations were rated as using less dominant interpersonal control strategies, and that the patients were perceived as having more control than patients in the unsatisfactory encounters.

A key finding from this study revealed that health professionals' management of the relationship and emotional needs of patients is an important dimension of communication. The relationship needs of patients are noted in the literature, but are often seen as secondary to information giving (Cegala *et al.*, 1996). The results presented here suggest that a patient's relationship and emotional needs deserve as much attention as does accurate information provision.

Study 3

The previous studies were based on retrospective accounts. In the final study reported here, we used actual video-taped interactions between health professionals and hospitalized patients. Initially a number of video-taped interactions were rated for intergroup and interpersonal salience. Six interaction video segments were selected. Three had been rated as high on intergroup salience, and three rated as highly interpersonal.

One hundred and thirty-four participants rated these six videotaped interactions for levels of emotional expression, discourse management, interpretability and interpersonal control (see Watson & Gallois, 1998, for details). Participants watched the interactions and rated the six health professionals on emotional expression items concerning the extent to which they reassured the patient, showed liking for the patient, and acted to reduce the patient's anxiety. Results revealed that, in all cases, health professionals in the interpersonal interactions were rated as using the communication strategy of emotional expression more than those in the intergroup ones. This finding was the key difference between the two types of interactions. With respect to the other strategies, judges perceived few differences between more interpersonal and more intergroup interactions in terms of attention to role relations. Rather, they perceived all health professionals as attending to controlling and leading the interactions. In addition, they perceived all health professionals as attending to the capacity of the patients to give information and understand them clearly, although this appeared more strongly in the intergroup interactions. The finding that information giving was important complements the fact that patients in the segments were rated as possessing goals that related to communication competence (e.g., obtain information).

When we examine the importance of achieving an optimal balance of intergroup and interpersonal salience, the results suggest that combining intergroup communication behaviors (e.g., health professionals acknowledge their role as "expert" and manage the interaction process – asks questions) with interpersonal communication behaviors (e.g., show concern, provide some self-disclosure) leads to participants reporting higher levels of satisfaction than when only intergroup communication behaviors occur.

Conclusions and Future Directions

Satisfactory and effective communication is crucial for both patients and health professionals, which is why so much research has been conducted in the area (e.g., Ley, 1988; Pendleton, 1983; Thompson, 1994). However, much research in health communication has been criticized because of its atheoretical nature (e.g., Pendelton, 1983; Thompson, 1994). As discussed above, such studies do not provide theoretical explanations for satisfactory or unsatisfactory interactions between health providers and patients, which means that methods to ensure good communication cannot be systematically developed. Through the three studies briefly described here, we have begun a systematic examination of the role of emotional expression in medical encounters and the related importance of achieving optimal levels of intergroup and interpersonal salience. Across all three studies we found that participants describe interactions which are rated as satisfactory or interpersonal as being more positive, effective and pleasant than the corresponding unsatisfactory or intergroup interactions.

If patients find interactions more positive, effective and pleasant, there are clear implications that the patients may be more disposed to treatment regimen compliance and follow-up consultations, than they will be if they find the interaction anxiety provoking and ineffective. These outcome measures merit more investigation in order to match the patients' perceptions of communication effectiveness with compliance and good patient health care management.

In the descriptions of conversations rated as satisfactory and the video-taped segments rated as interpersonal, not only did participants rate the health professionals as engaging in strategies of accommodative discourse management and interpretability, but importantly, participants noted that the health professionals used accommodative emotional expression (e.g., reassuring or calming a patient).

By contrast, in the unsatisfactory conversations and intergroup segments, the only accommodative strategy used by health professionals was interpretability. Thus all patients, irrespective of the type of interaction, perceived that health professionals provided clear information and answered patients' questions. However, in the unsatisfactory conversations, health professionals were also attributed with non-accommodation in discourse management. These results suggest that health professionals' use of accommodative strategies of discourse management and emotional expression is a key component of interactions judged as either satisfactory or interpersonal. While several researchers have stressed the importance of accommodation in discourse management strategies (e.g., Coupland, Coupland, Giles & Henwood, 1988; Giles *et al.*, 1991; Jones, 1994) there has not been a similar emphasis on emotional expression. Our findings across three studies suggest that, in the health context, this is a valuable strategy which can substantially improve the quality of the interaction. Further, these findings highlight the importance of incorporating the role of emotional expression into the CAT model.

With respect to understanding optimal levels of intergroup and interpersonal salience in a medical context, our results provide evidence that when health professionals combine the use of accommodative interpersonal and intergroup communication behaviors, the interaction is judged as more effective and positive for the patients. This finding suggests that when the health professional appropriately emphasizes the intergroup nature of the health consultation (moves into role as "expert" with high levels of control) this is not necessarily viewed negatively by the patient. Negative appraisal by the patient would appear to occur when such communication behaviors are not accompanied at some time during the interaction with more interpersonally appropriate communication strategies.

In the three studies reported here, we found that irrespective of the type of interaction (interpersonal/satisfactory or intergroup/ unsatisfactory), patients reported, or were rated by participants as, focusing on goals that related to communication efficiency, e.g., obtaining information. This finding suggests that for patients clear communication with health professionals is *always* an important goal. It also suggests that patients do not desire an entirely interpersonal interaction, because they depend on the health professional for help, expertise, and accurate information. The functional nature of the interaction (i.e., the patient and health professional communicate clearly to facilitate accurate diagnosis and treatment) is always a key aspect of the interaction and reflects the task-oriented nature of the interaction.

Interestingly, the results for the use of interpersonal control suggest that patients also expect health professionals to have control in interactions. If health professionals manage this control with appropriate accommodation in discourse management and emotional expression (particularly reassurance and attention to the patient's anxiety), the findings here suggest that patients do not regard them negatively. If, however, only interpretability strategies are used in conjunction with control, patients are likely to view the interaction less positively. This last point is important because it reflects the premise that when interactions between health professionals and patients are perceived as highly intergroup, this need not denote overt negativity on the part of the health professional. Rather, it demonstrates a failure to acknowledge the patient in sufficiently interpersonal terms.

This research provides important new directions for CAT. The optimal balance of intergroup and interpersonal salience in effective communication requires more exploration. Our research suggests that where effective interactions combine aspects of intergroup salience (e.g., role as health professional salient in terms of levels of control, and role as expert) with interpersonal salience (e.g., health professional engages in appropriate emotional expression, and discourse management) they were perceived positively by partici-pants, and analyses of subsequent outcome measures confirmed this finding. Conversely, the combination of accommodative interpretability strategies (which did not suggest high interpersonal salience) with high interpersonal control was not rated positively by participants, and was perceived as intergroup. One explanation for this finding is that in the medical context, interpretability strategies are perceived as task-oriented, and therefore do not represent strong interpersonal salience. Analyses of outcome measures confirmed that these interactions were not rated favourably.

Thus we propose that, in the medical context within a hospital situation, positive interactions may occur when there is a combination of high intergroup and high interpersonal salience. The term "high" is used cautiously as it clearly needs more elaboration and may vary according to the sociohistorical history and length of relationship between the individual patient and health professional.

CAT researchers need to formally theorize how attention to relationship needs and emotional needs are expressed in sociolinguistic strategies, as has already been noted. Emotional expression as a strategy needs to be further extended and should perhaps include strategies such as self-disclosure, communication repair and facework. All these strategies need to be theorized more clearly and related to an addressee focus of relationship needs. Our research has found that mutual self-disclosure was most strongly related to attention to role relations. However, given the non-orthogonal nature of sociolinguistic strategies, mutual self-disclosure, while representing a reduction in interpersonal control in the current medical context, also served to build a relationship between the two interactants. Thus, self-disclosure was most probably also motivated, at least for the health professional, by an attention to the relationship needs of the patient. The role of self-disclosure and its importance in relational needs is the focus of our future research.

At the practical level, our findings highlight the need for health professionals to attend to the communication process during a consultation. Health professionals should attend to the emotional state of the patient and respond with appropriate concern and reassurance. They should focus on the verbal and non-verbal behaviors of the patient to assess anxiety levels and change their interaction style to fit the patient's needs. They need to be aware that their non-verbal behavior can inhibit or promote the well-being of the patient during a consultation (see Buller & Street, 1992).

Our findings indicate that intergroup identification as patient or health professional is not necessarily negative, provided that it is combined with other accommodative strategies that denote interpersonal salience. Thus the health professional may lead the conversation and be directive towards the patient, but he or she should also allow the patient an opportunity to help manage the interaction. Sharing the management of the interaction (to varying degrees according to patient needs) facilitates the communication process. Specifically, our research to date has offered evidence that health professionals need to focus on the individual as both a patient (his or her presenting problem), and as someone who possesses other personal interests and group identities (e.g., lover of fine wine, member of the local bowls club). The health professional who endeavours to know a little more about the patient's personal interests, encourages the patient to interact, and gives reassurance, provides a balance of intergroup and interpersonal salience that facilities an effective and positive consultation.

The current research focussed on hospital interactions, but is readily applicable to other types of medical contexts. Contexts of interest in terms of the dynamics of interactions include doctors' consulting rooms and patients' homes. The study of interactions with allied health workers would also extend the understanding of such interactions to a wider health domain. Currently, we are conducting research which broadens the range of health professions. Our future research will explore the strategy of emotional needs from both the health professional's and the patient's perspective. Future work should examine how health professionals differ in their perceptions of work satisfaction and well-being when they encounter interactions perceived as more satisfying.

References

Buller, D. B., & Street, R. L. Jr. (1992). Physician-patient relationships. In R. S. Feldman (Ed.), *Applications of nonverbal behavioural theories and research* (pp. 119–141). Hillsdale, N.J.: Lawrence Erlbaum.

Cegala, D. J., McGee, D. S. & McNellis, K. S.(1996). Components of patients' and doctors' perceptions of communication competence during a primary care interview. Health *Communication, 8,* 1–27.

Cegala, D. J., McNellis, K.S., & McGee, D. S. (1995). A study of doctors and patients perceptions of information processing and communication competence during the medical interview. *Health Communication, 7,* 179–203.

Coupland, N., Coupland, J., Giles, H., & Henwood, K. (1988). Accommodating the elderly: Invoking and extending a theory. *Language in Society, 17,* 1–41.

Gallois, C., Franklyn-Stokes, A., Giles, H. & Coupland, N. (1988). Communication accommodation in intercultural encounters. In Y. Y. Kim & W. B. Gudykunst (Eds.), *Theories in intercultural communication* (pp. 157–185). Newbury Park, CA: Sage

Gallois, C., & Giles, H. (1998). Accommodating mutual influence in intergroup encounters. In G. A. Barnett (Series Ed.) & M. T. Palmer & G. A. Barnett (Vol. Eds.), *Progress in communication sciences: 14. Mutual influence in interpersonal communication: Theory and research in cognition, affect, and behaviour* (pp. 135–162). Stamford, CT: Ablex.

Gardner, J. & Jones, E (1999). Problematic communication in the workplace: Beliefs of superiors and subordinates. *International Journal of Applied Linguistics, 9,* 185–205.

Giles, H. (1973). Accent mobility: A model and some data. *Anthropological Linguistics, 15,* 87–105.

Giles, H., Coupland, J. & Coupland, N. (1991). Accommodation theory: Communication, context, and consequence. In H. Giles, J. Coupland, & N. Coupland (Eds.), *Contexts of accommodation: Developments in applied sociolinguistics* (pp. 1–68). Cambridge: Cambridge University Press.

Giles, H. & Powesland, P. F. (1975). *Speech style and social evaluation.* London: Academic Press.

Hall, J. A., Roter, D.L. & Katz, N. R. (1988). Meta-analysis of correlates of provider behavior in medical encounters. *Medical Care 26,* 657–675.

Harwood, J., Giles, H., Fox, S. Ryan, E. B., & Williams, A. (1993). Patronizing young and elderly adults: Response strategies in a community setting. *Journal of Applied Communication Research, 21,* 211–226

Hummert, M. L. & Ryan, E. B. (1996). Towards understanding variations in patronizing talk addressed to older adults: Psycholinguistic features of care and control. *International journal of psycholinguistics, 12,* 149–169.

Hummert, M. L. & Ryan, E. B. (2001). Patronizing. In W P Robinson & H Giles (Eds.). *The new handbook of language and social psychology.* (pp 253–269). New York : J. Wiley.

Inui, T. S. & Carter, W. B. (1985). Problems and prospects for health services research on provider-patient communication. *Medical Care, 23,* 521–538.

Jones, E. (1994). *Communication in an academic context: The effects of status, ethnicity and sex.* Unpublished doctoral dissertation, University of Queensland, Brisbane, Australia.

Korsch, B. M. & Negrete, V. F. (1972). Doctor-patient communication. *Scientific American, 227,* 66–74.

Kreps, G. (1988). Relational care in health care communication. *The Southern Speech Communication Journal, 53,* 344–359.

Ley, P. (1988). *Communicating with patients: Improving communication, satisfaction and compliance.* London: Croom Helm.

Pendleton, D. (1983). Doctor-patient communication: A review. In D. Pendleton & J. Hasler (Eds.), *Doctor-Patient Communication* (pp 5–53). London: Academic Press, Inc.

Roter, D. L. & Hall, J. A.(1991). Health education theory: An application to the process of patient-provider communication. *Health Education Research, 6,* 185–193.

Roter, D. L. & Hall, J. A. (1992). *Doctors talking with patient/patients talking with doctors: Improving communication in medical visits.* Westport, CT: Auburn House.

Ryan, E. B., Giles, H., Bartolucci, G. & Henwood, K. (1986). Psycholinguistic and social psychological components of communication by and with the elderly. *Language and communication 6,* 1–24.

Ryan, E. B., Hummert, M. L., & Boich, L. H. (1995). Communication predicaments of aging: Patronizing behavior toward older adults. *Journal of Language and Social Psychology, 14,* 144–166.

Shepard, C.A., Giles, H., & Le Poire, B. A. (2001). Communication accommodation theory. In W. P. Robinson & H. Giles (Eds.). *The new handbook of language and social psychology.* (pp 33–56). New York : J. Wiley.

Street, Jr., R. L. (1991). Accommodation in medical consultations. In H. Giles., J. Coupland, & N. Coupland (Eds.), *Contexts of accommodation: Developments in applied sociolinguistics* (pp. 131–156). Cambridge: Cambridge University Press.

Street, Jr., R. L. (1993). Analyzing messages and their outcomes: Questionable assumptions, possible solutions. *Southern communication journal, 58,* 85–90.

Street, Jr., R. L. (2001). Active patients as powerful communicators. In W. P. Robinson & H. Giles (Eds.), *The new handbook of language and social psychology* (pp 541–560). New York: Wiley.

Street, Jr., R. L., Mulac, A., & Wiemann, J. M. (1988). Speech evaluation differences as a function of perspective (participant and observer) and presentational medium. *Human Communication Research, 14,* 333–363

Street, Jr., R. L. & Wiemann J. M. (1988). Differences in how physicians and patients perceive physicians' relational communication. *The Southern Speech Communication Journal, 53,* 420–440.

Tajfel, H. & Turner, J. (1979). An integrative theory of intergroup conflict. In W. G.Austin & S. Worchel (Eds.), *The social psychology of intergroup relations.* Belmont: Wadsworth Inc.

Thompson, T.L. (1994). Interpersonal communication and health care. In M. L. Knapp & G. R. Miller (Eds.), *Handbook of interpersonal communication (2nd Edition* (pp. 696–725). Newbury Park, CA: Sage.

Watson, B. & Gallois, C. (1998). Nurturing communication by health professionals toward patients: A communication accommodation theory approach. *Health Communication, 10,* 343–355.

Watson, B. & Gallois, C. (1999). Communication Accommodation between patients and health professionals: Themes and strategies in satisfactory and unsatisfactory encounters. *International Journal of Applied Linguistics, 9,* 167–183.

Watson, B. & Gallois, C. (2002). Patients' interactions with health providers: A linguistic category model approach. *Journal of Language and Social Psychology,* 21, 32–52.

Williams, A., Giles, H., Coupland, N., Dalby, M., & Manasse, H. (1990). The communicative contexts of elderly social support and health: A theoretical approach. *Health Communication. 2,* 123–143.

3

A Self-Categorization Perspective on Gender and Communication: Reconciling the Gender-as-Culture and Dominance Explanations

Nicholas A. PALOMARES
Scott A. REID
James J. BRADAC

Since the 1970s there has been sustained empirical and theoretical debate on the form, substance, and implications of gender differences in communication. Taken as a whole, research has established that there are indeed gender differences in communication, albeit differences that occur for specific linguistic forms in specific social circumstances (see, for reviews, Aries, 1996; Weatherall, 2002). For example, there is evidence that men are more likely than women to interrupt and dominate the floor when the conversational topic is masculine or gender neutral, whereas the reverse is true when the topic is feminine (e.g., Dovidio, Brown, Heltman, Ellyson, & Keating, 1988). Further, there is evidence that women engage in more communicative support and topic building than men (e.g., Fishman, 1978; Maltz & Borker, 1982; Makri-Tsilipakou, 1994).

Theoretical approaches that address these gender differences posit different explanatory mechanisms. On the one hand, the dominance approach explains how male socio-structural advantages over women manifest communicatively in mixed sex interactions

85

(e.g., Henley & Kramarae, 1991; Lakoff, 1975; Thorne & Henley, 1975). In short, men are conversationally dominant, and women conversationally submissive, because men have more social power than women. On the other hand, scholars claim that gender differences result from early learning and socialization that places men and women in distinct sub-cultures, with separate rules, norms, and communicative orientations (Maltz & Borker, 1982; cf. Gilligan, 1982). Men and women communicate differently, not because of power and patriarchy, but because they are culturally distinct.

Importantly, there are a number of weaknesses in both of these lines of reasoning. Both explanations encounter difficulty in accounting for situational variation in communicative behaviors. For example, there is evidence that both men and women display conversational dominance *and* submissiveness. Furthermore, for any given individual, such differences surface on some occasions but not on others. Seemingly, then, these theoretical approaches explain main effect differences in male/female communication, but not interaction effects with social contexts. A broader theoretical account needs to explain: (1) differences in communicative form *and* content (broadly speaking, and most importantly for our paper, the frequencies of "cooperative" and "competitive" communication); *and* (2) situational dynamics. Stated differently, research on gender and communication would benefit greatly from a theoretical account that explains what communicative behaviors men and women will use, under what circumstances, and why.

The objective of this chapter, then, is to offer such a theoretical account from the perspective of self-categorization theory (Turner, 1985; 1987). By understanding the social context in which inter-gender contact takes place, we can predict concomitant effects upon the salience of gender identity, its normative character, and the emergence of descriptive and prescriptive rules for communication. Some social contexts promote gender identity salience, while others encourage the salience of different identities. Further, depending upon the details surrounding a particular context, we can predict whether gender will or will not be salient, and *if* gender is salient, what normative standards will prevail. The specific normative standard has implications for communication in general and, specifically, language use, language attitudes, and the degree of social influence speakers can generate.[1] In providing this account, we will review research on gender and communication with the aim of reconciling unexplained and inconsistent results in the literature. Next, two extant theoretical approaches are described and representative findings discussed. Following this, self-categorization theory is discussed with a focus on gender identity salience, illustrating how this concept can provide a unified account for empirical and theoretical discrepancies within the literature. Finally, a set of propositions that flow from self-categorization theory is elaborated. Along the way, we attempt to reconcile, and show points of contact between, the dominance and gender-as-culture explanations for communicative differences between men and women.

Research on Gender and Communication

The gender and communication literature provides evidence for situational variation in the content and incidence of male/female differences. For example, Carli (1990) reported a greater frequency of tentative language use (i.e., *tag questions*, *hedges*, and *disclaimers*) for women in mixed-sex but not same-sex interactions, while Brouwer, Gerritsen, and De Haan (1979; see also Crosby & Nyquist, 1977) failed to detect differences for men and women interacting in a public setting with service people. Further, McLachlan (1991) demonstrated that the occurrence of male/female language difference depended on the nature of the conversation. During disagreements men and women used similar communication patterns (e.g., *overlapping speech* and *back channels*), but when in agreement men and women used divergent patterns.

Some of the most stable gender differences in the literature – the language differences detected in research demonstrating the gender-linked language effect (see, for a review, Mulac, 1998)[2] – are not entirely free from inconsistent results. In this research, across a variety of situations, men used language features such as *directives* (e.g., "Read this book.") more frequently than women, while women used features such as *references to emotion* (e.g., "I am happy.") more frequently than men. There is evidence for gender-linked language differences in public speeches (Mulac & Lundell, 1982), written discourse (Mulac & Lundell, 1994), impromptu essays (Mulac, Studley, & Blau, 1990), same-sex and mixed-sex problem solving dyadic interactions (Mulac, Wiemann, Widenmann, & Gibson, 1988), small groups interacting anonymously via asynchronous computer-mediated communication (Mulac, Flanagin, Tiyaamornwong, Palomares, & Hallett, 2001), and other forms and contexts (e.g., Mulac & Lundell, 1980; 1986). The majority of these studies have used university students' language, but a number have sampled the language of fourth- and fifth-grade students, graduate teaching assistants and lecturers, and people in their 50s and 60s. In fact, knowing particular combinations of features of an individual's language use alone allows for high accuracy in predicting communicator sex (at times as high as 97 percent accuracy using discriminant analysis; Mulac, 1998). Nevertheless, Mulac and associates (Mulac, Seibold, & Farris, 2000) recently found evidence for a partial reversal in gender-linked language use. In this study, Mulac *et al.* examined managers and working professionals during role plays of criticism-giving to colleagues and found that men used more *references to emotion* than women. Clearly, inconsistencies exist in the gender and communication literature, as even Mulac and colleagues' research, which primarily has found the same main effect for gender across studies, contains anomalous findings at times.

While communication differences can exist between men and women as a main effect, the specific nature of these gender differences and the extent to which they manifest interact with contextual variables. Indeed, if anything, apart from the aforementioned research of Mulac and associates, situational interaction effects seem to be more prevalent than gender main effects. For example, research has demonstrated mutual convergence between men and women (e.g., Mulac *et al.*, 1988), while other research has shown unilateral convergence (i.e., language divergence of men and convergence of women; e.g., Hogg, 1985). Moreover, Aries (1996) conducted an extensive review and critique of male/female communicative differences and reached the conclusion that the similarities far outweigh differences; she went on to state "that knowledge of a person's gender will give us little ability to accurately predict how a person will behave in many situations" (p. 189). What is needed, then, is a theoretical mechanism to account for such differences relative to the context. This need is especially concerning given that the two prominent theoretical explanations of gender-based communication differences (subsequently discussed) are limited and often unnecessarily viewed as competing and divergent.

Explanations for Gender and Communication

Both major explanations for gender-based communication differences – the gender-as-culture and dominance explanations – predict only main effects for gender. The reasoning, however, for such main effects diverges across these explanations, which often are seen as competing (unnecessarily). We propose that, while they both have some merit, these explanations and their predicted main effects do not account for contextual shifts in gendered communication. In what follows, we review these explanations and supporting evidence, and conclude that another theoretical mechanism is needed to explain the dynamics of gender and communication.

Gender-as-Culture and Communication

Maltz and Borker's (1982) gender-as-culture argument is that men and women are socialized from an early age in two different normative/sociolinguistic sub-cultures. Because men and women for the most part grow up communicating with same-sex peers, they develop different communicative patterns. Boys are socialized to be competitive, independent, and assertive, whereas girls are socialized to be cooperative, dependent, and nurturing. Language use patterns reflect these socialization differences. Competitive boys tend to interrupt and dominate conversation, while cooperative girls tend to ask questions with the aim of supporting conversational flow. This same idea is even reproduced and dramatized in the popular press (e.g., Gray, 1992).

Mulac, Bradac and Gibbons (2001) have provided the most direct evidence supporting the gender-as-culture explanation. In three studies, Mulac *et al.* found that gender-linked language variables were perceived to vary along intercultural dimensions of style such as directness and instrumentality (Gudykunst & Ting-Toomy, 1988), dimensions that other research demonstrated covary with national cultures (Gudykunst *et al.*, 1996). Despite the fact that sex of speaker was not indicated nor detectable, language variables typically associated with men (e.g., *directives*, *references to quantity*) were perceived as more direct, succinct, personal and instrumental compared to female language variables. On the other hand, variables typically associated with women (e.g., *references to emotion*, *intensive adverbs*) were perceived to be more indirect, elaborate and affective compared to male language. Thus, typical male language differs from typical female language across intercultural dimensions of communication style in ways consistent with other research that shows national cultures vary along these same dimensions. The gender-as-culture explanation and supportive research, nevertheless, do not preclude the possibility that power and status play important roles in male/female language differences, as Mulac *et al.* (2001) note.

Male Dominance and Communication

The male dominance perspective is the second major attempt to account for gender-based communicative differences (Henley &

Kramarae, 1991; Lakoff, 1975; Thorne & Henley, 1975). The underlying assumption of the dominance approach is that communicative differences between men and women reflect wider socio-structural differences that favor men. In other words, one finds gender-based communication differences as a result of men's power over women. Indeed, some research shows that men interrupt and control the conversation more than women, and this is interpreted as male dominance (e.g., Fishman, 1977, 1978; Swan & Graddol, 1988; West & Garcia, 1988; Zimmermann & West, 1975). *Interruptions*, however, do not necessarily indicate dominance, as they can be affiliative or disaffiliative; nevertheless, research addressing this issue has shown that women use *interruptions* for support and agreement, while men use them indiscriminately usually directing *interruptions* toward female speakers (Makri-Tsilipakou, 1994). The dominance explanation, thus, holds that men assert and maintain their higher status over women communicatively.

There is, however, a significant problem with the gender-as-culture and dominance explanations. Namely, these two theoretical approaches cannot easily account for the many aforementioned contextual variations in male and female communication. In other words, these two approaches have little success in explaining and predicting what gender-based communicative differences will emerge, under what circumstances, and for what reasons. Why do differences emerge in some instances but not others, and how is it that across studies inconsistencies exist regarding the specific aspects of the detected differences? Both approaches are difficult to reconcile with data that show that women are more dominant than men in conversations when the topic is stereotypically feminine (e.g., Dovidio *et al.*, 1988; Postmes & Spears, 2002). Similarly, both approaches are difficult to reconcile with evidence that men and women at times use the language pattern typical of the opposite gender group (e.g., Mulac *et al.*, 2000; Palomares, 2003). Quite simply, these approaches, while offering some explanatory insights, still cannot fully account for gender-based communicative differences. For this reason, a theory comprehensive enough to reconcile the discrepant findings and unify the extant theoretical perspectives is essential, if gender-based communicative phenomena are to be fully understood.

Self-Categorization Theory and Social Identity Salience

Self-categorization theory (Turner, 1985, 1987) provides the theoretical basis for an account of the gender-based communicative differences presented above. According to self-categorization theory, individuals make sense of the world through the lens of self-categorizations. On the grossest level, people can represent themselves in terms of any of three levels of abstraction. People can represent themselves as idiosyncratic individuals in the context of an ingroup (e.g., what defines a person at work, in the family, etc.), as members of a collectivity in the context of other groups (e.g., what defines a person as an American in contrast to an Iraqi), or as a human being in the context of other species. Of course, people can define themselves in any number of ways within these levels of abstraction. In short, the theory was conceived to capture these variations in self-definition – that is, to provide an account of identity salience and its behavioral effects.

Two factors determine which particular social identity will become salient (i.e., operate psychologically/cognitively) for an individual in any given social context – accessibility and fit. Accessibility, also known as perceiver readiness, is an individual's contribution to categorization. People are more likely to identify themselves with some groups than others, and this can reflect, among other things, schemata, goals, needs, interests, prior experiences, and the degree of commitment to a group. The contextual contribution to fit is composed of comparative and normative elements. Following comparative fit, people are more likely to internalize categories that are objectively represented in the social environment. For example, one would be more likely to categorize using gender if in a particular context there were differences between men and women. These differences can be based in any number of things; a far from complete list might include attitude positions, accents, phrases, voice pitch, spatial location, hair color, and physical stature. Furthermore, following the meta-contrast principle, when people internalize comparative information, they do so in a way that maximizes the ratio of inter-category differences to within-category differences. This serves to clarify the salient self-categorization. Importantly, people are more likely to internalize comparative differences when they correlate with normative expectations (i.e., normative fit). For example, a categorization based on gender would be more likely if men were to take a stereotypically competitive stance and women a stereotypically cooperative stance in a discussion. Taken together, people most likely internalize (i.e., make cognitively salient) categories that are accessible to them personally, especially when that category is cognitively present in the social world, and the behavior of group members is normatively consistent with those categories.

Salient self-categorizations are represented as prototypes. Prototypes are cognitive representations of descriptive and prescriptive features that capture the essence of a particular identity within a given social context. For example, at the time of writing (March 29, 2003; 10 days into the war in Iraq), a number of American women might define themselves as powerful, aggressive, freedom loving, and patriotic in comparison with Iraqis. On the other hand, in comparison to American men, these same American women might define themselves as cooperative, nurturing and gentle. Clearly, in different social contexts the same social identity can take on a different normative character depending upon the intergroup relationship with the comparison other. These self-definitions have behavioral consequences. Prototypical definitions of groups are not just descriptive, they are also prescriptive. For example, the media in the United States is currently awash with information that supports the war with Iraq; as a consequence, anyone who chooses to oppose the war is likely to face argument. In contrast, within France, and a great number of other countries, the prevailing national self-definition is anti-war, and expressing a pro-war position is likely to produce angry disagreement.

Gender Identity Salience and Communication

Of importance to the current line of reasoning is the idea that communicative behaviors are determined in large part by one's self-conception as it reflects social group membership in specific social contexts. Following from this logic, we would predict gender-based communicative differences to manifest only when gender identity is salient. Further, the specific normative character (i.e., normative fit) of the salient gender identity will reflect the intergroup relationship (broadly speaking, the degree to which the relationship is cooperative or competitive), and the degree to which gender fits a particular context.

When power relations privilege men over women, we would expect communication to reflect this status discrepancy. Research by Hogg (1985) offers indirect support for this claim. When interacting in either cooperative same-sex dyads or competitive mixed-sex groups, where men and women disagreed about a controversial topic, men and women's language was perceived by naïve raters as more masculine and less feminine in the competitive intergroup context than in the intragroup context. Notwithstanding the fact that language features were not analyzed by trained coders, this research suggests that unilateral accommodation can occur under conditions of gender identity salience where intergroup relations favor men (as research demonstrates that men by default have the power advantage in mixed sex interactions; Dovidio *et al.*, 1988). Specifically, men will diverge in their language from women, and women will converge to the male standard. We speculate further and suggest that studies in support of the dominance explanation, which find that men tend to interrupt and control the conversation more than women (e.g., West & Garcia, 1988; Zimmermann &

West, 1975), were examining communication differences in situations where participants had a salient gender identity that emerged from a conversation with a topic in which higher status for men was normatively appropriate (see Dovidio *et al.*, 1988).

The specific nature of gender identity salience not only accounts for male communicative dominance, but also female communicative dominance (e.g., Dovidio *et al.*, 1988; Postmes & Spears, 2002). Dovidio *et al.* (1988) showed that during mixed-sex dyadic conversations on a stereotypically feminine topic, women displayed more verbal and non-verbal dominance over men. Thus, when women have higher status than men (because of the implicit expertise granted to women due to the feminine topic), this difference is reflected in communicative behaviors. We suggest that in this condition gender identity was salient because higher status for women over men was normatively relevant. Indeed, other research demonstrates that men only dominate conversations with women when they have a salient social identity and the topic is masculine, but not when the topic is feminine or when a personal identity is salient (Postmes & Spears, 2002). Although no research directly tests our explanation, it seems theoretically logical that when gender identity is salient as a result of status differences favoring women, women will demonstrate this discrepancy over men communicatively.

The previous discussion demonstrates how inconsistencies in previous research, especially research within the explanatory realm of the dominance approach, can be accounted for when considering gender identity salience and the specific nature of normative fit (i.e., including status differences or not). More can be said, however, to account for research within the gender-as-culture domain. Relations between cultural groups in general and even between sub-cultural groups, as in the current case of gender, can result in an intergroup distinction (Tajfel, 1982). These intergroup relations between cultures can also result in competition and status hierarchies.

This pattern, however, need not occur in all cases. Specifically, men and women belong to two different groups within society with each group having certain normative differences reflecting their (sub-)cultural group identities. As previously demonstrated, status differentials can easily become a part of their intergroup relationship. However, what happens when status is not a primary part of intergroup relations for men and women yet gender identity maintains its salience? Research by Mulac *et al.* (1988) offers one possible answer. Men and women exhibited mutual convergence when interacting in same-sex problem-solving dyads. Specifically, when working cooperatively to solve a problem (a superordinate goal, perhaps; see Sherif, 1958), men and women linguistically demonstrated solidarity by adopting language more typical of the opposite gender group. Thus, we suggest that when gender identity is salient as a result of cooperative intergroup relations normatively fitting for both men and women, language use will reflect this unity. In this case cooperation is the variable conducive to normative fit, whereas in our previous examples status difference was the normative variable. Interestingly, cooperation and status are themes emphasized in the peer-group socialization of women and men, respectively, according to Maltz and Borker (1982). This suggests an important point: Although men and women may have dissimilar behavioral tendencies as a result of socialization, members of each group are capable of manifesting the tendencies of the opposite-sex group. This pattern is also apparent in the case of gender-linked language, where each group adopts the language of the other group to some extent, as in a situation of mutual accommodation. (We advance these ideas in the following section.)

Recent research directly supports our claim that gender identity salience affects the production of language. Reid, Keerie, and Palomares (2003) predicted, and found, that when a shared student identity was salient (and gender identity was not salient) men and women used similar levels of tentative language (as defined by Carli, 1990; Lakoff, 1975). Given that tentative language use is not prototypical for undergraduate students, differences not emerging in that condition should not be surprising. However, in conditions designed to elevate gender salience, women used more tentative language, and men tended to use less. Here, tentative language was prototypical for females, and non-tentative language was prototypical for males. These findings suggest that previous research that has failed to detect gender-based communicative differences may have tested in contexts where gender identity was not salient, and that research that has found differences conducted tests under conditions where gender identity was salient. Theoretically, this makes sense – only when gender plays a role in one's cognitions should it influence one's communication.

More support for the ability of gender identity salience to incorporate extant discrepant research and the two theoretical approaches comes when considering another component of gender identity salience – gender identity accessibility. As previously stated, the adherence to a group's social norms, according to self-categorization theory, is affected by the accessibility of the category salience. One measure of (chronic) gender identity accessibility derives from gender schema theory (Bem, 1981; 1983; 1985). This theory states that certain individuals possess gender schemata, which are cognitive structures or networks of associations that predispose individuals to process information in terms of the learned cultural definitions of gender. Individuals with a gender schema have a chronic readiness "to encode and to organize information – including information about the self – according to the culture's definitions of maleness and femaleness" (Bem, 1985, p. 186). Thus, gender schematic (or sex-typed) individuals view themselves as being more typical of their gender and adopt consistent behaviors. Palomares (2003) tested these ideas in an examination of the effects of gender schematicity and gender identity salience (without reference to status differences) on Mulac's (1998) definition of gender-linked language. This study revealed that, on the whole, only gender-schematic individuals with a salient gender identity used gender-linked language. Specifically, when gender was salient, gender schematic individuals used more gender-linked language than both non-gender schematic individuals and gender-schematic individuals with low gender identity salience (i.e., high student identity salience). These results suggest that gender identity salience only affects gender-linked language for those with a schema regarding the cultural definition of gender.

The main purpose of this section has been to provide a comprehensive theoretical account of male/female communicative differences. Specifically, answers to the following questions were sought: When do men and women differ in their communication and when do they not? What factors play a role in determining the extent and specific character of such differences? Why do gender-based communication differences manifest at all? We have also suggested points of contact between the ostensibly competing dominance and gender-as-culture explanations for male/female communication differences. These two explanations are reconciled when the contextual salience of gender identity is considered.

Specifically, men and women will differ communicatively when the social context warrants such differences. Gender identity salience and, more importantly, the specific normative nature of the salience are major factors in determining the extent to and precise ways in which gender-based communication differences will occur. Finally, communicative gender differences reflect the socio-historical and contextually relevant differences between men and women that are accessible and (comparatively and normatively) fit the context.

Explaining Mutual Accommodation and Linguistic Gender Reversal

As indicated above, in particular contexts, such as when cooperation is normatively appropriate for both men and women, linguistic convergence may occur such that women will use forms that are typically masculine (e.g., *judgmental adjectives*) and men will use forms that are typically feminine (e.g., *uncertainty verbs*). Also, more broadly, men may adopt an indirect style that is also emotional and elaborate, while women may adopt a direct, instrumental, and succinct style (Mulac *et al*, 2001). Not surprising is that men can be indirect or that women can be direct; some roles demand counter-typicality, as in the cases of male diplomats or female physicians. What is perhaps more surprising is that in linguistic accommodation, men may use many specific feminine linguistic forms and women may use many specific masculine forms, many of which are not usually monitored or even noticed by speakers or hearers in spontaneous speech (e.g., *intensive adverbs* and *locatives*).

More specifically, some of the language variables associated with male/female differences and implicated in mutual accommodation and linguistic gender reversal are syntactic variables (e.g., *dependent clauses* and *sentence initial adverbials*) and there is evidence that speakers and hearers are usually unaware of syntactic variation and that they have poor memory for syntax (see, Mulac, Bradac, & Palomares, 2003). Other non-syntactic features also are implicated in mutual accommodation between men and women and linguistic gender reversal (e.g., *references to quantity* and *judgmental adjectives*). Responding to the latter fact, Mulac *et al.* (2003) suggest that "it seems highly unlikely that speakers monitor their performance in order to produce more or fewer of [these forms] in spontaneous interactive speech with the purpose of appearing masculine or feminine. Such monitoring would appear to greatly exceed the attentional capacity and computational abilities of most speakers" (p. 14).

The question then becomes: If at least some of the language features that are implicated in mutual mixed-sex accommodation and linguistic gender reversal exist with low or no speaker or hearer awareness, and if speakers *cannot manipulate* these features because they are unaware of them, then how is it that sometimes men exhibit a feminine language style and women a masculine language style? What mechanism accounts for this kind of linguistic cross-over?

One possibility is that in a mixed-sex interactive situation men quickly copy the language style of the women with whom they are interacting based on the woman's preceding turn or turns. This would demand a subtle and powerful information-processing device, especially given that some of the gender-linked language features exist outside of communicator's awareness and given the attentional demands of substantive interaction. Also, such an "on-line" copying device would not explain linguistic gender reversal in non-accommodative situation where individuals are communicating monologically (Mulac & Lundell, 1982; Palomares, 2003).

An alternative to a copying device is what Mulac *et al.* (2003) have labeled "gender-linked language schemata." These are implicit cognitive structures existing outside awareness, analogous to knowledge of grammatical rules, differing from linguistic stereotypes about gender, which are beliefs about language and gender available to introspection (e.g., "girls use flowery words"). Gender-linked language schemata are similar to Bem's (1985) notion of gender schemata in that they are learned though interaction with others and through observation of models, perhaps on television (see Mulac, Bradac, & Mann, 1985). These cognitive structures are energized (i.e., made salient) variously by different contexts. They enable the production of gender-linked language. Both men and women learn feminine and masculine gender-linked language schemata, which allows for mutual accommodation in mixed-sex groups and for linguistic gender reversal. The suggestion that both men and women learn both types of schemata deviates to some extent from the position of Maltz and Borker (1982).

A third possibility exists however. Men and women may adopt language typical of the other gender without being aware of it because such language can be prototypical of different social categories. So, for example, female physicians may use relatively direct "male" forms of language, but it seems quite likely that these forms are also prototypical of physicians in general. Objectively speaking, this language may be categorized as "male-typical," but psychologically it remains "physician-typical." Similarly, male diplomats who use female-typical indirect language are unlikely to be conscious of gender because they actually find being a diplomat salient – along with associated norms of being judicious, non-confrontational, and secretive. If this is indeed the relevant prototype for diplomats, then we would expect that the diplomat identity is salient, and gender identity is not, even though we researchers might notice that the language is objectively feminine. Possibly, then, there is considerable overlap between the kinds of language that can be prototypical for gender and prototypical for other social groups, but the degree to which people are conscious of a particular form being relevant to gender will depend upon whether gender is salient in the particular social context.

Indeed, data from Reid *et al.* (2003) speak to this point. Reid and colleagues found that their manipulation check on the salience of gender varied as a function of: (1) their manipulation of salience (gender vs. student identity); (2) the gender of the speaker; and (3) the degree to which the speakers' (opposite sex) conversational partner used tentative language. In conditions where student identity was salient, people rated the salience of gender as low, regardless of their gender, or their partner's use of tentative language. When gender salience was high, men felt that gender was more salient the *more* that their female conversational partner used tentative language, and females reported that gender was more salient the *less* that their male conversational partner used tentative language. These findings demonstrate that language use and the perception of it are tied closely to the degree to which language fits a given social context both comparatively (i.e., objectively) *and* normatively.

There is, however, another phenomenon yet to be explained. Namely, the research examining the gender-linked language effect shows that men and women use language differently across a great number of social contexts, and at least a sub-set of which seem unlikely to be associated with comparative divisions, or normative expectations for gender. In these situations we would argue that the chronic salience of gender in society produces a carry-over effect – gender is relevant to most of everyday experience, and it serves to structure many of our everyday interactions, so much so that such gendered behavior becomes automatic. In short, the chronic nature of gender in the social world makes gender chronically accessible and, therefore, frequently salient. However, should the social relations between men and women actually change socio-structurally, we would expect this pattern to decrease, disappear, or even reverse.

The latter two explanations (i.e., schemata and prototypes) of mutual accommodation and linguistic gender reversal need not preclude each other, however. That is to say, what is prototypical of male/female communicative behaviors may be determined in large part by one's gender-linked language schemata (the reverse may also be the case, suggesting a reciprocal relationship between what is prototypical and what is cognitively socialized regarding gender-linked language). Further, these gender-linked language schemata may be salient by default, such that the schemata determine what is prototypical in most interactions, and gender-based communication differences frequently occur outside of awareness. However, when other identities become salient, making gender a non-factor for communication, gender-linked language schemata will not be energized and therefore have no effect on language use. With this line of reasoning, men and women can demonstrate divergent or convergent language patterns and even linguistic gender reversal when a salient gender identity is active via energized gender-linked language schemata and prototypes. The existence of gender-based communicative patterns, however, depends on whether gender identity is salient or not, whereas the specific nature of the gender-based communicative patterns (e.g., divergence, convergence, etc.) are determined by the normative fit of the salient gender identity.

Propositions

Several propositions follow from the line of reasoning offered throughout this chapter, a few of which are briefly explicated in this section.

One of the first ideas derived from the theoretical foundation outlined above is that gender-based communicative differences will *not* occur at all times. Language differences occur when gender plays a role in one's self-conception and when the language differences are socially meaningful and lend to intragroup and intergroup relations. Thus:

> P_1: Communication differences between men and women are only manifest in contexts where gender identity is

salient (either by default or contextually activated) and the communicative differences serve to reflect the salient normative dynamics within and between gender groups.

Much too can be said regarding the specific nature of gender identity salience. The specific type of salience depends on the accessibility and fit of the gender differences, as the nature of the gender identity salience and the history of the gender groups (in relation to each other) will impact the extent to which and the specific ways in which gender-based communicative differences emerge. In general, determining if the comparative relations between men and women are mostly cooperative or competitive will allow for considerable predictive success, although specific contextual factors will minimize or maximize cooperative or competitive tendencies. When status differences are part of the salient gender prototype, then communication patterns of interacting men and women will reflect these differences. From this, two additional propositions result:

P_2: When gender identity with reference to men's higher status over women is normatively fitting, then the communicative behaviors of men and women will reflect this gender power inequality.

P_3: When gender identity with reference to female's higher status over men is normatively fitting, then the communicative behaviors of men and women will reflect this gender power inequality.

However, if gender relations are cooperative, then communication should reflect this normative dynamic. Accordingly, the following proposition is offered:

P_4: When gender identity with reference to cooperative intergroup relations between men and women normatively fits, communication will reflect this underlying cooperative relationship.

The second and third propositions suggest that when the social context makes dominance (e.g., aggression, power, and control) a part of the normative fit of gender identity salience, then perhaps the dominant gender group will use more *directives* (e.g., "Stop what you are doing now."), more direct *elliptical sentences* (e.g., "Good idea."), more negative *judgmental adjectives* (e.g., "stupid," "ugly"), more *disaffiliative interruptions*, and less tentative/hesitant language features (e.g., *tag questions, disclaimers*) than the other gender group who will be more submissive communicatively. Importantly, the dominant gender group could be either men or women (depending on the specific normative nature of gender identity salience); thus, the previous language features are *not* inherently male or female, rather they simply reflect the dominance of one gender group over the other which *is* inherent in the contextually dependent normative nature of gender identity salience. On the other hand, the fourth proposition suggests that when the normative fit of gender identity salience includes cooperation (e.g., solidarity, camaraderie, collaboration), then language of both men and women will perhaps contain more *references to emotion* (e.g., "I am thrilled to see you."), more *affiliative interruptions*, and more *intensifiers* (e.g., "I really like it.") to demonstrate this cooperative intergroup relation. But what happens when gender identity is salient and competition between men and women is normative such that both gender groups try to achieve dominance over the other? Perhaps language differences in this context do not emerge because both groups exhibit similar frequencies of using *directives*, disaffiliative *interruptions* and other communicative indicators of dominance. Extant research has not yet attempted to manipulate the normative fit of gender identity salience; thus, significant research examining the gender-based communicative patterns (differences and similarities) that emerge under various types of gender identity salience awaits. Overall, by accounting for the nature of the normative fit between men and women when gender identity is salient, we suspect that interesting predictions could be made regarding what gender-based communicative patterns will emerge, when and why.

Predictions also can be made for the specific nature of gender identity salience within same-sex social contexts. Intragroup relations for one gender group can vary in normative fit as well, which can influence their intragroup communicative patterns. For example, when gender identity including feelings of solidarity is salient for a group of women, then perhaps they will communicatively enact this identity to express their intragroup camaraderie via specific language patterns (e.g., use more *references to emotion* and *intensifiers*) that may distinguish them from a group of men trying to enact their own male ingroup identity. Thus, we would expect the following to be demonstrated empirically:

P_5: The specific nature of gender identity salience in same-sex encounters will determine the ways in which communication patterns are established for men interacting with other men and women interacting with other women.

We outlined the propositions above to offer a flavor of the potential for self-categorization theory and, more specifically, the concept of gender identity salience to account for many of the phenomena within the area of gender and communication. These propositions, needless to say, are not exhaustive and await direct empirical confirmation. Further, related propositions regarding language attitudes (e.g., the gender-linked language effect) and social influence follow from our theoretical account, although we have chosen not to discuss these possibilities in the current chapter. Nonetheless, in current work underway, we expand on Reid *et al.*'s (2003) findings in an experimental study where participants in either a high gender or high student (i.e., low gender) identity salience condition listen to a recording of a persuasive speaker using either tentative or direct language. From this study we anticipate several findings predicted from our self-categorization theoretical explanation of gender and communication, some of which examine language convergence and divergence of participants to speakers, the degree of social influence, and participants' judgments of speakers.

Conclusions

The following idea underpins our theoretical argument: Communication reflects the relevant similarities and differences of men and women in any given social context. With this rationale, a theoretical unification of much of the theoretical and empirical record on gender and communication materializes. Specifically, one can predict when gender-based communicative differences should or should not be detected and the specific content and patterns of such differences. A gender-as-culture dynamic, a male dominance dynamic, or perhaps some other dynamic of gender-based communication patterns can come to the fore in a particular context depending on the salience of gender identity and, specifically, its normative character. In other words, the gender-as-culture and dominance explanations can mutually co-exist when considering the normative nature of gender identity salience. Different cultures *can* have a power/dominance component to their intergroup interactions; whether or not this power/dominance component plays a role in a particular interaction depends on and can be predicted from knowing the normative nature of gender identity salience. Advancing this theoretical reasoning along with pertinent research may well cast a brighter light on the *dynamics* of gender and communication.

Notes

1. We, however, focus our current attention just on communication and language use.

2. The gender-linked language effect is the consistent finding that typical male language is judged more dynamic than typical female language, whereas typical female language is judged more aesthetically pleasing and socio-intellectual than typical male language (Mulac, 1998). As mentioned, language attitudes, such as the gender-linked language effect, are outside the scope of the current argument. However, the gender-linked language patterns, that significantly determine the gender-linked language effect (see Mulac & Lundell, 1986), are of concern.

References

Aries, E. (1996). *Men and women in interaction: Reconsidering the differences.* New York: Oxford University Press.

Bem, S. L. (1981). Gender schema theory: A cognitive account of sex typing. *Psychological Review, 88,* 354–364.

Bem, S. L. (1983). Gender schema theory and its implications for child development: Raising gender-aschematic children in a gender-schematic society. *Signs: Journal of Women in Culture and Society, 8,* 598–616.

Bem, S. L. (1985). Androgyny and gender schema theory: A conceptual and empirical integration. In T. B. Sonderegger (Ed.), *Nebraska symposium on motivation: Psychology and gender* (pp. 179–226). Lincoln: University of Nebraska Press.

Brouwer, D., Gerritsen, M. M., & De Haan, D. (1979). Speech differences between women and men: On the wrong track. *Language in Society, 8,* 33–50.

Carli, L. (1990). Gender, language, and influence. *Journal of Personality and Social Psychology, 59*(5), 941–951.

Crosby, F., & Nyquist, L. (1977). The female register: An empirical study of Lakoff's hypotheses. *Language in Society, 6,* 313–322.

Dovidio, J. F., Brown, C. E., Heltman, K., Ellyson, S. L., & Keating, C. F. (1988). Power displays between women and men in discussions of gender-linked tasks: A multichannel study. *Journal of Personality & Social Psychology, 55,* 580–587.

Fishman, P. (1977). Interactional shiftwork. *Heresies: A Feminist Publication on Art and Politics,* 1, 99–101.

Fishman, P. (1978). Interaction: The work women do. *Social Problems, 25,* 397–406.

Gilligan, C. (1982). *In a different voice: Psychological theory and women's development.* Cambridge, MA: Harvard University Press.

Gray, J. (1992). *Men are from Mars, women are from Venus.* New York: Harper Collins.

Gudykunst, W. B., Matsumoto, Y., Ting-Toomy, S., Nishida, T., Kwangsu, K., & Heyman, S. (1996). The influence of cultural individualism-collectivism, self-construals, and individual values on communication styles across cultures. *Human Communication Research, 22,* 510–543.

Gudykunst, W. B., & Ting-Toomy, S. (1988). *Culture and interpersonal communication.* Newbury Park, CA: Sage.

Henley, J. M., & Kramarae, C. (1991). Gender, power, and miscommunication. In N. Coupland & H. Giles & J. M. Wiemann (Eds.), *"Miscommunication" and problematic talk* (pp. 18–43). Newbury Park, CA: Sage.

Hogg, M. A. (1985). Masculine and feminine speech in dyads and groups: A study of speech style and gender salience. *Journal of Language & Social Psychology, 4*, 99–112.

Lakoff, R. (1975). *Language and women's place.* New York: Harper & Row.

Makri-Tsilipakou, M. (1994). Interruptions revisited: Affiliative vs. disaffiliative intervention. *Journal of Pragmatics, 21*, 401–426.

Maltz, D. J., & Borker, R. A. (1982). A cultural approach to male-female miscommunication. In J. J. Gumpertz (Ed.), *Language and social identity* (pp. 196–216). Cambridge: Cambridge University Press.

McLachlan, A. (1991). The effects of agreement, disagreement, gender and familiarity on patterns of dyadic interaction. *Journal of Language & Social Psychology, 10*, 205–212.

Mulac, A. (1998). The gender-linked language effect: Do language differences really make a difference? In D. J. Canary & K. Dindia (Eds.), *Sex differences and similarities in communication: Critical essays and empirical investigations of sex and gender in interaction* (pp. 127–155). Mahwah, NJ: Lawrence Erlbaum Associates.

Mulac, A., Bradac, J. J., & Gibbons, P. (2001). Empirical support for the gender-as-culture hypothesis: An intercultural analysis of male/female language differences. *Human Communication Research, 27*, 121–152.

Mulac, A. Bradac, J. J. & Mann, S. K. (1985). Male/female language differences and attributional consequences in children's television. *Human Communication Research, 11*, 481–506.

Mulac, A., Bradac, J. J., & Palomares, N. A. (2003, May). A general process model of the gender linked language effect: Antecedents for and consequences of language used by men and women. Paper presented at the annual conference of the International Communication Association, San Diego, CA.

Mulac, A., Flanagin, A. J., Tiyaamornwong, V., Palomares, N. A., & Hallett, J. (2001, November). *Gender-linked language differences in virtual group deliberations.* Paper presented at the annual conference of the National Communication Association, Atlanta, GA.

Mulac, A., & Lundell, T. L. (1980). Differences in perceptions created by syntactic-semantic productions of male and female speakers. *Communication Monographs, 47*, 111–118.

Mulac, A., & Lundell, T. L. (1982). An empirical test of the gender-linked language effect in a public speaking setting. *Language & Speech, 25*, 243–256.

Mulac, A., & Lundell, T. L. (1986). Linguistic contributors to the gender-linked language effect. *Journal of Language & Social Psychology, 5*, 81–101.

Mulac, A., & Lundell, T. L. (1994). Effects of gender-linked language differences in adult's written discourse: Multivariate tests of language effects. *Language & Communication, 14*, 299–309.

Mulac, A., Seibold, D. R., & Farris, J. L. (2000). Female and male managers' and professionals' criticism giving: Differences in language use and effects. *Journal of Language & Social Psychology, 19*, 389–415.

Mulac, A., Studley, L. B., & Blau, S. (1990). The gender-linked language effect in primary and secondary students' impromptu essays. *Sex Roles, 23*, 439–469.

Mulac, A., Wiemann, J. M., Widenmann, S. J., & Gibson, T. W. (1988). Male/female language differences and effects in same-sex and mixed-sex dyads: The gender-linked language effect. *Communication Monographs, 55*, 315–335.

Palomares, N. A. (2003, May). *Gender schematicity, gender identity salience, and gender-linked language use.* Paper presented at the annual conference of the International Communication Association, San Diego, CA.

Postmes, T., & Spears, R. (2002). Behavior online: Does anonymous computer communication reduce gender inequality? *Personality & Social Psychology Bulletin, 28*, 1073–1083.

Reid, S. A., Keerie, N., & Palomares, N. A. (2003). Language, gender salience, and social influence. *Journal of Language & Social Psychology, 22*, 210–233.

Sherif, M. (1958). Superordinate goals in the reduction of intergroup conflict. *American Journal of Sociology, 63*, 349–356.

Swan, J., & Graddol, D. (1988). Gender inequalities in classroom talk. *English in Education, 22*, 48–65.

Tajfel, H. (Ed.). (1982). *Social identity and intergroup relations.* Cambridge: Cambridge University Press.

Thorne, B., & Henley, N. M. (1975). *Language and sex: Difference and dominance.* Rowley, MA: Newbury House.

Turner, J. C. (1985). Social categorization and the self-concept: A social cognitive theory of group behavior. In E. J. Lawler (Ed.), *Advances in group processes* (Vol. 2, pp. 77–122). Greenwich, CN: JAI Press.

Turner, J. C. (1987). A self-categorization theory. In J. C. Turner & M. A. Hogg & P. J. Oakes & S. D. Reicher & M. S. Wetherell (Eds.), *Rediscovering the social group: A self-categorization theory* (pp. 42–67). New York: Basil Blackwell.

West, C., & Garcia, A. (1988). Conversational shift work: A study of topical transitions between women and men. *Social Problems, 35*, 551–575.

Weatherall, A. (2002). *Gender, language, and discourse.* New York: Routledge.

Zimmerman, D. H., & West, C. H. (1975). Sex roles, interruptions, and silences in conversation. In B. Thorne & N. M. Henley (Eds.), *Language and sex: Difference and dominance* (pp. 105–129). Rowley, MA: Newbury House.

4

Seeing the Difference, Feeling the Difference: Emergent Adults' Perceptions of Communication and "Good" Communication with Peers and Adolescents

Angie WILLIAMS
Peter GARRETT
Rosalind TENNANT

Introduction

Emerging Adulthood

Recently, theorists of human development have begun to argue that we need to distinguish between adolescence and "emergent adulthood" as phases of the lifespan in many Western societies. Evidence for these distinct life-stages is presented by Arnett (2000), who argues that a lifestage we know as "adolescence" occurs between (approximately) 10 and 18 years of age, whereas the period between 18 and 25 years of age should more properly be labelled "emergent adulthood". This is despite what appears on the surface to be too short an age-gap as characterized in previous

111

developmental theories such as Erikson's (1968) life stages where adolescence was a stage that spanned the teenage years. In part, this new life stage is due to the conditions of contemporary Western culture and lifestyles, the demands they make on, and opportunities they offer to, young people. Arnett asserts that emergent adults are distinct from adolescents in at least three major ways. They are distinct *demographically*, in that they typically have more variable living arrangements (e.g., they do not live with parents). They are distinct *subjectively* because numerous surveys show that while they believe they have completed adolescence, they do not define themselves as "adults" (e.g., accepting responsibility, making independent decisions and becoming financially independent). They are also distinct, according to Arnett, because of the nature of their *identity exploration*. Emergent adulthood is a period of the lifespan when there is the greatest opportunity for identity exploration in the three main areas of love, work and worldview. In matters of love, emergent adults are beyond early explorations and are beginning to focus on more enduring and emotionally intense relationships. At work they are free to experiment with a range of possibilities such as short-term volunteer jobs away from home. In terms of their worldviews, Arnett cites research (e.g., Arnett, 1997) that shows that emergent adults have reached a point where they are more likely to discard ready-made viewpoints that they may have previously taken on board from their family, and to form their own opinions more independently. Adolescence, according to Arnett, is characterized by common experiences that differ from those of emergent adults. Adolescents typically "live with their parents, are experiencing the physical changes of puberty, are attending secondary school, and are part of a school-based peer culture" (p.476). And if emergent adulthood is different from adolescence, it is also distinct from adulthood (achieved at approximately 30 years old), because of the fluidity of life experience and opportunities. Emergent adults are typically not married, not parents, and not settled into a career. In addition, young adults aged thirty are more likely to see themselves subjectively and define themselves discursively as "adults".

Adolescence

As can be gleaned from the above, identity development is a major issue for adolescents and emergent adults (and may indeed be an issue in numerous ways at numerous stages of life). Scholars interested in adolescence recognize the importance of both autonomy from family of origin (Noom, Dekovic and Meeus, 1999), and attachment for psychosocial adjustment during adolescence (e.g., Baltes and Silverberg, 1994; Noller, 1994; Silverberg and Gondoli, 1996). Autonomy is "the ability to regulate one's own behavior", while attachment is "the quality of the relationship with significant others". Baltes and Silverberg (1994) suggest that "the developmental task of adolescence seems to be complicated in that it calls for a negotiated balance between an emerging sense of self as a competent individual on the one hand, and a transformed, but continued, feeling of connection with significant others on the other" (p. 57).

Beyers and Goossens (1999) distinguish three types of adolescent autonomy (Noom, 1999), *emotional autonomy* is when teenagers are not emotionally dependent on parents and they see parents not as ideals but as real individuals. *Behavioral autonomy*, also known as decisional autonomy, reflects the youngsters' ability to make independent decisions regarding all types of behavior. *Attitudinal autonomy* is achieved as teenagers move towards the development and expression of a set of independent opinions outside the realm of parental influence.

Beyers and Goossens suggest that autonomy achieved too rapidly in early adolescence may be associated with negative patterns of adjustment. Older adolescents in their Dutch study reported more autonomy than the younger ones and there was no relationship between autonomy and distress for older adolescents. It is thought that adolescents who are in the middle of autonomous transitions find life most stressful and those who gain various types of autonomy too hastily are most at risk. In contrast, increased autonomy during late adolescence comes to be associated with positive adjustment.

Much developmental research into adolescence has focused on identity building revealing that the early to mid-teen years are generally associated with rapid change and development both in terms of physical changes and self-concept, and a move away from family to peer-group identity (e.g., Baker, 1992). Adults' overseeing of peer relationships lessens, and teenagers have to negotiate their peer terrain to a large extent on their own. Fortman (2002), too, points to the balance between the development of one's own identity as an individual personality autonomous from parents and family towards a more social identity as a member of various peer networks and social groups. Thus, at the same time as developing more autonomy from parents, these teenagers must forge rewarding and supportive relationships with peers. One important feature of this process is the exploration of "crowds" (Bradford Brown, Mory and Kinney, 1994). Allegiance to or interest in a crowd, and the awareness of social distance among crowds, help these young teenagers decide which peers to seek relationships with and which to ignore. At its most conspicuous, this process tends to involve the allocation of evaluative names to groups and their members, such "brainies", "druggies", "normals", "dirtbag". Here then, we see the discursive aspect of social identity, as these teenagers align and distance themselves in relation to the alternative relationships and identities around them. Labels such as "brainies", "normals" etc. can be seen as an intriguing shorthand for such evaluative discourses (see also, Garrett, Coupland and Williams, 1999, 2003: chapter 8, in press; Thurlow, 2001).

There are developmental trends with respect to peer groups that seem to reflect the move from adolescence to emergent adulthood and the increasing importance of social contacts and networks beyond the family of origin – their communication worlds. Kinney (1993) found that adolescents moved from a relatively strongly demarcated 2-crowd system at around 13–14 years to a far more diverse range of crowds at 15–16 years, with the importance of crowds declining thereafter as older teenagers seek to express their personal attitudes and interests (Bradford Brown *et al*, 1994: 160). Catan, Dennison and Coleman (1996), in their survey of 12–19 year olds from all over the UK, found that at different lifestages, young people had varying amounts of contact with friends. As older teenagers gained independence from their families, their communication worlds opened out.

Social Identity and Communication Accommodation Theory

The teenage years and, as Arnett argues, emergent adulthood, are crucial periods for developing a sense of *social identity* (that aspect of a person's self concept based on his or her memberships of various social groups), as well as personal identity. Differentiating between one's own and other crowds is an early indication of a growing awareness and exploration of social group membership (Tarrant, North, Edridge, Kirk, Smith and Turner, 2001). Social identity and group membership is as much a discursive construction as it is a cognitive awareness (e.g., Williams, Coupland, Folwell and Sparks, 1997). Social identity theory asserts that one derives a sense of self-identity as a social being from the groups of which one is a member (Tajfel, 1978; Hogg and Abrams, 1988) and this is partly a product of the social interaction between and within groups. Social identity is an important part of a person's self-concept and because of this we strive to achieve and maintain positive social identities. To do this we may try to belong to positively valued and high status social groups and/or to discursively construct our own groups as positive and valued when compared with other groups (e.g., see Edley and Wetherell, 1997; Williams, Coupland, Folwell and Sparks, 1997). Thus, establishing clearly differentiated boundaries between groups where one's own group is construed more positively than other groups is a fundamental intergroup process.

Communication accommodation theory (CAT) draws on social identity and intergroup theory to explain the processes by which individuals attune their language and communication to one another both as individuals and social group members (for a review see Giles, Coupland and Coupland, 1991). Importantly CAT details communication strategies that bring us closer to or distance us from our interactional partners. Accommodation is one means by which we may attempt to move linguistically and communicatively closer to partners by performing acts such as attending to their conversational needs, adjusting the topics, the pace and timing of conversations. Non-accommodation may signal psychological and communicative distance from a partner as for example when we do not attend carefully to what they say, we may be distracted or push our own agenda for talk and so forth. Processes of accommodation tend to correlate with interactional satisfaction. We feel better about conversations where our partner is accommodative and we feel dissatisfied when our partner is non-accommodative (Williams, 1992). CAT also draws our attention to the fact that we attempt to adjust our language and communication to where we *think* our partner is psychologically and communicatively, and this perception can be associated with various problems such as when we over-adjust or under-adjust to our partner's language and communication needs. Over-accommodation occurs when we over-adjust our speech and communication – for example when we "baby talk" a very capable elderly or young person. Under-accommodation occurs when we are not able for one reason or another to adjust our language and communication adequately to meet our partner's language and communication needs. For example, under-accommodation might occur when a computer expert uses technical language to explain a process to lay people who are not technically trained.

Good Communication

Over the past two or three decades in particular, there has been growing importance attached to the notion of "good communication", with more individuals and organzations setting out recommended or required versions of communication in various contexts (see Cameron, 2000). In the post-industrial West, the growth of the service sector, and the parallel decline in manufacturing industries have led to a stronger emphasis on professional communication between service sector workers and clients. Moreover, the impact of late modernity and the associated fragmentation of individual identities (Giddens, 1991; 1994) have been associated with decreasing clarity with respect to various social roles (parent, consumer, salesperson, colleague etc.), such that people may often experience uncertainty with regard to the enactment of these roles and associated responsibilities. For example, under the conditions of late modernity, they may be more unsure of how to produce and interpret new ways of speaking and writing required for successful professionals, and indeed for professional success. Designing new "competences" is increasingly seen as crucial for the conduct of contemporary life. And this has led to various codifications of communication skills (Cameron, 2000).

In the UK, first moves in the direction of enhancing the communication skills of young people were introduced in the 1970s, and "communication" lessons now feature prominently in schools. Drury, Catan, Dennison and Brody (1998) note that, in large part, such educational input addressing "good communication skills" (in both school and adult schemes) is based on the assumption that communication can be analysed into component parts, which can be defined in behavioral terms. As they note, contemporary theories of interpersonal communication have taken a very different direction, towards shared and negotiated meanings (e.g. Burgoon, Hunsacker and Dawson, 1994) which lead to different conclusions about what constitutes "good communication". Hence, Drury *et al.* note that we need to investigate in what areas young people *themselves* experience their communication successes and difficulties. Although there is some research in this area, it has tended to focus on communication in relatively intimate relationships such as peer groups and families (p. 178). In the study we report below, we analyse our data to see how our young respondents view "good communication" with non-family members.

In Drury *et al.*'s (1998) own study of young people's accounts of good communication, they found some interesting differences between their two age groups of 16–20 year olds and 12–15 year olds. For example, in communication experiences with friends and workmates, with family members, and with non-family adults, the 16–20 year olds reported significantly more good communication and less bad communication than did 12–15 year olds. In addition, the younger teenagers tended to blame bad communication on other people more than did the older age group. To return to our starting point in this introduction, such differences would seem to provide some support for the notion of a distinct "emergent adulthood" developing out of the adolescent phase of the lifespan.

Adults tend to view adolescents as being fairly unskilled communicators (Thurlow, 2003). For example, Drury and Dennison (1999) found benefits officers making negative generalzations about their communication encounters with adolescents compared to those with adults. Negative views have also been reported from data collected from police officers (Drury and Dennison, 2000) and teachers also may view encounters with teenagers as problematic (Williams and Cockram 2002). Recently, our own research with a large sample of UK adults aged from 20 to 59 years old indicated that adults of all ages perceive adolescents as relatively non-accommodative, uncommunicative, and self-promotional as compared to peers and much older people (aged 65 to 85) (Williams and Garrett, 2002). From this, we might also expect to find important differences in comparative communication experiences and judgements of 18–25 year olds when considering 13–16 year olds.

Rationale for this Study

Building on the theoretical work of Arnett (2000), can we say that the relatively small age gap between young adults aged 18–25 and those aged 13–16 is enough to indicate two distinct perceptual lifespan groups with subsequent communication indices? If so, then would young adults predictably differentiate between their own age group (same age peers) and adolescents? Also on the basis of intergroup differentiation and our previous work, can we predict that young adults would favor their peers in comparison to adolescents in terms of their perceptions of others' (same age peers and adolescents) and their own communication behaviors. In other words, do young adults perceive their interactions with adolescents as "intergroup" in terms of the age difference?

Following the work of Drury *et al.* (1998) regarding "good" communication, we wanted to explore the emotions young people associate with conversations with peers, and whether they are different to those they report when reflecting on conversations with adolescents. In line with our predictions for communication behavior, we expected that more positive and less negative emotions would be associated with conversations with peers than with adolescents. Previous studies (e.g. Williams and Giles, 1996) have shown how positive emotions may be associated with satisfying and accommodative interactions. In addition, we were interested to find out: what are the predictors of "good communication" for young people (18–25) in conversation with peers, and are they different from those that predict "good communication" when in conversation with adolescents? Finally, is an awareness of the interaction as intergroup in age terms related to evaluations of satisfaction?

Here, then, we set out our research questions.

RQ1:   Do young adults differentiate their perceived communication experiences with peers from those with young teenagers?

RQ2:   Do young adults associate different emotions with conversations with peers, compared to conversations with young teenagers?

RQ3:   Do young adults perceive communication with young teenagers in intergroup terms?

RQ4:   What variables do young adults associate with "good communication" in conversations with peers, compared to conversations with young teenagers?

Method

Participants

Participants were 243 students enrolled on introductory Communication courses at a large UK University. Their participation in this project was voluntary. Participants who were ethnically non-Anglo-Celtic and over age 30 were excluded from the analysis. This reduced the final sample size to 208. All were aged between 18 and 25 years old and the average age was 19.3. 170 were female and 38 were male.

Materials and Procedure

Participants completed a questionnaire based on previous questionnaires pertaining to perceptions of intergenerational communication (e.g., see Williams and Garrett, 2002; Williams, Ota, Giles, Pierson, Gallois, Ng, Lim, Ryan, Somera, Maher, Cai, Harwood, 1997). The questionnaire sought information about communication experiences of respondents with peers, adolescents, along with general demographic information. One section of the questionnaire asked respondents to evaluate their perceptions of *others'* communication behavior when "others" were same aged peers and adolescents (aged 13 to 16) respectively. This section began, "During conversations with (target group) who are not family or who I do not regard as "like family", I found, in general, they . . .". Thirty items followed that included phrases such as "were out of touch", "negatively stereotyped my age group", "were attentive", "initiated conversation" and "gossiped". Respondents were also asked about their perception of *their own* communication with peers and adolescents respectively. This section began "During conversations with (target group) who are not family or who I do not regard as like family, in general I have . . . ." This time seventeen items asked respondents to agree or disagree that they "avoided certain topics", "spoke slower", "did not act like myself" and "talked down to them". A third section asked respondents assess their own feelings when communicating with peers and adolescents respectively. This section began "During conversations with (target group) who are not family or who I do not regard as like family, I have generally felt . . .". The twenty-four items in this section included "satisfied", "angry", "supportive", "secure" and "sympathetic". Feelings were drawn from those used by Williams (1994): defensive, guarded anxious, emotionally positive, satisfied, age did not matter, anxious to leave, emotionally negative, happy, frustrated, angry, relaxed, interested, helpful, supportive, kind, generous, good about myself, secure, bored, loved, powerless, sad, sympathetic. Each item was rated by participants on a 7 point Likert scale where 1 = strongly disagree and 7 = strongly agree.

The questionnaire also included five questions designed to evaluate respondents' awareness of age in intergroup terms in interactions with adolescents. These questions were devised from Hewstone and Brown's (1986) intergroup contact theory that suggests that an interaction is intergroup when the participants are aware of group differences and see themselves and their partner as typical representatives of their respective groups (see Williams, 1994). When reflecting on conversations with adolescents, participants were asked whether or not they agreed that they: "were aware of the age differences"; "felt like a typical older person"; "acted like a typical older person"; "were treated like a typical older person" and whether the younger person acted like a typical younger person. All questions were set out on a Likert scale with 1 = strongly disagree and 7 = strongly agree. A final section asked for information concerning respondents' age, sex, ethnicity, younger siblings and experience working with adolescents. Respondents were also asked how frequently they interacted with peers and adolescents respectively on a 7 point Likert scale where 1 = not at all frequently and 7 = very frequently.

Results and Discussion

Perceptions of others' communication, perceptions of own-communication and perceptions of feelings were each subjected to

Figure 1
Final factor structure and alphas
for perceptions of other's communication behavior:

Nonaccommodation	Accommodation
closed minded	compliments
out of touch	advice
forced attention	stories
angry complaints	support
complaints about health	humor
complaints about life	attention
negatively stereotyped my age group	initiated conversation
talked down to me	sought information
	talkative
Cronbach's alpha	Cronbach's alpha
Peers = 0.6964	Peers = 0.8150
Adols = 0.7143	Adols = 0.7106

Noncommunication	Self-promotion
dried up	over confident
short answers	tried to impress
uncommunicative	superior
	talked about own life
	were cheeky
	gossiped
Cronbach's alpha	Cronbach's alpha
Peers = 0.7376	Peers = 0.6156
Adols = 0.6454	Adols = 0.6593

principle components factor analysis with varimax rotation. Resultant factors were judged as closely analogous to those described in the Williams and Garrett (2002) study described above. The validity of the factor structure was supported by reasonable to very good scale reliabilities calculated using Cronbach's alpha (see Figures 1 and 2). In line with previous research, the factors pertaining to perceptions of others' communication behavior were labelled "accommodation", "non-accommodation", "non-

Figure 2
Final factor structure and alphas
for perceptions of self-behavior

Communication adjustments	Discomfort
talk louder	did not know what to say
talk slower	tried to end the conversation
simplified vocab	did not act like self
avoid certain words	
talk down to them	
Cronbach's alpha	Cronbach's alpha
Peers = 0.7585	Peers = 0.7676
Adols = 0.7066	Adols = 0.6103

Respect/obligation	Topic accommodation
obliged to be polite	talked about topics they enjoy
bite tongue	tried to find common topics
make allowances for age	had to initiate conversation
avoid certain topics	
show respect	
Cronbach's alpha	Cronbach's alpha
Peers = 0.7103	Peers = 0.6300
Adols = 0.7106	Adols = 0.6300

communication" and "self promotion". For perceptions of own-communication behavior, factors were labelled "communication adjustments", "discomfort", "respect/obligation" and "topic accommodation" Factors, items and reliabilities can be seen in Figures 1 and 2.

The "feelings" items were factor analysed using the same procedure and seeking a compatible solution for peers and adolescents. The final factor structure judged as satisfactory across both age target groups was as follows:

Factor 1 was labelled "support/nurturing" and was comprised of: "kind", "helpful", "supportive" and "generous". Cronbach's alpha reliabilities were peers = 0.8155, adolescents = 0.7978. Factor

2 was labelled "negativity" and was comprised of: "angry", "bored", "frustrated" and "emotionally negative". Reliabilities: peer = 0.8344, adolescents = 0.7183. Factor 3 was labelled "satisfaction" and was comprised of satisfied, happy, emotionally positive, relaxed, and interested. Reliabilities: peer = 0.7598, adolescents = 0.7794. Factor 4 was labelled "tension" and was comprised of "guarded", "defensive", "anxious" and "anxious to leave". Reliabilities: peer = 0.7721, adolescents = 0.8059.

RQ1 asked whether young adults would differentiate communication with peers from communication with adolescents. To evaluate this, two within-subjects MANOVAs were calculated. The factors for perceptions of others' communication and perceptions of own-communication were used in turn as dependent variables. The independent within-subjects factor was the conversational target (peer versus adolescent).

The overall MANOVA for perceptions of others' communication was significant (Wilks' lambda (4, 192) = 0.39, $p<0.001$ eta^2=0.61). Drop down univariate analyses of variance showed significant effects for accommodation (F (1, 195) = 275.49, $p<0.001$, eta^2 = 0.59), nonaccommodation (F(1, 195) = 57.10, $p<0.001$, eta^2 = 0.23), and noncommunication (F (1, 195) = 51.78, $p<0.001$ eta^2 = 0.21). Effects for self-promotion were not significant. Further inspection of the means revealed that these young adults tended to perceive peers as relatively more accommodative (M (peers) = 4.93; M (adols) = 3.74), less nonaccommodative (M (peers) = 2.77; M (adols) = 3.40) and less noncommunicative (M (peers) = 3.10, M (adols) = 3.79) than adolescents. They tended to disagree that either peers or adolescents were self-promotional (M (peers) = 2.66, M (adols) = 2.77).

For perceptions of own-communication behavior the overall MANOVA was also significant (Wilks' lambda (4, 196) = 0.66, $p<0.001$ eta^2 = 0.35). Drop down univariate analyses of variance showed significant effects for communication adjustments (F (1, 199) = 85.33, $p<0.001$, eta^2 = 0.30), discomfort (F (1, 199) = 29.72, $p<0.001$, eta^2 = 0.13) and topic accommodation (F (1,199) = 19.53, $p<0.001$, eta^2 = 0.09). Effects for respect/politeness were not significant. Inspection of the means revealed that respondents reported they were less likely to adjust communication to peers than to adolescents (M (peers) = 2.56, M (adols) = 3.32). They also reported that they were less likely to feel discomfort with peers (M (peers) = 2.97, M (adols) = 3.45) as opposed to adolescents. While they perceived that they accommodated the topic of conversation for both groups, they reported less accommodation to adolescents than to peers (M (peers) = 4.81, M (adols) = 5.14).

Our first research question therefore receives an affirmative answer from our data. On six of the eight factors, there is a significant difference in the way that communication experiences with the two age-groups are judged, and communication with peers is consistently judged in what can reasonably be regarded as a more favorable light. With peers, there is more accommodation and less non-accommodation, there is less non-communication, less discomfort, less adjustment of communication and of topic. In our earlier study (Williams and Garrett, 2002) of communication evaluations across the lifespan, essentially the same eight factors were present. The two factors "non-communication" and "self-promotion" had not featured in previous studies (which had tended to focus on communication with the elderly) but were new, and, we felt, pertinent to adolescents in particular. Our present study confirms these. The two studies differed, though, with regards to respondents. In the previous study, the four respondent age-groups were 20–29, 30–39, 40–49 and 50–59, and the three age-groups being judged were peers (for each respondent age group), 13–16 year olds, and 65–85 year olds. Hence it is difficult to make direct comparisons with the present study. But broadly speaking the results of the two studies are close with regard to these eight factors. For example, in the previous study, the 13–16 year olds were seen to be less accommodative than peers or elder targets, as well as the most non-communicative of the three groups. And respondents reported that they were more likely to accommodate the conversation topic with elders and teenagers than with their peers. The teenagers were also seen as the most self-promoting of the three groups, but peers were lumped together across groups. The lack of significance for self-promotion in the study we report here may mean that this is still a common ground (perhaps in slightly different forms) for our young adults and young teenagers. And this may explain one of our findings for "good communication", discussed below.

RQ2 asked whether different emotions were associated with conversations with peers and adolescents. To answer this, a further MANOVA analysis with the target age group as the within-subjects variable and the emotion factors as dependent variables was calculated. Results for the overall MANOVA were significant (Wilks' lambda (4, 195) = 0.683, p<0.001 eta^2 = 0.317). Univariate analyses of variance revealed significant effects for satisfaction (F (1,198) = 39.96, p<0.001, eta^2 = 0.17), tension (F (1,198) = 6.63, p<0.02, eta^2 = 0.03), negativity (F(1, 198) = 4.19, p<0.05, eta^2 = 0.02), results for support/nurturance were not significant.

Inspection of the means revealed that although respondents tended to disagree that they felt tension (M (peers) = 2.95, M (adols) = 2.72) or negativity (M (peers) = 2.78, M (adols) = 2.94) in these interactions in general, they reported less tension and less negativity when judging interactions with peers than when judging interactions with adolescents. In addition, respondents perceived that they felt more overall satisfaction when reporting conversations with peers as opposed to adolescents (M (peers) = 5.05, M (adols) = 4.62). However, they reported that they felt supportive and nurturant in both types of interaction and did not differentiate between peers and adolescents on these dimensions (M (peers) = 4.98, M (adols) = 4.98). Overall, then, our second research question is also answered in the affirmative. Within three out of the four factors, the two age groups are evaluatively distinguished. And again, it is reasonable to interpret these findings as favoring the peers over the adolescents, with communication experiences with peers seen as involving less tension and negativity, and giving more satisfaction.

RQ3 asked whether or not respondents would perceive communication with adolescents as intergroup encounters, in terms of age. To evaluate this, means for the five intergroup questions were examined and are displayed in Table 1. As can be seen from the table, all means were over the midpoint of the scale in the direction of agreement. It was not possible, of course, to include any kind of control group for comparison to address this question, but the positive scale ratings on all five items are a strong suggestion that respondents do indeed perceive their communication encounters in intergroup terms, and lead us to consider this a reasonable conclusion.

Table 1
Means and standard deviations for intergroup questions

I was aware . . .	Mean	SD
Other much younger	4.45	1.37
Other acted typical young	4.60	1.41
Self much older	4.56	1.43
Self acted typically older	4.37	1.42
Self treated typically older	4.37	1.39

Thus far, then, we have established a clear differentiation between conversations with peers and with adolescents (aged 13–16 years old). However, our research questions also included the exploration of variables that might be related to perceptions of "good communication" from the perspective of young adults (RQ4). To address this question, we took "satisfaction" to be a core component of "good communication" that was available to us in our data (see Williams and Giles, 1996), and we employed regression analysis to examine the contribution of each of the measured variables to our respondents' perceptions of satisfaction. Two regression analyses were performed on the data. The first analysis focused on conversations with peers with "satisfaction" as the dependent measure. The independent variables were the communication factors (accommodation, non-accommodation, non-communication, self promotion, communication adjustments, discomfort, respect/obligation, topic accommodation), the emotion factors (support/nurturing, negativity, satisfaction, and tension), "frequency of interaction", "sex of respondent", "experience with adolescents" and "respondent age". For peers, the full model was significant but the best predictors of accommodation were a linear combination of "nurturing/support", "tension" (negatively related), "accommodation", and "self promotion" ($R = 0.76$, $R^2 = 0.57$), F (4, 192) = 65.86, $p < 0.001$). Beta weights and t values are presented in Table 2.

Table 2
Regression analysis predicting evaluations of
satisfaction in conversations with peers

Variable	Beta	T
Accommodation	0.37	6.82**
Self promotion	0.11	2.17*
Tension	−0.26	−5.07**
Positive emotions	0.40	7.70**

** $p<0.01$ *$p<0.05$

Overall then, the degree to which these young adults report feeling satisfied with their interaction with peers is positively related to the degree to which their peers accommodate and self-promote and the degree to which they themselves feel nurturing and supportive and experience low levels of tension. Notably the degree of satisfaction was not predicted from own-communication behaviors – communicative and linguistic (e.g., communication adjustments, respect and topic accommodation) ways that they might influence the interaction – but more from others' behavior (e.g., self-promotion, accommodation) and the emotional properties (e.g., lack of tension, and positive emotions) of the conversation.

A second regression analysis was performed for perceptions of satisfaction in conversations with 13 to 16 year olds. In this analysis, the dependent and independent measures were the same as for the first analysis but with the addition of the intergroup variables combined to make a scale. Reliability for the intergroup scale was good, calculated using Cronbach's alpha at 0.78. Results indicated that although the full model was significant, the best predictors of young adults' satisfaction in conversations with people aged 13–16, was a linear combination of "accommodation", "self-promotion", "topic accommodation", "support/nurturing" "tension" (negatively related), "negativity" (negatively related), and intergroup awareness (negatively related) (R = 0.80, R^2 = 0.64), F (7, 187) = 47.51, $p < 0.001$). Beta weights and t values are presented in Table 3.

Table 3
Regression analysis predicting evaluations of
satisfaction in conversation with adolescents

Variable	Beta	T
Accommodation	0.38	7.46**
Self promotion	0.13	2.63**
Topic accommodation	0.14	2.71**
Negative emotions	−0.13	−2.40*
Positive emotions	0.33	6.07**
Tension	−0.16	−2.80**
Intergroup awareness	−0.11	−2.42*

** p < 0.01 *p< 0.05

In fact, we find a considerable degree of similarity in the way that good communication (by the criteria we have employed here) is perceived to operate with peers and young teenagers. Accommodation and self-promotion by the other party in the interactions are seen as core properties, along with the respondent's own feelings of supportiveness (kindness, helpfulness, generosity), and low levels of tension (guardedness, defensiveness, anxiety, eagerness to leave). In addition, it seems that non-accommodation and non-communication from the others in the interactions do not hold any salience as far as these judgements are concerned. This is particularly interesting, given that in this and in earlier studies, findings have shown that these are well-documented factors characterizing dissatisfying intergenerational communication. Indeed, it suggests that properties of what is deemed to be "good communication" may vary across the lifespan, both in terms of the producers and the evaluators. This is an important finding with potentially crucial implications for current approaches to communications training of the kind that we find in many educational settings and that we referred to earlier in this paper. Indeed, given the contemporary emphasis on and codifications of good communication, this finding suggests an important avenue for further research.

What can we say then about the differences between the respondents' judgements of their peers and their judgements of teenagers? Our findings show that there are additional requirements for communication with young teenagers for them to be satisfying, compared to that with young adult peers. The young adults must not experience feelings of negativity (anger, boredom, frustration, negative emotions). They should also not perceive that age-difference has high salience in the conversation or that participants are typical of their age group. In other words, perception of the interaction as intergroup in age terms may be associated with less overall satisfaction (see also, Williams 1994). On the more behavioral level, the young adults see a link between their own topic accommodation and the experiencing of good communication. With young teenagers, then, compared to their peers, they seem to expect that they will need to make an effort themselves in communicating about suitable topics in order to gain satisfaction from the encounters.

There are two further aspects of our findings that are worth mentioning here, because, although not central to our research questions, they connect with pertinent issues in other research, and to some degree run counter to earlier work. One is that our findings showed no differences as far as the sex of our respondents was concerned. It seems that, in terms of the questions we asked at least, the body of findings pointing to sex/gender differences in the communication literature are not reflected in these judgements of good communication.

The second is our finding that the young adults' self-reported frequency of contact with non-family teenagers had no impact on their judgements. It would appear that perceptions and judgements of their communication with teenagers do not change if they have more contact with them, but that insofar as such communication encounters have an intergroup nature, the influence of stereotypes persists. This contrasts with findings of studies looking at the communication perceptions of young adults with elders. Young students who report more frequent contact with elders have been found to perceive them as more accommodative and less non-accommodative than those who report less contact (Williams *et al*, 1997). However, it echoes findings in our own earlier research (Williams and Garrett, 2002: 119). There, we looked at communication evaluations of and by age groups across the lifespan, and found no relationships between self-reported frequency of contact across the age-groups and their evaluations. Our best explanation at the time was that our sample of community adults probably had much more varied cross-generational experiences at work, at leisure, and within the family than the campus-bound college students whose judgements were affected by frequency of contact in earlier studies. However, in the study we are reporting here, our respondents were also university students, who are not likely to have had more varied cross-generational experiences than the college students in previous studies. We are unable to find any alternative explanation, and feel that the difference is worth pursuing in more depth, perhaps through qualitative data.

Conclusion

This study has proved to be a useful development of our earlier research in which we have extended the intergenerational communication research paradigm, with its earlier heavy focus on perceptions of communication with the elderly, to encompass the wider lifespan. Continuing the focus on adolescence in particular (Garrett *et al.*, 2003; Williams and Garrett, 2002), we have now more firmly established the evaluative dimensions of self-presentation and non-communication, and continue to work towards a more inclusive factorial matrix. The identification of these factors has enabled us to sketch out differentiating communication characteristics of additional groups across the lifespan, to draw a more detailed evaluational life-line. More details emerge. In Williams and Garrett (2002), we were able to gain more insights into the comparative evaluations of young adolescents and the 30–39 year age group in particular. In our present study, we have found a further communicative subdivision between young teenagers and young adults, as well as debated the notion of "emergent adulthood". We have also extended our work beyond the realm of perceived behaviors and experiences to embrace emotional reactions. This seems a particularly crucial ingredient in notions of "good communication", and certainly our respondents were able to make such important connections within the design-confines of this study. The behavioral skills approach to fostering "good communication" through formulaic training of a checklist of competencies inevitably bypasses, indeed fails to acknowledge, such emotional and affective features. And, indeed, some of the miscommunication that directly results from such communication skills approaches (see for example Cameron, 2000) arguably stem from a lack of awareness of their affective oversights or deficiencies. As Cameron herself (p. 181) has emphasized, with such a narrow view of "good communication", communication training cannot only be criticized for "dumbing down" competent speakers, but the practices involved can also be oppressive.

Further discussion on this theme concerns the "self-promotion" factor that we previously (Williams and Garrett, 2002) identified with 13–16 year olds, but which it seems in this study does not differentiate young adults from young teenagers, yet is a core criterion for "good communication" with both peers and with the younger age group. The scales for this factor (over-confident, tried to impress, superior, talked about own life, were cheeky, gossiped) suggest that a great deal of satisfaction in communication for people at this stage of the lifespan in particular is derived from a degree of self-assertion and also exploring the ludic properties of communication. Cameron (2000), in her criticism of the communication skills approach, emphasizes how "our choices about speaking are one important aspect of our self-presentation, of the identities we construct for public display" (pp.180–181). Perhaps these are particularly important too in the process of identity building, where people are experimenting with alternative available identities and testing others' reactions as they go along. To the degree to which "good communication" programmes are arguably stifling some fundamental experimental and boundary-testing processes of identity building through adolescence and emerging adulthood in particular, they might indeed be said to be oppressive.

The question of "good communication" (and its bedpartner "bad communication") has a much broader basis than the one with which this study could engage. Yet it appears to be of increasing importance in people's lives, featuring large in the growing debate on globalzation. With the burgeoning literature in this area, so much of it so influential and yet only modestly informed, there is much more for our field to contribute.

References

Arnett, J. J. (1997). Young people's conceptions of the transition to adulthood. *Youth and Society, 29*, 1–23.

Arnett, J. J. (2000). Emergent adulthood: A theory of development from the late teens through the twenties. *American Psychologist, 55*, 469–480.

Baker, C. (1992). *Attitudes and Language*. Clevedon, UK: Multilingual Matters.

Baltes, M. M., & Silverberg, S. (1994). The dynamics between dependency and autonomy: illustrations across the lifespan. In D. L., Featherman, R. M., Lerner, & M. Perlmutter (Eds.), *Life-span development and behavior, Vol. 12*, (pp. 41–90). Hillsdale, NJ: Lawrence Erlbaum.

Beyers, W. & Goossens, L. (1999). Emotional autonomy, psychosocial adjustment and parenting: Interactions, moderating and mediating effects. *Journal of Adolescence, 22,* 753–769.

Bradford Brown, B., Mory, M. & Kinney, D. (1994). Casting adolescent crowds in a relational perspective: caricature, channel, and context. In R. Montemayor, G. Adams & T. Gullotta (Eds.) *Personal Relationships during Adolescence,* (pp.123–167) Thousand Oaks, CA: Sage.

Burgoon, M., Hunsacker, F. & Dawson, E. (1994). *Human Communication.* Beverly Hills, CA: Sage.

Cameron, D. (2000). *Good to Talk? Living and Working in a Communication Culture.* London: Sage.

Catan, L., Dennison, C. & Coleman, J. (1996). *Getting Through: Effective communication in the teenage years.* London: The BT Forum.

Drury, J., Catan, L., Dennison, C. & Brody, R. (1998). Exploring teenagers' accounts of bad communication: a new basis for intervention. *Journal of Adolescence, 21,* 177–196.

Drury, J. & Dennison, C. (1999). Individual responsibility versus social category problems: benefit officers' perceptions of communication with young people. *Journal of Youth Studies, 2,* 171–192.

Drury, J. & Dennison, C. (2000). Representations of teenagers among police officers: some implications for their communication with young people. *Youth and Policy, 66,* 62–87.

Edley, N., & Wetherell, M. (1997). Jockeying for position: The construction of masculine identities. *Discourse and Society, 8,* 203–217.

Erikson, E. H. (1968). *Identity: Youth and crisis.* New York: Norton.

Fortman, J. (2003). Language skills and identity in adolescence. *Journal of Language and Social Psychology, 22,* 104–111.

Garrett, P., Coupland, N. & Williams, A. (1999). Evaluating dialect in discourse: teachers' and teenagers' responses to young English speakers in Wales. *Language in Society, 28,* 321–354.

Garrett, P., Coupland, N. & Williams, A. (2003). *Investigating Language Attitudes: Social meanings of dialect, ethnicity and performance.* Cardiff, UK: University of Wales Press.

Garrett, P., Coupland, N. & Williams, A. (in press) Adolescents' lexical repertoires of peer evaluation: boring prats and English snobs. In A. Jaworski, N. Coupland & D. Galasinski (Eds.) *Metalanguage: Social and ideological perspectives.* The Hague: Mouton.

Giddens, A. (1991). *Modernity and Self-Identity.* Cambridge: Polity Press.

Giddens, A. (1994). Living in a post-traditional society. In U. Beck, A, Giddens & S. Lash (Eds.), *Reflexive modernization: Politics, tradition and aesthetics in the modern ocial order* (pp.56–109). Cambridge: Polity Press.

Giles, H., Coupland, N. & Coupland, J. (1991). Accommodation theory: communication, context, and consequence. In H. Giles, N. Coupland & J. Coupland (Eds.) *Contexts of Accommodation: Developments in applied sociolinguistics,* (pp.1–68). Cambridge: Cambridge University Press.

Hewstone M., & Brown, R. (1986). (Eds). *Contact and conflict in intergroup encounters.* Oxford: Blackwell.

Hogg, M. A., & Abrams, D. (1988). *Social Identifications: A social psychology of intergroup relations and group processes.* Florence, KY: Taylor & Francis/Routledge.

Kinney, D. (1993). From "nerds" to "normals": adolescent identity recovery within a changing social system. *Sociology of Education, 66,* 21–40.

Noller, P. (1994). Relationships with parents in adolescence: process and outcome. In Montemayor, R., Adams, G. R. and Gullotta, T. P. (Eds.), *Personal relationships during adolescence: Vol. 6, Advances in adolescent development* (pp. 37–77). Thousand Oaks, CA: Sage.

Noom, M. J., Dekovic, M. & Meeus, W. H. J. (1999). Autonomy, attachment and psychosocial adjustment during adolescence: A double edged sword? *Journal of Adolescence, 22,* 771–783.

Silverberg, S.B. & Gondoli, D.M. (1996). Autonomy in adolescence: A contextualized perspective. In G.R. Adams, R. Montemayor & T.P. Gullotta (Eds), *Psychosocial Development during Adolescence: Progress in Developmental Contextualism.* Thousand Oaks, CA: Sage.

Tajfel, H. (Ed.) (1978). *Differentiation between social groups.* London: Academic Press.

Tarrant, M., North, A., Edridge, M., Kirk, L., Smith, E., & Turner, R. (2001). Social identity in adolescence. *Journal of Adolescence, 24,* 597–609.

Thurlow, C. (2001). The usual suspects? A comparative investigation of crowds and social type labelling among young British teenagers. *Journal of Youth Studies, 4,* 319–334.

Thurlow, C. (2003). Teenagers *in* communication. Teenagers *on* communication. *Journal of Language and Social Psychology, 22,* 50–57.

Williams, A. (1992). *Intergenerational communication satisfaction: An intergroup analysis.* Unpublished Masters thesis. University of California, Santa Barbara.

Williams, A. (1994). "Attention, attention, . . . I love attention": Younger person's perceptions of satisfying and dissatisfying intergenerational conversations with older people. Unpublished Doctoral thesis. University of California, Santa Barbara.

Williams, A. & Cockram, M. (2002). *Authority versus affiliation: Dialectics of teachers' communication with adolescent pupils.* Paper presented at the 8th International conference on Language and Social Psychology, Hong Kong, July 2002.

Williams, A., Coupland, J., Folwell, A., & Sparks, L. (1997). Talking about Generation X: Defining them as they define themselves. *Journal of Language and Social Psychology, 16,* 251–227.

Williams, A. & Garrett, P. (2002). Communication evaluations across the lifespan: from adolescent storm and stress to elder aches and pains. *Journal of Language and Social Psychology, 21,* 101–126.

Williams, A. & Giles, H. (1996). Retrospecting intergenerational conversations: the perspective of young adults. *Human Communication Research, 23,* 220–250.

Williams, A., Ota, H., Giles, H., Pierson, H. D., Gallois, C., Ng, S-H., Lim, T-S., Ryan, E. B., Somera, L., Maher, J., Cai, D., & Harwood, J. (1997). Young people's beliefs about intergenerational communication: An initial cross-cultural analysis. *Communication Research, 24,* 370–393.

Section II
Cultural Processes

5

Making Sense of Differences: Language, Culture, and Social Reality

Terry Kit-fong AU

"Language is a guide to 'social reality.' . . . No two languages are ever sufficiently similar to be considered as representing the same social reality," mused the linguistic anthropologist Edward Sapir (1949, p. 162). His student Benjamin Lee Whorf (1956, p. 213) went further, "The world is presented in a kaleidoscopic flux of impressions which has to be organized . . . largely by the linguistic systems in our minds."

If language indeed shapes social reality, one would expect to see: (1) differences in language structure paralleled by differences in social reality, and (2) evidence of language structure shaping social reality rather than the other way around. In recent years, language and culture as well have become two exciting and fast-growing areas in social psychology. Sapir and Whorf's theoretical framework still sets much of the research agenda for understanding how language and culture may be related to social reality. Much research energy has focused on, and succeeded in, uncovering cross-linguistic and cross-cultural differences in social cognition and social behaviors. But are those differences real or only apparent?

Real versus Apparent Differences

As more and more cross-linguistic/cultural differences are uncovered, it becomes increasingly important to tell apart real differences from apparent ones. Can the field come up with some "gold standard" for evaluating such observed differences? Trained in cognitive rather than social psychology, good sense dictates that I talk about research stories in language and cognition rather than social psychology per se. But I hope that, in due course, the relevance of these research stories to social psychology will become clear.

One more comment before I go on: This essay focuses on language structure rather than communication (or cooperative use of language *à la* Grice, 1975). Elsewhere I (Au 1988) have discussed how misleading questions, helpful hints, sexist language, and the like can influence the listeners' cognition and even behavior – most likely because people generally try to be informative, truthful, relevant, and clear when they use language, and expect others to do the same. But that is another story for another time. Here I will focus primarily on the relation between language structure and cognition.

The first research story began when I was at Harvard enrolled in a seminar taught by Roger Brown. One day after class, he asked me to take a look at a fascinating book manuscript by Alfred Bloom soon to be published by Erlbaum (Bloom, 1981) and to give him my opinion as a native speaker of Chinese. I dutifully read the manuscript and told him that what Bloom claimed could not be true, and that if he (i.e., Brown) would agree to be my undergraduate honors thesis advisor, I would try to make my case empirically. He did.

Alfred Bloom's (1981) claimed that without a distinct counterfactual marker in the Chinese language, Chinese speakers have to struggle to think counterfactually – that is, to think hypothetically about what is not true. In a nutshell, here is Bloom's argument: Like other Indo-European languages, English has a distinct counterfactual construction, the subjunctive, whereas other languages including Chinese do not. To talk about something counterfactual in the present in English, one could say, "If I were you, I would be grateful." When talking about the past, one could say, "If he had been there, this would have been avoided." Simply put, when entertaining a counterfactual, the English verb tense is pushed further into the past: the past tense for the present; the past perfect tense for the past. Quite possibly, these linguistic devices were adopted in the evolution of English to put some psychological distance between the reality and the counterfactual world.

By contrast, Bloom explained, there are no verb tense markers in Chinese and hence nothing like the English subjunctive. In order to say, "If I were you, I would be grateful" in Chinese, one can say "If I being you, I will be grateful." This might not seem difficult, but what happens if a counterfactual argument is very abstract, complex, and long? Consider "If Wittgenstein had been able to read Chinese, he would have done X, he would have done Y, and he would have done Z." Chinese speakers, Bloom speculated, could become confused in dealing with its Chinese equivalent: "Wittgenstein cannot read Chinese. If he can read Chinese, he will do X, he will do Y, and he will do Z." That is, Chinese speakers may lose track of the fact that Wittgenstein could not read Chinese in the first place, thereby becoming unsure if he actually did X, Y, or Z. To support his speculation, Bloom presented counterfactual stories to Chinese and English speakers in their native language. Lo and behold, he found that Chinese speakers failed miserably whereas English speakers were virtually perfect in grasping the counterfactuals in those stories.

When I finished reading Bloom's book manuscript, my first thought was, "It can't be true!" Back then in the late 1970s, there was a very popular play in Mainland China called, "If I were the real. . . " (*假如我是真的*). It was about someone imagining if he were the real Mayor of Shanghai and all the things he would do and would have done. If millions of Chinese speakers saw and understood this play, I wondered, how could it be difficult for Chinese to handle counterfactual stories?

More generally, in everyday life, people across cultures and language communities must engage in counterfactual reasoning often. For instance, when we feel lucky, we know that things could have turned out badly but did not; when we are grateful to someone who has lent a helping hand, we know that we could have been in deep waters without the help. When we regret having said or done something stupid and wish we had not, we will be mentally undoing those rash acts and imagining the counterfactual bliss of ourselves and others unharmed by those rash acts. When children engage in pretend play and adults become engrossed in movies or novels, counterfactual thinking is in center-stage for the children, screenwriters, actors, audience, novelists, and readers. In these everyday activities, we freely enter and exit counterfactual worlds of our own and others' creation. How can something so fundamental and pervasive in human thinking and social interaction be difficult in any human language? The human need to think about the counterfactual world should create counterfactual markers in languages all over the world (see also Au, 1992a.) So, I launched my honors thesis research project with this motto: If some research findings seem too fantastic to be true, they are probably too fantastic to be true. This is an especially important motto in cross-linguistic and cross-cultural research, where researchers often have to navigate minefields filled with assumptions about languages and/or cultures in foreign terrains.

In my honors thesis and follow-up studies, Chinese speakers' purported difficulty in understanding counterfactual stories disappeared when Bloom's stories were rewritten in idiomatic Chinese with proper counterfactual markers (Au, 1983, 1984, 1988; see also Liu, 1985). As it turns out, there are a number ways to mark counterfactuality in Chinese, and Bloom focused on but one of them (namely, not X, if X then Y). Other markers include *shi* and *jie* in Classical Chinese (使, 藉), and *hai yiwei* (還以爲), *yaobushi* (要不是), and *yaoshi . . . zao jiu / zenme hui . . . le* in Modern Chinese (要是 . . . 早就 ／ 怎麼會 . . . 啦; see also Au, 1992a, in press). Bloom used none of these counterfactual markers in Chinese. Moreover, he mistakenly considered the hypothetical markers *jiu hui* (就會 meaning "will") optional and omitted them from his Chinese version of the counterfactual stories. When Au (1984) added the hypothetical markers to Bloom's stories, Chinese speakers understood the stories just fine.

In cross-linguistic studies, mastery of foreign languages is an obvious challenge. Alfred Bloom actually had some command – although not native-like mastery – of the Chinese language. But partial knowledge could be a double-edged sword. Through academic grapevine, I later pieced together this story. Because this story was built entirely on hearsay, it ought to be treated as such. Treat it, if you will, as a fable.

"Once upon a time, an American professor went to China to compare how Chinese and English speakers think. He had learnt Chinese as a foreign language but could neither speak nor write it like a native speaker, so he enlisted the help of a native Chinese speaker who was also a Chinese language instructor to make up some questionnaires in Chinese. Short of telling the Chinese language instructor how to write the questionnaires, he gave lots of input in the process. . . ." The asymmetry of power relationship in the creative process told here, observed from a distance, can be rather obvious to most (and especially to social psychologists). But engrossed in a research project near and dear to one's heart, it could be a different story.

Elsewhere, I have written about methodological safeguards such as having research materials checked by multiple native speakers, using back translations to check the fidelity of translation, and so forth (Au, 1992b). There are also other safeguards to minimize the impact of "foreign" researchers' preconception of the "natives' conceptions." One way is to let the natives speak in their own words. Anthropologists and developmental psychologists (whose young research participants at times seem to come from a different culture) have warned against yes/no and other forced-choice questions (e.g., Carey, 1995; Au & Romo, 1999). Once we get the natives' own words, we can translate them into the coders' native language and keep the coders blind to the research participants' language and cultural backgrounds. . . . But as my "fable" suggests, the social psychology – or social dynamics in a research team – is as much at the core of cross-linguistic/cultural research methodology as other methodological safeguards.

How to Deal with Real Differences?

The second research story has to do with color names and color perception. Compared to counterfactual reasoning, this topic would seem even further afield from social psychology – the focus of this book. But I hope the relevance of this story to cross-linguistic/cultural research in social psychology will too become evident.

Lenneberg and Roberts (1956) were among the first to hit upon promising evidence for a parallel between language differences and cognitive differences. They discovered that monolingual speakers of Zuni, a native American language, name the colors yellow and orange with the same word *lhupzʔinna*; Zuni-English bilinguals often used *ʔolenchianne* (derived from English *orange*) for the orange color, reserving *lhupzʔinna* for yellow. Lenneberg and Roberts found that all four monolingual Zuni speakers in their study failed miserably in a memory test for yellow and orange; the eight Zuni-English bilinguals remembered these two colors better but not as well as native English speakers. One problem with this study was that the participants' language background was completely confounded with their age and education level: The Zuni monolinguals were elderly with little or no formal education, the English monolinguals were Harvard students, and the bilinguals fell in between these two in age and education (Au, 1992b, in press). Nonetheless, subsequent studies have offered prima facie support for Lenneberg and Roberts' (1956) classic findings: Speakers of languages lacking certain basic color names (e.g., *green* and *blue*) tend not to have distinct corresponding color categories (green and blue, in this example; see e.g., Kay & Kempton, 1984; Lucy, 1992; Roberson, Davies, & Davidoff, 2000).

A major challenge in interpreting such a correlation between language and cognition is what causes what. Does the lack of distinct names for different colors in a language make its speakers less attuned to the differences between those colors so compellingly perceived by people who have distinct names for the colors? Or, quite the contrary, do languages lack distinct names for colors such as "green" and "blue" because – for reasons that have nothing to do with language – their speakers cannot see green or blue?

As it turns out, people living in the tropics – thereby exposed to chronically high dose of ultraviolet-B (UV-B) – tend to speak languages without a basic color name for blue. Instead, they refer to blue with a term akin to *grue* (a color name covering the blue-green spectrum) or *dark* (Bornstein, 1973). By contrast, languages that have distinct basic color names for blue and green tend to situate much further away from the equator. Lindsey and Brown (2002) speculated that premature aging of the eye due to high, chronic exposure to UV-B in sunlight may lead to loss in sensitivity to shortwave-length light and hence to blue and green colors. If people living in the tropics cannot see blue and green very well, it would make sense that their languages do not have distinct names for these two color categories. Lindsey and Brown asked native English speakers to name colors seen through dense lenses – to simulate the lenses of human eyes prematurely aged due to high and chronic exposure to UV-B in sunlight – and clear lenses. As predicted, the native English speakers named blue and green colors accurately when looking through clear lenses. When seeing through the dense lenses, however, they named the colors as if they were speaking a "grue language."

This research story started out offering prima facie support for the Sapir-Whorf hypothesis of language shaping cognition; it ends up supporting quite the opposite view, namely, how we see the world may shape how we talk. It also highlights the importance of going beyond documenting a parallel between language and human cognition or behavior. Such a parallel could mean language shaping cognition/behavior, but it could also mean exactly the opposite. To be fair, Whorf did recognize possible cognitive constraints on language use:

> The tremendous importance of language cannot, in my opinion, be taken to mean necessarily that nothing is back of it of the nature of what has traditionally been called "mind." My own studies suggest, to me, that language, for all its kingly role, is in some sense a superficial embroidery upon deeper processes of

consciousness, which are necessary before any communication, signaling, or symbolism whatsoever can occur, and which also can, at a pinch, effect communication (though not true AGREEMENT) without language's and without symbolism's aid (Whorf, 1956, p. 239).

Researchers focusing on the language-shaping-thought story in Whorf's writings understandably might be tempted to extrapolate a parallel between language and thought to language shaping thought. But this research story illustrates why finding a parallel is only half of the fun; the real reward lies in uncovering the origins or underlying causes of such a parallel (see also Au, 1998).

Keeping Track and Making Sense

As we uncovered more and more differences across cultures and languages, how can we best keep track of them, sort them out, and explain them? This challenge is not unlike the one faced by language acquisition researchers a few decades ago. In the late 1960s and early 70s, Roger Brown spearheaded a pioneering project at Harvard on how children learn language. He worked with a team of extremely talented post-doctoral research fellows and graduate students; the lab roster now reads like the "Who's Who" in the study of language acquisition. They started with English and soon branched out to other languages. It became clear quite quickly that languages can be structured very differently, and the process of language acquisition can also look very different.

The field went through an "oooh and aaah" stage: Isn't it amazing that 2- and 3-year-olds learning Turkish already know their number, gender, person, case marking, verb tense and aspect marking, etc. so well, while 4- and 5-year-olds learning English still say things like, "two sheeps and deers" instead of "two sheep and deer" and "brang" instead of "brought" and "I meaned" instead of "I meant"? Isn't it interesting that Japanese children acquire such a complicated honorific system so well, whereas Chinese children are barely getting simple distinction between the polite versus informal form of you (*nin* and *ni)?*

But once the field had got beyond this stage, it became clear that a most urgent task was to figure out how to organize all those cross-linguistic differences in a meaningful way. The task is likewise urgent in understanding the origins of variations in social cognition and behavior across cultures and language communities. Can the latter task be informed by the former?

An Analogy between Language and Culture

Virtually all human babies are born to learn a language if exposed to the language; virtually all of them are also born to learn to become a competent social and cultural being. Pinker (1994) has written much on the language instinct. Likewise, much evidence has accumulated for a culture instinct: Human newborns are pre-wired to track faces, imitate facial gestures, and preferred human voice. By age one year, human babies will look to trusted adults for clues in novel situations. If the adults show fear, the babies will flee to the adults for protection; if the adults look relaxed, the babies will venture out to explore. They seek joint attention (by pointing) and share their joy (by flashing big smiles) and distress (through tears) with people around them. They are curious about others' thoughts and feelings and begin to build a theory of mind even before they learn to read and write (e.g., Astington, Harris, & Olson, 1988).

Like language acquisition, there too seems to be a critical period for acquiring social and cultural competence. Most who try to learn a language beyond childhood never quite master its accent or grammar (e.g., Flege, 1987; Newport, 1990). Trying to become a full-fledge member of a culture or social group too seems to have a limited window of opportunity. Late comers often behave with a "foreign accent" in social situations, making faux pas without knowing that they have done so. And, like language, culture has complex systems of implicit rules. Cultural "rules" tend to be learned by immersion; such rules are often induced from observation rather than acquired from explicit teaching.

To understand the origins of variations in social cognition and behavior across cultures or language communities, then, it may be instructive to see how language acquisition researchers have approached their analogous task. Here are a few highlights:

1. Characterize the input, the endpoint, and the acquisition mechanisms.
2. Look for universals in starting point (what all babies are born with) and in learning principles.
3. Uncover variations across cultures or languages.
4. Try to understand the origins of such variations in a principled way.

Organizing Principles in Understanding Cultural/Social Variations

To meet the challenge of organizing and understanding the many observed differences in social cognition and behavior across cultures and languages, several dichotomies have been invoked in major research programs: East *vs.* West; collectivism *vs.* individualism; holistic vs. analytic; men *vs.* women. What can these dichotomies do for us? Are these categories mere labels? Or do they have explanatory power?

To explain cultural differences, we need to know how these "cultures" came about. Cultures are alive and can change over time (e.g., Schaller & Crandall, 2003). In what sense are the college students in China nowadays – a popular population in cross-cultural/linguistic research – *bona fide* exemplars of members of a collectivistic culture?

In speculating on the origins of a collectivistic culture or an individualistic culture, one oft-cited source is ancient philosophy. For example, ancient Chinese philosophers endorsed "collectivistic' virtues in their writings and teaching. But how did their elitist teaching filter down to hundreds of generations of illiterate peasants? If such teaching has managed to survive and shape Chinese college students nowadays, might it not be just a case of passing on the cultural torch among elites? How representative is this highly-selected sample of the whole Chinese population?

Likewise, to explain why Americans are so "individualistic," ancient Greek philosophers teaching and wisdom have been invoked. But how did their elitist teaching filter down to generations of peasants, serfs, and landlords in Europe? How about the Irish, Italian, and Jewish immigrant families pouring into the U.S. in the early 1900s, who must have looked much like families in the supposedly "collectivistic" cultures? How did ancient Greek philosophers' teaching skip all those people and generations of serfs and peasants to shape the American college students now?

Where are the missing links? How did ancient philosophies shape the mass and survive? Like languages, cultures have to be learnable to survive. To understand observed cultural differences in social cognition and behavior, then, an indispensable part of the story would be cultural learning (Tomasello, 1993) and cultural teaching (Maynard, 2002).

Beyond Labeling

The third research story offers an example of going beyond labeling group differences and getting to the underlying of causal mechanisms. In her book *The Tending Instinct*, Taylor (2002) explored why and how men and women react to stress differently. The point of departure was the then conventional wisdom in theoretical and empirical research in stress and coping, namely, the "fight or flight" as a response to stress. However, when she interviewed breast cancer survivors in her health psychology research, she discovered quite a different repertoire of coping strategies. What she saw repeatedly was a "tend and befriend" response pattern. Those cancer survivors turned outward rather than inward; they actively sought to take care of others and made new friends. Puzzled by these surprising findings, she dug deeper into the "fight or flight" research studies and discovered that almost all "research participants" of those studies had been male – men, mice, and more. She speculated that the "fight or flight" response characterizes male reaction, and the "tend and befriend" response characterizes female reaction. But she did not stop there with mere labels for the gender differences.

Instead, in a theoretical tour de force grounded in sound empirical findings, Taylor explores how socialization could join force with biology to shape men's and women's neuro-circuitries for tending and befriending, their hormonal responses to stress, and their social cognition and behavior. The benefits of being tended and befriended are clear. A case in point: Children growing up in risky families characterized by harsh and/or cold parenting are at risk for not only poor social relationships and mental health, but also – perhaps because chronic stress compromises their cardiac-vascular and immune system – poor physical health including higher rates of cardiac-vascular diseases, cancer, and premature death (Repetti, Taylor, & Seeman, 2002). The benefits for the women doing the tending and befriending were, at least *a priori*, more surprising. Importantly, Taylor (2002) went on to try to work out the underlying mechanism – including the neuro-circuitries for tending and befriending, and hormonal, cognitive, and behavioral responses to stress – for these intriguing observed gender differences in stress and coping. In the end, a gender difference story became a Human story.

Much has been said about men and women growing up and living in two cultures. What Taylor (2002) has done is to show how we can go from documenting "cultural differences" (or any other group differences, for that matter) to understanding the why and how of such group differences. Such "Why's and How's" – that is, the causes and causal mechanisms for observed differences in social reality among cultures or language communities – may well turn out handy in organizing and making sense of the myriad of group differences documented to date and in the future in social psychology. I re-tell this research story here not because it is unique in social psychology (and thank goodness it is not unique; see e.g., Schaller & Crandall, 2003), but simply because it is a good exemplar of how going after the underlying causal mechanisms for observed differences between social groups can pay off handsomely.

Concluding Remarks

Three research stories – counterfactuals, colors, and coping – spun into one tale: It is the tale of an outsider with little expertise but nonetheless a long-standing interest in social psychology and its relation to language and culture. Pray take whatever messages you want from it, and leave whatever you don't alone – as one would with any tale.

References

Astington, J. W., Harris, P. L., & Olson, D. R. (1988). *Developing theories of mind*. London: Cambridge University Press.

Au, T. K. (1983). Chinese and English counterfactuals: The Sapir-Whorf hypothesis revisited. *Cognition, 15*, 155–187.

Au, T. K. (1984). Counterfactuals: In reply to Alfred Bloom. *Cognition, 17*, 289–302.

Au, T. K. (1988). Language and cognition. In L. Lloyd and R. Schiefelbusch (Eds.), *Language perspectives II* (pp. 125–146). Austin: Pro-Ed.

Au, T. K. (1992a). Counterfactual reasoning. In G. R. Semin and K. Fiedler (Eds.), *Language, Interaction and Social Cognition* (pp. 194–213). London: Sage.

Au, T. K. (1992b). Cross-linguistic research on language and cognition: Methodological challenges. In H. C. Chen and O. Tzeng (Eds.), *Language processing in Chinese: Eastern and Western perspectives* (pp. 367–381). London: Elsevier Science Publisher B.V.

Au, T. K. (1998). Language and thought. An entry in *The MIT encyclopedia of the cognitive sciences* (pp. 444–446). Cambridge, MA: MIT Press.

Au, T. K. (In press). The relationship between language and cognition. In P. Li (General Ed.), *Handbook of East Asian psycholinguistics, Part I: Chinese psycholinguistics* (E. Bates, L. H. Tan, & O. J. L. Tzeng, Eds.). London: Cambridge University Press.

Au, T. K., & Romo, L. F. (1999). Mechanical causality in children's "folkbiology." In D. Medin and S. Atran (Eds.), *Folkbiology* (pp. 355–401). Cambridge, MA: MIT Press.

Bloom, A. H. (1981). *The linguistic shaping of thought: A study in the impact of language on thinking in China and the West*. Hillsdale, NJ: Erlbaum.

Bornstein, M. H. (1973). Color vision and color naming: A psychophysiological hypothesis of cultural difference. *Psychological Bulletin, 80,* 257–285.

Carey, S. (1995). On the origin of causal understanding. In S. Sperber, D. Premack, and A.J. Premack (Eds.), *Causal cognition* (pp. 268–302). Oxford: Clarendon Press.

Flege, J. E. (1987). A critical period for learning to pronounce foreign languages? *Applied Linguistics, 8,* 162–177.

Grice, H. P. (1975). Logic and conversation. In P. Cole and J. L. Morgan (Eds.), *Syntax and semantics: Vol. 3. Speech Acts* (pp. 41–58). New York: Seminar Press.

Kay, P., & Kempton, W. (1984). What is the Sapir-Whorf hypothesis? *American Anthropologist, 86,* 65–79.

Maynard, A. E. (2002). Cultural teaching: The development of teaching skills in Maya sibling interactions. *Child Development, 73,* 969–982.

Lenneberg, E. H., & Roberts, J. M. (1956). The language of experience: A study in methodology, *International Journal of American Linguistics* (Memoir No. *13;* Suppl. 22), 1–33.

Lindsey, D. T., & Brown, A. M. (2002). Color naming and the phototoxic effects of sunlight on the eye. *Psychological Science, 13,* 506–512.

Liu, L. G. (1985). Reasoning counterfactually in Chinese: Are there any obstacles? *Cognition, 21,* 239–270.

Lucy, J. A. (1992). Language diversity and thought: A reformulation of the linguistic relativity hypothesis. London: Cambridge University Press.

Newport, E. L. (1990). Maturational constraints on language learning. *Cognitive Science, 14,* 11–28.

Pinker, S. (1994). *The language instinct: How the mind creates language*. New York: Morrow.

Repetti, R. L., Taylor, S. E., & Seeman, T. E. (2002). Risky families: Family social environments and the mental and physical health of offspring. *Psychological Bulletin, 128,* 330–366.

Roberson, D., Davies, I.R. L., & Davidoff, J. (2000). Color categories are not universal: Replications and new evidence from a stone-age culture. *Journal of Experimental Psychology: General, 129,* 369–398.

Sapir, E. (1949). In Mandelbaum (Ed.), *Selected writings in language, culture and personality.* Berkeley and Los Angeles: University of California Press.

Schaller, M., & Crandall, C. (2003). *The psychological foundations of culture.* Mahwah, NJ: Erlbaum.

Tomasello, M., Kruger, A. C., & Ratner, H. H. (1993). Cultural learning. *Behavioral and Brain Sciences, 16,* 495–552.

Taylor, S. E. (2002). *The tending instinct: How nurturing is essential to who we are and how we live.* New York: Times Books.

Whorf, Benjamin. L. (1956). In J.B. Carroll (Ed.), *Language, thought, and reality: Selected writings of Benjamin Lee Whorf.* Cambridge, MA: MIT Press.

6

Symbols and Interactions: Application of the CCC Model to Culture, Language, and Social Identity

Chi Yue CHIU
Jing CHEN

What language seems to carry is a set of symbols answering to certain content which is measurably identical in the experience of the different individuals. If there is to be communication as such the symbol has to mean the same thing to all individuals involved. (G. H. Mead, 1934/1962, p. 54)

The self-conscious human individual, then, takes and assumes the organized social attitudes of the given social group or community . . . to which he [sic] belongs . . . Of these abstract social classes or subgroups of human individuals the one which is most inclusive and extensive is, of course, the one defined by the logical universe of discourse (or a system of universal significant symbols) determined by the participation and communicative interaction of individuals . . . (G. H. Mead, 1934/1962, p. 1156–158)

The CCC Model

Symbols and interactions are the keystones of George Herbert Mead's social psychology. Following Mead's intellectual tradition, we seek to describe the inter-relationship of language, culture, and group identity. Our analysis starts out from the general assumption epitomized in the above quotations: Language is a shared system of symbols, a carrier of shared meanings, as well as a marker of group identity. Guided by the Culture-Carrier-Context (CCC) model of culture, we explore the intricate interactions between language, culture, and group identity, and the symbolic significance of expressing or applying a piece of cultural knowledge in concrete situations. Figure 1 depicts the three major conceptual components of the model: culture, carriers, and context. The *reciprocal interactions* between these three components constitute the model's substantive contents. We will begin this chapter with a description of the assumptions and postulates of the model. Next, we will apply the model to explicate the relationship between language, culture and group identity.

Figure 1
The CCC model of culture and psychology

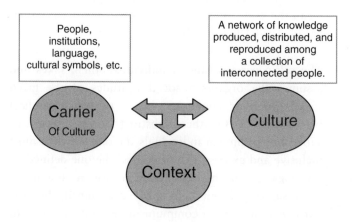

Definition of Culture

The word *culture*, a French word that entered the English language in the sixteenth century, originally meant "a piece of tilled land." By metaphorical extension, it came to signify "cultivate" or "developing the land." In social sciences, culture is often defined as "socially transmitted knowledge and behavior shared by some group of people" (Peoples & Bailey, 1994, p. 23).

However, in much current usage in cross-cultural and cultural psychology, culture is attributed to a specific *group*. In practice, many psychologists have studied the influence of culture by comparing national groups or ethnocultural groups residing in the same nation (e.g., Japanese, South Koreans, Hong Kong Chinese). This practice has the undesirable consequence of giving *culture* the unwelcome connotation of being a bounded, homogenous, coherent, and stable entity.

In the 1990s, some anthropologists had written against this usage of *culture*. In a disparaging tone, Keesing (1994) wrote, "our conception of culture almost irresistibly leads us into reification and essentialism" (p. 302). To a similar effect, Appadurai (1996) wrote,

> The noun *culture* appears to privilege the sort of sharing, agreeing, and bounding that fly in the face of the facts of unequal knowledge and the differential prestige of lifestyles, and to discourage attention to the worldviews and agency of those who are marginalized or dominated. (p. 12)

In a recent review, Brumann (1999) defended the theoretical value of culture. He pointed out that the unwelcome connotations of culture are not inherent in the concept of culture, but associated with the practice of attributing culture to a demarcated population. According to Brumann, although learned routines are never perfectly shared in a population, they are not randomly distributed. Thus, it is advisable to retain culture as a term for designating "the clusters of common concepts, emotions, and practices that arise when people interact regularly." (p. 1)

Many contemporary theorists agree with Brumann that cultural knowledge is distributed (vs. shared diffusely) in a population (Barth, 2002; Kashima, 2000; Latané, 1996; Lau, Lee, & Chiu, 2004; Sperber, 1996). In the present chapter, we use the term culture to designate a network of knowledge that is produced, distributed, and reproduced among a collection of interconnected people. The term "knowledge" has been used in the cognitive, behavioral and social sciences literatures to refer to different concatenations of cognitions. Our usage of the term is most similar to what Barth (2002) referred to as knowledge. In Barth's (2002) usage of the term, knowledge includes "feelings (attitudes) as well as information, embodied skills as well as verbal taxonomies and concepts: all the ways of understanding that we use to make up our experienced, grasped reality." (p. 1)

People and Culture: Separate Theoretical Entities

We avoid the problem of reifying culture by treating culture as a network of distributed knowledge, and by separating culture and carriers of culture (including people). More important, by treating people and culture as separate theoretical entities, our model permits us to describe the different ways people participate in and interact with culture. For example, we can theorize how people create a need for culture, create culture, use culture as guides for their social practices, reflect on the strengths and liabilities of a cultural tradition, identify or dis-identify with a culture, use culture as a tool to attain their personal goals, reproduce culture (by spreading it to other territories and transmitting it to new generations), and change culture. Thus, people are not treated as passive recipients of cultural influence; they also express and actualize their agency via culture.

People are not the only carriers of culture. Other carriers of culture include popular songs, language, mass media, proverbs, advertisement, law, cultural symbols or icons, and social policies (Briley, Morris, & Simonson, 2000; Cohen, 1996; Han & Shavitt, 1994; Ho & Chiu, 1994; E. Kashima & Kashima, 1998; Hallahan,

Lee, & Herzog, 1997; Kim & Markus, 1999; Lee, Hallahan, & Herzog, 1996; Menon, Morris, Chiu, & Hong, 1999; Morris & Peng, 1994; Rothbaum & Tsang, 1998; Rothbaum & Xu, 1995). These different carriers of culture do not exist in isolation; interactions between different cultural carriers often set off a chain of reciprocal influences. For example, people may use another carrier of culture (e.g., mass media) to interact with culture (e.g., change culture). In the process of doing so, people may change their attitudes and ideas in the direction of the shared meanings carried by the other carrier.

By treating people as carriers of culture, we do not mean that people cannot serve other roles. For example, as we will argue later, people also play an important part in the ontogenesis of culture. Similarly, other carriers of culture (e.g., songs, idioms or languages) are also sense-making "tools." As such, they are also a part of culture. These tools, suffused with cultural meanings, are often used to transmit cultural meanings from one human group to another and from one generation to another. People, including researchers, often infer culture from these tools. In this sense, these tools are also carriers of culture.

Coherence of Culture

As mentioned, we assume that cultural knowledge is distributed in a human group in a nonrandom fashion. In addition, we assume that culture changes and develops as social interactions take place. According to the dynamic social impact theory (Latané, 1996), through frequent interactions and social influence, previously unrelated beliefs, values, or practices will become strongly associated (or correlated), even without any necessary logical or semantic connections among them. The coalescence of shared knowledge this process produces corresponds to what some writers have referred to as cultural syndromes (Triandis, 1996), foundational schemata (Shore, 1996), or cultural paradigms (Fiske, 2000). In other words, through repeated human interactions and via a set of self-organizing principles, people in a human group may come to share a coalescence of many elements, meanings, practices and mental events that are loosely organized around a common theme. The self-organization processes described in the dynamic social impact theory have been demonstrated in computer simulation studies (Latané & Bourgeois, 1996; Latané & L'Herrou, 1996), computer-mediated communication games, and in a longitudinal study of college students' political socialization in their academic discipline (Guimond & Palmer, 1996).

Although repeated interactions could ultimately result in complete amalgamation, persuasive minority opinion leaders, through their interactions with people surrounding them, will be able to influence others, resulting in clusters of minority opinions in the group, and thus ensuring continuing diversity (Latané, 1996). Accordingly, dissimilar and even contrastive cultural paradigms may coexist in a group, although they differ in the likelihood of being sampled or adopted in a particular context (Triandis, 1989). Once a particular cultural paradigm is made salient in a concrete situation, the likelihood of applying that cultural paradigm will increase. For example, although individualism is a relatively prevalent cultural paradigm in North America, American students mention more group attributes and fewer idiocentric attributes when their collective self is primed than when their private self is primed (Gardner, Gabriel, & Lee, 1999; Trafimow, Triandis, & Goto, 1991). This finding indicates that both individualistic and collective self-constructions are available to some American students, and contextual priming could call out one of these two kinds of self-constructions.

Frequent human interaction facilitates the development of cultural paradigms. At the same time, frequent use of a cultural paradigm promotes differentiation of cultural knowledge (Triandis, in press). As Triandis (in press) puts it,

> Differentiation is important in culture change. A tool that works well may be replaced by a tool that works slightly better, but frequently the culture retains both tools. Random variation and selective retention result in different species of tools, just as they also result in

different dimensions of cultural variation. Campbell (1965) argued that random variation provided the bases of cultural evolution. It is followed by selective retention, and propagation of the positively selected variants. The more a dimension of culture is being used, the greater is the probability that variations will appear.

Functions of Culture and Cultural Learning

People do not just carry culture; they play a special role in the ontogeny of culture. First, the interdependent nature of everyday social interactions creates a need for culture. Consider the following example. The visitor said, "It is hot here," and Pat turned on the air-conditioner. Pat could have understood the visitor's utterance as a comment on the room's temperature instead of an indirect request to turn on the air-conditioner. The mundane nature of this daily exchange could easily mask the complex social coordination that is required in interpersonal interaction (Ho & Chiu, 1998; Krauss & Chiu, 1998; Sperber, 1996). In the above example, for the intended meaning of this utterance to be properly understood, when the visitor formulated this utterance, he needed to know that Pat would know his intended meaning, and that Pat would also know he knew she knew his intended meaning, and *ad infinitum*. The significance of solving complex coordination problems could not be emphasized more, because almost every kind of social activities (e.g., cooperation, competition, communication, exchange, division of labor, conducting a ritual, making joint decisions, and relating to outsiders) involves solution of complex coordination problems (Fiske, 2000).

Some writers have proposed that culture provides solutions to complex coordination problems by offering shared background knowledge, conventionalized solutions to recurrent coordination problems, as well as shared, schematized approaches to solving emerging coordination problems (Cohen, 2001; Fiske, 2000; Kashima, 1999; Sperber, 1996). Fiske (2000) refers to the cultural devices for resolving complex coordination problems as cultural coordination devices. According to him, cultural coordination devices are cognitive, motivational mechanisms that permit complementarity of human actions. These mechanisms develop from the interactions of universal psychological proclivities to coordinate social interactions and the cultural paradigms available to the cultural group.

After a cultural coordination device is discovered or invented to solve a coordination problem, the coordination device is deposited into the repository of cultural knowledge. This device may or may not be used again to solve other coordination problems. When it does, and does this often enough, it becomes a learned routine, and a part of "routinized" culture (Ng & Bradac, 1993).

Second, humans are endowed with several proclivities toward coordination of perspectives, which is crucial for constructing shared knowledge that gives rise to culture. Comparative studies of chimpanzee and human cultures have revealed a unique human capacity for cultural learning. Humans can learn to represent others' behaviors as intentional acts, and learning from the actors' perspectives the acts' intended consequences. In this sense, cultural learning is more than imitation of the actor's behavior. It involves learning through others' perspective the pragmatic meanings of social behavior (Boesch & Tomasello, 1998). Cultural learning is supported by a number of innate abilities. At the end of their first year of life, most infants are able to demonstrate the ability to engage in joint attention activities; they look where adults are looking, use adults as social reference, and act on objects in the way adults are acting on them (Carpenter, Nagell, & Tomasello, 1998). These cultural learning abilities have greatly facilitated human adaptation for complementation of social activities, and form the psychological foundation for the generation, transmission, consolidation, maintenance, and adaptation of cultural practices.

Effects of Context

Thus far, we have focused on the interaction between culture and its carriers. Now, we turn to the role of context.

There is good evidence that context can modify the interaction between culture and its carriers. First, studies comparing perceptual and cognitive characteristics of different groups have shown that the context of assessment often determines whether group differences in these characteristics would be found (Choi & Nisbett, 1998; Ji, Peng, & Nisbett, 2000; Miyamoto & Kitayama, 2002; Norenzayan, Choi, & Nisbett, 2002; see Lehman, Chiu, & Schaller, in press). For example, differences between South Koreans and North Americans in the tendency to make situational inferences are accentuated when the relevance of situational determinism is highlighted in the judgment context, and attenuated when it is obscure (Choi & Nisbett, 1998; Norenzayan *et al.*, 2002).

In addition, consistent with the idea that cultural knowledge is a shared epistemic tool for sense making (DiMaggio, 1997), people in a group are likely to apply cultural knowledge when it offers a broadly accepted, conventionalized solution to an interpretive problem, and when the problem solver lacks the capability, motivation, or resource to consider alternative solutions. For example, the likelihood of using a cultural causal theory to guide judgment and decision making increases when people need to recruit widely accepted reasons to justify their decision (Briley *et al.*, 2000), have a high need for cognitive closure (Chiu, Morris, Hong, & Menon, 2000; Fu, Morris, Lee, Chiu, & Hong, 2003), are cognitively busy (Knowles, Morris, Chiu, & Hong, 2001), or need to make judgments under time pressure (Chiu *et al.*, 2000).

Finally, contextual cues can increase the accessibility of a particular piece of cultural knowledge in a concrete situation, and hence the likelihood of applying that piece of knowledge in the situation (Briley & Wyer, 2001; Gardner *et al.*, 1999; Hong, Chiu, & Kung, 1997; Hong, Morris, Chiu, & Benet-Martinez, 2000; Verkuyten & Pouliasi, 2002). Furthermore, cognitively accessible cultural knowledge will be applied in a particular situation only when it is applicable in the situation (Hong, Benet-Martinez, Chiu, & Morris, 2003).

In short, context can increase (or decrease) the likelihood of applying a particular piece of cultural knowledge in a concrete situation, by rendering that piece of knowledge more (or less) cognitively accessible, applicable, relevant, and useful in the situation.

Language as a Carrier of Culture

A person learns a new language and, as we say, gets a new soul. He puts himself into the attitude of those that make use of that language. He cannot read its literature, cannot converse with those that belong to that community, without taking on its peculiar attitudes. He becomes in that sense a different individual. (Mead, 1934/1962, p. 283)

According to Mead, language is not a passive carrier of culture; it socializes the mind, and gives rise to group consciousness. Indeed, the development of the ability to use human languages to represent the reality symbolically is an important cognitive transition in the evolution of human cultures (Donald, 1993).

Language and culture are related in several ways. First, language encodes culture (Tong, Chiu, & Fu, 2001). For example, there is a strong correlation between group averages of individualism (vs. collectivism) and language practices in the group (E. Kashima & Kashima, 1998). In some languages, the use of first and second person pronouns is mandatory. Other languages allow pronoun drop. The use of first and second person pronoun in a sentence makes the self and the addressee stand out in the sentence context. As the group's average individualism decreases, permissiveness of pronoun drop in the group language increases systematically.

Second, shared meanings encoded in human languages facilitate solution of complex coordination problems. However, as Mead (1934/1962) pointed out, shared meanings are not essential for solving complex coordination problems:

If it is a co-operative process requiring different sorts of responses, then the call on the part of one individual to act calls out different responses in the others. The conversation of gestures does not carry with it a symbol which has a universal significance to all the different individuals . . . It is not essential that the individuals should give an identical meaning to the particular stimulus in order that each may respond properly ... Such a universal discourse is not at all essential to the conversation of gestures in cooperative conduct. (pp. 54–55)

Instead, as some writers posited, language plays a more important role in supporting our culturally adapted way of life by providing "shared modes of discourse for negotiating differences in meaning and interpretation." (Bruner, 1990, p. 13) Specifically, language allows constructions of multiple complementary perspectives (*I lent him 10 dollars.* vs. *He borrows 10 dollars from me.*), and thus leaves room for negotiation of meanings, and for construction of shared meanings (Lau, Chiu, & Lee, 2001; Lau *et al.*, 2004). It is in part through this meaning negotiation and shared meaning construction processes that people's thoughts are socialized (Chiu, Krauss & Lee, 1999).

To elaborate, in communication, members of a group would collaborate to construct a shared reality (Krauss & Chiu, 1998). Take the example of a professor trying to describe a psychological phenomenon to her students. Although there are many different ways to describe this phenomenon, how this phenomenon will be described depends on how much the students have already known about this phenomenon. In other words, how widely distributed a piece of knowledge in the intended audience is major determinant of how that piece of knowledge will be communicated (Lau, Chiu, & Hong, 2001). In interpersonal communication, knowledge widely distributed in the group is likely to be included in the message, and subsequently be incorporated in the shared representation of the referents in the conversation (Chiu, Krauss, & Lau, 1998). In short, culture shapes the construction of shared representations through communication, and is reproduced in communication.

In a similar vein, Kashima, Woolcock and Kashima (1998) have

developed a connectionist model to account for the reproduction
and consolidation of cultural meanings in a group. This model also
assumes that cultural knowledge is not evenly distributed in a
group. Individuals in a group resemble a network of simple
processing units that receive information from each other and
reproduce the information through the network. The network of
connections is updated as serial reproductions proceed. Due to
memory decay and schema-driven distortions, errors are introduced
in the reproduced messages. In addition, to overcome the cognitive
limits of the individual processing units, cognitive division of labor
and externalization of memory are implemented. Through these self-
organization processes, cultural knowledge that is widely shared
among group members (e.g., stereotypic knowledge) will be
reproduced and consolidated. Kashima *et al.*'s connectionist model
explains how cultural knowledge and meanings are reproduced and
maintained via interpersonal interactions. The model is specific
enough to permit precise simulation of the postulated cultural
meaning reproduction processes in controlled experiments. Findings
from such experiments have lent support to the model (Lyons &
Kashima, 2001).

In summary, when a group of people interact with each other,
more widely distributed knowledge has a greater probability of
being evoked in communication, a higher likelihood of being
reproduced in communication, greater persuasive force, and greater
influence on how individuals experience and grasp the reality.
Meanwhile, representations that are frequently communicated will
have a higher chance of being reproduced in the culture (Kashima *et
al.*, 1998; Schaller, Conway, & Tanchuk, 2002; Sperber, 1996).

Language as a Marker of Ethnocultural Identity

Language is a marker of group identity. There are several ways to
make sense of this assertion (Krauss & Chiu, 1998). First, the
language one speaks is the most salient dimension for social
categorization (Giles, Taylor, & Bourhis, 1977). Second, perceivers

often infer a speaker's group identity from his or her dialect, and attribute to the speaker stereotypic characteristics associated with the inferred group identity (Ryan & Giles, 1982).

In addition, people may accentuate the speech style characteristic of their group to affirm their group identity and maintain intergroup distinction. Speakers from different social categories often attenuate their distinctive speech styles and display speech convergence in order to reduce the psychological distance between themselves and others (Giles & Smith, 1979). However, they may also react to identity-threatening circumstances by accentuating speech differences between themselves and members of the other group (Bourhis, Giles, & Tajfel, 1973). Speech divergence is particularly likely to occur when group identities are emphasized in interactions, and when people expect competitiveness and hostility from outgroup members (Taylor & Royer, 1980).

Furthermore, language use can play a role in maintaining group identity by reinforcing intergroup perceptions (Maass & Arcuri, 1992). For example, people tend to describe undesirable outgroup behaviors and desirable ingroup behaviors with abstract verbs. By contrast, desirable outgroup behaviors and undesirable ingroup behaviors are likely to be described with concrete verbs (Maass, Salvi, Arcuri, & Semin, 1989). This pattern of lexical choice gives rise to the impression that undesirable outgroup behaviors and desirable ingroup behaviors are overt manifestations of global dispositions, whereas desirable outgroup behaviors and undesirable ingroup behaviors are responses to specific situational inducement.

Language, Culture, and Group Identity

Assimilation Effect

According to the CCC model, language, being a carrier of culture, may call out knowledge widely distributed in an ethnolinguistic group. Consistent with this idea, Earle (1969) reported that bilingual Hong Kong Chinese students are less dogmatic when they respond to the Dogmatism scale in English than when they answer the same scale translated into Chinese. The language priming effect Earle reported is similar to the culture priming effect reported in Hong *et al.* (1997). In the Hong *et al.* experiments, Westernized Hong Kong Chinese undergraduates responded to a causal attribution measure after they were exposed to images that symbolize Chinese culture (e.g., a Chinese dragon), images that symbolize US culture (e.g., American flag), or some neutral perspective drawings (control condition). Although Chinese undergraduates typically make fewer internal and more external attributions than their American counterparts (Morris & Peng, 1994), compared to the baseline in the control condition, exposing participants to symbols of Chinese culture effectively activated the causal knowledge widely distributed in Chinese culture, increasing the likelihood of making external attributions. Similarly, exposing participants to symbols of American culture effectively activated the causal knowledge widely distributed in the United States, increasing the likelihood of making internal attributions.

The explanation Earle offered for the language priming effect is similar to the explanation Hong *et al.* (2000) offered for the culture priming effect. Earle (1969) argued that bilingual Hong Kong Chinese undergraduates had learned Chinese and English in distinct settings, at the same time acquiring two language cultures. The Chinese version of the questionnaire activated the more dogmatic Chinese language culture, and the English version activated the less dogmatic language culture. As a result, the participants' responses to the Dogmatism Scale were assimilated into the activated language culture.

Other researchers (Bond, 1983; Ross, Xun, & Wilson, 2002) have reported similar assimilation effect of language priming. Bond (1983) found that bilingual Hong Kong Chinese undergraduates endorsed Western values to a greater extent when they responded to the original (English) Rokeach Value Survey than when they responded to a Chinese translation of it. In a series of studies by Ross *et al.* (2002), Canadian-Chinese undergraduates reported more collective self-statements in open-ended self-descriptions and lower self-esteem, when they completed measures of these variables in the Chinese language than when they responded in English. The effects of language manipulation on self-concept and self-esteem paralleled findings in previous cross-cultural studies.

In the experiments described above, the research participants belonged to the same ethnic group (Hong Kong Chinese or Canadian Chinese). Thus, the human carrier of culture is the same in the different experimental conditions. Through their experiences and participation in both Chinese and North American cultures, they have acquired both Chinese and North American cultural knowledge. A major determinant of whether they would apply Chinese or North American cultural knowledge to guide their responses in a test situation depends on the activation cues in that particular situation. The activation cues in the culture priming experiments were cultural icons, and those in the language priming experiments were languages. Both cultural icons and languages are also carriers of culture. Taken collectively, these culture priming and language priming experiments illustrate how interactions between different carriers of culture in a particular behavioral context might influence the application and expression of cultural knowledge in that context.

Contrast Effect

How does group identity enter the picture? To begin with, group identity influences how likely people would use cultural knowledge to guide their responses (Hong, Ip, Chiu, Morris, & Menon, 2001). People often express or affirm their ethnocultural identities by engaging in behaviors that are widely practiced in their ethnocultural group. Not surprisingly, psychological differences between ethnocultural groups are particularly pronounced when ethnocultural identities are salient (Rhee, Uleman, Lee, & Roman, 1995), or when there is strong identification with the ethnocultural group (Jetten, Postmes, & McAuliffe, 2002).

Similar phenomena are observed in people's use of language in intergroup communication. People may change their dialect or speech style to make it more like that of the outgroup partner (speech convergence), as a means to communicate a willingness to accommodate to the social psychological differences between themselves and outgroup members. Alternatively, people may display divergence in group-specific speech characteristics to show that they are trying to distance themselves psychologically from outgroup members (see Hogg & Abrams, 1988).

Group identity also influences how perceivers evaluate speech convergence and speech divergence. In one study (Tong, Hong, Lee, & Chiu, 1999), Hong Kong undergraduates listened to a conversation between a Hong Kong person and a Mainland Chinese. When the speaker converged to Putonghua (the Mainland official language), those who claimed a Hongkonger identity judged the speaker less favorably than did those who claimed a Chinese identity (a more inclusive identity that applies to both Hong Kong Chinese and Mainland Chinese). In addition, participants who claimed a Chinese identity judged the speaker more favorably when he converged to Putongua than when he maintained Cantonese (a Chinese dialect most commonly used in Hong Kong).

Among bicultural individuals, they have a choice of applying knowledge from one of the two cultures to guide their response. One factor that affects the choice they would make is how they manage their multiple cultural identities. Some bicultural individuals view their dual cultural identities as independent or complementary, while others see them as oppositional (Benet-Martinez, Leu, Lee, & Morris, 2002; Tsai, Ying, & Lee, 2000). Among bicultural minorities, some seek to assimilate into the majority group, while others seek to affirm their ethnocultural identity. Those who choose to assimilate may do so by aligning their values with those in the majority group (Tafarodi, Kang, & Milne, 2002). By contrast, those who choose to affirm their group identity may adhere to the dominant values in their ethnocultural group or distance themselves from the majority group (Kosmitzki, 1996). Variations in how dual identities are managed are related to bicultural individuals' responses to culture priming. Those who view their dual identities as independent or complementary display responses expected from the primed cultural knowledge. Those who view their dual identities as oppositional and those who seek to affirm their ethnocultural identities respond reactively to the culture primes; they show responses that are contrastive to the responses expected from the primed cultural knowledge (Benet-Martinez *et al.*, 2002).

Some researchers have found analogous contrast effects in language priming studies. In one study (Yang & Bond, 1980), Chinese-English bilingual participants responded to a Chinese value survey. They showed greater identification with Chinese values when the survey was in English than in Chinese. In another study (Bond & Cheung, 1984), Cantonese-speaking Hong Kong Chinese undergraduates filled out a survey of traditional Chinese beliefs. Participants who received oral instructions in Putonghua responded more like Westerners, compared to those who received instructions in Cantonese. Mainland Chinese are generally seen as more traditional than Hong Kong Chinese. It seems clear that the presence of an outgroup language can call out one's ethnolinguistic identity.

If language priming could result in assimilation and contrast effects, when would assimilation versus contrast effect emerge? A critical factor is how explicit or implicit the connection between the dependent measure and culture is. In studies finding contrast effect, the dependent measures were traditional Chinese values and traditional Chinese beliefs. The connection between the dependent measure and culture was obvious to the participants. Endorsing Chinese values or agreeing to Chinese beliefs is an expression of one's identification with Chinese culture. In the language of Self-categorization Theory (Turner, Hogg, Oakes, Reicher, & Wetherell, 1987), there was a good fit between group identity (Chinese vs. Westerner), the social environment (the presence of ingroup or outgroup language), and the normative expectations of how Chinese should respond to Chinese values and beliefs. In this context, the presence of an outgroup language reminded the participants of their ethnolinguistic identity, making the identity salient in the context. The activated group identity in turn guided their responses to the dependent measures, leading to a contrast effect.

In studies finding assimilation, the dependent measures were measures of dogmatism, spontaneous self-concepts, and self-esteem. The connection between these measures and Chinese culture was obscure to the participants. Thus, participants did not know that their responses to these measures could serve an identity affirmation function. In the language of Self-categorization Theory, the fit between group identity and the social environment was low. Hence, ethnolinguistic identity was not activated, and assimilation effect was observed.

The interactions between language, group identity, and context described above have clear implications for understanding the relationship of culture and psychology. At least in test situations, the likelihood that people would use cultural knowledge to guide their responses increases when group identity is emphasized in the situation, and when people identify strongly with the group. In these situations, people would affirm their ethnolinguistic identity by endorsing cultural values or subscribing to cultural beliefs, particularly when the presence of an outgroup language calls out their ethnolinguistic identity. These phenomena indicate that people do not passively receive influences from culture; they may use culture as a tool to accomplish emerging goals in the situation (e.g., affirmation of ethnocultural identity).

Intercultural Interaction

In our model, communicative acts are symbolic actions directed towards a specific target in a particular context. As mentioned, in social interactions, individuals will retrieve *representations of how knowledge is distributed* in the interaction partner's culture, and use these retrieved representations to guide social interactions. For example, when communicating to a member of a certain group about X, they will retrieve their representation of how knowledge about X is distributed in the group (as opposed to their own knowledge of X), and tune their communication message in the direction of the retrieved knowledge distribution. Consistent with this idea, Isaacs and Clark (1987) found that speakers describing

New York City landmarks refer to them differently depending on their listener's identity. When the listener is a New Yorker, who apparently is familiar with New York City, the descriptions of the landmarks tend to be briefer than when the listener has not been in New York City before.

This tuning process is particularly useful for understanding intercultural interaction. In intercultural communication, the communicator often needs to identify the communication partner's cultural group membership, and use the partner's group identity to construct or retrieve a culture- and situation-appropriate knowledge distribution to guide message formulation and comprehension. Such processes are particularly likely to emerge when the interaction is not identity-threatening, and when group identity is not emphasized in the interaction.

Conclusion

In the present chapter, we have outlined a CCC model of culture and psychology. In this model, we define culture as a network of knowledge that is produced, distributed, and reproduced among a collection of interconnected people. The major assumptions and postulates of the model are:

1. Culture knowledge is unevenly distributed (as opposed to perfectly shared) in a group.
2. The three major components in the model are culture, carriers of culture, and context. These three components are separate conceptual entities. Expression and application of culture in a particular situation should be understood in terms of the reciprocal interactions between these three components.
3. Humans, as a carrier of culture, create a need for culture, create culture, use culture as guides for their social practices, reflect on the strengths and liabilities of a particular cultural tradition, identify or dis-identify with culture, use culture as a tool to attain their personal goals,

reproduce culture by spreading it to other territories and passing it on to new generations, and change culture.

4. Cultural knowledge is distributed in a human group in a nonrandom fashion. Through a set of self-organizing principles, previously unrelated ideas and practices may organize themselves into thematic clusters. With frequent use, variations of cultural ideas and practices will appear.

5. Features of the context may attenuate or accentuate the likelihood of expressing or applying a piece of cultural knowledge in a particular situation. They may also call out a particular piece of cultural knowledge and render that piece of knowledge applicable (or inapplicable) in the situation.

The proposed model has some advantages. First, by defining culture as a network of distributed knowledge, and by conceptually separating culture and people, we avoid the problem of reifying culture. Second, we rely on a set of self-organizing processes to explain spontaneous production and maintenance of shared meanings in social interaction. Thus, our model does not require a homunculus-like agent or a collective will to oversee or manage the evolution of cultural knowledge. Third, cultural psychologists assume that people are cultural beings and that culture affects every aspect of social life. We agree that cultural influences are pervasive. However, we posit that people are cultural agents who actively participate in and interact with culture in various forms. Fourth, there are systematic variations in how people experience culture within a population. These variations may arise from individual differences, situational inducement, and their interactions. The CCC model recognizes these within-group variations, and seeks to understand both between-group and within-group variations within the same integrated theoretical model.

Finally, when culture is reduced to a fixed response pattern in a demarcated population, the absence of predicted group differences might pose a threat to the explanatory utility of culture (Briley & Wyer, 2001; Coon & Kemmelmeier, 2001). In a recent review of group differences in individualism and collectivism, Oyserman,

Coon and Kemmelmeier (2002) found that individualistic groups (North Americans) do not always have higher scores on measures of individualism and lower scores on measures of collectivism than do collectivistic groups (e.g., Chinese, Japanese, Koreans). On the face of it, these findings threaten the validity of the constructs of individualism and collectivism.

The threat is more apparent than real when we dissociate individualism and collectivism as cultural knowledge from group averages on measures of individualism and collectivism. Paradoxically, the explanatory utility of culture is most apparent if group differences emerge in a situation only when they are predicted in that situation, and disappear when they are not. Thus, the absence of group differences in some circumstances might highlight the explanatory utility of culture, instead of undermining it (Lehman *et al.*, in press). A critical test of the theoretical utility of a cultural account of psychological processes is whether we can predict contextual patterning of group differences based on known principles of cultural knowledge application. According to the CCC model, we can make these predictions only when we understand the intricate interactions between culture, its carriers, and the context. We have illustrated this point with findings from language and social identity research.

G. H. Mead (1934/1962) believed that the goal of social psychology is "to explain the conduct of the individual in terms of the organized conduct of the social group, rather than to account for the organized conduct of the social group in terms of the separate individuals belonging to it" (p. 7; see Bruner, 1990; Moscovici, 1988; Vygotsky, 1978 for similar ideas). Apparently, focusing on group processes at the expense of individual processes will compromise the prospect of achieving thorough understanding of the psychology of individuals-in-society. Nonetheless, to many social psychologists, Mead's emphasis on holistic social psychology is a good reminder of the need to correct the biases ensuing from methodological individualism in American social psychology. Language, culture, and group identity are the cornerstones as well as products of organized conduct of the social group. Not surprisingly, they have occupied the center stage in Mead's social psychology. We hope we have convinced readers that the CCC model offers a window of opportunity for researchers to bring together again the research literatures on language, group identity and culture. In the future, researchers will discover numerous other ways in which the three components in the CCC model interact to produce a dynamic, contextualized pattern of expressions of culture in situations. Through these discoveries, researchers will also find new ways to bring other seemingly unrelated research literatures together.

We end with another quotation from G. H. Mead (1934/1962), whose attempts to construct a holistic social psychology have inspired our thinking:

> The social act . . . must be taken as a dynamic whole – as something going on – no part of which can be considered or understood by itself – a complex organic process implied by each individual stimulus and response involved in it. (p. 7)

References

Appadurai, A. (1996). *Modernity at large: Cultural dimensions of globalization.* Minneapolis, MN: University of Minnesota Press.

Barth, F. (2002). An anthropology of knowledge. *Current Anthropology, 43,* 1–18.

Benet-Martinez, V., Leu, J., Lee, F., & Morris, M. W. (2002). Negotiating biculturalism: Cultural frame switching in biculturals with oppositional versus compatible cultural identities. *Journal of Cross-Cultural Psychology, 33,* 492–516.

Boesch, C., & Tomasello, M. (1998). Chimpanzee and human cultures. *Current Anthropology, 39,* 591–614.

Bond, M. H. (1983). How language variations affect inter-cultural differentiation of values by Hong Kong bilinguals. *Journal of Language and Social Psychology, 2,* 57–66.

Bond, M. H., & Cheung, M-k. (1984). Experimenter language choice and ethnic affirmation by Chinese trilinguals in Hong Kong. *International Journal of Intercultural Relations, 8,* 347–356.

Bourhis, R. Y., Giles, H., & Tajfel, H. (1973). Language as a determinant of Welsh identity. *European Journal of Social Psychology, 3,* 447–460.

Briley, D. A., Morris, M. W., & Simonson, I. (2000). Reasons as carriers of culture: Dynamic versus dispositional models of cultural influence on decision-making. *Journal of Consumer Research, 27,* 157–178.

Briley, D. A., & Wyer, R. S. Jr. (2001). Transitory determinants of values and decisions: The utility (or nonutility) of individualism and collectivism in understanding cultural differences. *Social Cognition, 19,* 197–227.

Brumann, C. (1999). Writing for culture: Why successful concept should not be discarded. *Current Anthropology, 40,* 1–27.

Bruner, J. (1990). *Act of meaning.* Cambridge, MA: Harvard University Press.

Campbell, D. T. (1965). Variation and selective retention in socio-cultural evolution. In J. R. Barringer, G. Blanksten, & R. Mack (Eds.), *Social change in developing areas* (pp. 19–49). Cambridge, MA: Schenkman.

Carpenter, M., Nagell, K., & Tomasello, M. (1998). Social cognition, joint attention, and communicative competence from 9 to 15 months of age. *Monographs of the Society for Research in Child Development, 63,* 1–174.

Chiu, C-y., Krauss, R. M., & Lau, I. Y-m. (1998). Some cognitive consequences of communication. In S. R. Fussell & R. J. Kreuz (Eds.), *Social and cognitive psychological approaches to interpersonal communication* (pp. 127–143). Hillsdale, NJ: Erlbaum.

Chiu, C-y., Krauss, R. M., & Lee, S-l. (1999) Communication and social cognition: A post-Whorfian approach. In T. Sugiman, M. Karasawa, J. Liu & C. Ward (Eds.), *Progress in Asian social psychology* (Vol. 2, pp. 127–143). Map-ku, Korea: Kyoyook-Kwahak-Sa.

Chiu, C-y., Morris, M. W., Hong, Y-y., & Menon, T. (2000). Motivated cultural cognition: The impact of implicit cultural theories on dispositional attribution varies as a function of need for closure. *Journal of Personality and Social Psychology, 78,* 247–259.

Choi, I., & Nisbett, R. E. (1998). Situational salience and cultural differences in the correspondence bias and actor-observer bias. *Personality and Social Psychology Bulletin, 24,* 949–960.

Cohen, D. (1996). Law, social policy, and violence: The impact of regional cultures. *Journal of Personality and Social Psychology, 70,* 961–978.

Cohen, D. (2001). Cultural variation: Considerations and implications. *Psychological Bulletin, 127,* 451–471.

Coon, H. M., & Kemmelmeier, M. (2001). Cultural orientations in the United States: (Re)examining differences among ethnic groups. *Journal of Cross-Cultural Psychology, 32,* 348–364.

DiMaggio, D. (1997). Culture and cognition. *Annual Review of Sociology, 23,* 263–287.

Donald, M. (1993). Precis of "Origins of the modern mind: Three stages in the evolution of culture and cognition." *Behavioral and Brain Sciences, 16,* 737–791.

Earle, M. (1969). A cross-cultural and cross-language comparison of dogmatism scores. *Journal of Social Psychology, 79,* 19–24.

Fiske, A. P. (2000). Complementarity theory: Why human social capacities evolved to require cultural complements? *Personality and Social Psychology Review, 4,* 76–94.

Fu, H-y., Morris, M. W., Lee, S-l., Chiu, C-y., & Hong, Y-y. (2003). *Why do individuals display culturally typical conflict resolution choices? Need for cognitive closure.* Manuscript under review.

Gardner, W. L., Gabriel, S., & Lee, A. (1999). "I" value freedom, but "we" value relationships: Self-construal priming mirrors cultural differences in judgment. *Psychological Science, 10,* 321–326.

Giles, H., & Smith, P. (1979). Accommodation theory: Optimal levels of convergence. In G. Giles & R. S. Clair (Eds.), *Language and social psychology* (pp. 45–65). Oxford: Blackwell.

Giles, H., Taylor, D. M., & Bourhis, R. Y. (1977). Dimensions of Welsh identity. *European Journal of Social Psychology, 7,* 165–174.

Guimond, S., & Palmer, D. L. (1985). The political socialization of commerce and social science students: Epistemic authority and attitude change. *Journal of Applied Social Psychology, 26,* 1985–2013.

Hallahan, M., Lee, F., & Herzog, T. (1997). It's not just whether you win or lose, it's also where you play the game: A naturalistic, cross-cultural examination of the positivity bias. *Journal of Cross-Cultural Psychology, 28,* 768–778.

Han, S-p., & Shavitt, S. (1994). Persuasion and culture: Advertising appeals in individualistic and collectivistic societies. *Journal of Experimental Social Psychology, 30,* 326–350.

Ho, D. Y. F., & Chiu, C-y. (1994). Component ideas of individualism, collectivism, and social organization: An application in the study of Chinese culture. In U. Kim, H. C. Triandis, C. Kagitcibasi, G. Choi & G. Yoon (Eds.), *Individualism and collectivism: Theory, method and applications* (pp.137–156). Thousand Oaks, CA: Sage.

Ho, D. Y. F., & Chiu, C-y. (1998). Collective representations as a metaconstruct: An analysis based on methodological relationalism. *Culture and Psychology, 4,* 349–369.

Hogg, M. A., & Abrams, D. (1988). *Social identifications: A social psychology of intergroup relations and group processes.* London: Routledge.

Hong, Y-y., Benet-Martinez, V., Chiu, C-y., & Morris, M. W. (2003). Boundaries of cultural influences: Construct activation as a mechanism for cultural differences in social perception. *Journal of Cross-Cultural Psychology 34,* 453–464.

Hong, Y-y., Chiu, C-y., & Kung, T. M. (1997). Bringing culture out in front: Effects of cultural meaning system activation on social cognition. In K. Leung, Y. Kashima, U. Kim, & S. Yamaguchi (Eds.), *Progress in Asian social psychology* (Vol. 1, pp. 135–146). Singapore: Wiley.

Hong, Y-y., Ip, G., Chiu, C-y., Morris, M. W., & Menon, T. (2001). Cultural identity and dynamic construction of the self: Collective duties and individual rights in Chinese and American cultures. *Social Cognition, 19,* 251–269.

Hong, Y-y., Morris, M. W., Chiu, C-y., & Benet-Martinez, V. (2000). Multicultural minds: A dynamic constructivist approach to culture and cognition. *American Psychologist, 55,* 709–720.

Issacs, E. A., & Clark, H. H. (1987). References in conversation between experts and novices. *Journal of Experimental Psychology: General, 116,* 26–37.

Jetten, J., Postmes, T., & Mcauliffe, B. (2002). "We're all individuals": Group norms of individualism and collectivism, levels of identification and identity threat. *European Journal of Social Psychology, 32,* 189–207.

Ji, L-j., Peng, K., & Nibsett, R. E. (2000). Culture, control, and perception of relationships in the environment. *Journal of Personality and Social Psychology, 78,* 943–955.

Kashima, E. S., & Kashima, Y. (1998). Culture and language: The case of cultural dimensions and personal pronoun use. *Journal of Cross-Cultural Psychology, 29,* 461–486.

Kashima, Y. (1999). Culture, groups, and coordination problems. *Psychologische Beitrage, 41,* 237–251.

Kashima, Y. (2000). Conceptions of culture and person for psychology. *Journal of Cross-Cultural Psychology, 31,* 14–32.

Kashima, Y., Woolcock, J., & Kashima, E. (2000). Group impressions as dynamic configurations: The tensor product model of group impression formation and change. *Psychological Review, 107,* 914–942.

Kessing, R. M. (1994). Theories of culture revisited. In R. Borofsky (Ed.), *Assessing cultural anthropology* (pp. 301–10). New York: McGraw-Hill.

Knowles, E. D., Morris, M. W., Chiu, C-y., & Hong, Y-y. (2001). Culture and process of person perception: Evidence for automaticity among East Asians in correcting for situational influences on behavior. *Personality and Social Psychology Bulletin, 27,* 1344–1356.

Kosmitzki, C. (1996). The reaffirmation of cultural identity in cross-cultural encounters. *Personality and Social Psychology Bulletin, 22,* 238–248.

Krauss, R. M., & Chiu, C-y. (1998). Language and social psychology. In D. Gilbert, S. Fiske-Emory & G. Lindzey (Eds.), *Handbook of social psychology* (4th ed., Vol. 2, pp. 41–88). New York: Guilford.

Latané, B. (1996). Dynamic social impact: The creation of culture by communication. *Journal of Communication, 46*, 13–25.

Latané, B., & Bourgeois, M. J. (1996). Experimental evidence for dynamic social impact: The emergence of subcultures in electronic groups. *Journal of Communication, 46*, 35–47.

Latané, B., & L'Herrou, T. (1996). Spatial clustering in the conformity game: Dynamic social impact in electronic groups. *Journal of Personality and Social Psychology, 70*, 1218–1230.

Lau, I. Y-m., Chiu, C-y., & Hong, Y-y. (2001). I know what you know: Assumptions about others' knowledge and their effects on message construction. *Social Cognition, 19*, 587–600.

Lau, I. Y-m., Chiu, C-y., & Lee, S-l. (2001). Communication and shared reality: Implications for the psychological foundations of culture. *Social Cognition, 19*, 350–371.

Lau, I. Y-m., Lee, S-l., & Chiu, C-y. (2004). Language, cognition and reality: Constructing shared meanings through communication. In M. Schaller & C. Crandall (Eds.), *The psychological foundations of culture* (pp. 77–100). Mahway, NJ: Lawrence Erlbaum.

Lehman, D., Chiu, C-y., & Schaller, M. (in press). Culture and psychology. *Annual Review of Psychology*.

Lyons, A., & Kashima, Y. (2001). The reproduction of culture: Communication processes tend to maintain cultural stereotypes. *Social Cognition, 19*, 372–394.

Maass, A., & Arcuri, L. (1992). The role of language in the persistence of stereotypes. In G. R. Semin & K. Fiedler (Eds.), *Language, interaction and social cognition* (pp. 129–143). London: Sage.

Maass, A., Salvi, D., Arcuri, L., & Semin, G. R. (1989). Language use in intergroup contexts: The linguistic intergroup bias. *Journal of Personality and Social Psychology, 38*, 689–703.

Mead, G. H. (1934/1962). *Mind, self, and society: From the standpoint of social behaviorist*. Chicago, IL: University of Chicago Press.

Menon, T., Morris, M. W., Chiu, C-y., & Hong, Y-y. (1999). Culture and the construal of agency: Attribution to individual versus group dispositions. *Journal of Personality and Social Psychology, 76*, 701–717.

Miyamoto, Y., & Kitayama, S. (2002). Cultural variation in correspondence bias: The critical role of attitude diagnosticity of socially constrained behavior. *Journal of Personality and Social Psychology, 83*, 1239–1248.

Morris, M. W., & Peng, K. (1994). Culture and cause: American and Chinese attributions for social and physical events. *Journal of Personality and Social Psychology, 67*, 949–971.

Moscovici, S. (1988). Notes towards a description of social representations. *European Journal of Social Psychology, 18*, 211–250.

Ng, S. H., & Bradac, J. (1993). *Power in language: Vernal communication and social influence.* Newbury Park, CA: Sage.

Norenzayan, A., Choi, I., & Nisbett, R. E. (2002). Cultural similarities and differences in social inference: Evidence from behavioral predictions and lay theories of behavior. *Personality and Social Psychology Bulletin, 28*, 109–120.

Oyserman, D., Coon, H. M., & Kemmelmeier, M. (2002). Rethinking individualism and collectivism: Evaluation of theoretical assumptions and meta-analyses. *Psychological Bulletin, 128*, 3–72.

Peoples, J., & Bailey, G. (1994). *Humanity: An introduction to cultural anthropology* (3rd ed.). St. Paul: West.

Rhee, E., Uleman, J. S., Lee, H. K., & Roman, R. J. (1995). Spontaneous self-descriptions and ethnic identities in individualistic and collectivistic cultures. *Journal of Personality and Social Psychology, 69*, 142–152.

Ross, M., Xun, W. Q. E., & Wilson, A. E. (2002). Language and the bicultural self. *Personality and Social Psychology Bulletin, 28*, 1040–1050.

Rothbaum, F., & Tsang, B. Y-P. (1998). Lovesongs in the United States and China on the nature of romantic love. *Journal of Cross-Cultural Psychology, 29*, 306–319.

Rothbaum, F., & Xu, X. (1995). The theme of giving back to parents in Chinese and American songs. *Journal of Cross-Cultural Psychology, 26*, 698–713.

Ryan, E. B., & Giles, H. (Eds.) (1982). *Attitudes toward language: Social and applied contexts.* London: Arnold.

Schaller, M., Conway, L. G. III; & Tanchuk, T. L. (2002). Selective pressures on the once and future contents of ethnic stereotypes: Effects of the communicability of traits. *Journal of Personality and Social Psychology, 82*, 861–877.

Shore, B. (1996). *Culture in mind: Cognition, culture, and the problem of meaning.* New York: Oxford University Press.

Sperber, D. (1996). *Explaining culture: A naturalistic approach.* Massachusetts: Blackwell.

Tafarodi, R. W., Kang, S-j., & Milne, A. B. (2002). When different becomes similar: Compensatory conformity in bicultural visible minorities. *Personality and Social Psychology Bulletin, 28*, 1131–1142.

Taylor, D. M., & Royer, L. (1980). Group processes affecting anticipated language choice in intergroup relations. In H. Giles, W. P. Robinson, & P. Smith (Eds.), *Language: Social psychological perspectives* (pp. 185–192). Oxford: Pergamon.

Tong, Y-y., Chiu, C-y., & Fu, H-y. (2001). Linguistic gender is related to psychological gender: The case of "Chinese characters." *Journal of Psychology in Chinese Societies, 2,* 107–117.

Tong, Y-y., Hong, Y-y., Lee, S-l., & Chiu, C-y. (1999). Language as a carrier of social identity. *International Journal of Intercultural Relations, 23,* 281–296.

Trafimow, D., Triandis, H. C., & Goto, S. (1991). Some tests of the distinction between private self and collective self. *Journal of Personality and Social Psychology, 60,* 640–655.

Triandis, H. C. (1989). The self and social behavior in differing cultural contexts. *Psychological Review, 96,* 506–520.

Triandis, H. C. (in press). Dimensions of culture beyond Hofstede. In H. Vinken, Soeters & Ester, P. (Eds.), *Comparing cultures, Dimensions of culture in a comparative perspective.* Leiden, The Netherlands, Brill Publishers.

Triandis, H.C. (1996) The psychological measurement of cultural syndromes. *American Psychologist, 51,* 407–415.

Tsai, J. L., Ying, Y-w., & Lee, P. A. (2000). The meaning of being Chinese and being American: Variation among Chinese American young adults. *Journal of Cross-Cultural Psychology, 31,* 302–332.

Turner, J. C., Hogg, M. A., Oakes, P. J., Reicher, S. D., & Wetherell, M. (1987). *Rediscovering the social group: A self-categorization theory.* Oxford: Blackwell.

Verkuyten, M., & Pouliasi, K. (2002). Biculturalism among older children: Cultural frame switching, attributions, self-identification, and attitudes. *Journal of Cross-Cultural Psychology, 33,* 596–609.

Vygotsky, L. S. (1978). *Mind in society: The development of higher psychological processes.* Cambridge, MA: Harvard University Press.

Yang, K. S., & Bond, M. H. (1980). Ethnic identification by Chinese bilinguals. *Journal of Cross-Cultural Psychology, 11,* 411–425.

7

Culture and Intergenerational Communication: Implications of Cultures for Communication across Age Groups

Hiroshi OTA

Population configuration has undergone transformation in many countries, witnessing the largest number of people aged over 60 in the history of the world. In this cultural milieu, older adults have increasingly been recognized as a salient and distinctive co-cultural group. Their health problems and need of care and assistance, among others, have called for serious policy considerations (e.g., Martin, 1988; Phillips, 2000). What further complicates this state is the presence of multi-cultural situations in many parts of the world where irreconcilable identities, languages, and cultural heritages often exist side by side. These contexts have been a driving force for the research on intergenerational communication around the world-wide (e.g., Pecchioni, Ota, & Sparks, in press). Among others, a program of research has been going on in various parts of the globe, framed, broadly, in the intergroup perspective (Harwood, Giles, & Ryan, 1995; Tajfel & Turner, 1986), drawing specifically on communication accommodation theory (Coupland, Coupland, Giles, & Henwood, 1988), and the communicative predicament of aging model (Ryan, Giles, Henwood, & Bartolucci, 1986; Barker, Giles, & Harwood, in press). A number of important theoretical and practical implications have been proffered to counteract the existing problems and advance the theories of intergenerational communication (Giles, McCann, Ota, & Noels, 2002).

In the present chapter, I will, following the tradition, view intergenerational communication from an intergroup perspective, with special focus on its relation to the macro-cultural context. Implications of "cultures" for communication across generational lines will be discussed by drawing on data from recent cross-cultural studies of intergenerational communication. Furthermore, I will discuss the importance of several social psychological factors for the studies of culture and intergenerational communication in this changing cultural milieu.

Culture and Intergenerational Communication

Intergenerational Communication in the Cultural Context

Communication and culture are inseparable as Hall (1973) astutely stated, "culture is communication" (p. 97). Culture may be viewed as a *system* made up of various social rules and norms, and also as people's *practice* of communicative interaction (Kashima, 2000). The two perspectives are complementary: Communication is often guided by the norms and rules of the cultural system, while it perpetuates, recreates or changes them. Culture, in this sense, is a symbolic process, and provides special meanings for the people concerned. Scholars in various academic fields have sought constructive approaches to the concept of culture in human social interaction. A number of cultural dimensions have been proffered with the hope of systematically explaining differences in human communication at collective as well as individual levels. For example, many countries located in East and Southeast Asia are collectivistic while those in "Western" regions, including the United

States, Australia, Canada, and northern European nations, are relatively individualistic (Triandis, 1995: for more recent arguments, Kitayama, 2002).

Numerous cross-cultural differences in cognitive, affective, and behavioral processes have been found to exit in Eastern and Western countries (Nisbett, 2003). Those differences may, in various ways, feed into people's views of intergenerational relationships and performance of such communication. Eastern countries share many features of communication between age-groups, despite their diverse socio-, politico-, and religio-cultural backgrounds (Phillips, 2000). Respect for the elderly, as exemplified by the ethical norm of filial piety in East Asia, is a key concept (Ho, 1994; Ingersoll-Dayton, & Saengtienchai, 1999; Sung 2001). Younger adults are expected to be polite, listen to, obey and provide practical support for older adults. Older adults are placed at a socially high and advantageous position to the extent that they are viewed in positive terms. Despite their lowered status due allegedly to the recent rapid societal transformation (Chow, 1999; Phillips, 2000), the norm of respect for older adults still remains in those countries (Sung, 2001).

In Western countries, intergenerational relations may be more bilateral. Because of this, people – young or old – may be more individualistic than their counterparts in Eastern countries.. Unlike the latter, Westerners may face intergenerational communication with less salient age-related social identities and, therefore, are less likely to encounter communication problems in such interaction. In this sense, older people would not occupy higher status positions over younger adults – and unequal power distribution based simply on age differences is *less* likely to be endorsed (Hofstede, 1991; Kim & Yamaguchi, 1995).

East-West Split in Communication across Age Groups

Against this background, cross-cultural research has been conducted to examine various aspects of intergenerational communication.

Participants have been recruited from countries around the Pacific Rim and elsewhere to share their perceptions of and attitudes to age-groups, and also their experiences of intra- and intergenerational communication. To summarize the major findings (e.g., see also Giles *et al.*, 2002), respondents' country of origin, as expected, plays a significant role in the way they judge their communication experiences. People from Eastern countries such as Japan, South Korea, and Hong Kong are more likely than their Western counterparts to report negative perceptions of older adults. They rate elders as non-accommodative, feel it necessary to be respectful, and take an avoiding stance toward them in communication. Elder respect stands out in their mind as an *obligation* although it is, paradoxically enough, less likely to be endorsed by them in communication than by their Western counterparts. Interestingly, intergenerational communication was less predictive of older adults' self-esteem and sense of coherence (as health indicators) in Asian than in Western countries. In the U.S.A. and Australia, negative intergenerational communication experiences (e.g., avoidance) were related to lower self-esteem and sense of control, while positive experiences (e.g., accommodation from young people) predicted higher self-esteem and personal control. In contrast, the Chinese (P.R. China, Hong Kong) older adults' self-esteem was predicted mainly by their communication with *other older* adults. Being respectful to other older adults in communication was found to *increase* their personal self-esteem. This last finding may point to a difference in the function of "respect/obligation" (e.g., self-restraint) in self-esteem across cultures (Lehman, Chiu, & Schaller, in press).

Beyond Eastern vs. Western Cultures

Acculturation. The foregoing notwithstanding, a simple East (Asia)-West dichotomy may not be sufficient to explain the cross-cultural variabilities in people's inter- and intra-generational communication experiences. One potent perspective with which to explain the cultural variety is *cultural change*, or acculturation. Acculturation may involve changes taking place both at societal and individual levels, due to internal (e.g., individual choice) and external forces (e.g., colonization). When societal transformation occurs, it is likely to favor the powerful and impose their values onto the powerless. Acculturation may prompt people to seek different self-views in social interaction (Heine & Lehman, 2003), and to use diverse modes of communication (see Ting-Toomey & Kurogi, 1998), whilst, at times, to adopt a defiant stance to outgroup members (Berry, Kim, & Boski, 1988). Acculturation effects were observed in Asian immigrants' attitudes toward care of older adults (e.g., Kim, Kim, & Hurh, 1991), and also in their communication across age-groups. Bicultural people, such as Chinese-Americans (Giles, Liang, Noels, & McCann, 2001), immigrant Chinese in New Zealand (Ng, Liu, Wetherall, & Loong, 1997), and the Filipinos (Williams *et al.*, 1997) appear, as do Westerners, to evaluate communication experiences in positive ways (greater others' accommodation, lower respect-obligation and sense of avoidance). However, this effect, curiously enough, was not observed among people in Hong Kong (Noels, Giles, Gallois, & Ng, 2001) despite their apparent biculturalism (Hong, Morris, Chiu, & Benet-Martinez, 2000).

Age-Groups as Culture. Respondents' age-groups have noticeable "cultural" implications on intergenerational communication. People go through a number of developmental stages, and move from one age-group to another. In this way, they experience the cultures of different age-groups (Giles, Fox, Harwood, & Williams, 1994). For instance, some people form age group associations or clubs, and thus separate themselves from others of a different age. Mass communication may contribute to the "culturalization" of age-groups by showing their members in particular programs to attract audience of same age (Harwood, 1997), and also by portraying them in certain (e.g., stereotype confirming or accentuating) ways (Robinson & Skill, 1995). Younger people visualize themselves having unique communication orientations and norms as they move to different age groups (e.g., Giles, Honeycutt, Fortman, & Ota, 2003; Hori, 1994).

Younger and Older Adult Communication in the U.S.A., Japan, and the Philippines

To further understand the implications of cultures for intergenerational communication, an investigation was conducted on younger and older adults' communication experience with people pf similar or different age in the U.S.A., Japan, and Philippines (Ota, Giles, & Somera, 2002). Examination was also conducted on the impact of older adults' communication on their self-esteem and sense of coherence as indicators of psychological health. Philippines is rather unique in that while it shares a multi-lingual and multi-cultural country located in Southeast Asia, sharing many interpersonal norms (e.g., maintenance of harmonious interpersonal relationship and observance of debts of gratitude) with other Asian countries (Natividad, 2000), it also has western cultural orientations such as the use of open/assertive communication (Niikura, 1999) inherited from its colonial (e.g., Spain, U.S.A.) and Christian background. English is widely used, which shows a legacy of American influence. No wonder, people there are sometimes called "Brown Americans of Asia" (Perdon, 1998).

The results of the study were in general, though not entirely, consistent with those of the previous studies (see Ota *et al.*, 2002, for details). Regarding between-country differences, American respondents rated communication with others most "positively" of the three nations. Their communication was featured by the greatest others' accommodation, the least others' non-accommodation, the lowest felt-obligation to be polite and the lowest sense of avoidance in communication. Filipino respondents reported a similar degree of others' accommodation as did their American counterparts, but their reported sense of respect and avoidance of their interlocutors were by far the greatest. An age-group effect was quite conspicuous. Younger adults were more likely than their older counterparts to perceive others to be non-accommodating, and to feel respect/ obligation and avoidance when communicating with others. With regard to the target age-group effect, both young and older adults showed the tendency to rate communication with younger adults *more favorably* than with older adults. As Figure 1 illustrates, American younger people, compared to the two Asian young groups, showed attenuation in this arguably "negative" view of communication with older people. American and Filipino older adults were less obliged to be respectful of younger than of older adults, whereas Japanese elders were obliged to be equally respectful of the young and the old. Younger Filipinos felt quite obliged to respect and avoid others in communication. However, their acknowledgment of a high level of accommodation from both older and younger others may suggest their attribution of positive meanings to intergenerational interactions, whilst observing traditional communication norms such as the respect for older adults (see Figure 1).

Figure 1
Respondents' rating of others' accommodation
and self's respect/obligation toward their communication partners

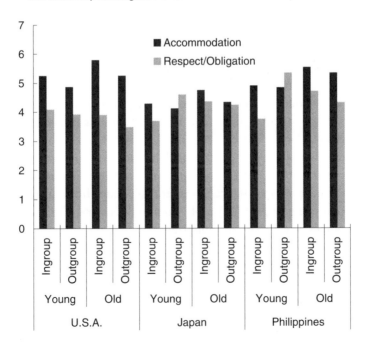

Older adults' self-esteem and sense of coherence were predicted by others' accommodation, similar to what the previous studies (e.g, Noels *et al.*, 2001) have found. Communicating with age peers (ingroup members) was a strong predictor across the three countries. In contrast, the effects of outgroup communication on the health indicators was more prominent in the U.S.A. and Philippines than in Japan. In Japan, being respectful to ingroup members and outgroup members' non-accommodation may lead to an *increase* in the sense of coherence. This relationship between seemingly negative communication (e.g., self-restraint and distancing) and increased psychological health was observed in the Philippines, especially between older people's non-accommodation and personal self-esteem. Nonetheless, younger and older adults' non-accommodation can potentially do harm to self-esteem and the sense of coherence there.

Some Issues for Cross-Cultural Intergenerational Communication Research

Stability-Change vs. Sharedness-Uniquess in Culture

The three-country study, in conjunction with others in the same program of research, has confirmed that cultures (i.e., age-groups, countries) have indeed significant implications for people's communication across generational lines. National and age-group cultures seem to provide people with unique intergenerational communication experience. Further, the data from members of different age-groups, and people from multicultural nations such as Philippines speak for the importance of cultural change in inter-generational communication. We need to deal with "stability-change" and "sharedness-uniqueness" when we study culture and intergenerational communication (see also Kashima, 2000; Martin & Nakayama, 1999).

On the one hand, using the static view of culture in research would be reasonable and perhaps practical. We are born into a certain cultural system where we learn its norms and rules through socialization, and abide by them to claim its full-fledged membership. In this way, we can communicate, and teach others to communicate, effectively and appropriately, and make sense of our communicative life therein. On the other hand, culture is far from being monolithic and stable. Contact with other countries may result in macro-structural change (e.g., modernization) as seen in a number of countries, including Philippines, Hong Kong and Singapore, to name a few. At the individual level, cultural changes may be reflected in psychological and communicative changes. A similar argument can be made about age-group culture. People may have a different sense of age group membership *via contact* with other people (Ryan *et al.*, 1986), seeing consequently various psychological and communicative transformations occurring in them (e.g., Giles *et al.*, 2003).

The stability-change dimension of culture leads to another related point requiring consideration. Various concepts, such as East-West (Yum, 1988) and individualism-collectivism (Hofstede, 1991; Triandis, 1995) have been constructed to classify countries. Although they may reasonably explain similarities and differences, they may fail to explain the uniquenesses of a country demonstrated in within-region differences and between-region similarities (e.g., McCann, Ota, Giles, & Caraker, 2003; Nadamitsu, Chen, & Friedrich, 2001; Williams *et al.*, 1997). At the same time, what lies behind those similarities and differences, has received limited attention so far (but see Triandis, 1995).

Suggestions for Future Research

Attending to the aforementioned cultural features is highly important for the study of intergenerational communication, given the rapid cultural transformation and heightened cultural awareness across the globe. This task, however, is easier said than done. To advance our understanding of how culture affects intergenerational communication, I would like to make three modest suggestions.

More Cross-Cultural Research. First, we should continue studying many more countries in different parts of the world. The program of research on intergenerational communication has not reached countries in South America or the Middle East, let alone those in Africa. Because many countries are multi-cultural, the acculturation perspective needs to be put to the rigorous test so as to examine whether, and how, the effects of multiple cultures are manifested in people's communication. Moreover, cross-cultural research in general tends to use Japan and the United States as the representatives of East and Western nations, and generalize the findings to other countries in the same cultural bloc. We should exercise great caution in the use of this approach because each country has features of communication that are unique.

Multiple Analytical Viewpoints. Second, using multiple analytical viewpoints is important. The use of the following three approaches may complement each other, and give deeper insight into intergenerational communication in different countries. A *group difference approach* has often been adopted to assess cross-nation and age-group differences in perceptions of intergenerational contact. The similarities and differences emerged are substantive and meaningful, and attributed to respondents' country and age group. However, this approach may be susceptible to confounding factors (e.g., response tendencies), and thus leaves room for alternative interpretations (Kitayama, 2002). Then, *a contextual approach* asks people to rate comparatively (thereby juxtapose) their intra- and intergenerational communication along different dimensions. This method may allow us to identify contextual differences in people's communication experiences. The climate of intra- and intergenerational communication in one country may be conjectured and "profiled" for further cross-cultural examination, when younger and older adults' intra- and intergenerational communication are examined simultaneously. Finally, *a factor-association approach* may be useful to identify cross-cultural similarities and differences in the psychological processes underlying intergenerational communication. This method has also been used and encouraged for adoption by scholars who follow the cultural psychology tradition (e.g., Uchida, Kitayama, Mesquita, & Reyes, 2001). By this method, we found possible Western (American) influences in the Philippines, observed in the relationship between older adults' intergenerational communication and their self-esteem and sense of coherence. It may be possible to observe the changes in people's psychological orientations over time by examining the patterns of association between variables through this approach.

Process View of Culture. Third, we may treat culture as a process involving communication as the central factor. As discussed earlier, communication and culture are mutually constitutive. Communication can be a causal factor to induce changes in some aspects of culture, while cultural transformation may result in some changes in people's communication. This approach, by giving attention to the concept of change, may allow us to explain some of the unique patterns of communication (e.g., those of Filipinos) that have been identified in previous studies of intergenerational communication.

I would like to bring several factors into the limelight for future studies of intergenerational communication across cultures, based on the intergroup perspective (Barker *et al.*, in press; Tajfel & Turner, 1986) and process view of culture. They include communication, group vitality, social identities, stereotypes, the norm of respect for the elderly, and psychological health. They have already been studied cross-culturally (see Giles *et al.*, 2002), but will be discussed again as the important building-blocks of culture.

Communication as contact is the most important factor. Communication, including intergenerational communication, is a powerful tool to sustain and change the cultural climate. It is a difficult and problematic process, as it involves potentials of miscommunication (Coupland, Giles, & Wiemann, 1991). This is because, for example, different social groups have differential expectations and evaluations of a particular communication style (Kim, 2002), and the dynamics of intergroup (i.e., intergenerational, interethnic) relations has been changed over the years (e.g., Ingersoll-Dayton & Saengtienchai, 1999). Careful and in-depth investigation of how people communicate with others in different age-groups (or ethnic groups) is indeed necessary in different countries (e.g., Zhang & Hummert, 2001).

Macro-cultural context is highly pertinent to people's communication behaviors. Amongst other macro-cultural indicators (see Georgas & Berry, 1995), power is a key theme (Ng, 1980), especially for the investigation of intergroup interactions. Which ethnic or age group *is perceived to* have more power in society at a particular time in history is deemed important in communication. In this sense, assessing group vitality (Giles *et al.*, 2000) is a promising approach (see also Barker *et al.*, in press). Group vitality indicates the relative power and status of one group in comparison to those of others in diverse facets of life such as politics, economics, education, and mass communication (e.g., media portrayal). The perception of group vitality may be susceptible to macro-structural transformation (Young, Giles, & Pierson, 1986), while their change may be context specific (Ota, Giles, & Gallois, 2002). The perceived vitality of a social group, ethnic or age-based, may be sustained, increased, decreased, or even manipulated through communication to serve particular purposes for the good of the group.

Peoples' sense of self is represented by social identities (Tajfel & Turner, 1986), including age-group identity (Ota, Harwood, Williams, & Takai, 2000). This may provide some social significance (e.g., security, threat, self-love and hate) for members. Indeed some people may accept and enjoy two different social identities at one time (Berry *et al.*, 1988). However, social identities, at times, may be quite problematic. Some people defy, and therefore change, the identities imposed by others in order to maintain their psychological consistency (Louw-Pottgieter & Giles, 1987). Others fail to do so and feel marginalized (Berry *et al.*, 1988). Social identities may serve as a motivational basis for one's interaction with ingroup and outgroup members (Berry *et al.*, 1988), and also for the use of communication strategies (Ting-Toomey & Kurogi, 1998).

Stereotypes may play an important role in intergenerational communication, as the CPA model and other theoretical perspectives (e.g., Hummert, 1994) suggest. Images of age-group members, as well as ethnic group members, are often expressed in communication (e.g., mass media discourse), and come to be shared widely by the people who are involved in it. With regard to its functions, the system justification function of stereotypes (Jost & Banaji, 1994) is especially relevant. People's beliefs about system justification is "shaped by chronic ideologies that people bring with them to specific situations, as well as by contextual cues that they encounter within a given situation" (Major & Schmader, 2002, p. 184). Stereotype-guided communication, in this sense, may mean the ideological treatment of the members of groups, and endorsement of the existing social system including hierarchical relationship between relevant groups. The connection between one's stereotypes of ingroup and outgroup members, and their perceived status and power (i.e., vitality) may be stronger in some countries than in others (Ota *et al.*, 2002).

Social norms also serve as guidelines on how people in different social groups should behave. People learn and internalize them as they are socialized into society. They have "ought-to" implications, just as stereotypes may also have. They may link a dyadic interaction between two persons from different groups with the macro-cultural context as they symbolize the power relationship that lies between the groups. The focal norm is respect for older adults. It exists across the world (Gallois *et al.*, 1999), but its salient meanings and impact on people may differ from one country to another, reflecting the societal climate (e.g., power structure) of the time. The change in the macro-cultural structure of a country may coincide with the changes in the status of age groups, the meanings people may attribute to the norm of elderly respect, and communication with older adults.

People's psychological health may, though indirectly, be associated with, and reflected in, the social climate of a culture. Cultural climate, such as cultural tightness, has been suggested to be pertinent to people's sense of anxiety (Triandis, 2000). It may then be possible that individuals' psychological health is represented in the cultural climate of society. In this sense, what constitutes psychological health in different society and how it is constituted there require further research. The research so far, based on the CPA model, used personal and collective self-esteem (i.e., evaluation of the self), and the sense of coherence (i.e., control over the environment) as indicators of psychological health. However, those three have been found relatively unrelated to older adults' *intergenerational* communication in Asian countries. Factors such as harmony, acceptance, interdependence, respect, and enjoyment (Ingersoll-Dayton, Saengtienchai, Kespichayawattana, & Aungsuroch, 2001) may also be considered as health indicators for older adults in Asia besides self-esteem and sense of coherence.

Conclusion

I believe it is highly important to consider culture in the research of intergenerational, or any type of, communication. As culture and communication are closely intertwined, it is not possible to study one without the other. As I suggested that they form a process together, the factors discussed in the previous sections, including communication and vitality perceptions, may be inter-related and be able to explain various cross-national similarities and differences, and perhaps problems people find, in intergenerational communication identified in the past studies.

Before closing this chapter, I would like to mention that the cross-national differences in people's cognitive and affective orientations, such as self-enhancement and self-criticism tendencies (Kitayama, 2002) and the strength of ingroup-outgroup distinctions (Triandis, 1995), deserve further pursuit in intergenerational communication research. Although I did not elaborate on them in this chapter, those differences in the fundamental psychological process may play an important role in how people communicate across generational lines and how people respond to the questions when they are asked about their intergenerational communication experiences.

References

Barker, V., Giles, H., & Harwood, J. (in press). Inter- and intragroup perspectives on intergenerational communication. In J. F. Nussbaum & J. Coupland (Eds.), *Handbook of communication and aging research 2nd Ed.* Mahwah, NJ: Lawrence Erlbaum.

Berry, J. W., Kim, U., & Boski, P. (1988). Psychological acculturation of immigrants. In Y. Y. Kim & W. B. Gudykunst (Eds.), *Cross-cultural adaptation: Current approaches* (pp.62–89). Newbury Park, CA: Sage.

Chow, N. (1999). Diminishing filial piety and the changing role and status of elders in Hong Kong. *Hallym International Journal of Aging, 1*, 67–77.

Coupland, N., Coupland, J., Giles, H., & Henwood, K. (1988). Accommodating the elderly: Invoking and extending a theory. *Language and Society, 17*, 1–41.

Coupland, N., Giles, H., & Wiemann, J. (1991). *"Miscommunication" and problematic talk.* Newbury Park, CA: Sage.

Gallois, C., Giles, H., Ota, H., Pierson, H.D., Ng, S.H., Lim, T-S., Maher, J., Somera, L., Ryan, E.B., & Harwood, J. (1999). Intergenerational communication across the Pacific Rim: The impact of filial piety. In J-C. Lasry, J. Adair, & K. Dion (Eds.), *Latest contributions to cross-cultural psychology* (pp. 192– 211). Lisse, The Netherlands: Swets & Zeitlinger.

Georgas, J. & Berry, J. W. (1995). An ecocultural taxonomy for cross-cultural psychology, *Cross-Cultural Research, 29*, 121–157.

Giles, H., Fortman, J., Honeycutt, J., & Ota, H. (2003). Future selves and others: A life span and cross-cultural perspective. *Communication Report, 16*, 1–22.

Giles, H., Fox, S., Harwood, J., & Williams, A. (1994). Talking age and aging talk: Communicating through the life span. In M. L. Hummert, J. M. Wiemann, & J. F. Nussbaum (Eds.), *Interpersonal communication in older adulthood: Interdisciplinary theory and research* (pp.130–161). Thousand Oaks, CA: Sage.

Giles, H., Liang, B., Noels, K.A., & McCann, R. (2001). Communicating across and within generations: Taiwanese, Chinese-Americans, and Euro-American's perceptions of communication. *Journal of Asia Pacific Communication, 11*, 161–176.

Giles, H., McCann, R.M., Ota, H., & Noels, K. (2002). Challenging intergenerational stereotypes across Eastern and Western cultures. In M.S. Kaplan, N.Z. Henkin, & A.T. Kusano (Eds.), *Intergenerational program strategies from a global perspective.*(pp. 13–28) Honolulu: University Press of America, Inc.

Giles, H., Noels, K., Ota, H., Ng, S.H., Gallois, C., Ryan, E.B., Williams, A., Lim, T-S., Somera, L., Tao, H., & Sachdev, I. (2000). Age vitality across eleven nations. *Journal of Multilingual & Multicultural Development, 21,* 308–323,

Hall. E. T. (1973). *Silent language.* Garden City, NY: Anchor Book.

Harwood, J. (1997). Viewing age: Lifespan identity and television viewing choices. *Journal of Broadcasting & Electronic Media, 41,* 203–310.

Harwood, J., Giles, H., & Ryan, E. B. (1995). Aging, communication, and intergroup theory: Social identity and intergenerational communication. In J. F. Nussbaum & J. Coupland (Eds.), *Handbook of communication and aging research* (pp. 133–159). Hillsdale, NJ: Lawrence Erlbaum.

Heine, S. J., & Lehman, D. R. (2003). Move the body, change the self: Acculturative effects on the self-concept. In M. Schaller & C. Crandall (Eds.), *Psychological foundations of culture* (pp. 305–331).. Mahwah, NJ: Lawrence Erlbaum.

Ho, D. Y-F. (1994). Filial piety, authoritarian moralism, and cognitive conservatism in Chinese societies. *Genetic, Social and General Psychology Monographs, 120,* 347–365.

Hofstede, G.H. (1991). *Cultures and organizations: Software of the mind.* New York: McGraw-Hill.

Hong, Y.-y., Morris, M. W., Chiu, C-y., & Benet-Martinez, V. (2000). Multicultural minds: A dynamic constructivist approach to culture and cognition. *American Psychologist, 55,* 709–720.

Hori, S. (1994). Beginning of old age in Japan and age norms in adulthood. *Educational Gerontology, 20,* 439–451.

Hummert, M.L. (1994). Stereotypes of the elderly and patronizing speech. In M.L. Hummert, J.M. Wiemann, & J.F. Nussbaum (Eds.), *Interpersonal communication in older adulthood* (pp. 162–184). Thousand Oaks, CA: Sage.

Ingersoll-Dayton, B., & Saengtienchai, C. (1999). Respect for older persons in Asia: Stability and change. *International Journal of Aging and Human Development, 48,* 113–130.

Ingersoll-Dayton, B., Saengtienchai, C., Kespichayawattana, J., & Aungsuroch, Y. (2001). Psychological well-being Asian style: The perspective of Thai elders. *Journal of Cross-Cultural Gerontology, 16,* 283–302.

Jost, J. T. & Banaji, M. R. (1994). The role of stereotyping in system-justfication and the production of false consciousness. *British Journal of Social Psychology, 33,* 1–27.

Kashima, Y. (2000). Conceptions of culture and person for psychology. *Journal of Cross-Cultural Psychology, 31,* 14–33.

Kim, K. C., Kim, S., Hurh, W. M. (1991). Filial piety and intergenerational relationship in Korean immigrant families. *International Journal of Aging and Human Development, 33,* 233–245.

Kim, M-S. (2002). *Non-Western perspectives on human communication: Implications for theory and practice.* Thousand Oaks, CA: Sage.

Kim, U., & Yamaguchi, S. (1995). Cross-cultural research methodology and approach: Implications for the advancement of Japanese social psychology. *Research in Social Psychology, 10,* 168–179.

Kitayama, S. (2002). Culture and basic psychological processes: Toward a systemic view of culture. *Psychological Bulletin, 128,* 89–96.

Lehman, D., Chiu, C-y., & Schaller, M. (in press). Culture and psychology. *Annual Review of Psychology.*

Louw-Potgieter, J. & Giles, H. (1987). Imposed identity and linguistic strategies. *Journal of Language and Social Psychology, 6,* 261–286.

McCann, R. M., Ota, H., Giles, H., & Caraker, R. (2003). Perceptions of intra- and intergenerational communication among young adults in Thailand, Japan, and the U.S.A. *Communication Report, 16,* 69–91.

Major, B., & Schmader, T. (2002). Legitimacy and the construal of social disadvantage. In J. T. Jost & B. Major (Eds.). *The psychology of legitimacy: Emerging perspectives on ideology, justice, and intergroup relations* (pp. 176– 204). Cambridge: Cambridge University Press.

Martin, L. G. (1988). The aging of Asia. *Journal of Gerontology: Social Sciences, 43,* 99–113.

Martin, J. N. & Nakayama, T. K. (1999). Thinking dialectically about culture and communication. *Communication Theory, 9,* 1–25.

Nadamitsu, Y., Chen, L., & Friedrich, G. (2001). Similar or different?: The Chinese experience of Japanese culture. In M. J. Collier (ed.), *Constituting cultural difference through discourse* (pp. 158–188). Thousand Oaks, CA: Sage.

Natividad, J. N. (2000). Ageing in the Philippines: An overview. In D. R. Phillips (Ed.), *Ageing in the Asia-Pacific Region: Issues, policies, and future trend* (pp. 267– 283). London: Routledge.

Ng, S.H. (1980). *The social psychology of power.* London: Academic Press.

Ng, S.H., Liu, J.H., Weatherall, A., & Loong, C.S.F. (1997). Younger adults' communication experiences and contact with elders and peers. *Human Communication Research, 24,* 82–108.

Niikura, R. (1999). The psychological process underlying Japanese assertive behavior: Comparison of Japanese with Americans, Malaysians, and Filipinos. *International Journal of Intercultural Relations, 23,* 47–76.

Nisbett, R.E. (2003). *The geography of thought: How Asians and Westerners think differently*. New York: Free Press.

Noels, K., Giles, H., Gallois, C., & Ng, S.H. (2001). Intergenerational communication and psychological adjustment: A cross-cultural examinations of Hong Kong and Australian adults. In M.L. Hummert & J. Nussbaum (Eds.), *Communication, aging, and health: Multidisciplinary perspectives* (pp. 249–278). Mahwah, NJ: Erlbaum.

Ota, H., Giles, H., & Gallois, C. (2002). Perceptions of younger, middle-aged, and older adults in Australia and Japan: Stereotypes and age group vitality. *Journal of Intercultural Studies. 23,* 253–266.

Ota, H., Giles, H., & Somera, L-B. (2002, July). *Communication across age groups in the* U.S.A., *Japan, and the Philippines: Younger and older adults' communicative experiences with younger and older adults*. Paper presented at 8th International Conference of Language and Social Psychology, Hong Kong, City University of Hong Kong.

Ota, H., Harwood, J., Williams, A., & Takai, J. (2000). A cross-cultural analysis of age identity in Japan and the United States. *Journal of Multilingual and Multicultural Development, 21,* 33–41

Pecchioni, L., Ota, H., & Sparks, L. (in press). Cultural issues in communication and aging. In Nussbaum, J. F., & Coupland, J. (Eds.), *Handbook of communication and aging research* Mahwah, NJ: Erlbaum.

Perdon, R. (1998). *Brown Americans of Asia*. Darlinghurst, N.S.W.: The Manila Prints

Phillips, D. R. (2000). *Ageing in the Asia-Pacific region: Issues, policies and future trends*. London: Routledge.

Robinson, J. D. & Skill, T. (1995). Media usage patterns and portrayals of the elderly. In J. F. Nussbaum & J. Coupland (Eds.), *Handbook of communication and aging research* (pp.359–392). Mahwah, NJ: Lawrence Erlbaum.

Ryan, E. B., Giles, H., Bartolucci, G., & Henwood, K. (1986). Psycholinguistic and social psychological components of communication by and with the elderly. *Language and Communication, 6,* 1–24.

Sung, K.T. (2001). Elder respect: Exploration of ideas and forms in East Asia. *Journal of Aging Studies, 15,* 13–26.

Tajfel, H., & Turner, J. C. (1986). The social identity theory of intergroup behavior. In S. Worchel & W. G. Austin (Eds.), *Psychology of intergroup relations* (pp. 7– 17). Chicago: Nelson-Hall.

Ting-Toomey, S., & Kurogi, A. (1998). Facework competence in intercultural conflict: Unupdated face-negotiation theory. *International Journal of Intercultural Relations, 22,* 197–225.

Triandis, H.C. (1995). *Individualism & collectivism*. Boulder, CO: Westview Press.

Triandis, H.C. (2002). Cultural syndromes and subjective well-being. In E. Diener & E.M. Suh (Eds.) *Culture and subjective well-being* (pp. 13–37). Cambridge, MA: MIT Press

Uchida, Y., Kitayama, S., Mesquita, B., & Reyes, J. A. (2001, June). *Interpersonal sources of happiness: The relative significance in three cultures.* 13th Annual convention of the American Psychological Society Toronto, Canada.

Williams, A., Ota, H., Giles, H., Pierson, H.D., Gallois, C., Ng., S.H., Lim, T.S., Ryan, E.B., Somera, L., Maher, J., Cai, D., & Harwood, J. (1997). Young people's beliefs about intergenerational communication: An initial cross-cultural analysis. *Communication Research, 24,* 370–393.

Young, L., Giles, H., & Pierson, H. (1986). Sociopolitical change and perceived vitality. *International Journal of Intercultural Relations, 10,* 459–470.

Yum, J. O. (1988). The impact of Confucianism on interpersonal relationships an communication patterns in East Asia. *Communication Monographs, 55,* 374–388.

Zhang, Y. B. & Hummert, M. L. (2001). Harmonies and tensions in Chinese intergenerational communication: Younger and older adults' accounts. *Journal of Asia Pacific Communication, 11,* 203–230.

8

A Comparative Study of Chinese and English Metaphorical Representation of Time

Rong ZHOU

Metaphors are considered as the way we live by and the basis for human cognition, thinking, experience, language and even acts (Carbonell, 1982; Honeck & Hoffman, 1980; Indurkhya, 1992; Lakoff & Johnson, 1980). Lakoff and Johnson (1980) even indicated that human conceptual systems are also metaphorical. Time representation, which is one of the basic concepts and essential dimensions of our human life, is certainly fundamentally metaphorical because without using metaphors, we could hardly represent time. Michon (1990) pointed out that the metaphorical representation of time is one of three basic forms of explicit representations of time and defined it as a conceptual structure that is borrowed or mapped onto time concept from another semantic domain (e.g. "time is money", "time is life"). No doubt, the metaphorical representation of time is not only important for understanding the nature of time but also useful for revealing the formation of time concepts, time reasoning, time thinking and time cognition.

We do not know, however, how the metaphorical representation of time is conceptually structured. What are the basic construction dimensions of the metaphorical representation of time concept? What is its prototype form? Do people in different cultures share similar or hold different metaphorical concepts of time? These questions prompted the author to carry out a cross-cultural study of the Chinese and English metaphorical representation of time. Based on an extensive pool of time-referencing phrases and sentences collected for the study, we first carried out a content analysis and then a factor analysis to find out the conceptual dimensions of the Chinese and English metaphorical representation of time, and on the basis of that, compared the two cultural representations of time metaphors.

Content Analysis

Method

Participants. The English participants were 81 first and second year university students randomly selected from Abertay-Dundee University, Scotland. They majored in engineering, information technology and chemistry. Their average age was 22.1, with 39 male students and 42 female students. The Chinese participants were 117 first and second year university students randomly selected from Southwest-China Normal University, mainland China. They majored in math, physics, and chemistry. Their average age was 19.8, with 45 males and 72 females.

Materials collection. We tried to obtain a comprehensive collection of English time metaphors and Chinese time metaphors. Two approaches were used:

(1) "What is time?" questionnaire. The participants were asked to give at most 20 answers to the question "What is time?" Back translations were made to make the instructions in the Chinese and English versions have as identical meanings as possible. The questionnaires were administered during classes. There was no time restriction for completing the questionnaire, but most of the

participants completed the questionnaire within 10 minutes. Interestingly enough, all their responses to the question were time metaphors. From the English participants, we obtained a pool of 1188 responses via the questionnaire, each participant producing 14.6 responses on average. After combining similar ones from different participants, we obtained 191 items of English time metaphors. From the Chinese participants, we obtained a pool of 1588 responses via the questionnaire, each person producing an average of 13.57 responses. After combining the same items, we got 216 items of Chinese time metaphors.

(2) Literature search. *The Oxford Dictionary of Quotations* (1992), *Bartlett's Familiar Quotations* (1992), etc., were consulted to find the English time metaphors used by English speaking people in the past and contemporary time. Chinese compendiums such as *Time Quotations* (Yue & An, 1987) were searched to collect the Chinese time metaphors used by Chinese people in the past and contemporary time. Such searching resulted in 180 items of English time metaphors and 145 items of Chinese time metaphors.

Combining the two sources of data, we obtained a pool of 361 Chinese time metaphors and a pool of 371 English time metaphors. Dropping out those metaphors whose frequency was below 3, we finally got 140 Chinese time metaphors and 131 English time metaphors. Examining these two pools of English and Chinese metaphors, we can see that there are 99 Chinese metaphors that use the same objects as the vehicles as the English metaphors do, that is to say, there are 99 metaphors that are exactly the same in the two cultures (see Table 1).

Hypothesized structural dimensions: Based on the meaning of the time metaphor sentences and the discussions in some literature (Lakoff & Johnson, 1980; Lakoff & Turner, 1989; Michon, 1990; 1998), we proposed preliminarily 12 structural dimensions of metaphorical concept of time: 1) time is a moving object, 2) time is a valuable object, 3) time is an instrument, 4) time is an evaluator, 5)time is its effect, 6) time is a container, 7) time is a changer, 8)time is space, 9) time is person, 10) time is a state, 11) time is a controller-the controlled, 12) others.

Interjudge consistency. Three English teachers in Abertay-Dundee University, Scotland, and three Chinese teachers in Southwest-China Normal University were trained and worked independently as judges of these sentences. They were instructed to classify these metaphor sentences into the first 11 dimensions mentioned above. Those items which could not be classified into the first 11 categories were put into "the other" type. The Kandall coefficient of concordance of the three Chinese judges was satisfactory ($w = 0.81$, $X^2 = 323.39$, $p < 0.001$). The Kandall coefficient of concordance of the three English judges was a bit lower, but still satisfactory ($w = 0.77$, $X^2 = 296.24$, $p < 0.001$). Thus the evaluation of all the three judges in both groups was quite consistent.

Results

The results of the content analysis of the Chinese and English time metaphors are presented in Table 1.

Table 1
Conceptual dimensions of Chinese and English time metaphors

Dimensions	Chinese metaphors	English metaphors
1. moving object	流水, 飞驰的列车, 阴影, 赛车, 带翼的马车, 长跑运动员, 流星, 无声的脚步, 瀑布, 呼啸而过的风, 波浪, 河流, 小溪, 滚动的车轮, 飞梭, 钟摆, 飞鸟, 潮汐, 飞跑的野兔, 急流, 慢爬的龟, 离弦之箭, 飘动的云, 过客, 闪电, 百驹过隙, 飞奔的骏马	river, stream, whirligig, tide, runner, winged chariot, violent torrent, flight, shadow, bird, rider, movement, hare, noiseless footsteps, galloping horse, shuttle, wheel, tortoise, wave, pendulum, moving object, arrow, lightning, travellor.
2. valuable object	金钱, 资本, 有限的资源, 珍宝, 贵重物品, 财富, 珠宝, 聚宝盆, 宝库, 奖金	precious jewel, money, valuable things, bonus, limited resources, wealth, treasure house, valuable commodity.

Dimensions	Chinese metaphors	English metaphors
3. medium (instrument)	尺度, 测量器, 桥梁, 锋利的刀, 利剑, 纽带, 刻刀, 机器	scale, measure, tooth, bridge, scythe, sword, measure of movement, plough, medium of narration, medium of life, machine.
4. changer (drive)	魔术师, 创造者, 追逐者, 机遇, 杀手, 雕刻家, 催化剂, 改变者, 警钟, 鞭子, 命令, 画笔, 力量, 复仇者, 征服者	innovator, avenger, whips, conqueror, order, opportunity, great physician, killer, pursuer, power, changer, devourer, transforming chisel.
5. effect	残迹, 良药, 忘情水, 青春的盗贼, 毁灭者, 美貌的凶手, 无情者, 效率, 遗憾, 皱纹, 灰尘, 恶梦, 负担, 收获	destroyer, thief of youth, burden, dust, ravages, soothing ointment, nightmare, reaper, merciless person, the Lethe, healer.
6. container	温床, 大海, 坟墓, 框架, 容器, 巨轮, 载体, 学校	carrier, container, sea, womb, grave, big ship, school, files.
7. evaluator	考官, 发言人, 法官, 镜子, 试纸, 检验真理的标准, 伟大的批评家, 试金石, 证人, 历史的见证	wisest counsellors, arbitrator, talker, greatest critic, mirror, evaluator, fair judge, measure of truth.
8. space	延绵的高山, 广阔的天空, 开放的空间, 长廊, 深渊, 最长的距离, 漫漫长路, 跑道, 直线, 迷宫	distance, stage, track, abysm, corridor, direction, open space, frame, long road.
9. person	老师, 顽童, 作家, 敌人, 老人, 吝啬鬼, 朋友, 慈母	kind mother, old man, miser, actor, teacher, child, author, friend, enemy, generous man.
10. state	生命, 一本读不完的书, 一幅画, 永恒, 知识, 环, 无尽的歌, 轮回, 圆, 青春, 一张白纸, 一部历史	soul of the world, endless song, book, preserver, essence, life, eternity, circle, loop, cycle, image of eternity, chronicle.
11. controller-controlled	仆人, 使者, 奴隶, 主人, 弹簧, 对手, 海绵, 礼物, 统治者, 主宰	slave, present, man's angel, master, sponge, servant, violent tyrant, warrior, rebel.
12. others	希望, 空气, 回忆, 口香糖, 魔鬼, 源泉, 速度, 效益	salt, seeds, fire, riddle, chewing gum, monster, threat, speed.

Note. Only the vehicle in each metaphor is given here due to space.

The result of the content analysis indicates that most of the Chinese and English time metaphors can be classified into the 11 conceptual dimensions of time metaphors. Only eight items in the Chinese set and another eight items in the English set of metaphors can not be put under these categories. This shows that Chinese and English time metaphors have highly systematic and similar internal organization and the representations of time metaphors are conceptually organized in similar ways in the two cultures. The 11 conceptual dimensions that we proposed can well represent the internal construction of this conceptual system. In order to further verify the conceptual construction of time metaphors, we carried out factor analysis.

Factor Analysis

Method

Participants. The Chinese participants were 370 first and second year students randomly selected from Southwest-China Normal University, Southwest-China Agricultural University and Southwest-China Law University, with 150 males and 220 females, and their average age was 20.1. The English participants were 320 first and second year students selected randomly from Abertay-Dundee University, with 145 males and 175 females, and their average age was 22.7.

Procedure. The 140 Chinese time metaphors and 131 English time metaphors we collected through the questionnaire and literature search (described above) were put into "Appropriate Chinese time metaphors questionnaire" and "Appropriate English time metaphors questionnaire". Twenty of the items were repeated in each questionnaire as a reliability check. To offset order effects, the items in the questionnaires were arranged in 4 different orders. The participants were asked to rate each item on a 5-point scale in terms of how appropriate each metaphor is in his or her own opinion (1 = not appropriate at all, 5 = very appropriate).

Most of the English participants were tested collectively in class hours, only a small number of them were tested individually. Chinese participants were also tested collectively in class hours. There was no time restriction, but most of them finished within 20 minutes.

Results

For the English group we collected back 294 valid questionnaires and for the Chinese group we got back 360 valid questionnaires. The value of the Bartlett's test of sphericity for the Chinese and English groups was 15660 and 15927 respectively, showing that there are shared factors within each set of variables. The value for the Kaiser-Meyer-Olkim was 0.71 and 0.73 respectively, indicating that the data of the samples are suitable for factor analysis.

The between-subject consistency was assessed by Cronbach alpha coefficients and they were 0.83 for the Chinese group and 0.85 for the English group. The presence of 20 repeated items helped us to examine the short-term temporal stability of those ratings. The correlations of the mean ratings over the repeated pairs of items were averaged 0.87 and 0.89 for the Chinese and English sets respectively, which indicated that the ratings had high stability and the participants were responding conscientiously.

A principal component analysis performed on each of the two sets of data indicated the presence of 33 factors with eigenvalues greater than 1, accounting for 80.06 percent of the total variance for Chinese data, and the presence of 32 factors with eigenvalues greater than 1, accounting for 78.4 percent of the total variance for English data. In order to compare with our *a priori* theoretical dimensions of the construct, we extracted 11 factors on both groups, which accounted 46.6 percent of the total variance for the Chinese data and accounted 40.7 percent of the total variance for English data. The results of the varimax rotation of those 11 factors for both groups are shown in Tables 2 and 3.

Table 2

Factor analysis of the Chinese conceptual dimensions of time metaphors

Factors (dimensions)	Eigen-value	Pct of Var (%)	Cum Pct (%)	Items and Loadings*
F1: space	13.476	13.342	13.342	容器(.60), 空间(.54), 高山(.52), 跑道(.51), 载体(.51), 恶梦(.50), 大海(.49), 遗憾(.44), 深渊(.43), 负担(.42), 源泉(.41), 过客(.42), 环(.41)
F2: valuable object	5.754	5.697	19.39	聚宝盆(.71), 奖金(.55), 宝库(.54), 财富(.51), 知识(.50), 珍宝(.45), 金钱(.44), 速度(.44)
F3: state	4.501	4.457	23.496	白纸(.68), 无尽的歌(.66), 画(.63), 画笔(.57), 朋友(.40)
F4: lapsing object	3.788	3.750	27.247	闪电(.58), 精灵(.56), 风(.54), 箭(.51), 瀑布(.49), 飞鸟(.41)
F5: effect	3.465	3.431	30.677	忘情水(.57), 青春的盗贼(.57), 良药(.53), 毁灭者(.52), 美貌的凶手(.41), 无情者(.47)
F6: changer	3.374	3.341	34.018	刻刀(.72), 雕刻家(.58), 催化剂(.57), 改变者(.44), 镜子(−.41)
F7: evaluator	2.947	2.917	36.936	批评家(.68), 历史(.60), 发言人(.60), 对手(.59), 试纸(.44)
F8: moving object	2.618	2.592	39.528	钟摆(.63), 飞奔的骏马(.60), 急流(.53), 飞跑的野兔(.51), 滚动的车轮(.41), 带翼的马车(.41)
F9: medium	2.472	2.447	41.975	尺子(.65), 纽带(−.42), 镜子(.42), 改变者(−.41)
F10: person	2.408	2.384	44.359	老人(.54), 顽童(.44), 法官(−.42)
F11: the controlled	2.319	2.296	46.655	主人(.51), 考官(.42), 礼物(−.46)

* The numbers in the brackets are factor loadings (greater than 0.4).

Table 3

Factor analysis of the English conceptual dimensions of time metaphors

Factors (dimensions)	Eigen-value	Pct of Var (%)	Cum Pct (%)	Items and Loadings*
F1: moving object	13.796	13.660	13.660	whirligig(.78), rider(.77), moving object(.76), torrent(.75), winged chariot(.67), ship(.68), lethe(.61), pendulum(.58), travellor(.42), sea(.41)
F2: changer	4.824	4.776	18.435	avenger(.67), transforming chisel(.48), innovator(.48), whips(.42), thief of youth(.41)
F3: space	3.620	3.585	22.020	corridor(.77), container(.56), space(.55), sea(.48), book(.45), school(.42), direction(.41)
F4: effect	3.216	3.184	25.204	destroyer(.67), merciless person(.54), dust(.49), plough(.44)
F5: state	2.619	2.593	27.797	eternity(.75), image of eternity(.74), soul(.52), circle(.45), space(.41), cycle(.41)
F6: valuable object	2.578	2.562	30.358	limited resources(.67), life(.61), money(.44), valuable thing(.44), bonus(.43), essence(.41)
F7: evaluator	2.407	2.383	32.741	counsellor(.59), evaluator(.55), changer(.40), measure of truth(.48)
F8: the controlled	2.202	2.181	34.922	order(.57), servant(.45), changer(.41), soul of the world(−.45)
F9: person	2.030	2.010	36.932	teacher(.66), old man(.60), physician(.54), evaluator(.49)
F10: lapsing object	1.916	1.855	38.829	arrow(.73), stream(.52), galloping horse(.41), runner(.41)
F11: medium	1.874	1.855	40.685	measure of movement(.68), measure(.52), medium of life(.57), distance(.51)

* The numbers in the brackets are factor loadings (greater than 0.4).

The items with high loadings in the extracted factors for both Chinese and English structural dimensions of metaphorical concepts of time had consistent tendency in meaning. For the Chinese set of factors, except factor 1, 4 and 8, the rest can all find corresponding dimensions in our hypothesized preliminary conceptual dimensions of metaphorical structure of time. Thus these dimensions were named accordingly: valuable object, state, effect, changer, evaluator, medium, person, the controller-controlled. The items in factor 1 were different from our hypothesized dimension. In our hypothesized dimension, "space" and "container" were two separated dimensions. But the items in our factor 1 seemed to cover both "space" and "container". Since "space" can be considered as a big container, the two categories were combined into one dimension and named "space". The items in factor 4 and factor 8 all belonged to "moving object" in our hypothesized dimensions. This initial classification seemed to be not suitable. In fact many items that compare time to moving objects describe the lapsing feature of time. So it is desirable to separate those items which describe this lapsing feature from other moving objects which do not have this feature. The items in factor 4 happened to have the feature of quick lapse, thus it was named "lapsing object", while factor 8 was still named "moving object".

For the English factor analysis, we also extracted 11 factors. There was also a factor (F1) whose items represented moving feature of time, and thus it was named "moving object". There was another one (F10) whose items embodied the feature of quick lapse of time, and thus it was named "lapsing object". Items in factor 3 covered both "space" and "container", and thus it was named "space". The rest of the factors all have corresponding dimensions in our proposed construct, and thus they were named after them accordingly.

Discussion

The dimensions obtained by factor analysis matched the preliminary results of our content analysis, although the match was not perfect.

This lends support to the underlying conceptual dimensions of metaphorical representation of time. It also indicates the validity of our hypothesized conceptual structural dimensions of metaphorical representation of time. Since only eight out of more than 130 of Chinese and English time metaphors could not be put into these 11 dimensions respectively, this shows that people's metaphorical representation of time, in both cultures, is largely based on these 11 conceptual dimensions.

From Tables 1–3, we can see that a lot of the items in the two cultures are quite similar, as a matter of fact, the majority of them (99 metaphors all together) are the same. For instance, within the "moving object" dimension, both cultures compared time to "pendulum", "torrent", "winged chariot", etc. This clearly shows that there is cross-cultural similarity in people' use of time metaphors. Even for those metaphors that use different vehicles to refer to time in the two cultures, their basic root concepts are still the same. Take the "moving object" dimension for example again, although the Chinese participants compared time to "飞奔的骏马" (galloping horse), "滚动的车轮 (rolling wheels)" while the English participants compared time to "ship", "travellor"(see Tables 2 and 3), these metaphors all share the same underlying root concept or conceptual metaphor as Lakoff and Johnson (1980) put it, that is, "TIME IS A MOVING OBJECT". Thus it seems that Chinese and English cultures share a lot of time metaphors in common.

From Table 2 and Table 3, we can also see that although the sequence of the Chinese dimensions and the sequence of the English dimensions are different, we could, however, find corresponding dimensions between them. For instance, factor 6 in the Chinese set matches with factor 2 in the English set, both representing the conceptual dimension "TIME IS A CHANGER". As for the differences in the varying eigenvalues and the percentage of variance for the same dimensions in the two cultures, they probably show the different weight and treatment of the dimensions given in the two cultures. The correspondence of dimensions in the two sets of factors indicates that the conceptual dimensions of metaphorical representation of time in the two cultures are similar and congruent.

The internal structural systems of the metaphorical representation of time in the two cultures thus can be said to resemble each other.

The similarity between the Chinese time metaphors and English time metaphors, and the correspondence and resemblance of the conceptual structural dimensions of Chinese and English metaphorical representation of time all seem to show that people's psychological experience of time, just like many other experiences in our human life, is largely based on panhuman experience and our general cognitive capacity. To put it in another way, our time perception, time experience and our mental representation of time are shaped and determined by human specific biological features and cognitive features, thus there must be cross-cultural similarity in them, just as Gell (1992) pointed out, "There is no fairyland where people experience time in a way that is markedly unlike the way in which we do ourselves, where there is no past, present and future, where time stands still, or chases its own tail, or swings back and forth like a pendulum. All of these possibilities have been seriously touted in the literature on the anthropology of time." In the light of this, it is easy to see why these two cultures are so congruent in their metaphorical representation of time. Actually, metaphorical representation of time is a common mechanism of people of different cultures.

When discussing the relationship between thought and meaning, Lakoff (1987) put forward the theory of experientialism, which holds the idea that thought fundamentally grows out of embodiment, that is, the structures used to put together our conceptual systems grow out of bodily experience and make sense in terms of it. "The core of our conceptual systems is directly grounded in perception, body movement, and experience of a physical and social character." (Lakoff, 1987, p. xiv) On the other hand, according to Lakoff (1987), thought is also imaginative, in that those concepts which are not directly grounded in experience employ metaphor, metonymy, and mental imagery. It is this imaginative capacity that allows for "abstract" thought and takes the mind beyond what we can see and feel. The imaginative capacity is also embodied – indirectly – since the metaphors, metonymies and images are based on experience, often bodily experience. The evidence we obtained in this study that there is strong cross-cultural similarity in the conceptual metaphorical representation of time provides support for Lakoff's view of experientialism.

The issues of conceptual structure, i.e. what are the components of concepts and how they are related, have attracted a lot of psychologists' attention for a long time, and there have been several theories concerning conceptual structures. Among them, the prototype theory is a very appealing one. According to prototype theory (Rosch, 1975; Rosch & Mervis, 1975), concepts are represented by its prototypes which are the central members that share features among all family members called "family resemblance". The representation of concept composes of both the prototype and specific features, i.e. the degree of category membership, which represents the variance of members of the same category. This prototype theory is very useful in the study of metaphors. Way (1991) points out that prototypes can be used in the formation of metaphors to depict what we commonly consider the outstanding or salient features of a concept. The results of our study on the conceptual structure of metaphorical representation of time seem to be consistent with this prototype theory. The 11 structural dimensions of metaphorical concept of time we obtained by the factor analysis may represent the degree of the category membership of metaphorical concept of time, i.e. the variance of the features. As a basic rational of factor analysis is to use fewer indexes to synthesize different types of information existing in all variables, there are reasons to say that the factor which has the highest eigenvalue represents maximal common features and thus can be considered as the prototype of a conceptual structure. In the light of this, we can say that "TIME IS SPACE", which has the highest eigenvalue among the Chinese set of factors and thus is the most salient, is the prototype of Chinese metaphorical concept of time. On the other hand, "TIME IS MOVING OBJECT", which has the highest eigenvalue among the English set of factors and thus is also the most salient, is the prototype of English metaphorical concept of time.

It is apparent that human experience and cognition cannot be independent of specific culture and society, thus the conceptual system of metaphorical representation of time in different culture inevitably bears some differences. The different prototypes of the metaphorical representation of time in Chinese and English cultures are a good indication of this. "TIME IS MOVING OBJECT" is prototypical in English culture and "TIME IS SPACE" is prototypical in Chinese culture, and this is because in the Western culture, time is more taken as a directional, irreversible, moving object whereas in the Chinese culture, the experience of time is more a matter of recycling and spatial-integrated experience (Wu, 1996). One important source of Western civilization originated from Christian culture, which believes that the beginning point of the world, according to Genesis, is God's act of creation, and this point is taken to be the starting point of time. From that point on, time flows forward in a linear, unidirectional way like a flying arrow. This dynamic linear experience of time leads Western people to take time as a constantly forward-flowing thing and thus there is no wonder that the prototypical metaphor of time for English culture is TIME IS MOVING OBJECT. On the other hand, Chinese people's early ontological experience of time is a kind of recycling experience. "Getting up to work at sunrise and retire at sunset" caused them to rely totally on the nature and became integrated with it. They not only achieved harmony with the universe but also formed recycling spatial perception and conceptualization of time. Their experience of the periodic motion of the universe such as the recycling seasons, the change of day and night, and the rotation of crops all led them to combine space and time together. Thus it is not surprising that the metaphor TIME IS SPACE is the prototypical metaphor of time for Chinese culture.

Different metaphorical representation of time will certainly influence our attitude and treatment of time. The metaphorical representation of time is not only the basic way of time thinking and time cognition but also useful dynamic carrier of time values. If a person always considers time as a snail moving slowly, difficult to kill, he must be having a negative attitude toward life and he must be wasting a lot of his time in his daily life. On the other hand, if a person tends to compare time to wealth, he must be holding positive view of life and values it very much. Our present study has found that in Chinese and English cultures a lot of time metaphors are the same and the structural dimensions of metaphorical representations of time are also quite similar. This does not mean that these two cultures hold exactly the same metaphorical representation of time. More studies are needed to examine those time metaphors that are used differently in the two cultures and to see how such differences reveal diverse cultural time attitude, time beliefs, time management and treatment.

References

Barlett, J. (1992). *Barlett's familiar quotations*, (16th ed.). Boston, MASS: Little, Brown and Company.

Carbonell, J. G. (1982). Metaphor: An inescapable phenomenon in natural language comprehension. In W. G. Lehnert & M. H. Ringle (Eds.), *Strategies for natural language processing* (pp. 415–435). Hillsdale, NJ: Lawrence Erlbaum.

Gell, A. (1992). *The anthropology of time: Cultural constructions of temporal maps and images*, Oxford: Berg.

Honeck, R. P. & Hoffman, R. R. (1980). (Eds.), *Cognition and figurative language*. Hillsdale, NJ: Lawrence Erlbaum.

Indurkhya, B. (1992). *Metaphor and cognition – An interactionist approach*. London: Kluwer.

Lakoff, G. & Johnson, M. (1980). *Metaphors we live by*. Chicago: University of Chicago Press.

Lakoff, G. & Turner, M. (1989). *More than cool reason: A field guide to poetic metaphor*. Chicago: University of Chicago Press.

Lakoff, G. (1987). *Women, fire, and dangerous things*. Chicago: University of Chicago Press.

Michon, J. A. (1990). Implicit and explicit representations of time. In R. A. Block (Ed.), *Cognitive models of psychological time* (pp. 37–58). Hillsdale, NJ: Lawrence Erlbaum.

Michon, J. A. (1998). On the modularity of time. *Teorie & Modelli, 1*, 7–32.

Partington, A. (1992). *The Oxford dictionary of quotations*, (4th ed.). Oxford: Oxford University Press.

Rosch, E. H. (1975). Cognitive representations of semantic categories. *Journal of Experimental Psychology: General, 104*, 192–233.

Rosch, E. H. & Mervis, C. B. (1975). Family resemblances: Studies in the internal structure of categories. *Cognitive Psychology, 7*, 573–605.

Way, E. C. (1991). *Knowledge representation and metaphor*. The Netherlands: Kluwer.

吴(Wu)国盛, (1996). *时间的观念*，北京：中国社会科学出版社.

岳(Yue)奇, 安(An)辉, (1987). *时间珍言录*，北京：明天出版社.

Section III

Social Identity

9

Social Identity, Self-Categorization, and Communication in Small Groups

Michael A. HOGG

What can contemporary social identity research offer to, and learn from the study of communication in groups? In order to answer this question I say a little about communication research in mainstream social psychology, give an overview and update of the social identity perspective in social psychology, and identify some contemporary social identity research that has potential for closer links with the study of communication and language.

My views are offered from the perspective of an experimental social psychologist who has been closely associated with the development of the social identity perspective for almost 25 years. As such I am a relative outsider to the language/communication area. But I have done social identity and language/communication research, and have long felt that the communication aspect of social identity processes is critical, but underdeveloped by social psychologists (Hogg, 1996a).

Social Psychology, Communication, and Language

Group Dynamics

During the 1940s, 1950s and into the 1960s, a rapidly developing experimental social psychology placed the study of small group processes centre stage. This group dynamics tradition (e.g., Cartwright & Zander, 1968) focused on interaction and influence among people in small face-to-face groups in order to understand group performance and productivity, group cohesion and solidarity, cooperation and competition among individuals, group decision-making, roles and communication networks, the development and influence of norms, leadership processes, and so forth. This tradition explicitly acknowledged that communication was important – people did indeed talk to one another in small groups.

Social Cognition

From the late 1960s the group dynamics tradition was gradually replaced by a mainstream social psychology that increasingly focused on how the isolated individual perceived and made inferences about others (i.e., attribution and social cognition processes), or on interpersonal processes divorced from their group context. Ivan Steiner is famous for his various lamentations in the 1970s about the demise of research on small interactive groups (e.g., Steiner, 1974). However, more recent commentators (e.g., Tindale & Anderson, 1998) have felt research on social interaction in groups has not died out but relocated to a more friendly environment outside mainstream social psychology – to organizational psychology, management science, and so forth. The new Zeitgeist of social psychology had little place for the study of language and communication at all, and certainly not in small interactive groups. People did not talk to one another, let alone in groups. A number of critiques of social cognition explicitly cited a lack of emphasis on communication as a regressive step that compromised the explanatory reach of a sub-discipline that needed to address social interaction and the emergent properties of such interaction (e.g., Kraut & Higgins, 1984; Markus & Zajonc, 1985).

Intergroup Relations and Social Identity

As social cognition gathered pace in the United States in the late 1970s and 1980s (e.g., Devine, Hamilton, & Ostrom, 1994; Fiske & Taylor, 1991) social psychology in Europe had taken a quite different direction. European social psychology had self-consciously pursued a more social social psychology (Taylor & Brown, 1979) that focused on intergroup relations, collective behavior, the collective self, social identity, and social conflict (Tajfel, 1984).

Bristol University in the 1970s was a key centre for this work, where Henri Tajfel and his colleagues developed the basic components of the social identity perspective (see below). Social identity research focused on what happens between groups, and on large social categories. Although it did not focus on intragroup processes or on small interactive groups, it provided an opening for a social psychology of language, largely because language and speech style were seen as group-, and thus self-, defining attributes that might be influenced by social identity processes. People did talk to one another, and speech was a powerful marker of collective identity and a central feature of group life and intergroup behavior.

This opening was successfully exploited by Howard Giles – with his collaborators such as Richard Bourhis, and Don Taylor and very quickly many others (see Clément, 1996; Giles, 1996; Noels, Giles, & Le Poire, 2003). An important aspect of this early focus on language and social identity was its firm home within social psychology – not just scientifically but also practically – Giles was one of the Bristol group of social identity researchers.

Unfulfilled Potential

During the early 1980s there were great hopes for a genuine multilateral integration of research on social identity, communication, language, social interaction, and group and intergroup behavior. However, to a great extent this potential was not fulfilled. The exciting new scientific nexus proved fragile. It quickly devolved into three groups that were distinct in terms of intellectual traditions, scientific practices, and communication venues and outlets. These groups seemed to be going in different directions, and to varying degrees failing to articulate with one another.

The main team of social identity researchers were first and foremost social psychologists. During the 1980s they were influenced by social cognition (cf. Farr, 1996), from which emerged a focus on the social cognitive underpinnings of social identity processes. This produced self-categorization theory (Turner, Hogg, Oakes, Reicher, & Wetherell, 1987) and a generally somewhat social cognitive emphasis (e.g., Oakes, Haslam & Turner, 1994). Small group interactive processes were still underplayed, if not largely ignored, and the link to language and communication had pretty much vanished.

Those who had brought language and communication to the table had gone in two separate directions that isolated them to some extent, and in different ways, from developments in mainstream social psychology and thus also from core social identity theory development. One group bedded down more soundly in the communication discipline, which was already well established, and the second group, mainly in the UK, allied themselves with the discourse analysis movement that had burgeoned in the UK in the early 1980s. Discourse analysis was an approach (e.g., Parker, 2002; Potter & Wetherell, 1987), that had very obvious and powerful relevance to communication research, but which set itself up in opposition to the "positivist" metatheory that underpinned mainstream social psychology and, therefore, by implication social identity research. With some exceptions, there was little love between the discourse analysis and social identity perspectives. For discourse analysts, people did talk to one another but social cognitive processes and small interactive groups were not really involved.

New Hope and New Opportunities

The mid- to late-1990s witnessed some significant changes that may create new opportunities for a closer articulation of social identity researchers in social psychology and communication and language researchers – an articulation that can benefit from advances made over the past 15 years in the conceptualization of social identity processes (Hogg, 1996a).

For many years social identity researchers took a rather closed-minded and oppositional stance to American social cognition – pretty much condemning and/or ignoring it. From a social identity point of view there still is little joy to be found in those aspects of conventional social cognition that are overly focused on memory and the individual cognizer taken out of social context. However some aspects of contemporary social cognition provide exciting new ideas that can help develop thinking about social identity and group phenomena – for example, recent work on entitativity (see Yzerbyt, Judd, & Corneille, in press) and on intergroup emotions (Mackie & Smith, 2003). There is now a much more open stance taken towards social cognition (e.g., Leyens, Yzerbyt, & Schadron, 1994), and there are now close links and a productive dialogue between social identity researchers and social cognition researchers (Abrams & Hogg, 1999).

The historic gulf between American small groups research and European social identity research has gone a long way towards narrowing (see Hogg & Tindale, 2001; Poole & Hollingshead, in press; Wheelan, in press). This is an important development as it allows an integration of the social cognitive and large-scale intergroup analysis provided by the social identity perspective, with the analysis of face-to-face interaction in small groups that underpins the small groups tradition. This new social identity focus on small group processes has also produced social identity analyses of organizational phenomena (see Haslam, 2000; Haslam, van Knippenberg, Platow, & Ellemers, 2003; Hogg & Terry, 2000, 2001). These developments help the study of communication to reappear more readily on the social identity agenda, and indeed invite a more serious consideration of communication processes by social identity researchers.

Related to this articulation is an increasing emphasis among social identity researchers on structural differentiation within groups. The classic social identity focus was on intergroup differentiation. Groups themselves were considered to be relatively homogenous and what happened within them was largely underemphasized or considered un-problematic. Newer research has focused on what happens within groups – for example, on role differentiation (e.g., Moreland, Levine, & McMinn, 2001), leadership process (e.g., Hogg & van Knippenberg, 2003), processes of deviance and marginalization (e.g., Abrams, Hogg, & Marqués, in press; Marqués, Abrams, Páez, & Hogg, 2001), and intragroup categorial diversity (e.g., Hogg & Hornsey, in press). There is also social identity research on power differentiation within and between groups, which focuses quite explicitly on the language and communication aspect of such differentiation (Brooke & Ng, 1986; Ng, Bell, & Brooke, 1993; Ng, Brooke, & Dunne, 1995).

Finally, some of the heat of the ideological stand-off between social identity and discourse analysis perspectives may have dissipated, giving social identity theorists the opportunity to work with students of language to advance theory about the relationship between language and social identity. A good case in point is Reicher and Hopkins's (e.g., 1996a) social identity research on how leaders use language to manage their leadership image.

Taken together these new currents place communication back on the agenda for social psychologists studying social identity processes. In this chapter I focus specifically on the way that social identity research is now addressing small interactive group phenomena via research on leadership and marginal group membership. Ironically, it is the avowedly cognitive concept of "prototype", from self-categorization theory, which opens the door to the study of intragroup differentiation and to communication within groups. The social identity conception of prototype allows us to look at small groups, to recognize the differentiated nature of small groups, and the dynamics of influence within small groups – all of which invite a better understanding of the relationship between communication and prototype structure and process.

Social Identity Perspective

Originating in Tajfel's early work in the late 1960s and early 1970s on social categorization, discrimination, and intergroup relations, the social identity perspective has developed into a general theory of group behavior, group membership, and the collective self-concept (Hogg & Abrams, 1988; Tajfel & Turner, 1986; Turner, Hogg, Oakes, Reicher & Wetherell, 1987; for up-to-date integrative statements see Abrams & Hogg, 2001; Hogg, 2001a, 2003; Turner, 1999).

People can conceive of themselves in many different ways, among which the most important distinction is between personal identity and social identity. Personal identity is a definition and evaluation of oneself in terms of idiosyncratic personal attributes and/or one's personal relationships. Social identity is a definition and evaluation of oneself in terms of the shared defining attributes of specific groups one belongs to. Personal identity is tied to the personal self, whereas social identity is tied to the collective self.

People have many different social and personal identities that vary in how subjectively important they are and how frequently they are used – how chronically accessible they are in one's self-concept. The interplay of chronic self-conceptual accessibility, immediate situational cues and deliberate personal or group goals, primes particular personal or social identities as a way to categorize oneself and other people. These social categorizations are then automatically used to make sense of the situation. If the social categorization seems to fit the ways that people differ in the context (called, comparative fit) and makes sense of why people are behaving in the way they are (called, normative fit), then that particular social categorization becomes psychologically *salient*. When a social categorization, self-conception or identity is psychologically salient it becomes real in the sense that it is one's subjective reality in that context. It is how one represents oneself and others, and it governs the way one perceives, thinks, feels and behaves.

The social identity approach focuses on social identity. It argues that social identity is associated with group and intergroup behaviors (e.g., conformity, stereotyping, normative behavior, cohesion, intergroup discrimination) that are quite different to the interpersonal and personal behaviors associated with personal identity. People cognitively represent groups in terms of *prototypes* (see below) – these are fuzzy sets of interrelated attributes that simultaneously capture similarities within each group and differences between the two groups, and prescribe group membership-related behavior. Prototypes are mental constructs that maximize entitativity – they enhance perceived similarity and structure within each group and differences between each group in order to make the groups seem as clear and distinct entities as possible. The prototype of a group you belong to, an ingroup, can therefore change as a function of what outgroup you are comparing your group with. In this way, prototypes are context-specific rather than trans-contextually invariant.

When you categorize someone, rather than seeing that person as an idiosyncratic individual you see them through the lens of the prototype – they become *depersonalized*. Prototype-based perception of outgroup members is more commonly called stereotyping – you vew "them" as being similar to one another and all having outgroup attributes. When you categorize yourself, exactly the same depersonalization process applies to self – you view yourself in terms of the attributes of the ingroup (self-stereotyping), and, since prototypes also describe and prescribe group-appropriate ways to feel and behave, you feel and behave normatively. In this way, self-categorization also produces, within a group, conformity and patterns of ingroup liking, trust and solidarity.

Social identity and self-categorization processes are psychologically motivated by uncertainty reduction and self-enhancement. People strive for a sense of relative certainty about their social world and about their place within it – they like to know who they are and how to behave, and who others are and how they might behave. Social categorization ties self-definition, behavior and perception to prescriptive and descriptive prototypes, and thus satisfies uncertainty reduction. People also strive to feel good about themselves, and to have relatively positive self-esteem. Prototypes are evaluative – they evaluate groups and thus those who belong to those groups. Therefore people strive to belong to groups that have favorable prototypes and thus have relatively higher status. The precise way in which people and the groups they belong to compete for status and evaluatively positive social identity is influenced by beliefs about the nature of intergroup relations – for example the stability and legitimacy of status differences, and the possibility of psychologically passing from one group to another.

Prototypes and Prototypicality

The prototype is the cognitive representation of the defining attributes of a group. It describes and prescribes all the attributes of an ideal group member. Prototypes are social-cognitively constructed according to the principle of metacontrast (maximizing the ratio of perceived intergroup differences to intragroup differences) in order to accentuate entitativity balanced by a concern to represent the ingroup favorably. As such, prototypes rarely describe average or typical ingroup members – rather they are polarized away from outgroup features and describe ideal, often hypothetical, ingroup members. Prototypes cannot form or be sustained purely by intragroup comparisons – they are dependent on intergroup comparisons. Thus, intragroup processes are inextricable from the wider intergroup context.

Prototypes vary from situation to situation as a function of the social comparative frame – that is, the specific ingroup members and the specific outgroup that are the basis for comparison. This variability may be dramatic (for example in relatively small and new groups), but it may also be more modest due to the inertial anchoring effect of enduring group representations (for example in large ethnic groups).

In salient groups, the prototype is the basis of perception, inference and behavior. Within groups people are highly attuned to prototypicality. Reactions to and feelings about fellow members are underpinned by perceptions of how prototypical those others are - how closely they match the group prototype. Hence, if the prototype changes, then feelings for and perceptions of specific members will change as their degree of prototypicality varies.

Communication and Prototype Construal

Most social identity research focuses on the social cognitive mechanisms that construct, modify, and contextually ground prototypes. Furthermore, experiments either operationalize and manipulate prototypes as unidimensional constructs (for example a single attitude dimension), or they prime pre-existing prototypes and measure their effects on social identity processes – see, for example, Oakes, Haslam & Turner, 1994). This research strategy has, in the service of operational ease, tended to strip down the richness of prototypes, and deprive them of their essentially dynamic nature. Notably absent is full discussion of the role of communication or language in prototype construction and change.

Prototypes define the nature of a group (its values, attitudes and customs) and the qualities of membership. They are normative properties of groups that rest on agreement among members about what the group is, what the group is not, how the group differs from other groups, and what sort of a group it might want to become. The entire process of prototype construal rests on communication among group members. People talk to one another to construe prototypes and correct prototype miscontruals, and to identify more or less prototypical members and to reject deviates. Ingroup prototypes are important as they define and evaluate self. Not surprisingly, the entire social process of prototype construal can be invested with passion – argument, persuasion, political intrigue, schism, and so forth.

People construe prototypes through communication in which they take into consideration how they would like their group to be different to other groups, what aspects of their group they would like to focus on and what to de-emphasize, and how their own qualities should be reflected in the group and therefore how prototypical they themselves should be. In the real word, prototypes certainly are cognitively represented and influenced by metacontrast and entitativity processes, but they are also arrived at by communication aimed at intragroup agreement and intergroup differentiation. They are subject to all the social influence and persuasion processes that operate where people communicate and interact with one another. This communication and language aspect has not been properly or systematically elaborated or articulated with the social cognitive aspects of the social identity perspective.

The need for a more communication-oriented treatment of prototype construal surfaces in many (new) areas of social identity research. Let me illustrate this point briefly with just two examples – deviance processes, and leadership.

Deviance and Leadership in Groups

Although largely researched as separate phenomena, from a social identity perspective deviance and leadership elegantly form two sides of the prototypicality coin – deviants are marginal members who are not very prototypical, whereas leaders are central members who are highly prototypical. Indeed social identity research on deviance and leadership rests on the self categorization theory-derived insight, which opened the door to research on structural differentiation within groups (e.g., Hogg, 1996b), that there is a prototypicality gradient within groups. Some people are more prototypical than others (groups are certainly not homogenous, they are structured at least as regards prototypicality), and members are highly attuned to prototypicality (prototypes are the yardstick of group life). The social attraction hypothesis (Hogg, 1993) then tells us that social evaluation and attraction in salient groups is depersonalized in terms of prototypicality, and is relatively consensual – rendering more prototypical members consensually liked/popular, and less protoypical members consensually disliked/unpopular.

Deviance

Marqués and his colleagues (e.g., Marqués & Páez, 1994) built on and extended the social attraction and prototypicality gradient ideas to describe how, in high salience groups, low prototypical ingroup members are marginalized and evaluatively downgraded. In particular they showed how a person located on an intergroup boundary would be evaluated more negatively if he or she were an ingroup member (i.e. a "black sheep") than an outgroup member. This analysis has recently been elaborated into the wider theory of subjective group dynamics (e.g., Marqués, Abrams, & Serôdio, 2001; see Marqués, Abrams, Páez, & Hogg, 2001), which argues that rejection of members who deviate from the group prototype occurs if and because such members compromise the group's social valence or relative status.

Hogg, Fielding and Darley (in press; also see Fielding, Hogg & Annandale, 2002) have suggested that how ingroup deviants are treated depends on two factors: (a) whether the deviant holds a prototypical position that borders the outgroup (a borderline, or negative, deviant) or is remote from the outgroup (an extremist, or positive deviant), and (b) whether the group members' dominant motivation concerns in the situation are for positive social identity or for uncertainty reduction and enhanced entitativity. As group membership becomes more salient, a borderline member is increasingly marginalized and evaluatively downgraded under conditions that threaten either the valence or entitativity of the group. Borderline/negative deviants compromise both the valence and entitativity of the group because they muddy group boundaries and lean towards the relatively less favorably evaluated outgroup prototype. Therefore threats to group valence or entitativity lead to marginalization of borderline deviants. In contrast, although extreme/positive deviants muddy the group's boundary they lean away from the outgroup prototype. This means that although under entitativity threat they will be marginalized just like borderlines, under valence threat they will be less marginalized and may even be celebrated as they contribute positively to group valence.

Marqués's work, and the associated research, does not incorporate an analysis of communication processes that might be the vehicle for marginalization or the justification of marginalization. However, in Fielding's work (e.g., Hogg, Fielding, & Darley, in press) we do explicitly build in a communication component that we have some preliminary support for (see Fielding, Hogg, & Annandale, 2002).

We argue that the treatment of prototypically marginal members may rest on how these people explain their prototypical borderline/negative or extreme/positive position. Specifically, positive deviants who publicly attribute their positive deviance to the actions of the group (modesty), and thus allow the group to own their contribution to the group's positive valence, will be favorably treated and embraced by the group as "one of us". Those who publicly take personal responsibility and deny that the group had anything to do with their positive deviance (self-aggrandizement), do not allow the group to own their contribution to the group's positive valence, and will be marginalized by the group. For negative deviants, the opposite is the case. If they take personal responsibility for their borderline position (self-blame) the group may have some sympathy and attempt to re-socialize them. If they do not take personal responsibility (blame the group) they will certainly be marginalized.

The communication and language component of this analysis needs to be further elaborated and investigated empirically. We may be able to learn from one area of social identity research on deviance that does integrate language and communication data to some extent. This is work by Emler and Reicher (1995) on adolescent delinquency. For Emler and Reicher, delinquency is reputation management. It is a matter of constructing a distinctive deviant identity that casts one as a deviant in society's eyes, but attracts some respect from one's peer group – as such, delinquency helps resolve adolescent identity problems for scholastic underachievers, particularly boys. The thing about delinquency is that it has to be publicly communicated for it to attract attention and serve its social identity function – if no one knows that you are a delinquent, then that identity is not validated. This communication can take many forms ranging from types of dress to boasting and telling tales of one's escapades.

Leadership

Over the past seven or eight years social identity theorists have developed a social identity model of leadership (Hogg, 2001b; Hogg & van Knippenberg, 2003; van Knippenberg & Hogg, in press). Leadership is defined as the ability to transform individual action into group action by influencing others to embrace as their own, and exert effort on behalf of and in pursuit of, new values, attitudes, goals, and behaviors. The core idea is that as group membership becomes increasingly salient group members pay more attention to prototypicality and endorse prototypical leaders more strongly than non-prototypical leaders. Prototypicality is a significant basis for effective leadership in high salience groups. This idea is now relatively well supported empirically across a number of studies that manipulate leader prototypicality and followers' social identity salience or strength of identification.

Prototypicality facilitates and enhances leadership in high salience groups through a number of processes. Group behavior conforms to the prototype and thus prototypical members are the focus of conformity within the group – follower behavior automatically conforms to their behavior. Prototypical members are the focus of consensual prototype-based depersonalized social attraction – they are 'popular' and thus not only able to gain compliance with their wishes but they appear to occupy a higher status position within the group than less prototypical members. Prototypical members are figural against the background of the group and thus their behavior is more likely to be dispositionally attributed so that they are seen to have a personality that suits them to effective leadership. Prototypical members often identify more highly with the group than do others, and as such they tend automatically to behave in more group oriented and group serving ways. These behaviors, which benefit the group as a whole and generate trust in the leader not to do things that will harm the group, cause followers to allow the leader to be innovative and to trust the leader to take the group in new directions that will benefit the group.

Communication is absolutely central to prototype based leadership – indeed to leadership in general. If prototypicality is a powerful basis of effective leadership in salient groups, then leaders need to be able to manage their prototypicality – they need to communicate their own image of their prototypicality to their followers (e.g., Reid & Ng, 2000). Indeed one's prototypicality is, as discussed above, not only a mechanical reflection of social cognitive metacontrast processes, but a dynamic product of influence, persuasion, and the perceptual manipulation of the comparative frame and of followers' perceptions of the prototype and one's own prototypicality.

Leaders can manipulate their prototypicality in many ways. They can talk up their own prototypicality and/or talk down aspects of their own behavior that are non-prototypical. They can identify deviants or marginal members in such a way as to highlight their own prototypicality or to construct a particular prototype for the group that enhances their own prototypicality. They can secure their own leadership position by vilifying contenders for leadership and casting them as non-prototypical. They can identify as relevant comparison outgroups those that are most favorable to their own prototypicality – that is, they can manipulate the social comparative frame and thus the prototype and their own prototypicality. They can engage in a discourse that raises or lowers salience. If one is highly prototypical then raising salience will provide one with the leadership benefits of high prototypicality; if one is not very prototypical then lowering salience will protect one from the leadership disadvantages of not being very prototypical.

In particular, leaders often accentuate the existing ingroup prototype, pillory ingroup deviants, and demonize an appropriate outgroup – many historical leaders have done this very effectively (e.g., Margaret Thatcher, Josef Stalin, Mao Zedong). Research by Reicher and Hopkins (e.g., Reicher & Hopkins, 1996a, 1996b; 2001) on the rhetoric used by political leaders shows that all three tactics are employed, and that the very act of engaging in these powerful rhetorical devices is often viewed as convincing evidence of effective leadership. Indeed, Reicher and Hopkins proposed that leaders are in this sense "entrepreneurs of identity" – as we might put it in the context of the present analysis, "prototypicality managers". Prototypicality management through talk is also central to the way that leaders of social movements can politicize members and mobilize them to engage in social action (Reid & Ng, 1999).

Other research suggests that high and low prototypical leaders of high salience groups actually need to behave somewhat differently in order to manage their prototypicality. For example, Rabbie and Bekkers (1978) show that leaders whose position is insecure are more likely to seek conflict with other groups. They may do this in order to be seen by the group to be behaving in a group-oriented manner. More generally, leaders who feel they are not, or are no longer, prototypical, may strategically engage in a range of group-oriented behaviors in order to strengthen their membership credentials (e.g., Platow & van Knippenberg, 2001).

The leadership behavior of low and high prototypical leaders may vary because they are differently positioned within the group, such that highly prototypical leaders do not need to establish their prototype-based leadership credentials as much as do less prototypical leaders. Highly prototypical leaders' membership credentials are not called into question, and so they do not need to behave in ways that either demonstrate prototypicality or confirm membership. They are trusted by the group to be doing the best for the group, because after all they are central members themselves and what benefits the group must benefit them. They can be innovative and creative, and ironically can actually behave in non-prototypical ways (cf. Hollander's, 1958, notion of idiosyncrasy credits). In contrast, low prototypical leaders' membership credentials are not confirmed and may be called into question. They therefore need to be much more careful to behave in ways that establish their prototypicality and valid membership of the group. They need to overtly behave in ways that confirm their prototypicality, and establish that they are good, loyal group members. Low prototypical leaders need to behave highly prototypically – they need to conform, engage in prototypicality talk and behavior, show greater outgroup derogation and ingroup loyalty, and display greater ingroup procedural justice.

Concluding Comments

My aim in this chapter has been to suggest that developments over the past 10 or 15 years in social identity research, and in the relationship between social identity research and social cognition and small groups research, have once again placed language and communication on the social identity agenda. From a social psychological and social identity point of view the scene is set for new advances in social identity research that require a sophisticated and central consideration of the role of communication and language.

The social identity perspective has advanced by leaps and bounds, much of it due to the social cognitive insights of self-categorization theory (Turner, Hogg, Oakes, Reicher, & Wetherell, 1987) and its analysis of the role of prototypicality in group life. We now know a great deal more about the social cognitive foundations of social identity processes than we did in the 1970s and early 1980s when there was a tighter link between social identity and language and communication researchers than there has been in recent years. We are now ready to build on this base, particularly in the context of influence and interactive processes among people in small face-to-face groups (see Ng, 2001). What is needed is systematic study and conceptualization of the communicative functions and processes associated with prototypicality – the way that people talk about and communicate prototypicality within groups and between groups. Self-categorization, depersonalization, entitativity, metacontrast, and so forth, are primarily the social-cognitive aspects of group life and social identity. The social-interactive aspect is symbolic communication in which people construct and use prototype information. It is this aspect that needs to be elaborated and linked/remarried to the social cognitive aspect.

To illustrate this claim I spoke about new research on deviance and on leadership in groups. But this only scratches the surface. The social construction and manipulation of prototypicality is integral to all social identity related group processes. For example, cohesion and solidarity require social organization around an agreed prototype, and group status and entitativity rest on communication-based social construction of an appropriate prototype. It is through communication that these things are accomplished – social cognitive processes provide critical parameters, but they need to be articulated with social interactive processes that are largely symbolic and communication based.

The importance of articulating social cognitive and social interactive processes in the explanation of group life actually lies at the heart of Tajfel's original vision for social identity theory (e.g., Tajfel, 1969). However, to a great extent the communicative dimension has not been fully integrated, or indeed explored. For example, the specific form that intergroup behavior takes is influenced by the beliefs that people have about the nature of the relations between their own and an outgroup (Tajfel & Turner, 1986). The way in which these beliefs or ideologies emerge and are internalized has not been elaborated. These representational and interpretative structures are not static or given – they are dynamic structures that emerge and change through the entire array of communication processes (see Thompson, 1990).

References

Abrams, D., & Hogg, M. A. (Eds.) (1999). *Social identity and social cognition.* Oxford, UK: Blackwell.

Abrams, D., & Hogg, M. A. (2001). Collective identity: Group membership and self-conception. In M. A. Hogg & R. S. Tindale, (Eds.), *Blackwell handbook of social psychology: Group processes* (pp. 425–460). Oxford, UK: Blackwell.

Abrams, D., Hogg, M.A., & Marqués, J., (Eds.) (in press). *The social psychology of inclusion and exclusion.* Philadelphia, PA: Psychology Press.

Brooke, M. E. & Ng, S. H. (1986). Language and social influence in small conversational groups. *Journal of Language and Social Psychology, 6,* 201–210.

Cartwright, D., & Zander, A. (Eds.) (1968). *Group dynamics: Research and theory* (3rd edn). London: Tavistock.

Clément, R. (1996). Social psychology and intergroup communication. *Journal of Language and Social Psychology, 15,* 222–229.

Devine, P. G., Hamilton, D. L., & Ostrom, T. M. (Eds.) (1994). *Social cognition: Impact on social psychology.* San Diego, CA: Academic Press.

Emler, N., & Reicher, S. D. (1995). *Adolescence and delinquency: The collective management of reputation.* Oxford, UK: Blackwell.

Farr, R. M. (1996). *The roots of modern social psychology: 1872–1954.* Oxford, UK: Blackwell.

Fielding, K. S., Hogg, M. A., & Annandale, N. (2002). *The effects of personal and group attributions for success on evaluations of high achievers.* Manuscript submitted for publication, University of Queensland.

Fiske, S. T., & Taylor, S. E. (1991). *Social cognition* (2nd edn). New York: McGraw-Hill.

Giles, H. (1996). Language, communication, and social psychology. *International Journal of Psychology, 31,* 4410–4410.

Haslam, S. A. (2000). *Psychology in organisations: The social identity approach.* London: Sage.

Haslam, S. A., van Knippenberg, D., Platow, M. J., & Ellemers, N. (Eds.) (2003). *Social identity at work: Developing theory for organizational practice.* New York: Psychology Press.

Hogg, M. A. (1993). Group cohesiveness: A critical review and some new directions. *European Review of Social Psychology, 4,* 85–111.

Hogg, M.A. (1996a). Identity, cognition, and language in intergroup context. *Journal of Language and Social Psychology, 15,* 372–384.

Hogg, M. A. (1996b). Intragroup processes, group structure and social identity. In W. P. Robinson (Ed.). *Social groups and identities: Developing the legacy of Henri Tajfel* (pp. 65–93). Oxford, UK: Butterworth-Heinemann.

Hogg, M. A. (2001a). Social categorization, depersonalization, and group behavior. In M. A. Hogg & R. S. Tindale, (Eds.), *Blackwell handbook of social psychology: Group processes* (pp. 56–85). Oxford, UK: Blackwell.

Hogg, M. A. (2001b). A social identity theory of leadership. *Personality and Social Psychology Review, 5,* 184–200.

Hogg, M. A. (2003). Social identity. In M. R. Leary & J. P. Tangney (Eds.), *Handbook of self and identity* (pp. 462–479). New York: Guilford.

Hogg, M. A., & Abrams, D. (1988). *Social identifications: A social psychology of intergroup relations and group processes.* London: Routledge.

Hogg, M. A., Fielding, K. S., & Darley, J. (in press). Deviance and marginalization. In D. Abrams, M. A. Hogg & J. Marqués (Eds.), *The social psychology of inclusion and exclusion.* New York: Psychology Press.

Hogg, M. A., & Hornsey, M. J. (in press). Self-concept threat and differentiation within groups. In R. J. Crisp & M. Hewstone (Eds.), *Multiple social categorization: Processes, models, and applications.* New York: Psychology Press.

Hogg, M. A., & Terry, D. J. (2000). Social identity and self-categorization processes in organizational contexts. *Academy of Management Review, 25,* 121–140.

Hogg, M. A., & Terry, D. J. (Eds.) (2001). *Social identity processes in organizational contexts.* Philadelphia, PA: Psychology Press.

Hogg, M. A., & Tindale, R. S. (Eds.) (2001). *Blackwell handbook of social psychology: Group processes.* Oxford, UK: Blackwell.

Hogg, M. A., & van Knippenberg, D. (2003). Social identity and leadership processes in groups. In M. P. Zanna (Ed.), *Advances in experimental social psychology* (Vol. 35, pp. 1–52). San Diego, CA: Academic Press.

Hollander, E. P. (1958). Conformity, status, and idiosyncracy credit. *Psychological Review, 65,* 117–127.

Kraut, R. E., & Higgins, E. T. (1984). Communication and social cognition. In R. S. Wyer, Jr & T. K. Srull (Eds.), *Handbook of social cognition* (Vol. 3, pp. 87–127). Hillsdale, NJ: Erlbaum.

Leyens, J-P., Yzerbyt, V., & Schadron, G. (1994). *Stereotypes and social cognition.* London: Sage.

Mackie, D. M., & Smith, E. R. (Eds.) (2003). *From prejudice to intergroup emotions: Differentiated reactions to social groups.* New York: Psychology Press.

Markus, H., & Zajonc, R. B. (1985). The cognitive perspective in social psychology. In G. Lindzey & E. Aronson (Eds.), *Handbook of social psychology* (3rd ed., Vol. 1, pp. 137–230). New York: Random House.

Marqués, J. M., Abrams, D., Páez, D., & Hogg, M. A. (2001). Social categorization, social identification, and rejection of deviant group members. In M. A. Hogg & R. S. Tindale, (Eds.), *Blackwell handbook of social psychology: Group processes* (pp. 400–424). Oxford, UK: Blackwell.

Marqués, J. M., Abrams, D., & Serôdio, R. (2001). Being better by being right: Subjective group dynamics and derogation of in-group deviants when generic norms are undermined. *Journal of Personality and Social Psychology, 81,* 436–447.

Marqués, J. M., & Páez, D. (1994). The "black sheep effect": Social categorization, rejection of ingroup deviates and perception of group variability. *European Review of Social Psychology, 5,* 37–68.

Moreland, R. L., Levine, J. M., & McMinn, J. G. (2001). Self-categorization and work group socialization. In M. Hogg & D. Terry (Eds.), *Social identity processes in organizational contexts* (pp. 87–100). Philadelphia, PA: Psychology Press.

Ng, S. H. (2001). Influencing through the power of language. In J. P. Forgas & K. D. Williams (Eds.), *Social influence: Direct and indirect processes* (pp. 185–197). Philadelphia, PA: Psychology Press.

Ng, S. H., Bell, D. & Brooke, M. (1993). Gaining turns and achieving high influence ranking in small conversational groups. *British Journal of Social Psychology, 32,* 265–275.

Ng, S. H., Brooke, M. & Dunne, M. (1995). Interruptions and influence in discussion groups. *Journal of Language and Social Psychology, 14,* 369–381.

Noels, K. A., Giles, H., & Le Poire, B. (2003). Language and communication processes. In M. A. Hogg & J. Cooper (Eds.), *The Sage handbook of social psychology* (pp. 232–257). London: Sage.

Oakes, P. J., Haslam, S. A., & Turner, J. C. (1994). *Stereotyping and social reality*. Oxford, UK: Blackwell.

Parker, I. (Ed.) (2002). *Critical discursive psychology.* New York: Palgrave Macmillan.

Platow, M. J., & van Knippenberg, D. (2001). A social identity analysis of leadership endorsement: The effects of leader ingroup prototypicality and distributive intergroup fairness. *Personality and Social Psychology Bulletin, 27,* 1508–1519.

Poole, M. S., & Hollingshead, A. B. (Eds.) (in press). *Theories of small groups: An interdisciplinary perspective.* Thousand Oaks, CA: Sage.

Potter, J., & Wetherell, M. S. (1987). *Discourse and social psychology: Beyond attitudes and behaviour.* London: Sage Publications.

Rabbie, J. M., & Bekkers, F. (1978). Threatened leadership and intergroup competition. *European Journal of Social Psychology, 8,* 9–20.

Reicher, S. D., & Hopkins, N. (1996a). Self-category constructions in political rhetoric: An analysis of Thatcher's and Kinnock's speeches concerning the British miners' strike (1984–5). *European Journal of Social Psychology, 26,* 353–371.

Reicher, S. D., & Hopkins, N. (1996b). Seeking influence through characterising self-categories: An analysis of anti-abortionist rhetoric. *British Journal of Social Psychology, 35,* 297–311.

Reicher, S. D., & Hopkins, N. (2001). *Self and nation.* London: Sage.

Reid, S. A., & Ng, S. H. (1999). Language, power and intergroup relations. *Journal of Social Issues, 55,* 119–139.

Reid, S. A., & Ng, S. H. (2000). Conversation as a resource for influence: Evidence for prototypical arguments and social identification processes. *European Journal of Social Psychology, 30,* 83–100.

Steiner, I. D. (1974). Whatever happened to the group in social psychology? *Journal of Experimental Social Psychology, 10,* 94–108.

Tajfel, H. (1969). Cognitive aspects of prejudice. *Journal of Social Issues, 25,* 79–97.

Tajfel, H. (Ed.) (1984). *The social dimension: European developments in social psychology.* Cambridge, UK: Cambridge University Press.

Tajfel, H., & Turner, J. C. (1986). The social identity theory of intergroup behavior. In S. Worchel & W. Austin (Eds.), *Psychology of intergroup relations* (pp. 7–24). Chicago: Nelson-Hall.

Taylor, D. M., & Brown, R. J. (1979). Towards a more social social psychology. *British Journal of Social and Clinical Psychology, 18,* 173–179.

Thompson, J. B. (1990). *Ideology and modern culture: Critical social theory in the era of mass communication.* Stanford, CA: Stanford University Press.

Tindale, R. S. & Anderson, E. M. (1998) Small group research and applied social psychology: An introduction. In R. S. Tindale, L. Heath, J. Edwards, E. J. Posavac, F. B. Bryant, Y. Suarez-Balcazar, E. Henderson-King & J. Myer (Eds.) *Social psychological applications to social issues: Theory and research on small groups* (Vol. 4, pp. 1–8). New York: Plenum Press.

Turner, J. C. (1999). Some current issues in research on social identity and self-categorization theories. In N. Ellemers, R. Spears, & B. Doosje (Eds.), *Social identity* (pp. 6–34). Oxford, UK: Blackwell.

Turner, J. C., Hogg, M. A., Oakes, P. J., Reicher, S. D., & Wetherell, M. S. (1987). *Rediscovering the social group: A self-categorization theory.* Oxford, UK: Blackwell.

van Knippenberg, D., & Hogg, M. A. (in press). A social identity model of leadership in organizations. In B. M. Staw & R. M. Kramer (Eds.), *Research in organizational behavior* (Vol. 25). Greenwich, CT: JAI Press.

Wheelan, S. A. (Ed.) (in press). *Handbook of group research and practice.* Thousand Oaks, CA: Sage.

Yzerbyt, V., Judd, C. M., & Corneille, O. (Eds.) (in press), *The psychology of group perception: Contributions to the study of homogeneity, entitativity, and essentialism.* New York: Psychology Press.

10

Language and the Situated Nature of Ethnic Identity

Kimberly A. NOELS
Richard CLÉMENT
Sophie GAUDET

Multicultural milieux provide opportunities for many instances of inter-group contact. As a result, ethnic groups may experience a number of challenges including daily hassles (e.g., Lay & Nguyen, 1998), lower levels adjustment (e.g., Abouguendia & Noels, 2001; Clément, Noels, & Deneault, 2001), and, more globally, acculturation (e.g., Berry, 1990). Cross-cultural research on acculturation has focused mostly on acculturative attitudes (e.g., Berry & Sam, 1997). However, aspects and repercussions of acculturation are more numerous. Recent developments have, for example, begun to highlight ethnic identity and its related factors in order to examine consequences of inter-group contact (Phinney, 2003). Furthermore, cross-cultural interaction may evoke a variety of changes from maintaining, adopting, or displaying single versus plural ethnic identities (Clément & Noels, 1992; Landry & Allard, 1992). These multifaceted aspects of identity may be especially apparent in multicultural contexts and among minority or immigrant groups. Members of these groups and in these situations, may choose to alternate between cultural identities and feel part of different groups at different times or, alternatively, may choose to maintain a single identity regardless of the context. Thus, contextual variations, combined with personal characteristics (i.e., language and status), influence the experienced identity and displayed behavior.

The present paper discusses aspects of a 10-year research program on the relation between language and ethnic identity. How context affects the manifestation of different patterns of identity will be examined first. Two key aspects to be discussed are (1) the socio-structural status or ethnolinguistic vitality of the groups under consideration, and (2) the immediate interpersonal situation in which intercultural contact takes place. Second, in the interest of understanding the process of acculturation, consideration will be given to how inter-group contact and communication variables, particularly one's anxiety and confidence in using a second language, are related to these patterns of ethnic identity. In doing so, the relevance of context and interactions will be highlighted as key factors to identity formation and acculturation.

Situated Ethnic Identity

Since Barth's (1969) analysis, researchers generally adopt a subjective perspective to defining ethnic identity, such that it corresponds to that aspect of the self derived from real or perceived common bonds with an ethnic group (Edwards, 1977). Like many definitions of ethnic identity, we believe that, in contexts of intercultural contact, at least two ethnic referent groups contribute to both groups' self-definition. Following the terminology proposed by Berry (1990) to describe patterns of attitudes toward acculturation strategies, at least four profiles of ethnic identity are possible. An individual may decide to maintain the original identity and not adopt the other cultural group as a reference group, which is termed *separation*. Conversely, as reflected by *assimilation*, a person may wholeheartedly engage in the new cultural group and relinquish the original cultural referent group. It is also possible that both identities may be fostered (i.e., *integration*) or neither identity may be acceptable (i.e., *deculturation*). Thus, cross-cultural and inter-group situations may result in the adoption of single or multiple identities. To elaborate, and along the premises of self-presentation and impression management perspectives of the self (Alexander & Beggs, 1986; Schlenker, 1985), identity is not an inveterate characteristic but rather a product of negotiations between individuals in a given situation. For example, a person born in Canada is not *ipso facto* Canadian but develops a Canadian identity as a result of interacting with Canadians and non-Canadians. Individuals have many goals in any social interaction and will behave in a way that best supports the identity-image that will help in attaining that goal. Whether or not a goal is achieved depends upon the acceptability of that image to the interactants. Accordingly, the self is "formed and maintained through actual or imagined interpersonal agreement about what the self is like" (Schlenker & Weigold, 1989, p. 245). The implication of this assumption is that identity not only determines behavior, and vice versa via reactions. Endorsed identities are thus based on social consensus as to which identity is most tenable in a particular interaction.

This negotiation process does not occur in a vacuum, but in the particular interactive social contexts. Situational characteristics are one important aspect of these social contexts. Although social psychological researchers have proposed many taxonomies and frameworks for conducting situational analyses (e.g., Argyle, Furnham, & Graham, 1981; Forgas, 1982), researchers interested in the social nature of linguistic behavior suggest that the setting, the relationship between the interlocutors, and the activity engaged in are three key aspects that define any interpersonal situation (e.g., Brown & Fraser, 1979). Moreover, although many situational domains can be identified, they generally vary in their level of intimacy (Côté & Clément, 1994; Noels, 1998). It is frequently found that individuals use one speech register for communicative purposes in public, less intimate situations (e. g. with clerks in stores) and another style in private, more intimate settings (e.g. at home with family members). In intergroup interactions, Edwards (1985) suggests that individuals are more likely to encounter members of other ethnolinguistic groups in public domains and hence the possibility of acculturative change regarding their language and identity. Lower levels of inter-group contact in more intimate situations shelter feelings of ethnicity and ethnic markers from acculturative processes. Accordingly, it is expected that identification with one's membership group is greater in intimate domains than in less intimate domains, and the converse pattern is true with regards to identification with the other ethnic group.

Edwards' (1985) contention is, however, relatively unique in attempting to describe the dynamics of identity in an interaction context. Although many social psychologists have commented on the situational nature of ethnic identity (e.g., Okamura, 1981; Phinney, 1991), there is rather little empirical work describing the situational domains across which ethnic identity can vary. Christian, Gadfield, Giles and Taylor (1976), for example, varied situational saliency of ethnic identity by asking Welsh adolescents to write an essay about either a neutral topic or a topic concerning English-Welsh conflicts. Subjects who wrote the latter essay rated themselves on a semantic differential scale as more highly Welsh and accentuated the polarization of the English and Welsh groups. Rosenthal, Whittle and Bell (1988) asked Greek-Australian adolescents to write an essay either about the advantages or disadvantages of their ethnic group membership or about a neutral topic. They found that sensitizing the respondents to their ethnic group membership through the essay topic resulted in increased salience of Greek identity. In sum, these and other studies (e.g., Benet-Martínez, Leu, Lee, & Morris, 2002; Yip and Fuligni, 2002) indicate that situational cues of ethnicity influence the level of identification with one's own or another ethnic group. It follows that ethnolinguistic identity should be conceived as situationally bound, such that individuals move in and out of memberships as required by the immediate contextual constraints (Collier & Thomas, 1988; Liebkind, 1989).

These studies did not, however, examine how identity alternates between the ethnic and target groups across a range of intimate and public situations. To that end, Noels and Imaike (2000) examined the issue of situational variation with 121 international students at a Canadian university. All were non-native speakers of English, 77.9% of whom originated from East and Southeast Asia, including the People's Republic of China, Hong Kong, Japan, Taiwan, Malaysia, India, Indonesia, and Pakistan. They were asked to complete a questionnaire regarding their ethnic identity. The items were developed based on a survey of activities that people engaged in on a more or less daily basis. These activities were defined in terms of the setting, the person with whom they interacted, and the task performed (Noels, 1998) and were meant to depict relatively intimate situations, including family and friendship domains, as well as less intimate situations such as those found in the school and public domains. For each situation the participants indicated the extent to which they identified with two target groups, their own ethnic group and the Canadian group, on separate 7-point Likert-type scale.

The results (see Table 1) revealed that, overall, ethnic identity was significantly stronger than Canadian identity. This pattern is not unexpected given the participants were short-term sojourners not committed to remain in Canada. When the identity patterns were examined across the four situational domains, however, it became clear that the pattern for overall identity told only part of the story. In intimate settings with family and friends, identification with the ethnic group was stronger. In the less intimate situations, at school or in public, Canadian identity was as strong as the ethnic identity. It is particularly noteworthy that there was little difference between the school and public domains in terms of ethnic identity and Canadian identity. Such a pattern is consistent with the idea that acculturation may occur in some situations before others; the friendship domain, and particularly the family domain, are relatively sheltered from acculturative contact.

Table 1
International students:
Identity as a function of target group and situational domain

| Situational Domains | Target Identity Group | | | |
| | Ethnic | | Canadian | |
	M	SD	M	SD
Family	5.71	1.28	2.92	1.71
Friends	5.27	1.13	3.48	1.60
School	4.35	1.54	4.29	1.30
Public	4.43	1.23	4.66	1.40
Global	4.94	1.30	3.84	1.50

These results, then, underline the point that global measures of ethnic identity may underestimate the variability of feelings of ethnic identity across situations and present a misleading picture of ethnic identification. In the family and friends domains, the pattern indicated that the ethnic identity is likely to be retained, and identification with the host culture is not pursued. In the public and school domains, the pattern suggested an integration of the two identities. It is important to note, however, that the means of both ethnic identity and Canadian identity only approach the midpoint, suggesting that strong identification with both groups was not endorsed. Thus, where dual and negotiated identities are possible, situational characteristics (i.e., public versus private) will most likely influence the direction of identification and further reflect acculturation patterns in inter-group contexts.

Situated Ethnic Identity and Ethnolinguistic Vitality

International students represent a particular kind of minority group within Canada. Although many of these students come from areas of the world that are not well represented in Canada, they are usually not committed to spending a longer period of time in the host society than the duration of their studies, work, or travel purposes necessitate. Consequently, these people do eventually return to their majority status in their country of origin and, as such, temporarily constitute a minority group within the host country. Considerable research, from a variety of theoretical perspectives, suggests that minority group status, whether temporary or not, has an important influence on identity formation and change. Drawing from Ethnolinguistic Identity Theory, Giles and his colleagues (e.g., 1979) have argued that minority groups may shift their identification from the group of origin to the group of higher vitality. Coupled with this observation, it is argued that since minority group members are more likely than majority group members to experience opportunities for contact with the other, higher-status group, and engage in greater second language use across situations, the effects of this acculturative contact should be evident across a greater variety of situational domains. In other words, the impact of acculturation should be more pervasive across situations for minority than for majority group members.

Following the theoretical work of Lambert (1974) and Clément (1980), we believe that integration and assimilation would be evident but the manifestation of these two profiles would depend upon the vitality of the language group. Both Lambert and Clément have suggested that when members of a minority group (such as Francophones in Canada), learn a second language and acquire a second cultural identity, there is a tendency to lose the original group identity and language. This pattern is referred to as subtractive bilingualism and corresponds to assimilation indicative of ethnic cultural loss. On the other hand, when majority groups (like Anglophones in Canada) learn a second language and gain a second cultural identity, they are likely to remain secure in their original culture. This pattern is referred to as additive bilingualism and corresponds to integration in that there is an acquisition of other cultural characteristics and further permeability between groups (see also Ng & He, 2004; Ng, He & Loong, in press).

To examine the effect of group status on situational variations in ethnic identity, a study was conducted at the University of Ottawa, in Ottawa, Canada, which lies on the border of the provinces of Quebec, a predominantly French-speaking province, and Ontario, a predominantly English-speaking province. As a bilingual institution, the University of Ottawa draws Francophone and Anglophone students from both provinces, such that students may come from a high or low vitality context. A breakdown of participants as a function of their native language and province of origin yielded three sub-samples. The Franco-Ontarian group, composed of individuals with French as mother tongue but living in a mostly (over 94 percent) English-speaking context, is the lowest vitality group. At the other end, the Anglo-Ontarian group represents the highest vitality group. In an intermediate position are the Québécois (French speaking from Quebec) who are a majority in their province (85 percent) but, in this case, are currently in an Ontarian environment.

The means (Table 2) were compared via a three-way analysis of variance using as within-subjects factors the situation (intimate vs. non- intimate) and target identity group[1] (ingroup vs. outgroup) and, as the between-subjects factor, the ethnolinguistic group of the participant (Anglo-Ontarian vs. Franco-Ontarian vs. Québécois). The results revealed a significant 3-way interaction effect (target group X situation X ethnolinguistic group interaction; $F(2, 157) = 15.83$, $p < .001$, $eta^2 = .17$). Post hoc Tukey tests indicated that there were significant differences between in- and outgroup identification such that participants felt more strongly about their ingroup than about their outgroup identity. However, the groups differed from each other in their level of endorsement of each identity. The Franco-Ontarian group had a lower ingroup identity than Anglo-Ontarian and Québécois groups, who had equally strong ingroup identities. This pattern was consistent across both intimate and non-intimate settings. With regards to outgroup identity, the Franco-Ontarians identified more strongly to the Anglophones than the Québécois group, who in turn had a stronger out-group identity than the Anglo-Ontarians. This pattern was also consistent across both intimate and non-intimate settings.

Table 2
Identity means and standard deviations
as a function of ethnolinguistic group, situation and target group

| Group | Target Identity Group | | | |
| | Ingroup | | Outgroup | |
	M	SD	M	SD
Anglo-Ontarian				
Low Intimacy	6.11	1.34	1.88	1.09
High Intimacy	6.43	1.30	1.53	1.12
Québécois				
Low Intimacy	5.99	1.14	2.77	1.64
High Intimacy	6.43	1.11	2.14	1.66
Franco-Ontarian				
Low Intimacy	4.56	1.25	3.90	1.57
High Intimacy	5.73	1.02	2.67	1.60

At first glance, the preference for the original group identity relative to the target group identity might be described in terms of separation. Such an interpretation however is only partially correct, since identification with the native language group is lower, and identification with the outgroup is higher for the Franco-Ontarian group than for the Anglo-Ontarian or Québécois groups. For that minority group, it would seem that the distinction between the two identities is considerably attenuated compared to the two majority groups. Moreover, although the two majority groups maintained equal levels of native or ingroup identity, the Anglophone group identified significantly less to the Francophone group than the Québécois did to the Anglophone group. Consistent with the Clément and Noels, (1992) results, this pattern suggests that minority group status has the effect of increasing identification with the higher vitality group, and in the case of the minority, this status may also be associated with diminished feelings of identification with the original ingroup. Such a pattern suggests that an integration profile involving a rapprochement of the two identities is most closely achieved by minorities, but it is in the dynamic context of relatively high outgroup and low ingroup identification reflecting assimilation to the higher vitality group.

This pattern is further tempered by the situational characteristics in that the identity patterns across situations differed depending upon the vitality of the group. With regard to native language group identity, for both the Anglo-Ontarian and Québécois groups, identity was equivalent across intimate and non-intimate situations, but for Franco-Ontarians, ingroup identity was lower in non-intimate situations than in intimate situations. With regards outgroup identity, all three groups showed higher identification in non-intimate than in intimate situations. This pattern suggests that in non-intimate situations, where there is more opportunity for interaction with members of the outgroup, identification with that group increases. However, this opportunity may also mean a decrease in original ethnic identity for extreme minority group members. In that case, it appears that more intimate situations act as a shelter from the acculturative effects of interethnic interactions.

These results then suggest that, in accordance with Edwards' hypothesis, identity is relatively protected in the private setting. It is likely that majority group members are faced with greater opportunities for intergroup contact and second language use in public settings and the impact of this contact on identity is more evident in this setting. Minority Francophones, on the other hand, are faced with more contact and second language use across a wider variety of situations. Not only does this interaction contribute to a lower level of mgroup identification but concurrently, to a higher level of outgroup identification. Because the intercultural contact is not limited to public settings but extends to more intimate settings, the acculturative impact of inter-group interactions across all domains becomes evident. Thus, Edwards' hypothesis relating the distinction between public and private domains to identity may be influenced by the vitality of the group such that low vitality individuals are not as sheltered in private situations as the high vitality individuals.

Language and
Situated Ethnic Identity

While situated ethnic identity is key to the understanding of acculturation, language is also of central importance in identity and inter-group contact. Many researchers have demonstrated a distinct link between language use and ethnic identity (see for review, Abrams, O'Connor & Giles, 2002). Although there are some exceptions (e.g., Bond & Yang, 1982), several studies of bilingual speakers have shown that responses given in a particular language tend to be more similar to the modal responses of monolingual speakers from the corresponding community (e.g., Ralston, Cunniff, & Gustafson, 1995; Sanchez, 2000). Indeed, in Harzing and Maznevski's (2002) examination of this phenomenon in seven nations around the world, these researchers found this pattern of responses quite robust, particularly with regards to culturally loaded items. Among the several explanations proposed, Yang and Bond (1980) maintain that language acquisition comes with cultural attitudes and associated values. It has been argued that original cultural identity and the host cultural identity are stored as separate knowledge structures and that language use may prime specific knowledge structures (Hong, Morris, Chiu, & Benet-Martínez, 2000). As such, when cued with one language, the associated cultural characteristics are likely to be evoked.

However, variations in identity may not simply be primed through language, but negotiated through communication practices. This position is similar to that of Kim (1988; see also Collier & Thomas, 1988), who suggested that patterns of communication between members of a group become eventually a consensual system of coding and decoding information specific to individuals in that network. As language is the primary medium of communication of cultural information, it is intimately linked with identity. One implication of this assumption is that in the acquisition of new routines, as happens when learning a second language, cultural identity can change. That is to say, competence in a second language is a determinant of psychological identity in that a new identity is negotiated between interlocutors through language.

To look more directly at the link between second language competence and ethnic identity, the instrument assessing situated identity was modified such that various situations were presented to participants cued as to the ethnicity of the interlocutor (Noels, Clément, Côté, & Gaudet, 2003). Hence, one third of the participants, who were all Canadian Francophones, received a questionnaire in which the ethnolinguistic group of the interlocutor was not specified, one third received a questionnaire where the interlocutor was described as Anglophone, and one third received a questionnaire where the interlocutor was described as Francophone. Participants were asked to view themselves in the depicted situation and evaluate their degree of identification to both target groups, Francophones and Anglophones. The results (Table 3) showed a significant 2-way interaction for the ethnicity of the interlocutor by target identity ($F(2, 246) = 50.92$, $p = .000$, eta^2 = .29). In ethnicity-neutral conditions, a distinction was made between the Francophone and Anglophone identities, such that Francophone identity was greater than Anglophone identity. When interacting with a Francophone interlocutor, this pattern was accentuated such that Francophone identity became higher and English identity was even lower. When interacting with an Anglophone interlocutor, there was a switch – Francophone identity was lower and Anglophone identity was significantly higher than in the other two conditions, and the two identities, French and English were equally endorsed. These findings suggest that the ethnicity of the person with whom we interact influences our own feelings of identity, such that we adjust our identity to accommodate to the other person. It is plausible that this identity accommodation is accomplished through language and communication practices. According to Giles and his colleagues, in the absence of inter-group threat or conflict, there is convergence to the language style of others to achieve solidarity (c.f., Giles & Noels, 2002). Our results suggest that there is also identity convergence.

Table 3
Francophone Canadians:
Identity as a function of interlocutor ethnicity and target identity group

| Interlocutor | Target Identity Group | | | |
| | English | | French | |
	M	SD	M	SD
Neutral	2.42	1.19	4.11	1.02
Anglophone	3.04	1.25	3.12	1.3
Francophone	1.83	0.89	4.46	0.85

This analysis did not, however, directly examine the role of communication. To look at the effects of communicative competence in English on patterns of ethnic identity, feelings of confidence using English were assessed (Clément, 1988). The group was split into high and low confidence using a median split (4.63 on a 7-point scale). The respondents' perceptions of their group's vitality and that of the English was assessed by calculating a relative perceived vitality score as a ratio of the French group vitality relative to that of English group. Thus minority Francophones perceived their group as having a relative vitality score below 1.00 and majority group members perceived their group above 1.00.

A series of ANOVAs were computed to assess the Anglophone and Francophone identities and the intimacy of the situation (the within-subjects factors) as well as vitality and language confidence (the between-subjects factors). The results (Figures 1 and 2) revealed a significant 4-way interaction ($F(1,246) = 3.85$, $p = .05$, eta^2 = .02). Identity varied according to target identity, subjective ELV, anxiety and the situation. Under conditions of low language confidence (Figures 1a and 1b), for both vitality groups, Francophone identity was higher than Anglophone identity in both intimate and non-intimate situations. Moreover, there were no differences in the levels of each identity across situations or across vitality groups. Thus, regardless of the status of the group, when individuals are not comfortable using the other language, perceived ethnolinguistic vitality and situational variations have little impact on identity.

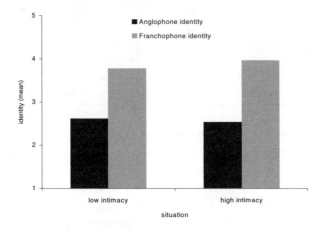

Figure 1a
Low English confidence and low group vitality:
Identity as a function of situation and target identity group

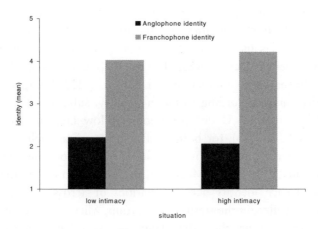

Figure 1b
Low English confidence and high group vitality:
Identity as a function of situation and target identity group

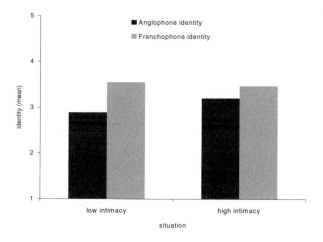

Figure 2a
High English confidence and low group vitality:
Identity as a function of situation and target identity group

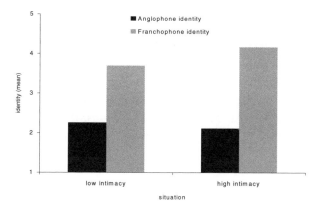

Figure 2b
High English confidence and high group vitality:
Identity as a function of situation and target identity group

Under conditions of high language confidence, however, different acculturative patterns are evident for the two vitality groups (Figures 2a and 2b). For high vitality groups, there was a clear distinction between identities across both situations, such that Francophone identity was higher than Anglophone identity. At the same time, although Anglophone identity was equivalent across situations, Francophone identity was stronger in high intimacy situations. This pattern is consistent with the idea that the original group identity is sheltered from acculturative influences in the high intimacy situation. The low vitality group showed a very different pattern: there was no difference between the two identities in either situation. Francophone identity was lower and Anglophone identity was higher relative to the other groups. Such a pattern suggests that low vitality group members comfortable interacting in the language of the high vitality group are more likely to experience a lessened sense of original identity and an increased sense of identity with the outgroup. Moreover, given there is no difference in the identity patterns across situations, this minority group is not advantaged in a sheltered intimate context.

Thus, despite the close association between language and identity, there are characteristics of language use and the group that need to be examined for a fuller appreciation of the inter-group contact. In the reviewed study, second language confidence moderated feelings of identification for high and low vitality groups. When there were perceptions of lower second language abilities, vitality and public versus private domains had little impact on identification. However, in instances of greater language confidence, low vitality groups demonstrated less in-group identification across all domains whereas for high vitality groups, there was a sheltered context of private domains to maintain in-group identity.

Conclusion

The present discussion had two major objectives. The first was to examine how ethnic identity varied depending on contextual factors, including the status of the group and the characteristics of the immediate social situation. The second was to consider how linguistic self-confidence relates to these contextual variations. With regards to the first objective, the contextual factors were systematically associated with variations in ethnic identity. The hypothesis that identity should be protected from acculturation pressures in private situations relative to public situations was generally upheld. Ethnolinguistic vitality modified this relation such that the distinction between the two identities was less pronounced for the minority group members. It is possible that majority members experience more intergroup contact and second language use in public than private settings and hence the acculturative impact of intercultural interaction on identity is more evident in this setting. Minority group members, on the other hand, may be faced with more contact and second language use across both intimate and non-intimate situations. Not only does this mean a lower level of heritage identification relative to their majority counterparts, but concurrently a higher level of identification with the other group.

These patterns of identification suggest that an individual may express different patterns of acculturation. Our research shows that although people may feel quite strongly about their first cultural identity particularly in intimate settings, these feelings may be lessened in public situations so that both identities are permeable, a phenomenon resembling integration, but also, arguably, resembling an identity shift or assimilation. Thus, context is an important predictor for patterns of acculturation for the situation as well as for the group's relative status and vitality.

With regards to the second objective, the results indicate that language and communication processes have an important moderating effect on patterns of identity. Under conditions of low confidence using English, there were no differences in the levels of identities across different vitality groups or situations. However, under conditions of high confidence in speaking English, differences in identification were evident depending on the vitality of the group and situation. This pattern is consistent with the position that communicative competence, and particularly confidence in using the language of the other ethnolinguistic group, is critical for acculturative changes in ethnic identity (Clément, *et al.*, 2001). These findings suggest a mechanism by which acculturative change occurs. That is, it proposes that identities are forced and modified to the extent that one possesses a sense of ease in communicating with people from other ethnic groups. This sense of confidence may be critical for negotiating identities in instances of cultural contact, in terms of both forming new identities and modifying old ones. Attention to the process by which acculturation occurs is relatively under-researched in psychology. Rather, research has tended to focus on states of acculturation in different groups, and how these different states are linked to various outcome variables, such as psychological well-being and socio-cultural adjustment. It is proposed and argued that researchers interested in the interface between language and social psychology need to examine more closely the social interaction and the communication that takes place between members of different cultural groups to better understand how, why and when, changes in identity occur as they do.

Notes

1. For the Franco-Ontarians and the Québécois, the target ingroup corresponds to the Francophones whereas, for the Anglo-Ontarians, the target ingroup is the Anglophone group. Conversely, the outgroup corresponds to the Anglophones for both French groups and to the Francophones for the Anglo-Ontarians.

References

Abouguendia, M., & Noels, K.A. (2001). General and acculturation-related daily hassles and psychological adjustment in first- and second-generation South Asian immigrants to Canada. *International Journal of Psychological, 36,* 163–173.

Abrams, J., O'Connor, J., & Giles, H. (2002). Identity and intergroup communication. In W. B. Gudykunst & B. Mody (Eds.), *Handbook of international and cross-cultural communication* (2nd ed., pp. 225–240). London: Sage.

Alexander, C. N., & Beggs, J. J. (1986). Disguising personal inventories: A situated identity strategy. *Social Psychology Quarterly, 49,* 192–200.

Argyle, M., Furnham, A., & Graham, J.A. (1981). *Social situations.* Cambridge, UK: Cambridge University Press.

Barth, F. (1969). *Ethnic groups and boundaries.* London: Allen & Irwin.

Benet-Martínez, V., Leu, J., Lee, F., & Morris, M.W. (2002). Negotiating biculturalism: Cultural frame switching in biculturals with oppositional versus compatible cultural identities. *Journal of Cross-Cultural Psychology, 33,* 492–516.

Berry, J. W. (1990). Psychology of acculturation. In J. J. Berman (Ed.), *The Nebraska symposium on motivation* (pp 201–234). Lincoln: University of Nebraska Press.

Berry, J. W., & Sam, D. (1997). Acculturation and adaptation. In J.W. Berry, M.H., Segall, & C. Kagitçibasi (Eds.), *Handbook of cross-cultural psychology* (Vol. 3, pp. 291–326). Needham Heights, MA: Allyn and Bacon.

Bond, M. H., & Yang, K. (1982). Ethnic affirmation vs. cross-cultural accommodation: The variable impact of questionnaire language on Chinese bilinguals in Hong Kong. *Journal of Cross-Cultural Psychology, 13,* 169–185.

Brown, P., & Fraser, C. (1979). Speech as a marker or situation. In K.R. Scherer & H. Giles, (Eds.), *Social markers in speech* (pp. 33–62). Cambridge: Cambridge University Press.

Christian, J., Gadfield, N.J., Giles, H., & Taylor, D.M. (1976). The multidimensional and dynamic nature of ethnic identity. *International Journal of Psychology, 11,* 281–291.

Clément, R. (1980). Ethnicity, contact, and communicative competence in a second language. In H. Giles, W.P. Robinson, & P.M. Smith (Eds.), *Language: Social psychological perspectives* (pp. 147–154). Oxford: Pergamon.

Clément, R. (1988). *Echelles d'attitude et de motivation reliées aux rapports inter-ethniques.* [Scales of attitude and motivation related to inter-ethnic relations]. (Tech. Rep.), University of Ottawa, Ottawa.

Clément, R., & Noels, K. A. (1992). Towards a situated approach to ethnolinguistic identity: The effects of status on individuals and groups. *Journal of Language and Social Psychology, 11,* 203–232.

Clément, R., Noels, K. A., & Deneault, B. (2001). Interethnic contact, identity, and psychological adjustment: The mediating and moderating roles of communication. *Journal of Social Issues, 57*, 559–577.

Collier, M. J., & Thomas, M. (1988). Cultural identity: An interpretive perspective. In Y. Y. Kim & W. B. Gudykunst (Eds.), *Theories in intercultural communication* (pp. 99–120). Newbury Park: Sage.

Côté, P., & Clément, R. (1994). Language attitudes: An interactive situated approach. *Language and Communication, 14*, 237–251.

Edwards, J. (1977). Ethnic identity and bilingual education. In H. Giles (Ed.), *Language, ethnicity and intergroup relations* (pp. 253–282). London: Academic Press.

Edwards, J. (1985). *Language, society and identity*. Oxford: Basil Blackwell.

Forgas, J.P. (1982). Reactions to life dilemmas: Risk taking, success and responsibility attribution. *Australian Journal of Psychology, 34*, 25–35.

Giles, H., Llado, N., McKirnan, D. J., & Taylor, D. M. (1979). Social identity in Puerto Rico. *International Journal of Psychology, 14*, 185–201.

Giles, H., & Noels, K.A. (2002). Communication accommodation in intercultural encounters, Second Edition. In J.N. Martin, T.K. Nakayama, & L.A. Flores (Eds.) *Readings in cultural contexts: Experiences and contexts* (pp. 117–126). Boston, MA: McGraw-Hill.

Harzing. A.W., & Maznevski, M. (2002). The interaction between language and culture: A test of the cultural accommodation hypothesis in seven countries. *Language and Intercultural Communication 2*, 120–139.

Hong, Y-Y., Morris, M.W., Chiu, C-Y., & Benet- Martínez, V. (2000). Multicultural minds: A dynamic constructivist approach to culture and cognition. *American Psychologist, 55*, 709–722.

Kim, Y.Y. (1988). *Communication and cross-cultural adaptation*. Clevedon, UK: Multilingual Matters.

Lambert, W. (1974). Effects of bilingualism on the individual: Cognitive and socio-cultural consequences. In P.A. Hornby (Ed.), *Bilingualism: Psychological, social and educational implications*. New York: Academic Press.

Landry, R., & Allard, R. (1992). Ethnolinguistic vitality and the bilingual development of minority and majority group students. In W. Fase, K. Jaspaert, & S. Kroon (Eds.), *Maintenance and loss of minority languages* (pp. 223–251). Amsterdam: John Benjamin.

Lay, C., & Nguyen, T. (1998). The roles of acculturation-related and acculturation non-specific hassles: Vietnamese-Canadian students and psychological distress. *Canadian Journal of Behavioural Science, 30*, 172–181.

Liebkind, K. (1989). Conceptual approaches to ethnic identity. In K. Liebkind (Ed.), *New identities in Europe* (pp. 25–40) Hants, England: Gower.

Ng, S.H., & He, A. (2004). Code-switching in tri-generational family conversations among Chinese immigrants in New Zealand. *Journal of Language and Social Psychology, 23,* 28–48.

Ng, S.H., He, A., & Loong, C. (in press). Tri-generational family conversations: Communication accommodation and brokering. *British Journal of Social Psychology.*

Noels, K. A. (1998, August). *Vitality, contact and situational language norms: The acculturation experience of Latinos and Anglo-Americans.* Paper presented at the 1998 Congress of the International Association of Cross-Cultural Psychology, Bellingham, WA, August 3–8, 1998.

Noels, K. A., Clément, R., Côté, P., & Gaudet, S. (2003). Context and the acculturation of ethnic identity: Group status, situations and language. Manuscript under review.

Noels, K. A., & Imaike, E. (2000, July). *Acculturation-related daily hassles and psychological and socio-cultural adjustment in international university students.* Paper presented at the 15th International Congress of the International Association of Cross-Cultural Psychology, Pultusk, Poland, July 16 – 21, 2000.

Okamura, J. Y. (1981). Situational ethnicity. *Ethnic and Racial Studies, 4,* 452–465.

Phinney, J. S. (1991). Ethnic identity and self-esteem: A review and integration. *Hispanic Journal of Behavioral Sciences, 13,* 193–208.

Phinney, J. S. (2003). Ethnic identity and acculturation. In K. M. Chun, P. B. Organista, & G. Marín (Eds.), *Acculturation: Advances in Theory, Measurement, and Applied Research* (pp. 63–81). Washington, DC: American Psychological Association.

Ralston, D. A., Cunniff, M. K., & Gustafson, D., J. (1995) Cultural accommodation: The effect of language on the responses of bilingual Hong Kong Chinese managers. *Journal of Cross-Cultural Psychology, 26,* 714–727.

Rosenthal, D., Whittle, J., & Bell, R. (1988). The dynamic nature of ethnic identity among Greek-Australian adolescents. *Journal of Social Psychology, 129,* 249–258.

Sanchez, J.I. (2000). *Linguistic effects in translated organizational measures: A study of bilinguals.* Paper presented at the Academy of Management meeting (4–9 August) Toronto.

Schlenker, B.R. (1985). Identity and self-identification. In B. Schlenker, (Ed.), *The self and social life* (pp. 65–99). New York: McGraw-Hill.

Schlenker, B.R. & Weigold, M.F. (1989). Goals and the self-identification process: Constructing desired identities. In L. Pervin (Ed.), *Goal concepts in personality and social psychology* (pp. 243–290). Hillsdale, NJ: Lawrence Erlbaum.

Yang, K. S., & Bond, M. H. (1980). Ethnic affirmation by Chinese bilinguals. *Journal of Cross-Cultural Psychology, 11,* 411–425.

Yip, T., & Fuligni, A. J. (2002). Daily variation in ethnic identity, ethnic behaviors, and psychological well-being among American adolescents of Chinese descent. *Child Development, 73,* 1557–1572.

11

Exploring Social Support and Social Identity within a Multigenerational Community of Women

Margaret Jane PITTS
Amanda Lee KUNDRAT

> Social support is simply "being friendly, interested, and helpful to your neighbors" (Rachel).

The Montrose Women[1], a multigenerational neighborhood community of women, serves as the focus of this investigation. These women, who have monthly luncheons and daily garden chats, at first proclaimed no similarity with each other except that they live on the same street. Yet, we uncovered significant support, strength, friendship, and knowledge within this group. Together, they welcome new residents, bake cookies for local fraternities, plow each other's snow, and offer assistance during times of need. Of its many distinctive qualities, one of the most interesting is the community support and interaction among all members from the twenty-three year old bride-to-be, Katie, to the seventy-three year old widow, Cardie.

The purpose of our study is to present a holistic, descriptive account of the functions and uses of social support among the Montrose Women. This study responds to a call from Harwood,

Giles, and Ryan (1995) for more community-based intergenerational research and exploration into positive intergenerational relations. In this study, we also enter Carbaugh's (1996) conversational scenes, "actual scenes where people are living together . . . in which selves are fashioned and conducted" (p. 22), in order to capture the essence of the everyday, community lives of the Montrose Women. This allows for the natural illumination of the role of social support in a multigenerational community, will add to our previous knowledge of social support, and may influence future communicative research in the areas of identity, social support, and aging as they naturally occur in intergenerational settings.

Introduction and Guiding Literature

The intergenerational context in which this study was conducted seems to be a rarity in modern times. Presently, the study of intergenerational communication exists mostly in the realm of family communication, or amongst strangers (Williams & Nussbaum, 2001). It appears that few meaningful interactions between generations occur outside the family (Hummert & Nussabum, 2001; Nussbaum, Pecchioni, Robinson, & Thompson, 2000). In spite of the fact that intergenerational contact has more recently been encouraged through formal programs (Kuehne, 1999), very little research has been conducted with intergenerational encounters among people who are close, yet not bound together through family (Williams & Nussbaum, 2001). The community of women explored in this study spans an age range from early twenties to early seventies. Each woman is engaged in a different stage of the lifespan making it a rich context to study intergenerational communication among close, non-family relations.

Lifespan communication scholars suggest rewarding intergenerational social relationships are a rare, but important, aspect of successful, healthy aging (Nussbaum, 1983, 1985; Nussbaum *et al.*, 2000; Williams & Nussbaum, 2001). The necessity of a strong support network with which a person can share life events is notable. For the Montrose Women, it is not only their continual physical and social activities that lend to their healthy lifestyles, but the social support they derive from each other through these activities.

Social support can be understood as "a pattern of continuous or intermittent ties and mutual assistance that plays a significant role in maintaining the psychological, social, and physical integrity of the individual over time" (Cantor, 1980, p. 133). For aging adults, the informal support system, typically consisting of family, neighbors, and friends is frequently activated during times of need (Cantor, 1980; Nussbaum *et al.*, 2000). "Intangible" social support in the form of companionship, advice, and feedback promotes feelings of self worth (George, 1989). Many of these benefits are received through social interaction with friends and companions (Reis, 1984). Perhaps this is because friends offer support voluntarily, depending on the mutual gratification achieved through the offer and acceptance of social support, whereas family are more obligated to provide such support (Crohan & Antonucci, 1989).

To frame our study within a theoretical rubric, we employ Tajfel and Turner's (1986) Social Identity Theory (SIT). SIT offers perspective on the role of communication in maintaining the Montrose Women's social identity. SIT purports that when faced with an out-group against which a group is forced to compete for resources, an in-group will form, increasing group identity salience. In this study, two adjoining neighborhoods competed for various resources including zoning rights, number of private owners versus renters, and community activities. Thus, SIT explains how the Montrose Women is formed with implications for social support among this group. Moreover, SIT has been used in previous intergenerational communication studies and has proven to be useful in enhancing and generating such knowledge (Harwood *et al.*, 1995; Williams & Nussbaum, 2001). It is for this reason that we explored the functions of social support in the everyday lives of this multigenerational community with SIT providing us with the necessary borders encasing this group.

In order to investigate social support within this community, we proposed the following research question:

RQ: What is the role of social support among this multi-generational community of women?

Method

This study included nine female participants (See Table 1) living on the same street ranging in age from 23 to 73 years. The participants were all community active as well as employed full or part time, volunteers, members of various community groups, and/or caring for family members. Seven of the women were Caucasian and born in the United States, one was from Korea, and one was from Japan[2].

Table 1
Participant demographics

Participant	Age	Stated Group Status	Relational Status	Stated Occupation
Ruthie	59	"Leader"	Married	"Politician"
Nelly	48	"Event planner"	Married with children	"Artist"
Cardie	73	"Historian"	Widow with (grand) children	"Volunteer"
Sandy	54	"Comedian"	Married	"Housewife"
Mrs. Redbird	37	"New Kid"	Married	"Professor"
Katie	23	"Newcomer"	Engaged	"Student"
Patty	57	"Member"	Married with children	"Former Teacher"
Rachel	68	"Participant"	Married with children	"Retired"
Kim	34	"New Member"	Married	"Housewife"

We purposefully selected (Taylor & Bogdan, 1984) this community of women to represent a naturally occurring multigenerational neighborhood. The study proceeded in three phases. The first was a participant observation opportunity in which we participated in one of the Montrose Women's monthly luncheons. This introduction sensitized us to the group culture and establish personal rapport. We took an active part in the luncheon setting and wrote extensive notes on their behaviors and communicative interaction.

The second phase was an individual interview conducted with each woman at home. We conducted semi-structured interviews in order to solicit narrative accounts about social support within the group. Only one researcher was present during each interview. Interviews ranged in duration from one to three hours and were audio-taped for transcription. For two of the interviews, husbands were present to facilitate with translation, because English was not the participant's first language.

The final observational phase of the study took place during a potluck lunch hosted by Nelly. The observation served to gather further descriptive data and enhance the study's holistic view. The observer specifically looked for themes that were found in the previous observations and preliminary analyses of data, and any new patterns.

We analyzed the data in stages concurrent with those of the study. We first conducted the preliminary analysis of observational data. For this, we transcribed our observational notes and wrote conceptual memos from the data. We then coded the observations and identified participant roles noting any recurrent behaviors. This process led to questions that structured the individual interviews while enriching our descriptive knowledge of the group.

During the next phase of the analysis we transcribed the interviews and systematically coded key concepts and recurrent patterns that offered insight into our research question. We analyzed our own interviews first, then exchanged transcripts and re-coded. For each transcript we categorized responses from the participants. These categories were then read and rearranged, resulting in some new categories, and collapsing and elimination of others. The final categories were examined and refined in formal codes. After individually completing the process described above, we compared our findings and finalized the themes. Through discussion and extensive cross-comparison and analysis, we agreed on the themes and their attributes. We were then able to interpret the data and draw conclusions, applying them to previous research findings with new interpretations.

Results

In answering our research question, *What is the role of social support among this multigenerational community of women?* we identified 7 themes: (1) Offers Emotional Support, (2) Encourages Communication, (3) Provides Connection, (4) Provides a Sense of Community, (5) Provides Resources, (6) Provides Help, and (7) Sustains Independence, and 14 sub-themes (see Table 2). The following section offers descriptions of these themes and their attributes.

Table 2
Functions of social support

Themes	Sub-themes
Offers Emotional Support	Availability Kindness
Encourages Communication	Openness Request Interaction
Provides Connection	Enrichment Inclusion
Provides a Sense of Community	Building and Maintenance Protection Neighborhood issues
Provides Resources	Sharing Goods Sharing Information
Provides Help	Health Physical Aid
Sustains Independence	no sub-themes

Offers Emotional Support

The theme "Offers Emotional Support" consisted of *members' expressions "just knowing others are there if needed," and general acts of kindness between members, promoted well-being.* This theme runs through consistent remarks from members. Although social support was infrequent, just knowing that others were available to offer support put members' minds at ease. In addition, members' continual gestures of kindness and caring showed their willingness to offer support when needed, thus offering further emotional support for everyone.

Availability. The members believed that emotional support existed by the perception that others were around and able to lend a hand when needed. This sub-theme is centered on *members' expressions of perceived support derived from a feeling of social availability of others.* Nelly reported "keeping the door open . . . having [others' support as] a possibility" served as emotional support. Cardie noted, "I would hope that the neighborliness would come through, that people would know that they could come to me, I mean that we just don't go around saying that to each other, but if I knew that somebody was in trouble . . . " She followed with, "I think it's there if you need it, but you don't tap it unless you need it."

Kindness. The perception that members were kind to one another created another dimension of emotional support. This sub-theme is made up of *members' expressions that general kindness was an aspect of support.* Sandy said "most of the benefit is that we know each other . . . and [are] kind to each other." Kim disclosed that even though she is "a foreigner," the women talk with her and "show kindness." Nelly described the group as "very pleasant" without "cliquey stuff . . . nobody is nasty to anybody." She added, "we've defined ourselves that way." Being nice and doing kind things (often without being announced) is normative for this group. This was expressed among members in not only *doing* kind things, but also offering compliments and praise. For example, at luncheons it was common within the first few minutes of greeting to hear a round of compliments on new haircuts or stylish clothing. Later in the conversation, talk of past activities often spurred praise for the entertaining hostess. All of these acts of kindness served as emotional support for these women by offering a way to escape from everyday hassles.

Encourages Communication

In addition to offering kindness, a general open-style of communication defined the underlying pattern of interaction for this group. Social support functioned to encourage communication by allowing members to communicate directly and openly in order to manage important business without stepping on toes. We defined this theme as *members' expressions of open lines of communication for both task and social reasons.*

Openness. Members expressed a feeling of "openness" in their communication, indicating *members' beliefs that they could talk to each other about anything.* Ruthie expressed this point clearly, "when we get together there is total openness and we can talk about anything and everything." Katie felt as though she was able to "go and talk [to the women] without having any problem." Although they communicated and shared information openly, they did not see it as "gossip." Instead, they perceived the sharing of personal information, or "free-talking," important, and rarely passed on that information to others without the discloser's consent.

Members also valued honesty. The expression of opinions was strongly encouraged, and often led to lively discussions. Cardie, in discussing a recent book-swap, said she appreciated the ability to express opinions freely, "and that's what I like, that somebody can be that honest and say, 'I just don't think that, I just don't think that's me,' or you know, 'I tried it, but I didn't like it." Open communication encouraged the expression of identity among members and have that identity supported.

Request. Although support was available, members agreed someone would have to be asked directly for support if needed. We conceptualized this sub-theme as *members' beliefs that social support must be asked for directly*. In respect to her local government position, Katie said that when the women needed informational support they could "just call anytime." Similarly, Patty remarked that if someone were in need of support, "they would just have to tell me."

Interaction. A few of the women noted that without directly asking for support, they would not necessarily know if someone was in need. These women believed it was equally important to interact with each other frequently and through multiple channels of communication. It was through informal communication that members became aware of what was going on in the neighborhood, and who was in need of support. This sub-theme was conceptualized as *members' expressions that the need for social support was communicated indirectly through interaction*. When asked how she would know if someone was in need of support, Mrs. Redbird shook her head and stated, "I don't think I would, it's too bad, but I don't, at this point, I don't think I would." She then added, "I've not had anybody come and say to me I need your help, and part of that, I think, is because I'm the new kid on the block. Literally." Yet, even without this direct communication, many of the women were able to sense a need for support through their everyday interactions. Ruthie offered the following in expressing the importance of her interaction with the women, "just being aware of where we all are in our life situation, and knowing who needs to be connected with us periodically."

Provides Connection

Members' expressions of establishing connection and deriving personal fulfillment composed the theme "Provides Connection." Statements about personal enrichment and group inclusion from members made salient their desire for community connection and familiarity. This desire for interpersonal connection was a catalyst for socially supportive interactions and opportunities.

Enrichment. Members of the Montrose Women felt they gained life enrichment from their involvement with each other. We conceptualized "Enrichment" as *members' expressions of a feeling of nurturance and sharing as support.* They discussed enrichment in various ways from networking to "sharing and enjoying [time with] each other." Cardie described one humorous example of self-enrichment through this group. Several of the women discovered they were middle children. This discovery was of interest and amusement to the women, so they decided to hold a luncheon just among themselves to find out more about birth order implications. This luncheon enriched their personal knowledge, furthered interpersonal knowledge, strengthened relational bonds, and brought to surface generational differences and similarities among the women.

Members felt social support within this group led to both self and group enrichment in various ways. For some, like Kim, who was new to the United States, it was a learning and social opportunity. She was pleased to learn about U.S. customs and social interactions by engaging in them. Ruthie also expressed how much the group enriched her life.

> I consider these women my friends, I really care about them, it really makes me feel so good about myself to live in a place where we know each other and we can talk openly and there's a benefit that's just indescribable. I do it because I love it. I really like them, and I really want us to keep [our closeness] . . . it's really heartfelt. I guess nurturing would be the word that comes to mind.

Similarly, Nelly not only believed she benefited personally from the group, but she saw it as a source of enrichment for the other members as well. She stated, "There's huge payoffs being connected to people, it just enriches your life . . . there's a lot to be gained from talking to [the Montrose Women], seeing what they're like, sharing stuff, you know that enriches your life." Many of the members expressed forms of life-enrichment derived directly or indirectly from this group. Some had dramatic, life changing effects, as in the case of Mrs. Redbird who found "a real sisterhood" among the women, and was enabled to cope while recovering from a serious illness with their help. Patty felt enriched through her connection to this group because they provided her with an outlet for voicing her concerns about the neighborhood. In general, membership in this group enriched the women's lives by supporting their personal endeavors, social quirks, and differing needs for social interaction.

Inclusion. The Montrose Women felt it important to maintain neighborhood ties and continually involve members in the group. The sub-theme "Inclusion" is composed of *members' expressed feelings of being "accepted and supported" by the other women.* Ruthie described the group as all-inclusive, regardless of individual involvement. When asked about introducing a "new" member to the group, she quickly replied, "I would not say a *new* member at all, I mean all women on this block are members, and I think when they can participate, they are so appreciated." If members had not been present for some time, or had recently moved into the neighborhood, the Montrose Women felt it was important to draw them (back) into the group. Cardie explained, "if you like the person you've been introduced to, you just pull them in!" This happened recently when the Redbirds bought their home. Ruthie remembered "de facto, they'[d] been included in our group." Further, when discussing new neighbors, Cardie explained that she always makes an attempt to welcome them by bringing a small gift. She said, "I just think that everybody should do that, and that sort of breaks the ice for people that are moving in, that they feel like, 'at least somebody's interested that we've moved into the neighborhood.'"

Members worked at providing a sense of connection for all current and potential members of the group. Faced with the possibility of a new home-owner in the area, the group assembled to speak to the woman while she was investigating the home. They introduced themselves and spoke about their neighborhood group to the woman, being sure to make her feel welcome as a possible new resident. Each woman felt a sense of pride and connection with this group and was grateful to have such an enriching, inclusive relationship with other members.

Provides a Sense of Community

This theme was formed through *members' comments that the growth of the community and the maintenance of neighborhood cohesion and safety promoted social support.* Three sub-themes compose "Provides a Sense of Community." However, Patty summarized the overall theme and illustrated the importance of their community nicely. In describing the bulk of their communicative interactions, she said, "we mainly talk about the neighborhood."

Building and Maintenance. This sub-theme was defined through *members' expressions that the growth and development of their neighborhood was of primary importance to them, creating a sense of commonality and support among members.* Members noted that they must be supportive of each other in order to build and maintain a community. Katie described the neighborhood as being "mobilized with transients" who live in apartments only for a few years. She noted the concern this brings to the other women who are interested in keeping the neighborhood together. Mrs. Redbird said the members feel especially "connected" to the neighborhood because of Ruthie's position on town council and their interest in the neighborhood's "thriving."

Holding monthly socials, hosting "Give-a-Greek-a-Cookie" night, organizing "Neighborhood Watch" and lobbying for community rights were all activities in which these women engaged to maintain the community. Patty mentioned that because of Ruthie's political position, she keeps the group "posted" so they can attend town meetings. Patty clearly articulated the connection between social support and neighborhood maintenance, "like this thing with the traffic. That to me is [social] support, because we're all banding together. We're really trying hard to come up with our own alternative solutions and proposals and what we want to see done." Trash, traffic, and real estate were all topics of maintenance and catalysts for areas of social support.

Patty was especially interested in the maintenance of the neighborhood. She exclaimed, "I think we all want to maintain the neighborhood, we *do* have to be vigilant!" This sense of vigilance was also a concern for Mrs. Redbird, "I think there's a sense of being very protective of the neighborhood, because of the encroachment of rental properties. And I think there's a fear that if we aren't careful then the neighborhood could just, you know, go to hell. So I think there's a real perceptiveness about trying to maintain it."

The Montrose Women felt a sincere sense of responsibility toward maintaining their neighborhood. For some, like Cardie, community responsibility stemmed from past experiences and a traditional approach towards community living. For others, like Ruthie, the neighborhood connection was a new, and much appreciated, experience in comparison to other places she has lived. The mutual aid and mutual caring for their community allotted the Montrose Women a focused direction for their social support, which then trickled into many other areas of their daily lives.

Protection. The members understood social support as creating a sense of safety and protection in the neighborhood. We defined "Protection" as *members' expression of social support through joint safeguarding and property maintenance.* Patty believed members found security in knowing their neighbors. Likewise, Katie said it is "nice to live in a neighborhood where you know who your neighbors are and you don't have to worry about who's living next door and what they are doing." Sandy especially thought the biggest benefit of being in the group was that they knew each other well. Because of this, she felt safe in the neighborhood and was not "afraid" of those around her. She emphasized that for safety reasons she wanted to know *all* the neighborhood news, "what's going on with the neighbors or with this town."

Other women agreed that it was important "to get to know your neighbors at an individual level." Nelly admitted,

> I've always been sort of a nosy neighbor, wanting to know who's living where . . . . I want to know what the people are going through around me; I don't have to know all the details, but just a little bit about where they're coming from, so if they need you, you can do something.

As evidence of the importance these women placed on neighborhood protection, they engaged in such activities as holding a neighborhood safety meeting to which they invited a local police officer, hosting a fraternity – neighborhood forum, and checking on the physical and mental health among all residents. The fact that this neighborhood is located adjacent to a university and surrounded by fraternity houses increased members' attention toward neighborhood protection. Their location gave members the impression that they were on the "front lines" without the protection of surrounding neighborhoods. Ruthie was especially attuned to this, "I feel a real protectiveness of it and I think living here on Montrose Lane makes one aware of the issues that are pressing down [on this town], because we don't feel particularly protected by anything . . . and we love living here, so it makes us more responsive, I think, to the issues."

Neighborhood issues. Members' statements indicating *support was activated when they felt the neighborhood was threatened by change* create this sub-theme. The women found social support in discussing "any kind of neighborhood issues, like traffic, building codes, anything to do with the fraternities." One example of this led Ruthie to persuade her neighbors to be proactive against a proposed zoning variance in their neighborhood. She activated the women to "march down together and testify." She described the experience as "quite wonderful," yet admitted they "felt guilty afterwards," because they were successful in ousting a proposed enlargement of a nearby homeowner's bed and breakfast. This particular incident was mentioned by several of the Montrose Women as being a turning point in their relationships and one of the first sources of social support.

Nelly suggested the neighborhood women "have to be diligent about the building of the town, the times that we get together is when there's a petition to be signed, you know about the parking, things that impede on us." The Montrose Women felt united against a common front in protecting their neighborhood and being active in its development and maintenance. From addressing proposed speed bumps and stop signs to discussing a variety of safety issues, the Montrose Women not only gained a sense of social support from their group, but were also able to initiate social action among members.

Provides Resources

The theme "Provides Resources" was defined by *members' expression that sharing material and intangible resources was social support*. The communicative style among the Montrose Women allowed for the asking, lending, and giving of items or information for a variety of reasons. This provision of goods increased trust, egalitarianism, and social reciprocity among members reinforcing feelings of social support and caring.

Sharing Goods. Food sharing was such a central part of this group that when asked about social support, often the first examples they mentioned were of this nature. "Borrowing spices," remembered Ruthie, "how nice it was to have that kind of sharing and I realized that that's social support, isn't it?" Sandy mentioned "cook(ing) dishes of soup (to) take over to people." She was proud to be able to share food with the other women. These women also never hesitated to *ask* for food staples when needed. Sandy said, "I call when I don't have the cream of mushroom soup that I need, or I need egg, I call them." Ruthie, Cardie, and Nelly found food sharing especially enjoyable. Ruthie explained that the three of them often share foods they cannot eat. After sending her husband into agony over a pumpkin pie one night because of a food allergy, Ruthie shipped it over to Nelly who returned the favor with a "gallon of some wonderful soup that her kids didn't like, but I loved it."

Ruthie, who felt for the first time that she was part of a "real" neighborhood, especially appreciated this type of social support:

> I thought I had as good a life as you could get and last year I was ill and [the Montrose Women] brought me food and I never had that happen. It really touched me deeply. I think about it, Cardie made me soup, it was

> really so sweet of them . . . It is an old-fashioned community. Really caring, and willing to, you know, to share themselves, to really do something and not just to buy something and hand it off, but to actually spend time creating something to share.

Mrs. Redbird concurred by reflecting that somebody "bringing you something they've made" served as social support, and was wholly appreciated because of the time and thought put into making it.

The Montrose Women shared other items such as gardening tools, plants, seeds, books, and household items. In one example, Rachel described a planned visit to Nelly's home, "She wanted a mount and frame and I knew that I have the exact frame that she needed." Sharing goods enabled the Montrose Women to obtain small necessary items without disrupting their daily routine by having to drive or ask for a ride to the store. The ability to freely exchange small items helped the Montrose Women to feel more like a community by providing each woman an opportunity to do her part to help others.

Sharing Information. Information provision, or "just meeting and exchanging information" was another way through which the Montrose Women were able to convey a sense of community interest and social support. This sub-theme was conceptualized as *members' expressions that sharing various forms of information with one another served as a form of social support.* When asked about different types of social support she was getting from the Montrose Women, Ruthie took a deep breath and sighed, "sharing, sharing of information."

The Montrose Women shared information about gardening, cultural norms, and shopping bargains among others. Kim noted that because she was new to the U.S. and not fluent in English, the others offered her "good information" about the town, restaurants, and upcoming events. Additionally, Rachel expressed that a major way in which *she* contributed social support toward her neighborhood was by relaying "information, what's going on, and what's coming into the neighborhood."

Other types of information were equally prevalent in

participants' discourse about social support. Mrs. Redbird found support in "just being able to ask people. Get information. Give me advice . . . You know, where to get our car fixed, where do we go to get our driver's license, who's shoveling the driveway, that kind of thing." Katie found social support in being able to look up to older members in the community. She offered this as an example, "I would maybe go and ask 'Hey, I'm doing this report, I'm having some trouble, would you help me?' Because I know Mrs. Redbird is a teacher and that other people are involved in the university." Katie contributed unique information to the group as she was the youngest member, a university student, and a local city employee. She offered important information to the group such as new trash and noise regulations. Each Montrose Woman offered unique information and knowledge to the group from knowing current museum exhibits to changes in neighborhood variances. Information sharing allowed each member to contribute equally to the general group knowledge and enhanced their sense of social support by increasing interdependence and well-being.

Provides Help

The theme "Provides Help" describes *members' beliefs that physical assistance, especially in terms of health and labor, was social support.* With the aid of some minor neighborly help, many of the Montrose Women were able to maintain healthy, active lifestyles while keeping up with their busy work schedules, necessary home repairs, and family obligations.

Health. This sub-theme is composed of *members' expressed beliefs that social support was activated when physical or psychological difficulties/illness made it a burden to carry out regular daily activities and other members offered assistance.* Many examples of this type of social support were given for situations involving surgery, cancer, attempted suicide, depression, broken bones, and abuse. For Mrs. Redbird, the social support she derived from the other Montrose Women served as a turning point in her life after a battle with a serious illness, "I had surgery right before we moved in and it was life changing, but life affirming too, just sharing that with them and really seeing how much they really cared. I mean they were like, they were just so supportive."

The Montrose Women not only offered aid when physical limitations made it difficult for a member to conduct her daily routine, but they also stepped in when they thought a member needed a "reality check," or a break from her everyday routine, in order to heal or cope. Each member took special notice of her direct neighbors, watching for signs of mental/physical distress. The group worked together to keep everyone informed about other's need of support. Nelly narrated the following about a distressed neighbor:

> We were just kind of keeping an eye on [a neighbor] . . . it's not like we spend that much time with each other where we can tell, so you kinda have to rely on each other to let you know if somebody's having an episode, and if it's something we can do as a group . . . [The others] were just very concerned about her, they didn't wanna gossip, but it's just, I mean she needs, she's in trouble, and it was sort of understood that we would keep an eye on her.

Other examples of social support in the arena of health included "long, intense conversations," "providing comfort," and "lending a shoulder" when somebody felt depressed or was enduring especially difficult times. In general, the Montrose Women offered support in the way of physical, and sometimes mental, help for women in need. In order to do so, they found it necessary to stay "tapped" into their community.

Physical Aid. "Physical Aid" consisted of *members' expressions that acts of physical help such as property maintenance and caregiving were social support*. The members indicated a reciprocal norm for help with property maintenance by looking after each other's homes and snow shoveling. For example, Cardie explained that when someone went on holiday she would, "watch [their] house and ask them for the same thing."

The members also spoke about wintertime and the chore of

shoveling snow. Several of the women explained that they were helped or would help others with snow removal. Cardie recalled, "when we had that last snow storm, that nine inch one . . . [Ruthie and her husband] both came over with their shovels and helped me finish the Montrose Lane side. . . . I've enjoyed having that kind of help." Mrs. Redbird also noted lending aid to the others. She explained that if she's shoveling her own yard, she'll "just go through the whole block."

In addition to poor health and inclement weather, the Montrose Women stepped in to provide help when there was a family crisis. For example, Sandy took special care of her widowed neighbor by helping with household chores and offering coffee, desserts, and a place of company and comfort. Recalling a similar instance, Cardie expressed, "it's nice to know that there are people who you can count on." The Montrose Women offered physical help from household chores to carrying one woman's sick mother to a car. All these acts of physical aid contributed to an overall sense of social support and allowed members to live relatively independent lives.

Sustains Independence

The final theme, "Sustains Independence," stems from *members' belief that by accepting their need for some interdependence, they were able to establish boundaries that allowed them to live independently*. Cardie bluntly stated, "we're not running in and out of each other's homes," later admitting that she frequently "has a lot of nice conversations over the fence" where each person was minding the property barriers. Nelly's thoughts coincided with those of Cardie. She stated, "nobody's running in and out of each other's homes, we're not that type." These women maintained privacy barriers by laying out strict territories and using more public spaces for social functions such as their luncheons.

In order for these women to maintain their independence, at times they had to give in to certain amounts of necessary and generally appreciated interdependence. Ruthie described social support as existing "When you're really sort of interdependent with each other, to be relying on each other." The women often spoke about feeling "bonded" to each other, and several even speculated that participating in this study, as well as participating in other neighborhood functions, might lead to even more cohesion. Moreover, they felt they were able to more fully appreciate dependent, active living because of their close, interdependent ties.

Interpretations

As evidenced by the findings above, the Montrose Women benefited from being active members in a multigenerational community. The purpose of this study was to provide a descriptive account of the Montrose Women's use and understanding of social support. We uncovered a total of seven themes describing the uses and benefits of social support for this group. Specifically, their relationships with each other offered a sense of emotional support, the ability to communicate openly, honestly, and directly with various neighborhood members, provided each of them with a strong sense of connection to each other and the larger community, provided members with needed im/material resources and physical/mental aid, and perhaps most significantly, offered all the women, regardless of age, a greater sense of independence and ability to maintain an active lifestyle. In these ways, each woman's life was enriched by the maintenance and formation of supportive multigenerational community ties. By applying theories of aging and social identity to the social support literature, the unique benefits of this community of women can be further explored.

Theories of Aging and Intergenerational Communication

As implied in numerous theories on successful aging, active social relationships and support bonds, such as those among the Montrose Women, are keys to successful aging and life satisfaction (Nussbaum *et al.*, 2000). The older Montrose Women fit Hummert and Nussbaum's (2001) description of healthy aging by demonstrating healthy bodies, minds, and social relationships, much of which the Montrose Women attribute to positive intergenerational relationships.

Activity Theory argues that for successful aging and life satisfaction, communication and social interaction should be maintained as long as possible (Burgess, 1954). For the women in this study, active social bonds were sought after and maintained across generational boundaries making it not only easier for older women to ask for specific types of instrumental support, but for younger members to obtain other forms of less physical support. Similarly, *Continuity Theory* suggests the communication and social interaction patterns enjoyed by a person throughout her lifespan should continue as she ages to increase successful aging and life satisfaction (Field, 1999; Neugarten, Havighurst, & Tobin, 1968). The life satisfaction felt among the Montrose Women is not only a reflection of some member's continued participation in activities such as reading circles and gardening, but also the addition of new activities brought into the lives of the older and younger members.

Finally, the *Selective Optimization with Compensation Model* suggests that as people age and become restricted in some ways, they select and focus their efforts into areas of high priority, such as social interaction (Baltes & Baltes, 1990). For example, individuals who were once engaged in a team sport may transform from participant to spectator due to increased physical limitations. Because of their close intergenerational bonds, the Montrose Women were not restricted in the many activities in which they wished to participate. Some older members enjoyed sharing advice with younger members about activities in which they no longer engaged. While Patty, Cardie, and Rachel spent much of their lives raising and teaching small children, they no longer were in a position to do so. However, some of the younger Montrose Women were balancing motherhood and careers; they relied not only upon the advice from the older women, but also the solitude and support they found in sending their children to visit them. This allowed the older members to care for and spend time with children, while providing a much needed break for younger mothers.

Identity as a Montrose Woman

As suggested by Harwood *et al.* (1995) we employed Social Identity Theory to glean a better understanding of the communication between generations and the formation of a community group. SIT holds that a group seeks to positively differentiate itself from an out-group, in this case the Knox Avenue Women. A primary assumption of SIT is that groups are defined by what they are not; a group only exists if it is in comparison to another group (Tajfel & Turner, 1986). Identity markers such as neighborhood, socio-economic status, and careers are meaningless if there are no other groups present. For example, as the Montrose Women became increasingly aware of the community action on Knox Avenue, they became more cohesive. They began interacting more frequently and behaving like a "club" in an attempt to establish their own neighborhood identity. The more achievements Knox Avenue made, such as entering a group decorated Christmas tree in a local competition, the more achievements Montrose Lane made, such as holding a "Vestal Virgins" or "Xena, Warrior Princess" party. The influence of social identity for the Montrose Women was evidenced in the findings of a strong sense of community and deep desire to enhance and protect their neighborhood.

SIT further suggests that as a result of identity salience and the desire to create a positive distinction from the out-group, greater in-group cohesion and perceived similarity will result. Group cohesion and increased similarity are brought about largely through communicative acts (Giles & Johnson, 1981). For example, their distinct language and open, direct communication helped to create and maintain cohesion and allow for the expression of social support. The Montrose Women had unique nicknames for each other, a self-imposed group name, and they reserved certain types of talk for group members only. Interestingly, it was through the specific topics addressed among group members and specialized language (verbal communication), as well as gestures and gifts (non-verbal communication), that group cohesion and social support was conveyed to members. Not only did the social support function within this group to encourage this type of communication, but it also bestowed upon the women a sense of sincere connection and life enrichment. The formation and maintenance of a distinct social identity for these women has, therefore, led to a mutually supportive group involved in community events.

Social Support in the Multigenerational Community

The Montrose Women held their community in grave importance and saw it as their responsibility to protect and maintain it. The women worked hard to maintain their identity as a "real neighborhood" while protecting it from over-development and welcoming each new and potential resident. Through their community interest and competitive spirit, the Montrose Women became a cohesive unit that served as a social support and friendship network, within which members were able to provide and receive personal support as they mutually assisted one another in various life realms offering emotional help and companionship. Moreover, they were communally supportive by providing a sense of connection to the community and sharing in/tangible resources for the betterment of the neighborhood.

The social support derived from this group was beneficial to the women and to the community as a whole. For example, instrumental support such as physical help and sharing resources afforded members the ability to continue healthy, active lives without disruption. As elsewhere noted, friends and neighbors actually enable people to lead independent lives through their supportive interaction, lessening the necessity of formalized support or institutions (Nussbaum *et al.*, 2000). The emotional support of availability and the pervasive feeling of kindness from one another illustrated deep friendship among the women. This type of relationship encourages healthy aging, as social support derived from friendship is "nonobligatory and egalitarian" (Nussbaum, 1994, p. 213). Interestingly, Ruthie explained that one of the most satisfying aspects of this group was a sense of egalitarianism in all that they did. The relationships among the Montrose Women reflect previous research findings in the area of intergenerational communication and life satisfaction. Nussbaum *et al.* (2000) note that the socially supportive bonds particularly found within a multigenerational community, "provide enough assistance for successful day-to-day living, for a level of independence, and for the maintenance of a positive self-identity" (p. 263).

As the women experienced support from the relationships, they also desired to maintain their independence. For the Montrose Women, there existed a dialectical pull between independence from and dependence on each other. These dialectical tensions are pervasive in all types of relationships (Montgomery & Baxter, 1998). This particular dialectic existed because although members perceived and enjoyed the interdependence of this group, especially in respect to community issues, they also enjoyed independence through respecting privacy and the help of others. This was true for the Montrose Women of all ages, but was especially evident among the older members who often needed more instrumental support than younger women.

Rawlins (1983) suggests that friendships hold the freedom for members to be independent from each other while also remaining dependent upon each other. The management of the dialectical tension between dependence and independence enabled the Montrose Women to sustain their independence while socializing with and relying upon others. Rawlins (1995) also describes a North American preoccupation with "individualism and self-reliance and its simultaneous tendency to underestimate and denigrate the capabilities and initiative of the elderly" which may ultimately result "in many older persons [who] are sensitive about their autonomy and are reluctant to rely on others" (p. 247). Often, elder persons turn to formal organizations when the informal kin or friend relations can no longer assist the person as needed (Nussbaum, 1991). However, the intergenerational relationships forged within this neighborhood offered an alternative to formal institutions by relieving members of some of their daily burdens. In turn, the extra support provided by the Montrose Women also freed immediate friend and kin relations from many of the tedious support tasks allowing them to focus on larger support needs. Finally, the social support available to the Montrose Women may have provided the necessary support to all members that enabled them to command more freedom than they would without such resources.

The different ways social support was given to each Montrose Woman, often depending upon the age of the member, enriched their lives. Although considered a peer-centered society, wherein people prefer to interact with members of their age group (Williams & Nussbaum, 2001), this group preferred multiple generations, where mentoring and living in a lively community were necessary for the sustained quality of life and happiness of these women. The different perspectives of the women from the various age groups brought about completeness, a sense of nurturing and enrichment, for each member.

The observation, "there appears to be very little sustained or meaningful overlap between these [generational] cultures" (Williams & Nussbaum, 2001, p. 36), is challenged, in part, by the findings of this study. Not only did we find the opposite, as expressed by various Montrose Women, but we also found some of the women actually changed their perception of the older neighborhood women through these community interactions. Mrs. Redbird recalled her first luncheon, "At the ladies lunch, I was so surprised, cuz I was thinking . . . 'oh these *old women*,' you know? And there *I* am fuddy-duddy."

Intergenerational relationships are different from many other forms of intergroup connections (Harwood *et al.*, 1995). This is evident in the participants' expressed needs to be involved with the community and established a connection with the Montrose Women. Their relationships filled a need for diversity and perspective in their personal and social lives.

Conclusion

With this study, we have taken a step toward increasing the little available knowledge about intergenerational interaction among persons who are not bound by family ties. We have also spoken of the call for more naturalistic investigations into communities of shared identities and scenes of everyday living (Carbaugh, 1996; Harwood *et al.*, 1995). What we found hints at an optimistic future for naturally developing multigenerational communities. The Montrose Women represent a hopeful community in our generally age-segregated, fast-paced U.S. culture. With little more than a competitive edge and a compassionate nature, the Montrose Women developed a strong multigenerational community of women out of a typical, university-town neighborhood. Reminiscent of traditional neighborhood living, the Montrose Women offer a modern twist on an old fashioned community wherein the women are community leaders as well as professionals, spouses, and mothers.

The findings from this study suggest the unique nature of multigenerational neighborhoods offers layers of social support and points of connectivity beneficial to all members that might not otherwise be afforded. According to Cantor (1980), social support networks enable persons to fulfill three basic needs; socialization, carrying out the tasks of daily living, and personal assistance during times of crisis. The layers of support available in multigenerational communities make fulfillment of those needs from the youngest to the eldest members not only possible, but less constrained. In particular, social support among the Montrose Women offered a sense of emotional support, encouraged open and honest communication, provided them with connection and a sense of community, provided in/tangible resources, provided help, and helped to sustain their personal independence by offering an interdependent community from which they could draw support. Although we established the Montrose Women as a unique group of community-active women, we do not doubt that similar pockets might be found elsewhere in the U.S. It is our hope that investigators in the near future continue this line of community-embedded research among close-knit, non-family groups. The strength in this research lies not only in the findings presented here, but in the possibilities they open for future researchers who wish to build upon these social support and identity findings to develop a more comprehensive understanding of the roles they play in intergenerational relationships.

Acknowledgments

The authors wish to thank Professor Jon Nussbaum for his continued guidance. I also thank my collegiate sister, Amanda Lee Kundrat, who passed away before this chapter is published.

Notes

1. All names and identifying information in this paper have been changed to insure confidentiality.

2. The descriptions of participants we offer here, with the exception of their names, are the way they introduced themselves to us as members of the group. We made every effort to use their own words and self-descriptions throughout this study to ensure presence of the participants' voice.

References

Baltes, P. B., & Baltes, M. M. (1990). Psychological perspectives on successful aging: The model of selective optimization with compensation. In P. B. Baltes & M. M. Baltes (Eds.), *Successful aging: Perspectives from the behavioral sciences* (pp. 1–34). Cambridge, England: Cambridge University Press.

Burgess, E. W. (1954). Social relations, activities, and personal adjustment. *American Journal of Sociology, 56,* 352–360.

Cantor, M. (1980). The informal support system: Its relevance in the lives of the elderly. In E. Borgotta, & N. McCluskey (Eds.), *Aging and society: Current research perspectives* (pp. 131–144). Beverly Hills, CA: Sage.

Carbaugh, D. (1996). *Situating selves: The communication of social identities in American scenes.* New York, NY: State University of New York Press.

Crohan, S. E., & Antonucci, T. C. (1989). Friends as a source of social support in old age. In R. G. Adams, & R. Blieszner (Eds.) *Older adult friendship structure and process* (pp. 129–146). Newbury Park: Sage.

Field, D. (1999). Continuity and change in friendships in advanced old age: Findings from the Berkeley older generation study. *International Journal of Aging and Human Development, 48,* 325–346.

George, L. K. (1989). Stress, social support, and depression over the life-course. In K. S. Markides, & C. L. Cooper (Eds.), *Aging, stress and health* (pp. 241–268). Chichester: John Wiley & Sons.

Giles, H., & Johnson, P. (1981). The role of language in ethnic group relations. In J. C. Turner, & H. Giles (Eds.), *Intergroup behaviour.* Chicago, IL: The University of Chicago Press.

Harwood, J., Giles, H., & Ryan, E. B. (1995). Aging, communication, and intergroup theory: Social identity and intergenerational communication. In J. F. Nussbaum & J. Coupland (Eds.), *Handbook of communication and aging research* (pp. 133–159). Mahwah, NJ: Lawrence Erlbaum Associates.

Hummert, M. L., & Nussbaum, J. F. (2001). *Aging, communication, and health: Linking research and practice for successful aging.* Mahwah, NJ: Lawrence Erlbaum Associates.

Kuehne, V. S. (1998/1999). Building intergenerational communities through research and evaluation. *Generations, 22 (Winter),* 82–86.

Montgomery, B. M., & Baxter, L. A. (1998). *Dialectical approaches to studying personal relationships.* Mahwah, N.J.: Lawrence Erlbaum Associates.

Neugarten, B. L., Havighurst, R. J., & Tobin, S. S. (1968). Personality and patterns of aging. In B. L. Neugarten (Ed.), *Middle age and aging* (pp. 173–177). Chicago, IL: University of Chicago Press.

Nussbaum, J. F. (1983). Relational closeness of elderly interaction: Implications for life satisfaction. *The Western Journal of Communication, 47,* 229–243.

Nussbaum, J. F. (1985). Successful aging: A communication model. *Communication Quarterly, 33,* 262–269.

Nussbaum, J.F. (1991). Communication, language, and the institutional elderly. *Aging and Society, 11,* 149–165.

Nussbaum, J.F. (1994). Friendship in old adulthood. In M.L. Hummert, J.M. Wiemann, & J.F. Nussbaum (Eds.), *Interpersonal communication in older adulthood: Interdisciplinary research* (pp. 209–225). Thousand Oaksica: Sage.

Nussbaum, J. F., Pecchioni, L. L., Robinson, J. D., & Thompson, T. L. (2000). *Communication and aging 2nd edition.* Mahwah, NJ: Lawrence Erlbaum Associates.

Rawlins, W. K. (1983). Negotiating close friendship: The dialectic of conjunctive freedoms. *Human Communication Research, 9,* 255–266.

Rawlins, W. K. (1995). Friendships in later life. In J. F. Nussbaum, & J. Coupland (Eds.), *The handbook of communication and aging research* (pp. 227–258). Mahwah, NJ: Lawrence Erlbaum Associates.

Reis, H. T. (1984). Social interaction and well-being. In S. Duck (Ed.), *Personal relationships. 5: Repairing personal relationships.* New York, NY: Academic Press.

Tajfel, H., & Turner, J. (1986). The social identity theory of intergroup behavior. In S. Worchel & W. Austin (Eds.), *Psychology of intergroup relations* (pp. 7–24). Chicago, IL: Nelson Hall.

Taylor, S. J., & Bogdan, R. (1984). *Introduction to qualitative research methods.* New York, NY: Wiley and Sons.

Williams, A., & Nussbaum, J. F. (2001). *Intergenerational communication across the life span.* Mahwah, NJ: Lawrence Erlbaum Associates.

12

Language, Tourism and Globalization: Mapping New International Identities

Adam JAWORSKI
Crispin THURLOW

From the outset, we would like to establish an understanding of globalization as a dense and fluid network of global *flows* (Appadurai, 1990) and *concentrations* (Smith, 2000) of people, technologies, financial resources, information, news images, and ideologies. Importantly, however, while these flows and concentrations may span the globe, they do not necessarily cover it. Furthermore, such global forces are evidently not neutral but always subject to economic privileges and political agendas.

In this context, and in what Appadurai (1990, 1996) calls "ethnoscapes", one of the widely acknowledged hallmarks of globalization is the mobility (or flow) of people, and especially tourism and travel-by-choice – in stark contrast to other global (though not "new") types of mobility such as forced and economic migrations. In Bauman"s (1998) terms, it is "tourists" rather than the "vagabonds" that we are concerned with – those whose travel is voluntary rather than enforced. Indeed, tourism and traveling elites act as powerful agents *and* channels for the kinds of economic and cultural re-orderings indicated by the label "globalization". In this sense, tourism can be viewed as an identity resource for members of post-industrial, late-modern societies (cf. Giddens, 1991, 1999), although we are less convinced than Giddens that the scale of such cultural effects of globalization transformations necessarily keeps pace with economic and technological globality.

Certainly, and as we suggest in the course of this paper, in the semiotic landscape of tourism, much of what takes the appearance of being global is, more often than not tour operators, tourists and hosts in pursuit of the cachet of globalization and the cash of global capital. Which is not to say that the context and conditions for social life are not shifting and being steadily transformed as a result of the economic and ideological re-orderings of globalism (i.e. global capitalism) and worldwide *interconnectedness* of capital and (mass) communication (Thompson, 2000). At the level of human interaction, however, we are less certain of the kind of interconnectedness invoked by the popular notion of the "global village", which appears to remain more at the level of myth than *universal reality*. In other words, it is aspirational rather than actual, with people commonly talking globalization into existence. Globalization, for us, is a discourse, an ideological construction, or even, as we shall show, an identity resource – all of which runs central to international tourism.

In fact, in these terms, there is a striking complicity and circularity in the relationship between tourism and globalization. A core assumption underpinning the discourses of tourism and globalization is that of the promise of the "global village" and the transformational potential of encounters with the Other. Just as tourists are often encouraged to think that the very act of travel and encountering cultural Other guarantees a broadened horizon and greater intercultural understanding, one of the major premises and justifications of globalization is the assumption of an increased tolerance for diversity and the harmonious integration of peoples (Waters, 1995). As such, while tourism is commonly conceived as a manifestation of globalization, it simultaneously justifies itself in terms of the aspirations of globalization.

As a major service industry in the developed world, tourism too has undergone (and helped perpetuate) the major shift by which service-oriented economies in general render goods more discursively mediated, or increasingly semioticized (Fairclough 1999). Not only does tourism involve face-to-face (or more mediated) forms of visitor-host interaction, like in many other types of service encounters, but the ultimate goods purchased by tourists during their travels are memories and their narrative enactments (de Boton, 2002) – the fantasy and performance of "going native", adventure, meeting new peoples, cultures and sites. Material goods such as souvenirs, artefacts not unlike snippets of language formulae brought back from foreign trips are useful props in the enactment of these performed narratives, and they serve as an extension of the tourist gaze (Urry, 2002) slowly turning into a tourist *haze*.

It is with all this in mind that we offer here a meta-analytic overview of an on-going program of research, in which discourse is presented as both talk in the interpersonal communication of host-tourist interactions, and in terms of the ideologies and organising practices of the tourism industry. Interpersonal communication between tourists and hosts is also invariably mediated at any number of stages of the tourist enterprise (e.g. from reading holiday brochures and watching TV holiday programs to following tour guides and visiting curio shops) and in many different forms (e.g. a hotel-based package or activity holiday to "grassroots" or adventure tours). However fleeting, any face-to-face interaction between hosts and tourists will also vary in frequency, duration and intensity of contact (e.g. from perfunctory service encounters to more involved exchanges).

More specifically, however, it is our intention to start mapping the ecologies of language/s (and discourse) in tourism – their (meta)functions, uses, contexts, speakers, symbolic and economic capital, and so on (cf. Haugen, 1972). In terms of the agenda outlined by Robinson and Giles (2001) for the social psychology of language, our concern is therefore primarily with the *perceptions* and *representations* of language and languages in the context of tourism. As such, and with reference to a select sample of the kind of data which we and our colleagues, Sarah Lawson and Virpi Ylänne-McEwen, have been working with in our broader program of research, what we have been interested to do is consider two general questions:

(a) how does tourism work as a key globalizing industry both in terms of creating a "global culture" and responding to the forces of global capitalism (or globalism)?

(b) what is the role of language(s) in symbolizing and constituting the tourist landscape, and in creating identities for hosts, tourists, and other agents?

In the light of our comments above, we also base our discussion in this chapter on a range of *different* tourisms, locations/sites, patterns of participation, and degrees of mediation of the tourist experience. It is, we believe, precisely these *discourses on the move* which turn people into tourists, understood here as part of what Cronin (2000:1) refers to when discussing tourists as "speaking subjects".[1] To this end, we start by considering the genre of international inflight magazines as a prototypical example of institutionally driven, heavily mediated tourist discourse, before examining the representations of tourist-host interactions in British television holiday programs. We then move on to less mediatized forms of tourism discourse, drawing on extracts from the "communication diaries" of British tourists in the Gambia, and then from our preliminary analyses of interviews with Polish farmers running holiday businesses. As a way of bringing together some of the key themes highlighted in our analyses, we end by discussing examples from British newspaper travelogues.

At each stage in the presentation of these different data, we are looking to illustrate briefly the variety of ways in which we see language and discourse construing global ideologies for tourism on the one hand, and local/national identities for hosts and tourists on the other. Despite these being seemingly contradictory impulses, we argue that they are ultimately complementary manifestations of the *globalist* ideology which underpins the mythologies of both globalization and tourism.

Communicating a Global Reach:
Inflight Magazines

Our first data sample comes from a study of 72 inflight magazines as a genre of tourism writing and one which exemplifies and embodies the idea of global mobility fashioned on the elite jet-setter – a predominantly urban, celebrity-engrossed, brand-conscious community of frequent-flyer cosmopolitans (see Thurlow and Jaworski, 2003). As a genre, inflight magazines are the ultimate global "glossies", not only in terms of ubiquity and uniformity, but also in selling the dream of global citizenship and the world as already globalized. Importantly, and following van Leeuwen's (2002) notion of genre, we also take these texts to powerfully represent and reconstitute familiar areas of social life. As we show, they epitomise the globalization myth and are premised on global capital – or, in other terms, globalism (cf. Held and McGrew, 2000).

It seems that an increasingly important part of the way airlines are able to achieve the kind of competitive brand they require is to position themselves as "global" and to promise their passengers the kudos of being global citizens and travelers. In order to communicate this global reach, the inflight magazines use a range of semiotic resources, including feature articles and advertisement which draw on the metonymic repertoires of "global" cities, celebrities, and brands, as well as the global cachet (or "worldliness" – Pennycook 1994) of English. For the purpose of our analysis here, however, perhaps the most striking, colourful instance of this discursive process is the visual semiotic of the genre-defining route map.[2]

Where imperial Britain once sought to paint the world-map pink, it seems national airlines nowadays look instead to criss-cross them in red, which is predominantly the color of choice for the representation of their flight paths. Airlines must be seen to be "in the world" even if their routes do not actually cover the world; an effect which is often amplified by also depicting the routes of all codeshare partners. What is most striking, however, is how these world maps graphically reveal how the global reach simultaneously depends on, and privileges, the nation state.

Maps are peculiar forms of representation, in that they usually represent the spherical, three-dimensional world drawn into a two dimensional shape such as a rectangle or ellipsis. As Jeremy Black (1997) explains, projections always involve distortions and are always political. For a long time, designs such the 16th century Mercator Projection or the 20th century Robinson Projection have struggled to bring as accurate and/or convincing a representation of the world as possible. What is interesting about both types of these rather familiar projections is that they usually represent the word in the same left-right, top-bottom orientation. The Americas appear on the left, Europe in the top-center position, New Zealand is shown bottom-right, etc. Maps like this have become one of the most hegemonic ways of representing the world – they are, according to Black, the archetypal European projections. Interestingly, and in the style of McArthur's *Universal Corrective Map of the World* (see, for example: <http://www.flourish.org/upsidedownmap/>), inflight magazine maps tend to subvert this typical spatial arrangement of the world invariably (except for most European airlines which are served well by the traditional maps) centering their hub/capital/ nation state.

Following Arnheim (1982), Kress and van Leeuwen (1996) discuss the privileging role of the center in visual images and observe:

> For something to be presented at Center means that it is presented as the nucleus of the information on which all the other elements are in some sense subservient (Kress and van Leeuwen,1996: 206).

As numerous examples in our sample demonstrate, in order to position themselves at the heart of any global network, these so called "flag-carriers" invariably center their capital-city as the hub of a vivid network of routes spanning out across the globe, not unlike the 14th century *Mappa Mundi* positioned Jerusalem as the center of the universe.

In sum, the maps in inflight magazines position themselves as global or globalist, but as one of the bearers of their nations' identity, their globalism is premised on the centrality of the nation in the world. Thus, they introduce an ambivalence of being rooted in the nation and surpassing, or obliterating the national boundaries.

(Inter)national Travel:
Television Holiday Programs

Perpetuating the notion of international travel as elite is the use of "celebrity" presenter in (British) holiday travel programs (see Jaworski, Thurlow *et al.*, 2003; Jaworski, Ylänne-McEwen *et al.*, 2003) – our second "discourse on the move". Significantly, we think, the presenters in these holiday programs are cast in a kind of two-fold tourist role: both as tourists in their own right (thus "presenter-tourist") and as role-models or proxies for "viewer-tourists" – in this sense, they serve as a kind of Every Tourist or "tourist-tourist". As such, whilst these programs constitute heavily mediated representations of tourism, we nonetheless take them to be indicative of, and promoting, some of the dominant discourses of tourism and actual or everyday tourism practices in Britain. Through participating in various holiday activities, the presenters' main allegiance is to the viewers, not hosts, and everything we see them doing in these programs, including conversing in host languages (especially when these are different than English), is geared towards creating involvement with the viewers, in part by demonstrating what a tourist can expect from or do on a holiday. We can explain better what we mean by this with reference to just two extracts.

The first extract typifies the central role-dynamic of tourists as consumers of the exotic and hosts as friendly servants and helpers. Notably, in this instance, the host language is also presented as a commodity and a prop in the staging of touristic authenticity.

Extract 1

Holiday 2001, BBC1, 30 January 2001
CD = presenter Craig Doyle;
M = Massimo, the shopkeeper in Siena, Italy.

1   CD: (voiceover) the Italians are passionate about food and no one more so than Massimo one of Siena's larger than life grocers

2   M: grande grande=
           large large

3   CD: =grande
           large

4   M: questo è pesto pesto genovese (.) guarda (picks up a packet of pasta)
           this is pesto pesto from Genoa (.) look
           [

5   CD: si si pesto fresh tomatoes si (voiceover) so I need these as well yeah (picks up a tray of blackberries)
           yes yes pesto

6   M: avanti
           let's go on

7   CD: oh yeah

8   M: tomatoes dried si chiamano ciliegini
           (shows CD some dried tomatoes)
           they're called cherry tomatoes

9   CD: (points over M's shoulder) look at that out there (pops a tomato in his mouth with a look of mock guilt-cum-innocence)
           [

     M: (looks away briefly)

10 CD: grazie grazie (.) (CD pays)
           thank you thank you

11 M: a posto cosi
           anything else?

12   CD: ciche ciche cento

13   M: no (.) ciche ciche ciu (.) ciao a presto (shakes hands
            with CD)
            [
            bye see you soon
14   CD: ciao grazie
            bye thank you
15   (walks out of shop; voiceover) thank you Massimo

This extract shows a service encounter framed (by the presenter at least) as a playful, phatic exchange. Massimo is thereby cast as an amusing caricature of a typical Italian who is "passionate about food" (line 1). In this extract, like in many others we and our colleagues have studied, a host language is used/exploited as a key resource for imagining a community of (international) tourists whereby code-crossing (Rampton 1995) i.e. stylized use of a language (or variety) of a group which the speaker cannot legitimately claim membership of (in this case the tourist using Italian) signals the encounter as play, in which the ordinary ways of behavior, including language use, are suspended (lines 3, 5, 10, 12). Here, the use of Italian – sometimes (deliberately) incorrect (see line 12) – for a predominantly non-Italian speaking TV audience therefore signals flirting with the idea of being Italian, a momentary performance of Italianness, allowing (and encouraging) the presenter-tourist and the viewer-tourist to remain firmly rooted in their national identification as "British".

The second of our two extracts briefly demonstrates this argument even more explicitly, by including not only the presenter-tourist's use of a "foreign" language, but also a typical instance of in-grouping/out-grouping through a metacommentary which pointedly draws viewers' attention to the idea that host languages (other than English) are "incomprehensible".

Extract 2

Wish You Were Here, ITV, 22 January 2001
LR = Lisa Riley in Spain

  1 LR: (voiceover) there's more to Marbella than sun glitz
  2   and glamour (.) take a short stroll up from the main
  3   street and you'll find the old town (2.0) this beautiful
  4   quarter is centerd around the Plaza de Naranjos
  5   (camera on sign) Orange Square to you and me

This extract exemplifies not only a brief moment of verbal (line 4) and visual (line 5) crossing into the host language, but also the presenter's strategic orientation to the viewers. First, LR offers a reinterpretation of the "foreign" as "familiar" through her translation (however inaccurate) of the place name into English (line 5), and secondly she introduces an instance of "othering" by an explicit positioning of herself and the viewers against local people through the inclusive pronominal reference "you and me" (line 5). In this respect, the presenters in both Extracts 1 and 2 are seen to rely on linguistic and discursive resources to align, and affirm, themselves and their viewers as "fellow nationals". It is in this respect that the ethos of international travel is seen again to be predicated on processes of national-linguistic identification.

One-way Global Flow: British Tourists in The Gambia

The adherence to the underpinning national identity of (international) tourists and their hosts is equally strongly manifested in other research in our collaborative program which focuses on West Africa, mainly The Gambia.

    The Gambia, with its approximate population of 1.3 million inhabitants, is a major, principally winter, sun-sea-sand tourist destination in West Africa, attracting around 80-90,000, mostly British, tourists per year. One of the most striking features of The Gambia as a "winter sun" package tourist destination is the pervasiveness of interaction between tourists and members of the local community. On leaving their hotels, tourists are met by (generally) young local people offering to show them around, take them bird-watching or to other tourist attractions. A major tourist activity is visiting craft markets to look at and sometimes buy local crafts, negotiating with the stall holder the while. Strolling along the beach, the tourist is also met by young people wanting to chat and accompany them on their walk. Clearly, all of these encounters need to be treated predominantly as a type of service transactions. Local people, even those described commonly as "bumsters", or unofficial guides, who may approach tourists and offer what seems like a social encounter, do that as part of their "trade" counting on some kind of material reward from the tourist.

Lawson and Jaworski (forthcoming) analyse 194 tourist-host interactions as recorded in "communication diaries" kept by British visitors to The Gambia. The participants were 20 British tourism lecturers and students on a study tour in the Gambia (Spring 2002). One of the more obvious characteristics with which to analyse these interactions is "topic types". These have been categorised as follows (percentages indicate the frequency of their occurrence):

1. Tourist-oriented personal information (20 percent): e.g. hosts' questions about tourists' place of origin/residence, occupation, family;
2. Services/goods for sale (19.8 percent): e.g. buying/selling goods at the craft market, beach/street stalls;
3. Host-oriented personal information (19 percent): e.g. tourists' questions about hosts' place of origin/residence, occupation, family;
4. Tourist experience of The Gambia (8.3 percent): e.g. how long the tourist has been in The Gambia, whether it is her/his first visit;
5. Greeting (7.8 percent): more or less elaborate exchanges of greeting formulae;

6. Culture & customs (7.4 percent): hosts explaining The Gambia to the tourists;
7. Request for friendship (7 percent): e.g. hosts asking tourists to "keep in touch", to exchange addresses, to receive an invitation to the UK;
8. Other (10.6 percent).

What is apparent in the above list of topic types is that most of them are phatic (1, 3, 4, 5, 7) rather than transactional (2) or referential (6). When we examine the qualitative comments made by the participants in their diaries about the sorts of phatic exchanges they had, it also transpires that the types of contrasts between tourists and hosts are predominantly of the type "British"/"English" – "Gambian" (less frequently "European" – "African"). Consider just a couple of reflections of tourist-host interaction expressed by some of the participants:

Extract 3

Communication Diary 7, Female, 22 years old (original spelling and punctuation)

People are surprisingly friendly and are very proud of where they're from. Very family-oriented people + express genuine interest of my own family life, Britain, Uni etc.

Despite my preconceptions of Gambia being unsafe at night etc, once I got to know how the people really behave, I never felt threatened – only irritated by endless bumsters.

Extract 4

Communication Diary 18, Female, 22 years old (original spelling and punctuation)

Never thought it would be so difficult to have a conversation. Most of the men are only interested in either our address or being special friend. At the markets the conversations were all one sided as tried not to talk to people as people just wanted our money and not interested in a conversation. The beach + hotel people are very friendly and usually interested to talk about England, our homes and their work + life here. However the conversations always end up with the men asking for our addresses. It makes the conversations boring as everyone you speak to you have to repeat yourself to every man you meet. Its very difficult not to be rude, as after a day of talking about same thing it gets a little boring

What we see in most of these interactions is some kind of rooting of shared information or establishing interpersonal relations on the re-affirmed individual identities of the tourists and hosts as "British" (or more commonly "English") or "Gambian", respectively. What is also apparent from the research participants' communication diaries is that hosts' orientation to the tourists is often underwritten by a certain reciprocity, expressed most clearly in their desire to visit the UK. Although the Gambian hosts (most notably the unofficial guides known as "bumsters") seem to buy into the common ideology of globalization through what is defined here as "requests for friendship", implying extended contact culminating in visiting the UK, these visits rarely, if ever, materialize. In this way, we suggest, the notion of the "global village" holds sway over the tourists and hosts, but only in their mutual engagement in the discourse. It is a (shared) aspiration rather than a practical reality.

The interactions between Gambian hosts and British tourists reported in the diaries are also invariably conducted through English. As is typical of so much "international" tourism, this suggests an accommodating orientation of hosts towards tourists; even if English continues to be a reminder of colonial subjugation, nowadays it appears to be a useful *instrument* attracting a specific group of tourists-clients (see Lawson, in preparation). Through these encounters, Gambian hosts further display their knowledge of the "world beyond" through references to English cities, football clubs, and occasional (sometimes fabricated) friends and family members residing in those cities. This is done in a way which is reminiscent of Thompson's (2000) notion of "social distancing", whereby people conceive of, and are influenced by, images and ideologies from geographically far-flung places without actually being able to take part in the lives of the people who produce these images and ideologies.

In terms of tourist-host relations, The Gambia, not unlike most other tourist destinations in the world, is marketed as a "friendly" place. Indeed, our data suggest that having overcome initial prejudices in meeting the local other, the tourists can derive much pleasure and "positive" intercultural experience from their encounters with local people. It is also clear that hosts benefit economically from the tourists' purchases of goods, services and offers of drinks and food. What we want to argue here, however, is that the obvious economic and socio-political asymmetries between British tourists and Gambian hosts, inevitably preclude these fleeting encounters from becoming lasting *friendships* based on symmetry and reciprocity. Probably even more than the mediated representations of tourist-host interactions in television holiday programs discussed above, the actual interactions between these two groups (at least in The Gambia case) exemplify the shared ideology of globalization despite the actual *flow* of people being sustained and sustainable in one direction: from the rich north to the poor south, with the participants predominantly juxtaposed in terms of their national identities: the British/English vs. Gambians.

Thinking global, Acting Local:
Polish Agritourists in Poland

In the first phase of a research project on the interaction between Polish farmers engaged in rural tourism, or agritourism, and their visitors, a series of interviews have been conducted which seek hosts' representations of their relations and communication with tourists (see Jaworski and Lawson, in press). The interviews took place in different locations in western Poland in 2001 and 2002, identified from an information guide to agritourism farms designed predominantly for the Polish market.[3] In contrast to The Gambia, Polish holiday farms present an image and experience of tourism which runs counter to the more familiar stereotype of international, sun-all-year-round mass tourism. In particular the holiday farms offer a style of tourism based on mass flows of people from *within* national boundaries. In both cases, however, what we would argue is that the tourist experience is underpinned by the implicit relations of movement around the globe – only in this case, through its predominant *absence*. For example, in the following indicative extract, the type of tourists most frequently visiting the farms are successfully defined against the absent "foreign" tourists. (All the interviews were conducted in Polish. The Polish originals and their English translations are reproduced here using standard orthography.)

Extract 5

AJ = interviewer; AD = farmer/tourism operator.

1 AJ: A skąd przyjeżdżają w większości goście?

2 AD: Z miasta.

3 AJ: A z miast których?

4 AD: No z miast. Poznań, no to w tej chwili już z Warszawy mieliśmy gości z Łodzi i z Bydgoszczy. Także już coraz szerszy, szerzej ta reklama się rozchodzi także już już coraz więcej gości, no ale przeważnie przez te pierwsze dwa lata to Poznań.

5 AJ: A czy mają państwo jakichś zagranicznych turystów?

6 AD: To znaczy się tak, mamy jednego pana, to znaczy to jest Polak, który mieszka w Niemczech. Był marynarzem, bo w ogóle Kapitan Żeglugi Wielkiej. Bardzo fajny pan, był ze swoim Bosmanem Belą, taki pies (laughs) bokserka

1	AJ:	Where do most of your visitors come from?

1   AJ: Where do most of your visitors come from?

2   AD: From towns.

3   AJ: Which towns?

4   AD: Well, towns, like now we've had visitors from Warsaw, from Łódz and Bydgoszcz, so that as our publicity spreads, so we get more and more visitors, but or the past two years it's been mostly [visitors from] Poznań.

5   AJ: And do you have any foreign tourists?

6   AD: Well we do have one gentleman. I mean it's a Pole who lives in Germany. He was a seafarer, indeed a Captain. He is a very nice man. He was here with his Bosun Bela the dog (laughs) a boxer

Indicated in Extract 5 above, is a recurring theme in these interviews identifying most tourists as "locals", perceived consistently by the hosts as "same" across different criteria, most notably their Polishness, defined through the geographical proximity of nearby large towns and industrial regions in Poland.

In noticeable contrast with our other research sites and texts, host-tourist interactions in these farms are often represented as reciprocal, enduring encounters between "people like us". This is demonstrated most clearly in the case of "returning" tourists as in the following extract.

Extract 6

AJ = interviewer; AD1 = farmer/tourist operator.

1   AJ: A jak jest z gośćmi, którzy wracają? Czy to oni już wracają jako znajomi?

2   AD: Tak, tak. Jako [że] utrzymujemy kontakty. Kartki świateczne to już obowiązkowo, a jeżeli nie kartka to ten telefon, co jakiś czas a jak tam zdrowie i to i tamto także utrzymujemy kontakty z gośćmi, którzy oczywiście chcą.

1   AJ: And what's it like with returning visitors? Do they
          return as friends?

2   AD: Yes, yes, we keep in touch. Christmas cards are
          obligatory, and if not cards, then a phone call from
          time to time, how's your health and this and that. Of
          course, we [only] keep in touch with the visitors who
          want that.

As the respondent in this second extract indicates, contacts with
"returning" tourists extend well beyond the time of the holiday on
the farm. Although she stresses her desire not to impose on the
tourists, extended contact is clearly maintained when mutually
desired. This, we contend, is afforded by the perceived *sameness* of
tourists and hosts due to their shared national, ethnic and linguistic
background.

What we have here, then, is an instance of highly localized
action, where the primary distinction between hosts and tourists lies
between "town" and "country" (Extract 5, line 2). This distinction,
however, is not posited so much in terms of contrast and difference
but rather as two types of locales which complement each other in
what is perceived "our" territory. Even the sole "foreign" visitor to
the farm in Extract 4 is more of a "local", sharing the same ethnic
and linguistic background as his farmer-hosts.

International tourists are conspicuous by their absence in the
case of this particular farm, but the discourse which describes
tourists as "locals" and "friends" is, in our view, still premised on
more general ideologies of tourism identified as global flows of
internationals. Communication with the visitors is unproblematic
and may extend well beyond the short period of the farm holiday
but it is not inter-national communication as described in The
Gambia example above, but intra-national communication based on
the understanding of "all of us" being members of the "same"
national community.

Centering the National:
Newspaper Travelogues

The last set of our data examples comes from a selection of 15 issues of British broadsheet newspaper travel sections, focusing on instances where the authors, traveling journalists, refer to their actual or hypothetical encounters with hosts in travel destinations. Not unlike the TV holiday programs, these encounters are heavily mediatized, staged, and occasionally fictionalized, while also being (re)presented as generic forms of contact: what the implied "reader-tourist" can expect in a particular destination. The mentions, uses and representations of interactions and languages in the travelogues display a whole array of global-local forms of mobility as well as the kinds of tourist identities implied in the interactions with hosts. Across the travelogues we have looked at, what we also find is a strong tendency to simultaneously exoticize the international while also rendering it familiar in relation to recognisable national signifiers (see also Galasiński and Jaworski, 2003).

Extract 7

Sunday Times Travel, 10 February 2002
Richard Green. Malta: On the cheap. p. 8.

> The locals are a friendly, tolerant lot and save you struggling with Malti (the unique blend of Arabic, Italian and Spanish) by speaking excellent English. They also drive on the left, use bright-red post-boxes and seem know to London as a Camden cabbie.

This first extract states implicitly the expectation of British travel writers for hosts anywhere in the world to speak English (well). This is especially welcomed in destinations where English is a second or foreign language, and, as in Malta (or The Gambia, cf. above) it comes with the promise of not only linguistic familiarity

(English being an official language in Malta), but also other cultural indicators of shared background (driving on the left, red post-boxes, orientation to a common capital city – London). It is in this context that the British traveler may enjoy the surrounding exoticity, epitomised through the reference to "Malti (the unique blend of Arabic, Italian and Spanish)", yet remain firmly "British".

Extract 8

The Guardian Travel, February 3, 2001
Patricia Fenn. Raiding the larder. pp. 10–11.

> Mantua deserves more than a few hours to explore the town's treasures and the 16th century Palazzo del Te, an imposing country house on the outskirts. For us, the visit was spoiled by gaggles of schoolchildren. Italians are noisy by nature and so are children. Combine the two and bedlam reigns. We shall just have to go back at a quieter time. (p. 11)

On the other hand, the value of host languages (other than English) lies not so much in their usefulness as means of communication, but in their symbolic/metonymic representation of the foreignness of the destination. In this sense, language fulfills a similar role to the use of foreign accents in English-language adverts which Cronin (2000: 6) notes offer the "exotic thrill of difference without the discomfort of incomprehension". In the case of Extract 8, this is taken a step further in that the content of hosts' talk is regarded as semantically and pragmatically irrelevant. It all becomes "gaggle" and "noise". To us, this is "crossing-in-reverse" (see p. 305 above). In other words, tourists here are seeking a language which they do not belong to, to create for themselves a distant but tangible sense of a transient identity as an *inter*-national. This is in contrast to Extract 1 in which the TV presenter-tourist engages in an act of crossing by attempting a few playful phrases of Italian.

Discussion:
Mapping "New Internationalisms"

In tying together our discussion of these five illustrative data sets, and as a way of concluding, we would like to highlight what we regard as the central, meta-analytic theme to have emerged. To begin, we considered how the unifying genre of inflight magazines (with their huge investment in international English) constructs the cosmopolitan, global jet-setter as transcending national boundaries. In fact, we could argue that there would be no cosmopolitan traveler, if there were no national boundaries to cross in the first place. As such, and with reference to the frequent claims of globalization, we find ourselves in agreement with Hannerz (1996: 90) who continues to view the nation as an important point of reference for the construction of individual and group subjectivities.

From a sociolinguistic viewpoint, and returning to our analysis here, host-tourist interaction which entails tourists *crossing* to the language of the host community, or hosts *switching* to the post-colonial language of their former master-tourists, further reinforces this orientation to the national as a default in tourist self- and other-identification. Tourists doing crossing merely stylize themselves as hosts in playful moments of liminal/liminoid (Turner, 1969, 1974) suspension of their *true* (or technical) national identities. Meanwhile, bumsters on the beach in The Gambia buy into the myth of global citizenship through the discourse of their *desire* of travel to the UK. In doing so, they too stylize themselves in similar ways – through their use of English, which is of course part of their post-colonial legacy, but especially through their displays of cultural references to English football, weather, geography, and so on, yet knowing that, with few exceptions, the asymmetry of economic globalism does not allow them to shrug off their national identity as "Gambians" and will not transform and transport them into the "British".

National identities are also re-confirmed and maintained in more localized forms of mobility where hosts and locals view themselves and their language varieties as "same" – as in the case of Polish agritourism. Hosts and tourists participate in the co-construction of a shared, albeit imagined national identity (cf. Anderson 1983) in the newly discovered friendships of like-minded peers through a *shared local* language. In this sense, therefore, the contemporary appeal of national identity may be regarded not only in terms of a reactionary, defensive response to fears and anxieties about the "runaway world" of globalization (Giddens, 1999). The nation (and national identity) is instead *re-imagined* as a means of experiencing and expressing the international and the "global".

In fact, in dismissing some of the exaggerated claims of, or anxieties about, globalization, Smith (2000:180) notes that the "greatest obstacle" to the emergence of any putative "global culture" is the persistence of modern and even pre-modern myths and sentiments. From what we have begun to see in the different data examples we discuss here, the tenacity of national identity is apparent. While tourism may promote an aura of globe-trotting and tourists (and local people) aspire to jet-setter lifestyles, nationality still has a strong hold on subjectivities, offering an important point of reference. In this way, and just as Smith (2000) talks about the nationalization of pre-modern ethnicities from the 19th century onwards, there appears to be a globalization of nationality – putting a "global" spin on traditional, modernist constructs such a nation-state and class.

It is precisely for this reason also that, just as Rampton (1995) argues for linguistic crossing to create new "inter-ethnicites", we propose that tourist crossing – both linguistic and territorial – creates "new internationalisms" which entail tourists playing with global identities but not fully embracing them (cf. Extract 1, "si si pesto fresh tomatoes si") and exploiting the double standard of dealing with the exotic in the familiar semiotic landscape (cf. Extract 7, hosts speak English, drive on the left, share a colonial history, etc.). While the popular notion of the "international jet-setter" is a largely modernist construct relying as it does on earlier discourses of the nation state and elite, privileged travel, it is precisely this "ideal" to which new internationals, as mass tourists, aspire through the mediated, consumerist discourses of glossy magazines, celebrity-oriented TV holiday programs, etc. In fact, we would further argue that appeals to global citizenship are fundamental to the ideology of globalism and the mythology of globalization; nevertheless, it is an image and identity which remains rooted in structuring processes of national identification.

> Nation is a discursive product that is perpetually marketed back to its own people and to other nations. Nation thus continues to function as a defining, unifying, reinforcing, reassuring socio-political and cultural resource of extraordinary importance [. . .].
> (Lull, 2001: 15-16)

In the context of globalization, much is often made of communications, not enough, we believe, is made of interactions. And yet, in many respects, host-tourist interactions and identities embody the essence of globalizing processes in that it is precisely at this level which the global and the (national) local interface, are negotiated and resolved – be it through processes of cultural absorption, appropriation, recognition, acceptance or rejection. As we hope we have begun to show, herein lies the most obvious potential for linguistic and discursive analysis; for it is through the alignment of micro-level, interactional moments and macro-level, structuring forces that scholars of language and communication can make their strongest contributions to more critical, complex understandings of the experiences, changes *and* identities commonly invoked by the term globalization.

Acknowledgments

We would like to thank our colleagues, Sarah Lawson and Virpi Ylänne-McEwen, for their ongoing collaboration which in part informs our analyses here. We also thank Nik Coupland for his useful and detailed comments, and we are grateful to Alison Phipps, Jan Blommaert and the editors of this volume for their ideas.

The research for this paper was supported by funding from the Leverhulme Trust (Grant No. F/00 407/D) to the Centre for Language and Communication Research, Cardiff University, for a larger project on Language and Global Communication (http://www.global.cf.ac.uk/index.asp).

Notes:

1. Cronin (2000:1–6) is concerned to promote the often neglected role of language in the construction of traveling (or tourist) identities; for him, travel is always a verbal event.

2. Route maps were found in all but two of the magazines in our data-set. For colour reproductions of some of these maps, please visit the following website, entering the username "guest" and the password "maps": http://faculty.washington.edu/thurlow/maps/

3. The two extracts cited below come from one interview conducted on 24 April 2001.

Referencec

Anderson, B. (1983). *Imagined Communities: Reflections on the Origin and Spread of Nationalism*. London: Verso.

Appadurai, A. (1996). *Modernity at Large: Cultural Dimensions of Globalization*. Minneapolis, MN: University of Minnesota Press.

Appadurai, A. (1990). Disjuncture and difference in the global cultural economy. *Theory, Culture and Society* 7, 295–310.

Arnheim, R. (1982). *The Power of the Centre*. Berkeley and Los Angeles: University of California Press.

Bauman, Z. (1998). *Globalization: The Human Consequences*. Cambridge: Polity.

Black, J. (1997). *Maps and Politics*. Chicago: Chicago University Press.

Cronin, M. (2000). *Across the Lines: Travel, Language, Translation.* Cork, Ireland: Cork University Press.

de Boton, A. (2002). *The Art of Travel.* London: Hamish Hamilton.

Fairclough, N. (1999). Global capitalism and critical awareness of language. *Language Awareness 8,* 71–83.

Galasiński, D. & Jaworski, A. (in press). Representations of hosts in travel writing: *The Guardian* Travel section. *Journal of Tourism and Cultural Change* 1.

Giddens, A. (1991). *Modernity and Self-identity: Self and Society in the Late Modern Age.* Cambridge: Polity.

Giddens, A. (1999). *The Runaway World: The Reith Lectures Revisited.* Available (19/06/01) at <http://www.lse.ac.uk/Giddens/pdf/10–Nov–99.pdf>.

Hannerz, U. (1996). *Transnational Connections: Culture, People, Places.* London: Routledge.

Haugen, E. (1972). *The Ecology of Language: Essays by Einar Haugen* [Selected and introduced by Anwar S. Dil.]. Stanford, CA: Stanford University Press.

Held, D. & McGrew, A. (2000). The great globalization debate: An introduction. In D. Held & A. McGrew (Eds.), *The global transformations reader: An introduction to the globalization debate* (pp. 1–45). Cambridge: Polity Press.

Jaworski, A. & Lawson, S. (in press). Discourses of Polish agritourism: Global, local and pragmatic. In A. Jaworski & A. Pritchard (Eds.) *Tourism, language and communication.* Clevedon: Channel View Publications.

Jaworski, A., Thurlow, C. Lawson, S. & Ylänne-McEwen, V. (2003). The uses and representations of local languages in tourist destinations: A view from British television holiday programmes. *Language Awareness 12,* 5–29.

Jaworski, A., Ylänne-McEwen, V. Thurlow, C. & Lawson, S. (2003). Social roles and negotiation of status in host-tourist interaction: A view from British television holiday programmes. *Journal of Sociolinguistics* 7, 135–163.

Kress, G. & van Leeuwen, T. (1996). *Reading images: The grammar of visual design.* London: Routledge.

Lawson, S. (in preparation). Postcolonial patterns of language use in global tourism.

Lawson, S. & Jaworski, A. (forthcoming). Shopping and chatting: Tourist-host interaction in The Gambia.

Lull, J. (Ed.) (2001). *Culture in the communication age.* New York: Routledge.

Pennycook, A. (1994). *The cultural politics of English as an international language*. Harlow: Longman.

Rampton, B. (1995). *Crossing: Language and ethnicity among adolescents*. London: Longman.

Robinson, P. and Giles, H. (Eds.). (2001). *The new handbook of language and social psychology*. Chichester: John Wiley & Sons.

Smith, A. D. (2000). Towards a global culture? In D. Held and A. McGrew (Eds.), *The global transformations reader: An introduction to the globalization debate* (pp. 239–247. Cambridge: Polity Press.

Thompson, J. B. (2000). The globalization of communication. In D. Held and A. McGrew (Eds.), *The global transformations reader: An introduction to the globalization debate* (pp. 202–215). Cambridge: Polity Press.

Thurlow, C. & Jaworski, A. (2003). Communicating a global reach: Inflight magazines as a globalizing genre in tourism. *Journal of Sociolinguistics 7*, 579–626.

Thurlow, C., A. Jaworski & V. Ylänne-McEwen. (in press). "Half-hearted tokens of transparent love": "Ethnic postcards and the visual mediation of host-tourist communication. *Tourism, Culture and Communication*.

Turner, V. (1969). *The ritual process: Structure and anti-structure*. Chicago: Aldine.

Turner, V. (1974) *Dramas, fields, and metaphors: Symbolic action in human society*. Ithaca: Cornell University Press.

Urry, J. (2002). *The tourist gaze*. 2nd edition. London: Sage.

Van Leeuwen, T. (2002). Genre and field in critical discourse analysis. In M. Toolan (Ed.), *Critical discourse analysis: Critical concepts in linguistics* (pp. 166–199). London: Routledge. [originally published in 1993].

Waters, M. (1995). *Globalization*. London: Routledge.

Section IV

Communicating Culture and Identity

in Natural Social Settings

13

Creating Caregiver Identity: The Role of Communication Problems Associated with Dementia

Marie Y. SAVUNDRANAYAGAM
Mary Lee HUMMERT

Dementia is a devastating disorder, affecting approximately 7.4 million people in developed countries around the world. Prevalence rates for dementia increase drastically from 1.4 percent for those in the 65–69 age group to 23.6 percent for those 85 years and above (Jorm, Korten, & Henderson, 1987). Cognitive deficits and memory impairments often characterize the dementias, including Alzheimer's disease (AD), disrupting abilities to complete the simplest activities of daily living. Moreover, the presence of mood and personality changes, including depression, confusion, agitation and paranoia, pose difficulties for symptom management (Davies, 1988). One of the most noticeable declines in persons with dementia is in their communicative competence (Burgio, Allen-Burge, Stevens, Davis, & Marson, 2000; Orange, 1991). These changes have a profound impact on family caregivers, with more than 80 percent reporting high levels of stress or burden (Alzheimer's Association and National Alliance for Caregiving, 2000). Moreover, family members are the source of care most preferred by older adults (Biegel & Blum, 1990). Eighty-nine percent of AD caregivers are relatives (Alzheimer's Association and the National Alliance for Caregiving, 2000), and most are female (Ory, Hoffman, Yee, Tennstedt & Schulz, 1999). The Family Caregiver Alliance (2000) reported that 33 percent of caregivers are wives and 29 percent are daughters.

In this chapter we explore how AD-related communication problems may contribute to caregiver stress by changing the nature of the relationships between caregivers and care-recipients. As we will show, the kinds of changes in language abilities that characterize AD make it difficult for family members to maintain their spousal or filial identities. The resulting disorientation of long-term, central identities may be a critical factor in caregivers' subjective experience of stress, and that stress may be resolved only by a redefinition of familial identities as caregiving identities. In the sections that follow we first describe the kinds of communication problems that accompany AD, illustrate how those problems can create identity challenges for family caregivers, and examine the ways in which identity processes could both contribute to and help ease caregiver stress. We conclude with consideration of directions for future research.

Dementia as a Communication Disorder

Declines in communicative competence are one of the most salient impairments associated with dementia. Communication problems affect various levels of language processing, with phonological and syntactic levels relatively spared, and pragmatic and semantic problems being the most noticeable (Appell, Kertesz, & Fishman, 1982; Hamilton, 1994; Hier, Hagenlocker, & Shindler, 1985; Kempler, 1991). Semantics involve the study of language content, specifically attaching meaning to word and phrases (Boone & Plante, 1993; Emery, 2000). Pragmatics includes the study of language use in context. It considers interpersonal communication beyond the word and sentence levels. It is concerned with how language is adapted to the situation (Boone & Plante, 1993). Semantics and pragmatics are not independent levels of language processing but work together in enabling communication.

Semantic Problems

In the early to middle stages of dementia, problems associated with semantic memory include anomia (word-finding difficulties), naming difficulties, semantic comprehension, and semantic paraphasia (choosing wrong words). Confrontation naming tasks, such as the Boston Naming Test where participants are asked to name line-drawn pictures, are often used to assess word-finding problems. Generally, in such tasks, persons with dementia may give a related name, indicating they understand the meaning but cannot find the target word (Bayles & Tomoeda, 1983; Kempler, 1988). In the following excerpt, Sabat (2001) offers a clear example of naming and word-finding difficulties common to those with dementia: "And, and I was looking for an article about, you know who was it that failed to get the – he, he wasn't, he, you know, his wife – he has a wonderful wife, was a wonderful nife, and he was, but he was um, doing, he ran for the privy" (p. 33).

In the middle to late stages of dementia, semantic problems include empty speech, neologisms, and loss of verbal fluency. In a longitudinal study of conversations with a person with dementia, Hamilton (1994) reported the use of semantically related words to maintain verbal fluency. However, as the disease progressed, the AD participant used more semantically unrelated words, empty words and created her own idiosyncratic words. Breakdown of the semantic system is observed through the overuse of deictic terms, such as "here" and "there". These terms indicate person, place or time, but in the case of AD, the referent is difficult to trace (Bayles & Kaszniak, 1987; Ulatowska *et al.*, 1988). Persons with AD use vague terms such as "thing" and pronouns frequently with no obvious referent. Utalowska *et al.* (1988) provide the following excerpt illustrating these types of semantic problems (p. 131):

> Well, first thing, *it's* – it's high enough that – that I couldn't reach *it* from the floor,
>
> But I do have a beautiful stand at the end of the bed and –
>
> And I have on this stand – I have a red velvet that I – my wife loves me to put it on the bed, and so we put that – It's folded up so I have to take this red velvet off of the bed – off of the stand and put it on the bed.
>
> Then I step up on that stand and then I can reach up and – and unscrew the *thing* from the glass.
>
> Now I did one in the kitchen and *it* had a *thing* that long.
>
> *It* was in a case like, so I don't know whether *this* would be the same or not.

In this excerpt, the person with dementia consistently uses indefinite references (i.e. "it", "thing" and "this"), making it difficult to decipher the referent. The overuse of vague terms and incomplete terms (such as "red velvet") make it difficult to understand what persons with dementia are trying to communicate.

Losses in verbal fluency are also prevalent in middle stages of dementia. Several studies have used narrative tasks to compare the verbal fluency of persons with dementia and normal controls (Hier *et al.*, 1985; Ripich & Terrell, 1988; Shekim & LaPointe, 1984; Ulatowska *et al.*, 1988). Such tasks are useful for understanding how semantic problems affect day-to-day communication because they place semantic problems in the context of naturally occurring language. For example, Shekim and LaPointe (1984) elicited a variety of narratives, such as telling memorable stories, procedural discourse and picture story descriptions. They found that in comparison to normal controls, participants with dementia had more incomplete utterances and more unattached sentence fragments that did not constitute a communication unit.

Pragmatic Problems

As mentioned earlier, semantic and pragmatic levels of language processing are not independent. The semantic problems, which are generally on the word and sentence level, do not underlie but contribute to pragmatic communication problems, which are concerned with language use in social contexts (Kempler, 1991). In early stages of dementia, pragmatic problems include talking too much at inappropriate times, digressing from the topic of a conversation, and repeating ideas (Ehrlich, 1994; Kempler, 1991; Powell, Hale, & Bayer, 1995).

In a study where dementia participants were asked to talk about a memorable experience, they made a significant number of irrelevant propositions categorized as digressions and redundant repetitions (Ulatowska *et al.*, 1988). Digressions and repetitions reflect a person's inability to remain focused and may be indicative of a person's inability to monitor the relationship between previous utterances and the current one. For instance, persons with dementia may repeatedly ask the same question, tell the same story a number of times, or have difficulty maintaining a conversation without prompts from the conversational partner. The following dialogue between a person with dementia (T) and the researcher (V) shows T's repetition of her husband's job and busy lifestyle, as well as the pauses that disrupt the continuity of the conversation (Ramanathan, 1997, p. 57):

V: tell me about your marriage Tina?
T: oh, I've oh my husband works for the
    Industrial Relations,
    For Cal Tech Industrial Relations,
    And ah he's a busy busy guy [laughs]
    [*pause*]
V: How did you meet him?
T: I met him with some friends and ah ah [*pause*]
    we got to talking about things,
    and we just sort of escalated.
V: how old were you?
T: oh I was not a youngster at that particular point in time,
    but he is always very busy,
    he works for Cal Tech.

Repetitions are particularly important because they are one of the more noticeable and disturbing communication behaviors that are reported by family caregivers in the early stages of dementia (Bayles & Tomoeda, 1991) and worsen as the disease progresses (Bourgeois, Burgio, Schulz, Beach, & Palmer, 1997; Hamilton, 1994).

As the disease progresses, persons with dementia have difficulty maintaining conversations and are ambiguous about what they are referring to in conversations (Nicholas, Obler, Albert, & Helm-Estabrooks, 1985; Mentis, Briggs-Whittaker, & Gramigna, 1995; Ripich & Terrell, 1988). Some pragmatic problems could be due to problems associated with attention and encoding of new information. During conversations, inappropriate topic changes, and breakdowns in cohesion and coherence are common (Ripich, 1994). This may occur as a result of attentional problems. If information is not attended to, it will not be encoded. Ramanathan (1997) offers an example of a conversation in which the person with dementia (T) suddenly becomes incoherent. In this excerpt, the person with dementia who was talking about her husband suddenly shifts topics to something that is not in line with her previous comments (i.e., "and then it's you hop up. . . . oh good") (p. 58):

and my husband is very busy
and ahm ah sometimes away a lot [*pause*] from home.
but tt it was something that you do,
and then it's you hop up and say hey look here I am,
I'm already coming up [*pause*]
did you drop somebody?
oh good [*pause*]

Other pragmatic problems may be due to poor sensitivity to social contexts and partners. Examples include using embarrassing words (e.g. swearing), speaking too loudly and talking at inappropriate times (Bayles & Kaszniak, 1987; Santro Pietro & Ostuni, 1997). In some cases of dementia, there is a tendency for blunt, insulting and accusatory comments. Mace and Rabins (1981) report that such behavior may be due to an inability to judge who the social partner is or lack of awareness of the social situation. For example, when a friend brings dinner, the person with dementia may make accusatory statements such as, "Get out of my house, you're trying to poison us" (Mace & Rabins, 1981, p. 107). They also report that when persons with dementia shout excessively, it may be because the situation overwhelms their cognitive ability. For example, when asked to perform an activity of daily living, such as bathing, persons with dementia may resist by shouting and arguing because the task involves a series of procedures including unbuttoning, finding the bathroom, turning on the faucets, etc.

Garcia and Joanette (1994) examined topic shifting in conversations with normal controls and participants with dementia. They found that there were more topic shifts in conversations with participants with dementia but that the social partner made those shifts because the AD participants had trouble elaborating on the topic. Hutchinson and Jensen (1980), on the other hand, found that participants with dementia initiated more new topics but did so inappropriately and also made more utterances with indeterminable intent. Ulatowska *et al.* (1988) obtained similar results on tasks that required participants with dementia and normal controls to summarize a story. The participants with dementia produced more irrelevant information than normal controls, suggesting a difficulty differentiating between useful and trivial information.

The literature has reported a general reduction in the information provided by persons with dementia during conversations (Ulatowska & Chapman, 1991; Ulatowska *et al.* 1988). On picture description tasks, persons with dementia produced fewer relevant observations, more aborted phrases and incomplete propositions compared to normal controls (Bayles, Tomoeda & Rein, 1996; Hier *et al.*, 1985; Ulatowska *et al.*, 1988). In the following excerpt, the person with dementia (E) failed to elaborate on the initial topic (the "kinds of jobs" he had) and instead, began another story (his boat trip to England), which was irrelevant to the initial question (Ramanathan, 1997, p. 68):

V: what kinds of jobs did you have?
E: well, I was I was essentially a teacher all my life,
V: mm
E: I uh uh I was a teacher in high school in Chicago,
      high school and uh I enjoyed that,
      Then I went to college, University of Chicago.
      and uh I was not married,
      Uh-huh I finally found out I had a chance to go to England
        on a boat,
      that had just come,
      in in a freighter that had been unloaded.

The excerpt also includes occasions with incomplete sentences, where E moved from topic to topic ("and uh I was not married, Uh–huh I finally found out I had a chance to go to England on a boat"). Hier *et al.* (1985) suggested that these problems occurred because persons with dementia do not recognize the need to complete the sentence, which reflects a pragmatic issue. Bayles *et al.* (1996), however, contend that these problems may be due to memory deficits; that is, they may simply forget what was said earlier and therefore see no need to continue. This reflects a semantic issue. Both explanations are plausible, illustrating the interrelationship between the pragmatic and semantic levels of language processing.

Impact of AD Communication Changes on Family Caregivers

The gradual breakdown in communicative ability restricts the level and quality of interaction between persons with dementia and their caregivers. Given the multitude of communicative impairments, caring for an individual with dementia can be a very difficult endeavor for a family caregiver (Poulshock & Deimling, 1984). As political and social policy agendas shift towards deinstitutionalization, primarily as a means of cost-containment in long-term care, more and more family members find themselves in the role of caregiver (Montgomery, Stull, & Borgatta, 1985; Ory & Dunker, 1992).

The relational dynamics associated with caregiving within a family makes these caregivers a unique group with many common concerns. The family context tends to include feelings of obligation, duty, affection and personal responsibility. As a result, most family members want to retain their caregiving role and postpone institutionalization as long as possible (Mittleman, Ferris, Shulman, Steinberg, & Levin, 1996), and therefore caregiving often becomes a career (Aneshensel, Pearlin, Mullan, Zarit, & Whitlach, 1995; Montgomery & Kosloski, 2000; Pearlin, 1992).

AD Communication Changes as Challenges to Familial Identity Maintenance

Interpersonal communication has been defined as including at least two communicators (Brochner, 1989) who through their interactions create shared meanings (Wood, 1999). Communication is reliant upon mutual awareness, an element that deteriorates for care-recipients and their family caregivers as the disease progresses. The impact of this deterioration in mutuality is particularly salient in the marital relationship. In a qualitative study of how wives of institutionalized husbands with AD managed contradictions in their marital relationship, Baxter, Braithwaite, Golish, & Olson (2002) noted that caregiving wives did all the communicative work because of their commitment to maintain some sort of relationship. Dealing with their husbands' dementia was stressful, so much so that they had to redefine their marital relationship in terms of the contradiction between their husband's physical presence and cognitive/emotional absence. One wife remarked, "he's not my husband anymore . . . I feel very little closeness to him...there's no closeness, no intimacy . . . he doesn't know I'm his wife. He knows me but he doesn't know I'm his wife. He talks to me about his wife"(p.10). This quotation illustrates how communication problems fail to reinforce the norms (i.e., closeness, intimacy, shared meaning) of a spousal relationship.

Communication is integral to a dyadic relationship because it allows for reciprocity. Reciprocity requires that each member of a dyad participates in the maintenance and transformation of the other's identity; as long as each member relates to the other according to expectations of the dyadic relationship, identity is maintained (Orona, 1990). Research on relationship quality has focused on the degree of reciprocity between caregivers and care-recipients (Chesla, Martinson, & Muwases, 1994; Walker, Pratt, & Oppy, 1992). Caregivers who considered their relationship with their family member with dementia to be discontinuous indicated no sense of reciprocity between themselves and the care-recipient (Chesla *et al.*, 1994). While there was no direct measure of communication problems, the implication is that lack of reciprocity may be an indication of increases in communication problems.

Elements of a marital relationship such as companionship, emotional support, shared responsibilities and decision-making, are lost as a result of the disease process. All these elements require communication. In a multi-national qualitative study on spousal caregiving across Europe, Murray, Schneider, Banerjee, & Mann (1999) reported that loss of understanding and conversation were the most difficult aspects of dementia because of the loss of companionship and reciprocity in the marital relationship. One caregiver in the Netherlands remarked, "He is not the man he once was. You lose your husband. When I come home now, full of stories, I don't tell them. It takes such a long time to explain. His language is seriously affected, understanding as well as saying things" (p. 664).

Shared memories play an important role in the continuity of relationships and in identity maintenance. The communication problems associated with AD result in a loss of reciprocal validation for the caregiver and the relationship becomes more unilateral. The caregiver loses a partner who was once able to validate his/her past. In a qualitative study on how loss of identity in a person with AD is perceived by family caregivers, Orona (1990) reported that when reciprocity in the relationship was no longer a possibility, caregivers lost part of their self-identity. Once invested in a relationship, the caregiver worked to save the relationship and its history. However, as the caregiving role consumed most of their lives and as ordinary chores took more time, the caregiver's familial identity deteriorated.

Communication is also an indication of social support, which contributes to relationship quality. Wright and Aquilino (1998) examined the degree of emotional support exchanged between ill husbands and their caregiving wives. The husbands had a variety of conditions, with Alzheimer's disease being the most common. The study asked caregiving wives to list persons in their social networks. While most included their ill husbands, 17 percent did not include them because of their husband's disability level. The marital relationship of caregiving wives of persons with Alzheimer's disease was characterized by lack of social support. Comments such as "because he is no longer my husband as such, and I am his caregiver," reflect a change in the wives' identities (p. 197). None of the spousal AD caregivers in another study (Wright, 1993) mentioned their afflicted spouses when asked to report who they went to for comfort and help. The marital relationship, which was once a primary source of comfort and companionship, undergoes a striking change, as caregivers seek support elsewhere. Wright and Aquilino (1998) also included a sample of non-caregiving wives and found that although there was no overall difference in the amount of social support/exchange, the impact of social support/exchange was greater for caregiving wives than non-caregiving wives. This implies that feedback becomes more important in situations with a growing lack of reciprocity. It also provides some evidence that finding ways to maintain and manage communication in persons with dementia is important to marital satisfaction of caregiving wives.

As noted above, feedback is crucial to the maintenance of the familial relationship and to the well-being of caregivers. Not receiving any meaningful feedback or receiving negative feedback (usually in the form of problem behaviors such as agitation) becomes increasingly frustrating for caregivers because their efforts are not positively reinforced. The following comment illustrates how exasperating it is for caregivers when they receive no feedback, "Sometimes I find it difficult when he is home that he sits there not talking. I have to do the talking, but it's like to the wall. I don't get anything back" (Small, Geldart, & Gutman, 2000, p. 297). The notion of not "getting anything back" is a common theme among caregivers who feel burdened.

It is just as distressing when caregivers receive feedback that appears to be meaningless and/or simply annoying. Repetitive behaviors have often been cited as highly noticeable. The following account provides a vivid picture of the stress associated with repetitive statements:

> The basic challenge is trying to be patient because he asks me questions repeatedly. We can go over the same thing over and over and over. In our marriage, when we had an issue that had to be worked, well, we would work it out. But now it's all undone an hour later or the next day. And we have to go through the same issue again, and sometimes I get angry with him. Yet, I know he can't help it, but I get tired (Kuhn, 1998, p. 193).

This excerpt shows that although the spouse acknowledges the changes in the quality of her relationship with the care-recipient, she still finds these communication problems difficult to handle on a constant basis.

However, there are other caregivers who appear to adapt to the situation and receive rewards from their experiences. Caregivers simplified their interactions with care-recipients as a means of adapting to the communication problems. One caregiver asserted, "I cannot confide in him anymore. It upsets him, and he couldn't understand. We talk about simple things – what to wear, what day it is, what time it is. I have been exhausted by his repeated questions" (Wright, 1993, p. 49). Small talk and superficial conversations were strategies caregivers used to maintain the feeling that a relationship exists and were also used to prevent the occurrence of any topics that would invoke problem behaviors (Baxter *et al.*, 2002).

Caregiving rewards were experienced when caregivers' efforts appeared to be appreciated by their relatives with dementia because any sign of appreciation was a reinforcement of the familial role and past relationship (Murray *et al.*, 1999). In order to retain their initial familial relationship, some spousal caregivers increased their interpretative work when interacting with care-recipients (Baxter *et al.*, 2002). Caregiving wives would over-interpret their husbands' moments of lucidity as certainty that they were communicating meaningfully. In effect, these spousal caregivers were attempting to create a cognitive/emotional response on behalf of their husbands and also used this strategy to differentiate the person from the disease.

For caregivers, the familial relationship does not end even as the disease progresses. Instead, it is greatly diminished while the caregiving relationship takes on a larger role. In a longitudinal study following persons with dementia and their caregivers before symptom onset to 18 months after diagnosis, Blieszner and Shifflett (1990) found lower levels of intimacy as the disease progressed. While the importance of the relationship remained stable 6 months after diagnosis, there was a sharp decline in confiding, enjoying time with the care-recipient, and relationship satisfaction, all of which indicate a loss in the initial familial relationship. The researchers termed the relationship between caregivers and care-recipients as "nonexistent but nonterminal" (p. 61), reflecting the idea that while the familial relationship does not technically end, it does change dramatically. Similar concepts alluding to this contradiction include, "lost but not gone" (Morgan & March, 1992, p. 566) and married widowhood (Rollins, Waterman, & Esmay, 1985). The following caregiver's reactions to the relationship loss poignantly highlight the deterioration of familial relationship, "I now know what it is like to be lonely. It's a good preparation (for widowhood)" (Wright, 1993, p. 53). Coping strategies family members employed to deal with the contradiction of having a nonexistent but nonterminal relationship included redefining the relationship, working on closure within the relationship, and changing their role identity from family member to caregiver (Blieszner & Shifflett, 1990). In doing so, caregivers redefined expectations for that relationship.

Thus far, we have shown that caregiving does not occur in isolation. It occurs within the historical context of past relationships between caregivers and their relatives and the caregiving role emerges out of this past familial relationship (Aneshensel *et al.*, 1995; Horowitz & Shindelman, 1983; Montgomery & Kosloski, 2000). What makes the caregiving situation with persons with dementia difficult is that while care-recipients are there in person, communicative declines make it challenging for them to interact as they did prior to the illness. As family members continue with caregiving and as care demands become more custodial, the nature of the relationship shifts from spouse or adult-child to "care-giver" (Montgomery & Kosloski, 2003).

Caregiver Stress: Impact of Communication Problems and Problem Behaviors

We have discussed how dementia-related communication changes put a strain on the relationship between family caregivers and care-recipients. It is the change in the nature of the familial relationship that causes caregiver stress. In addition to problems with communication, persons with dementia may exhibit behaviors that are viewed as problematic by their caregivers. Examples of such behaviors include wandering, incontinence, agitation, restlessness, inappropriate sexual behavior, etc. Some communication behaviors have also been classified as problematic behaviors, e.g., swearing, and repeating questions or stories. Some research suggests that communication difficulties may not only constitute problem behaviors, but also may trigger them (Burgio *et al.*, 2000; Rau, 1993; Vitaliano, Young, Russo, Romano, & Magana-Amoto, 1993). As the care-recipient's communication abilities decline, there are more opportunities for miscommunication and frustration on the part of both the caregiver and care-recipient. With their limited communication skills, care-recipients may respond to such communication breakdowns with problem behaviors (e.g., yelling, aggression, or agitation). Comments such as, "I cannot have a conversation with him. He cannot understand me and gets angry" reflect the consequences of communication breakdown for both the caregiver and care-recipient (Murray *et al.*, 1999, p. 664). The root of problem behaviors such as agitation, disruptive vocalizations, and lack of cooperation may be due to difficulties understanding verbal directions, difficulties finding words to express feelings/intent (Bourgeois, 2002) or inability to retrieve words to explain the need to engage in activities (Volicer & Bloom-Charette, 1999).

Problem behaviors have consistently and strongly predicted caregiver stress, commonly measured as caregiver burden (Coen *et al.*, 1997; Deimling & Bass, 1986; George & Gwyther, 1986; Kosberg, Cairl, & Keller, 1990; Talkington-Boyer & Snyder, 1994; Williamson & Schultz, 1993). Earlier, we described the various communication changes associated with dementia. Qualitative and descriptive studies presented reports of caregiver distress due to dementia-related communicative declines (Bourgeois *et al.*, 1997; Orange, 1991). Unlike those studies, we used quantitative measures to examine the relationship between communication problems, problem behaviors and caregiver burden (Savundranayagam, Hummert, & Montgomery, 2003). A communication problems scale, with semantic and pragmatic items, was developed and administered to 89 participants, along with measures of care-recipient status, problem behaviors and caregiver burden. Using structural equation modeling, the results revealed that care-recipient status predicted semantic and pragmatic problems but the direct effect of status on semantic problems was much stronger than the effect on pragmatic problems. Moreover, both semantic and pragmatic communication problems predicted problem behaviors, which in turn predicted caregiver burden. The indirect effects of pragmatic problems on caregiver burden were stronger than those of semantic problems. This finding adds support to research suggesting that communication problems may trigger problem behaviors (Burgio *et al.*, 2000) and that problem behaviors predict or are strongly related to burden (George & Gwyther, 1986; Kosberg *et al.*, 1990).

The fact that pragmatic problems had a stronger impact on burden than semantic problems confirms prior research suggesting that caregivers may find pragmatic problems more disturbing than semantic ones (Bourgeois *et al.*, 1997; Orange, 1991). Word-finding difficulties are one of the most common semantic problems described by family caregivers (Bayles & Tomoeda, 1991; Rabins, Mace, & Lucas, 1982), including the participants in our study. One explanation for the finding that semantic problems were weaker indirect predictors of burden is that word-finding difficulties are not only stereotypes associated with normal aging, but also tend to be viewed as a typical characteristic of dementia (Ryan, 1991). The latter was evident in the strong relationship between care-recipient status and semantic problems. Pragmatic problems, on the other hand, go beyond the word and sentence level to appropriate behavior in social contexts. For instance, repetitive questions have been reported to be distressing and frustrating to caregivers (Bourgeois *et al.*, 1997; Kuhn, 1998). When pragmatic problems are coupled with problem behaviors, caregivers may not feel that they can take a break or take advantage of respite opportunities. Consequently, caregivers may become housebound because they are afraid to take their relative out in public. Caregivers may gradually limit their interactions with others, becoming more and more isolated.

Development of Caregiver Identity

For family members of persons with dementia, caregiving is not simply about performing care tasks. It is an all-consuming, dynamic process that is an expression of their commitment to the well-being of their family members (Pearlin, Mullan, Semple, & Skaff, 1990). As such, the caregiver role emerges from the established familial role (i.e. spouse or adult-child) and caregivers perform the role in a manner that is consistent with expectations of the familial role (Montgomery & Kosloski, 2000). Because the caregiving role emerges from an established familial role, early in the career family members often perform care tasks without interpreting them as being any different from the familial role (Aneshensel *et al.*, 1995). The transition into the caregiving role is ambiguous because it does not have a discrete demarcation as in parenthood, for instance, where the role transition begins with the birth of a child (Seltzer & Li, 1996). The following is a discussion on the development of a caregiver identity, within the framework of the caregiving career.

While researchers agree that caregiving is a career, there are distinctions in the way the career is described. Aneshensel *et al.* (1995) presented a broad description of the career, with three components: role acquisition, role enactment and role disengagement. Role acquisition was described as performing care tasks while not noticing the growing lack of reciprocity within the familial relationship. Role enactment involved being a caregiver not only at home but after placing a loved one in a nursing facility. Role disengagement occurred most often when the family member passed away, however for a few caregivers, it involved leaving the caregiving to other family members or to nursing home staff. The disengagement process is often accompanied by a reengagement with one's self and other role-identities.

Aneshensel *et al.*'s (1995) conception of the caregiving career accounts for the continuity and diversity of the caregiving process but because of its broad nature, it does not offer a description of markers that signal change within the career. Information about such markers can be instrumental in the development of interventions that can ease transitions within the career. Montgomery and Kosloski (2000; 2003) provided a more detailed description of the phases within the career and markers that identify each phase. Implicit in the perspective on the caregiving career by Aneshensel *et al.* (1995) is the notion of "caregiver" as a role identity. Montgomery and Kosloski (2003) built upon this notion by proposing a theoretical evolution of the caregiver role as part of one's identity. In general, there is a gradual growth in the in the caregiving role as the caregiving career progresses. However, as was the case in the disengagement component of Aneshensel *et al.*'s model (1995), the latter phases of the career involve the regaining of the familial role and other role identities (Montgomery & Kosloski, 2003).

Each phase of the caregiving career begins with a marker that highlights a transition. The first marker occurs when the caregiver begins to perform care tasks associated with the care-recipient's increased dependency. However, the caregiver is not aware of tasks as caregiver tasks but simply views them as part of the fulfilling the obligations of a familial role. The second marker occurs when caregivers acknowledge care tasks as being beyond the familial role, and identify themselves as "caregivers". Montgomery and Kosloski (2000) suggested that self-definition as caregiver occurs sooner for adult-child caregivers than spousal caregivers because providing care for a parent in a dependency situation is a dramatic role shift. On the other hand, because of the shared responsibility involved in a spousal relationship, performing some care tasks may not be such a dramatic shift for spouses.

Marker three occurs when the care-recipient's needs increase in quantity and intensity, and when caregivers begin to perform personal care tasks, such as bathing or feeding their family member. This marker further accentuates the dramatic shift in the familial relationship for adult-children. Consequently, some adult children exit the caregiving role by considering placing their parent in a nursing facility or having less involvement as caregivers (Aneshensel *et al.*, 1995). For spousal caregivers, this marker makes the shift in the spousal role relationship more salient and either occurs at the same time as, or soon after, self-definition as caregiver. At this point, the caregiver role becomes an increasingly more dominant part in the caregiver's identity.

Marker four occurs when caregivers first consider placing their relative in an alternative living situation. The length of any phase is dependent upon the nature of the existing familial relationship and the level of commitment associated with that relationship. For adult children, this phase can be relatively short but for spouses it can be an extended amount of time. The caregiver role takes on a larger part of the caregiver's identity. Marker five occurs when the caregiver places the care-recipient in a nursing facility. Placing the family member in a nursing facility can be a means to restore the original familial relationship. Montgomery and Kosloski (2003) argue that placement is an opportunity to shift the caregiver's primary identity back to the initial familial role. Finally, marker six occurs when family members exit the caregiver role. In the case of dementia, this marker would occur either with the death of the care-recipient or when the caregiver terminates that role.

Caregiver Stress and Identity Change: Understanding the Link

Many researchers have argued that stress is a subjective response that is more likely an outcome of life events or situations that are closely related to one's identity than other events (Burke, 1991; Pearlin *et al.*, 1990; Thoits, 1991). In the context of caregiving, stress results from an involuntary transformation of a relationship that is closely tied to one's identity (Pearlin, 1983). The involuntary nature of this relationship transformation is a result of the cognitive and functional declines, problem behaviors, and communication difficulties associated with the disease process.

To explain the link between stress and identity change, Montgomery and Kosloski (2003) presented a model of the identity maintenance process for caregivers. Based on the work of Burke (1991), this model views identity not as a trait but as a continuous process with a set of standards that are applied to self in a social role (Burke & Tully, 1977). The identity maintenance process begins with an identity standard, which is closely linked with the familial role, particularly at the beginning of the caregiving career. The identity standard guides the caregiver's behavior, which includes the performance of care tasks and how he/she relates to the care-recipient. In turn, the caregiver's behavior influences the caregiving context, which includes the care-recipient, other family members, and/or formal caregivers. Those in the caregiving context provide feedback, which in turn, contributes to the caregiver's self-appraisal. Self-appraisal refers to the perception of self in a certain role. In other words, self-appraisal is a role-specific self-evaluation (Skaff, Pearlin, & Mullan, 1996). Caregivers evaluate how well they responded to the challenge of caregiving.

The next and arguably most important part of the identity maintenance process for caregivers is the comparison process, where the caregiver's self-appraisal is compared with the initial identity standard. The goal of the identity maintenance process is to maintain homeostasis by matching one's identity standard with self-appraisal (Burke, 1991). If self-appraisal is congruent with the initial identity standard, there are no disruptions in the caregiver's identity and no changes in the caregiving career. If the identity standard and the self-appraisal are incongruent, the caregiver will experience some stress, which will lead the caregiver to adjust behavior to be more consistent with the caregiver's current role. When there are large and persistent inconsistencies between self-appraisal and the identity standard, the caregiver feels pressure to change identity or reject the caregiver role (Montgomery & Kosloski, 2003).

The process of obtaining a match between self-appraisal and the identity standard involves negotiations with those who are part of the caregiving context. One source of stress comes from those who are part of the caregiving context. Recall that the caregiving context includes the care-recipient, other family members, and/or formal caregivers. As the disease progresses, the care-recipient's needs increase. Gradually, the familial relationship between the caregiver and care-recipient is transformed into a caregiving relationship. As the care tasks become increasingly inconsistent with the expectations of a familial relationship, a shift occurs in the caregiver's role identity. When the caregiving context provides feedback that is incongruent with the caregiver's identity standard, the result is stress. In the case of a care-recipient with dementia, the feedback necessary to maintain the identity standard is not always offered because of communication problems associated with the disease. In addition, persons with dementia may provide negative feedback to caregivers, particularly when communication breakdowns give rise to problem behaviors. For instance, accusatory comments such as calling the caregiver an imposter have a negative impact on the caregiver's self-appraisal. Therefore, the combination of lack of feedback and negative comments from care-recipients serve as unfavorable reflections (or evaluations) of care-givers' performance. Consequently, caregivers may experience stress because their identity standard is not reinforced by the care-recipient.

According to the identity maintenance process, to re-establish congruency between self-appraisal and identity standard, the caregiver makes a change in the initial identity standard. For instance, if the caregiver's initial identity standard was primarily a familial role, such as wife, and the care tasks are not reflective of that familial role, then the caregiver experiences stress/burden. To address the stress and maintain homeostasis within the identity maintenance process, the caregiver would incorporate more of the caregiving role into her identity standard. Montgomery and Kosloski (2003) argued that high levels of stress generally precede changes to one's identity standard. High stress levels also coincide with markers that signal a new phase in the caregiving career. If, however, the identity standard is primarily comprised of the caregiver role and care tasks are reflective of that role, then the caregiver experiences rewards (satisfaction with caregiving). In this case, the caregiver would be coping relatively well and low/moderate stress levels would occur within each phase of the career. Thus, the caregiving role involves the continual process of adjusting and readjusting to interactions with the care-recipient and also adjusting the caregivers' perceptions of themselves and their responses to changes in the care-recipient (Quayhagen & Quayhagen, 1996).

Directions for Future Research

In this chapter, we argued that dementia could be characterized as a communication disorder. As such, dementia-related communication changes put a strain on relationship quality and play a pivotal role in the gradual deterioration of the familial identity. We also presented a theory on the stress process for caregivers (Montgomery and Kosloski, 2003). Caregiver stress results from discrepancies between self-appraisal and one's identity standard. Simply put, when a caregiver's familial identity is persistently challenged, the result is stress.

Our discussion of how communication problems negatively affect the maintenance of familial identities focused largely on qualitative research. Relationship quality has been investigated using communication as one component of quality, along with other components such as closeness, having similar views, and getting along (Lawrence, Tennstedt, & Assmann, 1998). However, the communication component consisted of a single item, which is not as informative as examining how the types of communication problems (semantic versus pragmatic) that could affect relationship quality and familial identities. Future research should capitalize on the opportunity to empirically test the identity maintenance process for caregivers. Specifically, future research should investigate the effects of communication problems (and other stressors such a problem behaviors) on caregivers' self-appraisal, examining how communication problems contribute to discrepancies between their self-appraisal and identity standard.

What causes stress is different in each phase of the caregiving career because of the gradual emergence of the caregiver identity over the course of the career. The same variables operate differently in each phase. Future research should consider stages of the caregiving career in which communication problems are most likely to be an issue. This is particularly important because knowing critical stages of the career that cause the most relationship strain can offer guidance in terms of timing of communication interventions.

As mentioned earlier, the goal of research on family caregiving is to preserve the relationship between caregivers and care-recipients. Communication plays a critical role in relationship maintenance. Understanding how dementia-related communication changes interact with other stressors to challenge a caregiver's familial identity will provide opportunities not only to create the necessary support services for caregivers, but also intervene at the most critical phases of the career.

Acknowledgment

Preparation of this chapter was supported by U.S. National Institute on Aging/National Institutes of health 16352 to the second author.

References

Alzheimer's Association and National Alliance for Caregiving (2000). *Who cares? Families caring for persons with Alzheimer's disease.* Bethseda, MD: National Alliance for Caregiving.

Aneshensel, C. S., Pearlin, L. I., Mullan, J. T., Zarit, S. H., & Whitlach, C. J. (1995). *Profiles in caregiving: The unexpected career.* San Diego, CA: Academic Press.

Appell, J., Kertesz, A., & Fishman, M. (1982). A study of language functioning in Alzheimer patients. *Brain and Language, 17,* 73–91.

Baxter, L. A., Braithwaite, D. O., Golish, T. D., & Olson, L. N. (2002). Contradictions of interaction for wives with elderly husbands with adult dementia. *Journal of Applied Communication Research, 30*(1), 1–26.

Bayles K. A., & Kaszniak A. W. (1987). *Communication and cognition in normal aging and dementia.* Boston, MA: Little Brown & Co.

Bayles, K. A., & Tomoeda, C. K. (1983). Confrontation naming impairment in dementia. *Brain and Language, 19,* 98–112.

Bayles, K. A., & Tomoeda, C. K. (1991). Caregiver report of prevalence and appearance order of linguistic symptoms in Alzheimer's patient. *The Gerontologist, 31(2),* 210–216.

Bayles, K. A., Tomoeda, C. K., & Rein, J. A. (1996). Phrase repetition in Alzheimer's disease: Effect of meaning and length. *Brain and Language, 54*(2), 246–261.

Biegel, D., & Blum, A. (1990). *Aging and caregiving: Theory, research, and policy*. Newbury Park, CA: Sage.

Blieszner, R., & Shifflett, P. A. (1990). The effects of Alzheimer's disease on close relationships between patients and caregivers. *Family Relations, 39,* 57–62.

Boone, D. R., & Plante, E. (1993). *Human communication and its disorders.* New Jersey: Prentice-Hall.

Bourgeois, M. S. (2002). Where is my wife and when am I going home? The challenge of communicating with persons with dementia. *Alzheimer's Care Quarterly, 3*(2),132–143.

Bourgeois, M. S., Burgio, L.D., Schulz, R., Beach, S., & Palmer, B. (1997). Modifying repetitive verbalizations of community dwelling patients with AD. *The Gerontologist, 37,* 30–39.

Brochner, A. P. (1989). Interpersonal communication. In E. Barnouw, G. Gerbner, W. Schramm, T. L. Worth, & L. Gross (Eds.), *International encyclopedia of communication* (pp. 336–340). New York: Oxford University Press.

Burgio, L., Allen-Burge, R., Stevens, A., Davis, L., & Marson, D. (2000). Caring for Alzheimer's Disease patients: Issues of verbal communication and social interaction. In J. M. Clair & R. M. Allman (Eds.), *The gerontological prism: Developing interdisciplinary bridges* (pp. 231–258). Amityville, NY: Baywood.

Burke, P. J. (1991). Identity processes and social stress. *American Sociological Review, 56,* 836–849.

Burke, P. J., & Tully, J. (1977). The measurement of role/identity. *Social Forces, 55,* 880–897.

Chesla, C., Martinson, I., & Muwaswes, M. (1994). Continuities and discontinuities in family members' relationships with Alzheimer's patients. *Family Relations, 43,* 3–9.

Coen, R. F., Swanwick, G. R. J., O'Boyle, C. A., & Coakley, D. (1997). Behavior disturbance and other predictors of carer burden in Alzheimer's disease. *International Journal of Geriatric Psychiatry, 12,* 331–336.

Davies, P. (1988). Alzheimer's disease and related disorders: an overview. In M. K. Aronson (Ed.), *Understanding Alzheimer's disease* (pp. 3–14). New York: Scribner's.

Deimling, G. T., & Bass, D. M. (1986). Symptoms of mental impairment among elderly adults and their effects on family caregivers. *Journal of Gerontology, 41,* 778–784.

Ehrlich, J. S. (1994). Studies of discourse production in adults with Alzheimer's disease. In R. L. Bloom, L. K. Obler, S. De Santi, & J. S. Ehrlich (Eds.), *Discourse analysis and applications: Studies in adult clinical populations* (pp. 149–160). Hillsdale, N J: Lawrence Erlbaum.

Emery, V. O. B. (2000). Language impairment in dementia of the Alzheimer type: A hierarchical decline? *International Journal of Psychiatry in Medicine, 30*(2), 145–164.

Family Caregiver Alliance (2000). *Who are the caregivers?* Retrieved December 10, 2000, from http://www.caregiver.org

Garcia, L. J., & Joanette, Y. (1994). Conversational topic-shifting analysis in dementia. In R. L. Bloom, L. K. Obler, S. De Santi, & J. S. Ehrlich (Eds.), *Discourse analysis and applications: Studies in adult clinical populations* (pp. 161–183). Hillsdale, N J: Lawrence Erlbaum.

George, L. K., & Gwyther, L. P. (1986). Caregiver well-being: A multidimensional examination of family caregivers of demented adults. *The Gerontologist, 26*, 248–52.

Hamilton, H. (1994). *Conversations with an Alzheimer's patient.* Cambridge, England: Cambridge University Press.

Hier, D. B., Hagenlocker, K., & Shindler, A. G. (1985). Language disintegration in dementia: Effects of etiology and severity. *Brain and Language, 28*, 235–249.

Horowitz, A., & Shindelman, L. W. (1983). Reciprocity and affection: Past influences on current caregiving. *Journal of Gerontological Social Work, 5*(3), 5–20.

Hutchinson, J. M., & Jensen, M. A. (1980). A pragmatic evaluation of discourse communication in normal and senile elderly in a nursing home. In L. Obler & M. Albert (Eds.), *Language and communication in the elderly* (pp. 59–74). Lexington, MA: D. C. Heath.

Jorm, A. F., Korten, A. E., & Henderson, A. S. (1987). The prevalence of dementia: a quantitative integration of the literature. *Acta Psychiatrica Scandinavica, 76*, 465–479.

Kempler, D. (1988). Lexical and pantomime abilities of Alzheimer's disease. *Aphasiology, 2*, 147–159.

Kempler, D. (1991). Language changes in dementia of the Alzheimer type. In R. Lubinsky (Ed.), *Dementia and communication* (pp. 98–113). Philadelphia: B. C. Decker, Inc.

Kosberg, J. I., Cairl, R. E., & Keller, D. M. (1990). Components of burden: Intervention implications. *The Gerontologist, 30*(2), 236–242.

Kuhn, D. R. (1998). Caring for relatives with early stage Alzheimer's disease: An exploratory study. *American Journal of Alzheimer's Disease, 13*(4), 189–196.

Lawrence, R. H., Tennstedt, S. L., & Assmann, S. F. (1998). Quality of the caregiver-care recipient relationship: Does it offset negative consequences of caregiving for family caregivers? *Psychology and Aging, 13*(10), 150–158.

Mace, N. L., & Rabins, P. V. (1981). *The 36-hour day*. Baltimore, MD: The John Hopkins University Press.

Mentis, M., Briggs-Whittaker, J., & Gramigna, G. D. (1995). Discourse topic management in senile dementia of the Alzheimer's type. *Journal of Speech and Hearing Research, 38*(5), 1054–1066.

Mittleman, M. S., Ferris, S. H., Shulman, E., Steinberg, G., & Levin, B. (1996). A family intervention to delay nursing home placement of patients with Alzheimer's disease. *Journal of the American Geriatrics Society, 38*, 446–454.

Montgomery, R. J. V., & Kosloski, K. D. (2000). Family caregiving: change, continuity, and diversity. In M. P. Lawton & R. L. Rubenstein (Eds.), *Interventions in dementia care: Toward improving quality of life* (pp.143–171). New York: Springer.

Montgomery, R. J. V., & Kosloski, K. D. (2003). Pathways to a caregiver identity for older adults. Unpublished manuscript. University of Kansas.

Montgomery, R. J. V., Stull, D. E., & Borgatta, E. F. (1985). Measurement and the analysis of burden. *Research on Aging, 7*, 137–152.

Morgan, D. L., & March, S. J. (1992). The impact of life events on networks of personal relationships: A comparison of widowhood and caring for a spouse with Alzheimer's disease. *Journal of Social and Personal Relationships, 9*, 563–584.

Murray, J., Schneider, J., Banerjee, S., & Mann, A. (1999). Eurocare: A cross-national study of co-resident spouse carers for people with Alzheimer's Disease: II A qualitative analysis of the experience of caregiving. *International Journal of Geriatric Psychiatry, 14*, 662–667.

Nicholas, A. D., Obler, L. K., Albert, M. L., & Helm-Estabrooks, N. (1985). Empty speech in Alzheimer's disease and fluent aphasia. *Journal of Speech and Hearing Research, 28*, 405–410.

Orange, J. B. (1991). Perspectives of family members regarding communication changes. In R. Lubinsky (Ed.), *Dementia and Communication* (pp. 168–186). Philadelphia: B. C. Decker, Inc.

Orona, C. J. (1990). Temporality and identity loss due to Alzheimer's Disease. *Social Science and Medicine, 30*(11), 1247–1256.

Ory, M. G., & Dunker, A. P. (1992). *In-home care for older people: Health and supportive services.* Newbury Park, CA: Sage.

Ory, M. G., Hoffman, R. R., Yee, J. L., Tennstedt, S., & Schulz, R. (1999). Prevalence and impact of caregiving: A detailed comparison between dementia and nondementia caregivers. *The Gerontologist, 39* (2), 177–185.

Pearlin, L. I. (1983). Role strains and personal stress. In H. B. Kaplan (Ed.), *Psychosocial stress: Trends in theory and research.* New York: Academic Press.

Pearlin, L. (1992). The careers of caregivers. *The Gerontologist, 32,* 647–651.

Pearlin, L. I., Mullan, J. T., Semple, S. J., & Skaff, M. M. (1990). Caregiving and the stress process: An overview of concepts and their measures. *The Gerontologist, 30,* 583–594.

Poulshock, S. W., & Deimling, G. T. (1984). Families caring for elders in residence: Issues in the measurement of burden. *Journal of Gerontology, 39,* 230–239.

Powell, J. A., Hale, M. A., & Bayer, A. J. (1995). Symptoms of communication breakdown in dementia: Carers' perceptions. *European Journal of Disorders of Communication, 30,* 65–75.

Quayhagen, M. P., & Quayhagen, M. (1996). Discovering life quality in coping with dementia. *Journal of Nursing Research, 18*(2), 120–135.

Rabins, P., Mace, N., & Lucas, M. (1982). The impact of dementia on the family. *Journal of the American Medical Association, 248,* 333–335.

Ramanathan, V. (1997). *Alzheimer discourse: some sociolinguistic dimensions.* Mahwah, NJ: Lawrence Erlbaum

Rau, M. (1993). *Coping with communication challenges in Alzheimer's disease.* San Diego, CA: Singular Publishing Group.

Ripich, D. N. (1994). Functional communication with AD patients: a caregiving training program. *Alzheimer Disease and Associated Disorders, 8,* 95–109.

Ripich, D. N., & Terrell, S. (1988). Patterns of discourse cohesion and coherence in Alzheimer's disease. *Journal of Speech and Hearing Disorders, 53,* 8–15.

Rollins, D., Waterman, D., & Esmay, D. (1985). Married widowhood. *Activities, adaptation, and aging, 7,* 67–71.

Ryan, E. B. (1991). Normal aging and language. In R. Lubinsky (Ed.), *Dementia and Communication* (pp. 84–97). Philadelphia: B. C. Decker, Inc.

Sabat, S. R. (2001). *The experience of Alzheimer's disease: Life though a tangled veil*. Malden, MA: Blackwell.

Santro Pietro, M. J., & Ostuni, E. (1997). Positive techniques for successful conversation with Alzheimer's disease patients. In M. J. Santro Pietro & E. Ostuni (Eds.), *Successful communication with Alzheimer's disease patients: an in-service training manual* (pp. 131–144). Boston: Butterworth-Heinenmann.

Savundranayagam, M. Y., Hummert, M. L., & Montgomery, R. J. V. (2003). *Investigating the effects of communication problems on caregiver burden*. Unpublished manuscript. University of Kansas.

Seltzer, M. M., & Li, L. W. (1995). The transitions of caregiving: Subjective and objective definitions. *The Gerontologist, 36*(5), 614–626.

Shekim, L. O., & LaPointe, L. L. (1984). *Production of discourse in individuals with Alzheimer's disease*. Paper presented at the 12 annual meeting of the International Neuropsychological Society, Houston, TX.

Skaff, M. M., Pearlin, L. I., & Mullan, J. T. (1996). Transitions in the caregiving career: Effects of sense of mastery. *Psychology and Aging, 11*(2), 247–257.

Small, J. A., Geldart, K., & Gutman, G. (2000). Communication between individuals with dementia and their caregivers during activities of daily living. *American Journal of Alzheimer's Disease and Other Dementias, 15*(5), 291–302.

Talkington-Boyer, S., & Snyder, D. K. (1994). Assessing impact on family caregiver to Alzheimer's disease patients. *The American Journal of Family Therapy, 22*, 57–66.

Thoits, P. A. (1991). On merging identity theory and stress research. *Social Psychology Quarterly, 54*, 101–112.

Ulatowska, H., Allard, L., Donnell, A., Bristow, J., Haybes, S., Flower, A., & North, A. (1988). Discourse performance in subjects with dementia of the Alzheimer type. In H. Whitaker (Ed.), *Neuropsychological Studies of Nonfocal Brain Damage* (pp.108–131). New York: Springer Verlag.

Ulatowska, H., & Chapman, S. B. (1991). Discourse studies. In R. Lubinsky (Ed.), *Dementia and Communication* (pp. 115–132). Philadelphia: B. C. Decker, Inc.

Vitaliano, P. P., Young, H. M., Russo, J., Romano, J., & Magana-Amoto, A. (1993). Does expressed emotion in spouses predict subsequent problems among care recipients with Alzheimer's Disease? *Journal of Gerontology, 48*(4), P202–P209.

Volicer, L., & Bloom-Charette, L. (1999). Assessment of quality of life in advanced dementia. In L. Volicer, & L. Bloom-Charette (Eds.) *Enhancing the quality of life in advanced dementia* (pp. 3–20). Philadelphia: Taylor & Francis.

Walker, A. J., Pratt, C. C., & Oppy, N. C. (1992). Perceived reciprocity in family caregiving. *Family Relations, 41*, 82–85.

Williamson, G. M., & Schulz, R. (1993). Coping with specific stressors in Alzheimer's disease caregiving. *The Gerontologist, 33*(6), 747–755.

Wood, J. T. (1999). *Interpersonal communication: Everyday encounters* (2nd Ed.). Belmont, CA: Wadsworth.

Wright, D. L., & Aquillino, W. S. (1998). Influence of emotional support exchange in marriage on caregiving wives' burden and marital satisfaction. *Family Relations, 47*(2), 195–204.

Wright, L. K. (1993). *Alzheimer's disease and marriage.* Newbury Park, CA: Sage.

14

Communicating Disability: Stereotypes, Identity, and Motivation

Cindy GALLOIS

Research is burgeoning in the area of communication and disability, and the potential contribution of theory and method in language and social psychology (LASP) is great. This area cries out for study from an intergroup perspective, one that is surprisingly lacking in much of the research. In saying this, I should note that my own interest has developed from my personal experience with disability, which is common among researchers in this communication area (Thompson, 2000).

As the population in many countries ages and lives longer, as we cure many more acute illnesses and injuries, and as people survive horrific accidents that only twenty years ago would have killed them, the treatment and management of chronic illness and disability have become increasingly important issues for all of us. One salient variable in most people's thinking is the cost of treatment and rehabilitation, as the costs of maintaining health and treating illness soar. Because of their nature, such conditions require long and intensive treatment. Furthermore, while treatment often leads to a significant increase in function and quality of life, it is rare for no disability to remain – instead, there may be a lifelong need for medical or other treatment and management. Further, the culture of equality and rights that has developed over the past decades in many areas leads to intergroup tension between advocates for people with disabilities and those with other agendas, that go beyond cost.

In spite of this situation, there is surprisingly little research on the social-psychological aspects of disability and interability communication (i.e., communication between people with a disability and able-bodied people). There are, however, large related research traditions on identity, stereotypes, and disability and on motivation for treatment and rehabilitation. Many would argue, as Street (2001) does, that active participation by patients and others in their social environment is essential to achieving optimal results from treatment. This is particularly so for chronic illness and disability, where the relationships between health professionals, patients, and families are time-consuming and long-lasting.

This discussion leads to some questions for researchers, presented at the end of this chapter, which can form part of a research agenda on communication and disability from a LASP perspective. These questions include exploring the impact of stereotypes on communication between people with disabilities and health professionals (and others), and the resulting impact on motivation for rehabilitation or treatment and on outcomes. A key part of this process implicates individual differences in resources, self-stereotypes, goals, and motivation for rehabilitation.

Approaches to Communication and Disability

There are a number of literatures that exist largely independent of each other. One derives mainly from the health area and takes the perspective of health professionals. It emphasizes patient variables (and sometimes family variables) and their influence on motivation toward rehabilitation or further treatment, the course of rehabilitation, caregiver burden, and the like (e.g., V. Braithwaite, 1992: Diller, 2000; Grahn, Ekdahl, & Borgquist, 2000). This is a huge literature, and I will consider it only briefly here. Another approach, which takes the perspective of people with disabilities, concerns the management of identity by disabled people, their strategies for dealing with prejudice and bad behavior by others, and related issues, often from a rights perspective (e.g., see Braithwaite

& Thompson, 2000, for a number of papers in this line). Much of this work takes a critical perspective, arguing cogently for social change in the construction of disability, as well as for the rights of people with disabilities to participate fully in all aspects of social life. Still another approach examines the stereotypes about disabled people and communication with them by non-disabled others – the attitude of the larger society to people with disabilities – and the consequences for interability communication as a variety of intercultural communication (e.g., Emry & Wiseman, 1987; Fox & Giles, 1996). This last approach is the closest to LASP. I focus on it in this paper, because it has the potential to add a new perspective to this area.

All these approaches are useful – and interestingly, they all tell us something about the researchers themselves, and the way they (we) think about this area. This paper attempts an integration of the approaches, with a view to examining the impact of stereotypes (including self-stereotypes), identity, and interability communication on motivation and the course of rehabilitation and treatment. I believe that a fully intergroup perspective, but one that also recognizes the impact of individual differences, is essential to understanding the communication and miscommunication that takes place between people with a disability and those with whom they interact.

Types of Disability

There is an unfortunate tendency in the literature, as well as in the general population, to think of disability (and people with a disability or disabilities) as monolithic. Social policy, in the service of equity, generally makes no or only implicit and vague distinctions about the type or nature of disability. For example, there is policy on "disabled access" to buildings, streets, and other public areas, which is highly relevant to people with some disabilities (e.g., paraplegia, severe arthritis) and completely irrelevant to others (e.g., hearing impairment, laryngectomy). It is important for researchers not to fall into this trap, but to keep in mind the immensely diverse group of people with disabilities. No policy or practice fits all of them.

Congenital or Acquired Disability

One initial and important, but often neglected, distinction is when the disability was acquired, and in particular whether it is congenital (or acquired in early childhood) or acquired in late childhood, adolescence, or adulthood. Age of acquisition of a disability is likely to have a very major impact on stereotypes (both self and other), identity, and communication. This is in part because people with congenital or early-acquired disabilities have always belonged to a disabled group and have developed attitudes and behaviors that reflect this identity. Challenges for them in growing up include the development of identities not related to the disability, as well as to overcome the impact of stigma to their self-esteem. On the other hand, those who acquire a disability later in life move from the able-bodied (or temporarily able-bodied; Merrigan, 2000) majority to a disabled minority group, and thus have a very different relationship with both groups (cf. Braithwaite, 1990). It is important to consider these types of disability separately, as arguably they represent very different identity issues. This paper focuses on people with disabilities acquired after early childhood (called acquired disabilities here), whose situation brings into sharp relief the role of self and other stereotypes in communication.

Impact of Acquired Disability

The movement from non-disabled to disabled status is often very sudden, as in the case of a traumatic accident or injury (e.g., a car crash) or a sudden illness (e.g., a stroke). Whether the onset is sudden or gradual, people enter the disabled state with their ideas and stereotypes about disability, their personal and social identities, and their original qualities and resources more or less unchanged. These provide the first basis of self-stereotypes and identity. For this reason alone, it is worth examining the stereotypes of able-bodied people (including researchers) about disability.

In this paper, I consider stereotypes about people with disabilities by those in the larger society, themselves, and researchers. I also consider their identity and the impact of such stereotypes on it, looking at orientations to the larger society, and helped by the excellent theoretical work of Fox, Giles, Orbe, & Bourhis (2000). Next, the paper deals with the impact of identity on motivation for rehabilitation, and the consequences for the process of rehabilitation. Finally, I consider the role of others, including health professionals and those in the disabled person's social environment, on identity and motivation for rehabilitation.

Societal Stereotypes
about People with Disabilities

There are many definitions of stereotypes in psychology, communication, and related fields. A definition that is useful for this paper is that stereotypes are traits or expectations applied to a whole group of people by people in that group (self-stereotypes) or by those in other groups (other-stereotypes). Stereotypes may or may not contain a kernel of truth (i.e., they may be applicable to some people in the group, to some extent, or in some contexts), but in all cases they are over-generalized to the whole group and take little or no account of individual differences. Stereotypes may be overt, but more often they are subtle and covert, even automatic and unconscious. There is evidence of acquisition of stereotypes in early childhood (see Oakes, Haslam, & Turner, 1994) and they reflect the intergroup situation, including power relations between the stereotyped group and other groups (Fiske, 1993; Tajfel & Turner, 1979). As Tajfel and Turner theorize, stereotypes (and their normative analogue, prototypes) form the basis for social identity and interactions between members of different social groups.

Over the past 30 years or so, an interesting literature on stereotypes about people with disabilities has developed. Most studies involve questionnaire surveys of university students or (less commonly) other groups in the general population (e.g., Fox & Giles, 1996). They indicate that people with disabilities are perceived by able-bodied others as more angry, bitter, and frustrated, but less active, competent, happy, and sociable, than able-bodied people. People with disabilities are also perceived as patronized and ignored by non-disabled people, but as deserving of respect and kindness. These stereotypes are analogous to those about other minority groups (e.g., older adults; see Hummert, 2002), especially those perceived as low in social status and power.

Impact of Disability Type on Stereotypes

One striking feature of these stereotypes, as noted earlier, is that they assume a group of "people with disabilities" that is monolithic in character. Perhaps this is understandable, given legislative and other attempts to assert the rights of people with disabilities. Nevertheless, it does not reflect the situation of disabled people, who are often far more different from each other than they are from able-bodied people – who themselves do not represent a monolithic group.

In the first place, the distinction between people with and without a disability is subtle and blurred, and may have as much to do with social construction and social identification as it does with physical status. For example, when does a person whose hearing is fading become "hearing-impaired?" What is the distinction between "hearing-impaired" and "deaf" (or "Deaf")? How severe must rheumatoid arthritis be for the sufferer to be considered (and to consider himself or herself) as disabled? Such distinctions are even more difficult when the disability is cognitive, intellectual, or behavioral. There are myriad attempts to define disabled status, frequently for reasons of legislated rights or compensation, but the categorical cut points are nonetheless arbitrary. This fact turns out to be extremely important in the history of people with disabilities and their interactions with the larger society.

In fact, disability is highly multi-dimensional and individual. Besides age of acquisition, there are other distinguishing dimensions, including the degree of disability (from very slight to very severe), the extent to which disability is context-specific (e.g., exercise-induced asthma) or more context-general (e.g., quadriplegia), the extent to which the disability is visible (e.g., blindness) or invisible (e.g., deafness), and the type of handicap (e.g., sensory or motor, cognitive or affective). A further dimension that is of special relevance to LASP is the impact of the disability on communication. Arguably, all disabilities affect communication one way or another, but some of them (e.g., hearing impairment, upper limb paralysis, aphasia) have a direct impact on verbal communication, non-verbal communication, or both.

Most research on stereotypes about people with disabilities has done one of two things: (1) examined stereotypes about a single disability (this has been the case especially for deafness), or (2) examined disability in a generic sense, usually employing severe, visible motor disability (typically wheelchair status) as the stimulus (if any disability is mentioned at all). The "default" stereotype of disability for people in Western countries at the present time may well be wheelchair status. This is the Western icon for disabled parking (note that other cultures use other icons, which could mean they also have another default stereotype), even though the majority of people using the icons are not in wheelchairs. Furthermore, most disabled-access rules for buildings and the like are intended to accommodate people in wheelchairs. This may be a useful strategy, as structures that can accommodate wheelchairs can also accommodate many other motor disabilities, but it has the perhaps unintended consequence of glossing over important differences between disabilities, which are likely to be associated with different stereotypes and perceptions.

Tringo (1970) made this same point, eliciting social distance judgements by a number of population groups (high school students, undergraduate students, community residents, etc.) about a long list of disabilities, which produced a hierarchy of preference. The lowest social distance judgements in his study were about context-specific invisible disabilities like arthritis, asthma, and diabetes. Middle-range judgements were about sensory disabilities including blindness and deafness, along with motor disabilities such as paraplegia, stroke, and epilepsy. The highest social distance judgements were about serious cognitive disabilities like mental retardation and mental illness. As judgements of this type are often highly influenced by the immediate sociopolitical context, one might expect them to have changed significantly in recent times. To examine this possibility, Thomas (2000) replicated Tringo's study with appropriate changes in terminology, and largely replicated the earlier results; the social distance hierarchy has turned out to be surprisingly stable. It should be noted that this is not really a stereotype study as such, but it does give insight into how stereotypes might work.

There is also some research on stereotypes about a single specific disability. For example, Kiger (1997) found quite positive stereotypes about deaf people in judgements made by hearing people, with few distinctions between deaf and hearing people. This interesting result suggests that for some types of disability, the level of stigma may be much lower than for "disability" in general. If this is so, there is an interesting set of questions for research about the factors that determine level of stigma. The problem for this interpretation is that there are at present few comparative anchors in research.

Spencer and Gallois (2003), in a specific comparison of stereotypes about four disabilities, found more negative stereotypes by able-bodied university students about other university students with motor disabilities (paraplegia, aphasia) than sensory ones (blindness, deafness). Contrary to predictions, there were much more negative stereotypes about a less visible disability (aphasia) than a more visible one (paraplegia). As Kiger (1997) also found, the most positive stereotypes were about deaf people. These results, while they represent only a tiny step towards explicit comparison of types of disabilities, indicate that a disability that has a strong impact on expressive communication may provoke especially negative stereotypes.

Stereotypes, Identity, and Disability

The formation and management of identity by people with a disability has been approached in two main ways by researchers and others (Schultz, 2000). The first emphasizes the rights of people with disabilities and their strategies for dealing with discrimination by the larger society. This approach has gained in popularity through societal changes promoting such rights, for example the Disability Act in the USA and similar national, regional, and local legislation or policy in other places. The approach has as an underpinning assumption that disability involves impairment, and that people with disabilities are at a physical or social disadvantage – thus, they need and deserve special help and support to participate equally in all aspects of life. Often, the perspective is also critical, with social or system change assumed to be of paramount importance to gaining their rights by disabled people. The link between stereotypes and this approach to identity management gained a LASP theoretical focus when interability interactions were constructed as a form of intercultural interactions, in which disabled people were the lower-status or minority group (Emry & Wiseman, 1987; see Fox *et al.*, 2000, for a review).

From this perspective, identity management is centrally affected by discriminatory or inconsiderate communication from members of the majority, along with communication strategies on the part of disabled people to combat it (cf. Tajfel & Turner, 1979). Most research on this topic has examined the strategies of people with disabilities acquired in adulthood, most commonly through traumatic accidents (e.g., Braithwaite, 1990). People in this situation often use special social skills to "help" majority group members understand their situation and needs, such as polite assertion of preferences and desires (particularly the desire not to be helped) and the use of humour (Soule & Roloff, 2000). Braithwaite and Eckstein (2003), using interpretive analysis of interviews with people with visible motor disabilities, describe a series of communication strategies employed by the disabled person to forestall unwanted requests to help, to refuse them, and to control them, along with recommendations for non-disabled people to mange their interability communication. People with a disability may also develop communication strategies intended to achieve mutual treatment of themselves as individuals rather than as members of a disabled group (e.g., Merrigan, 2000), including the use of alternative media like computer-mediated communication, where their disability may be easier to ignore (e.g., Braithwaite, Waldron, & Finn, 1999; Fox, 2000). Finally, they may engage in assertion and advocacy of their rights (Schultz, 2000).

The second way in which the management of identity by people with disabilities has been approached has been labelled disability power (Schultz, 2000). This is perhaps best exemplified by the Deaf culture movement (e.g., McIntosh, 2000; Schultz, 2000), although there are other good examples, especially in the fight by people with congenital disabilities against genetic testing (cf. Newell, 2000). In the case of Deaf culture, disability is constructed not as disadvantage but as difference. Indeed, some advocates of Deaf culture, in a clear instance of social creativity strategies, characterize deafness as an advantage, in that it gives access to a language (sign languages such as Ameslan or Auslan) and a culture that is not accessible to hearing people. Those constructing disability in this way see no advantage in treatments that would cure or lessen the disability (such as cochlear implants); because they are not at a disadvantage in the first place, there is nothing to be gained.

The Deaf culture movement may reflect something special or unique in the context of profoundly deaf people, who are at a great communicative disadvantage that is dramatically lessened (even eliminated) through the use of sign language. It may also reflect the context of congenitally (or near-congenitally) deaf people, who have never had a hearing identity. In any case, people with disabilities acquired later in life tend not to think of themselves as members of a separate culture (although they acknowledge cultural aspects in their interability interactions), and they rarely eschew the possibility of a cure.

Individual Differences in Identity

These two radically different approaches to identity (and there are many more) suggest that there are important individual and group differences in the relationship desired by people with a disability between themselves and the able-bodied majority – not to mention others with whom they interact, including other people with their disability, people with another disability, and health professionals. Fox and her colleagues (2000) have presented a theoretical analysis of interability communication that touches upon such individual differences, using several theories from social psychology and communication.

A major contributor to this analysis is Berry's (e.g., 1997) model of intercultural adaptation, which deals with the orientation of immigrants or minority group members to their own (original) culture and the larger majority culture. Fox *et al.* (2000) argue that this model can be readily adapted to the situation of people with disabilities. Berry posits four main orientations of people in minority groups to the majority. *Assimilation* involves an orientation where the person highly values the majority group but not the minority, and thus attempts to pass as far as possible into the majority group. In the case of a person with a disability acquired in adulthood, this often means a *return* to the majority group (such people not really "immigrants," but more like forced expatriates). *Integration* involves an orientation where both the minority and majority groups are highly valued, and the person strives to develop an identity that blends them or to switch between them. This orientation could (but does not necessarily) involve advocacy for disabled people, as the person operates in the larger society on behalf of his or her group. *Separation* is an orientation where the minority group is highly valued but the majority is not, and the person tries to avoid interaction with the majority. In the case of people with a disability, this means spending as much time as possible with other disabled people (e.g., in support groups) and identifying mainly with them. This orientation does not necessarily imply hostility to the majority, but does imply avoidance of them. Finally, *individualism* is an orientation in which the person devalues both groups and strives for an individual identity apart from them, or alternatively interacts as much as possible from the position of another social identity (cf. Hogg & Abrams, 2001). In the case of people with a disability, this may come down to denying the disability or its impact on one's life altogether (more possible with some disabilities than others).

Bourhis, Moise, Perreault, and Sénécal (1997) extended Berry's model to include the ideology of the larger society. Fox *et al.* (2000) have applied this model to interability interactions, where the majority may be assimilationist, pluralist (allowing all groups to flourish), segregationist (wishing to isolate people with disabilities in special institutions) or individualist (wishing to interact through other identities and deny the importance of this one). In the view of Bourhis *et al.* and Fox *et al.*, it is the match between the orientation of the majority and the orientation of a person with a disability (or a disabled group) that determines the success of adaptation.

There are important consequences of individual differences among people with a disability, as well as among able-bodied people. One is that disabled people may disagree strongly with each other about how the relationship with each other or with able-bodied people should be carried out. They may also disagree about the most urgent and essential system changes – should there be more resources, more access, discontinuation or introduction of new treatments, special facilities for disabled people or mainstreaming, or another change? Similarly, they are likely to disagree about the best communication strategies. Members of the majority who construct disablement as monolithic (and thus attempt to privilege one orientation, such as integration) find themselves asking what people with disabilities want. It is only through a thorough understanding of individual differences that the range of appropriate strategies, and indeed underlying commonalities (e.g., a common desire for equity between able-bodied and disabled people), can be appreciated.

Stereotypes, Identity, and Motivation for Rehabilitation

For many (but far from all) people with a disability, particularly one acquired in adolescence or adulthood, the best treatment involves a long program of rehabilitation (in the case of chronic illness, rehabilitation may also be involved, or there may be a complex management program). It is not uncommon for rehabilitation from traumatic accident or illness to be a very time-consuming activity that lasts for several years or longer, and improvement is often very difficult to see (cf. Diller, 2000; Grahn *et al.*, 2000). The level of motivation needed to continue such a program, with the time, energy, expense, and interaction with strangers it entails, is extremely high, analogous to the training of an elite athlete (or a PhD student). The difference is that this is work the person did not choose, and the goal is to return to the level of function that he or she had prior to the trauma – or as close as possible – rather than to attain a new and higher goal (e.g., Gard & Sandberg, 1998). Not surprisingly, many people (both patients and health professionals) decide that the benefit is not worth the effort.

Most research on the impact of motivation on the course of rehabilitation comes from health professionals. Not surprisingly, the work generally indicates that higher motivation predicts better rehabilitation for many acquired disabilities (e.g., Diller, 2000; Gard & Sandberg, 1998). The background variables predicting good motivation are also not unexpected, and include higher level of education and socio-economic status, above-average intelligence, internal locus of control, and so forth (less intuitively, desire to return to work can predict lower motivation: see King, Humen, Smith, Phan, & Teo, 2001). A supportive but realistic family and social network predict better motivation for rehabilitation, and also help to re-integrate the person into the social environment. High self-esteem makes a positive difference to motivation here as in other contexts (Brumfitt & Sheeran, 1997).

Identity and Motivation

The literature on motivation for rehabilitation and success of rehabilitation also makes a number of assumptions. The most common perspective involves a deficit/rehabilitation model. In this type of model, the deficit (i.e., the disability) is located in the patient, who must participate in rehabilitation and other treatment to fix the problem. The solution to the problem is thus located in the health professional, who has the expertise to manage the rehabilitation program. Thus, a desire for assimilation (or return to the majority) on the part of the disabled person is assumed.

At the same time, there is an assumption that a complete return to the former state is not possible, and thus that the disabled person (and his or her family and other supporting people) will go through a series of stages in coming to terms with the disability. It is worth noting that these stages are also described by people with an acquired disability themselves, at least for some types of disability (cf. Braithwaite's, 1990, interviews with people with paraplegia). The first stage is denial of the disability, along with a belief that "things will return to normal soon." This is followed by a period of bargaining and anger, often accompanied by depression. Finally, there is an acceptance of the disability and an integration of the new status into the person's personal and social identity, implying an orientation of integration. Only at this point is the person in a position to develop new strategies, including new ways of communicating.

These dominant approaches (deficit-rehabilitation and stages of acceptance) have analogues in stage models of identity for other minority groups. They are derived from the grief and loss model of dying (Kubler-Ross, 1969), and indeed, acquired disability is an important loss. The materials commonly given to people who have recently acquired a disability reflect both models, particularly in encouraging patients and their families to "be realistic" about prospects for the future. Stage models are also applied to people with congenital disabilities.

These models represent an integrationist orientation on the part of health professionals; they match well with disabled people who believe that they must take on a disabled identity (integrationist orientation). Imagine, however, how a proponent of Deaf culture might react to a suggestion to accept and be realistic about his or her disability. Many people with disabilities reject acceptance of minority status altogether. For this reason, critical models of disability may locate the problem in the larger society, and the solution in a redistribution of power (cf. Newell, 2000; Schultz, 2000). Likewise, some intercultural models locate the problem for the disabled person in the patronizing or hostile communication of health professionals and others, which is based on the negative stereotypes of these people rather than on the disabled person's individual characteristics (cf. Merrigan, 2000; Ryan, Bajorek, Beaman, & Anas, in press; Ryan, Giles, Bartolucci, & Henwood, 1986). The assumptions underlying intercultural models are not likely to provide a good match to disabled people whose orientation is strongly assimilationist.

Arguably, none of the existing approaches to rehabilitation takes adequate account of the individual differences among people with disabilities. Given the difficulties of motivating people sufficiently highly to take on the formidable task of rehabilitation, models that do so are urgently needed to inform research as well as rehabilitation programs.

Conclusion

The discussion in this chapter leads to a number of questions, which can help form the basis for an intergroup research agenda in this area. First, how do the stereotypes held by people with and without a disability vary as a function of the severity and type of disability (and for researchers in LASP, what is the impact of communication disability in particular)? Next, what is the impact of severity and type of disability on interability communication? Thirdly, how does orientation to their disability vary with the type and severity of disability, and what is the impact of orientation on communication strategies by disabled people? Further, how does type and severity of disability affect the orientation and stereotypes of able-bodied people (including health professionals), and what is the impact of this orientation on the identity of disabled people? How do identity and self-stereotypes change over time or through the course of rehabilitation or treatment? Finally, what is the impact of orientation and identity on motivation for rehabilitation (where this is relevant) or other treatment, and how is this related to the course of treatment, if it is relevant and desired?

These are large questions, and they require an integration of the existing literature, so that the perspectives of people with disabilities, those around them, those who care for them, and the larger society are considered together. This necessitates a genuinely intergroup approach, where no perspective is privileged, and one in which interability communication is construed as a two-way (or multi-way) process. We must take seriously individual differences among people with disabilities, and among non-disabled people, including those in the disabled person's social environment and health professionals or service providers.

For researchers, this approach means that it is necessary to conduct multiple case studies or small N studies, as the context of interability communication is so diverse. It also means longitudinal research, in order to track the changes in stereotypes, identity, orientation, motivation over time and treatment. Most important, researchers in LASP should work with health professionals, disabled people and those in their social environments to examine the outcomes of stereotypes and interability communication, rather than assuming them. It is important to involve all stakeholders in theory-building, including patients, families, friends, health professionals, and the larger community. There is no *right* perspective – all voices must be heard.

In the end, research in the LASP tradition must take account of the ubiquitousness of disability, particularly when the full range of disabilities is considered. It is rare to go through life without acquiring a disability of any kind (hence Merrigan's, 2000, characterization of the larger society as temporarily able-bodied). Many people are able to disguise their disabilities and pass as normal. As this paper notes, many more would like to do so. Imperfections in body and mind, and consequently in communicative behavior, are a fact of life both private and public, personal and collective, however much one part of a society may choose to stereotype another as different or in deficit. Surely much about life can be learned from others' imperfections as well as our own, so that the study of disabilities is thus inherently humanistic. Hearing the voices of people with disabilities, in all their diversity, will enrich research and theory for language and social psychology.

References

Berry, J.W. (1997). Immigration, acculturation, and adaptation. *Applied psychology: An international journal, 46*, 5–68.

Bourhis, R.Y., Moise, L.C., Perreault, S., & Sénécal, S. (1997). Towards an interactive acculturation model: A social psychological approach. *International Journal of Psychology, 32*, 369–386.

Braithwaite, D.O. (1990). From majority to minority: An analysis of cultural change from ablebodied to disabled. *International Journal of Intercultural Relations, 14*, 465–483.

Braithwaite, D.O., & Eckstein, N.J. (2003). How people with disabilities communicatively manage assistance: Helping as instrumental social support. *Journal of Applied Communication Research, 31*, 1–26.

Braithwaite, D.O., & Thompson, T.L. (Eds.) (2000). *Handbook of communication and people with disabilities: Research and application.* Mahwah, NJ: Erlbaum.

Braithwaite, D.O., Waldron, V.R., & Fin, J. (1999). Communication of social support in computer-mediated groups for people with disabilities. *Health Communication, 11*, 123–151.

Braithwaite, V. (1992). Caregiving burden: Making the concept scientifically useful and policy relevant. *Research on Aging, 14,* 3–27.

Brumfitt, S.M., & Sheeran, P. (1997). An evaluation of short-term group therapy for people with aphasia. *Disability and Rehabilitation, 19,* 221–230.

Diller, L. (2000). Poststroke rehabilitation practice guidelines. In A.-L. Christensen & B.P. Uzzell (Eds.), *International handbook of neuropsychological rehabilitation* (pp. 167–182). New York: Kluwer/Plenum.

Emry, R., & Wiseman, R.L. (1987). An intercultural understanding of ablebodied and disabled person's communication. *International Journal of Intercultural Relations, 11,* 7–27.

Fiske, S. T. (1993). Controlling other people: The impact of power on stereotyping. *American Psychologist, 48,* 621–628.

Fox, S.A. (2000). The uses and abuses of computer-mediated communication for people with disabilities. In D.O. Braithwaite & T.L. Thompson (Eds.), *Handbook of communication and people with disabilities: Research and application* (pp. 319–338). Mahwah, NJ: Erlbaum.

Fox, S.A., & Giles, H. (1996). Interability communication: Evaluating patronizing encounters. *Journal of Language and Social Psychology, 15,* 265–290.

Fox, S.A., Giles, H., Orbe, M.P., and Bourhis, R.Y. (2000). Interability communication: Theoretical perspectives. In D.O. Braithwaite & T.L. Thompson (Eds.), *Handbook of communication and people with disabilities: Research and application* (pp. 193–222). Mahwah, NJ: Erlbaum.

Gard, G., & Sandberg, A.C. (1998). Motivating factors for return to work. *Physiotherapy Research International, 3,* 100–108.

Grahn, B., Ekdahl, C. & Borgquist, JL. (2000). Motivation as a predictor of changes in quality of life and working ability in multidisciplinary rehabilitation. *Disability and Rehabilitation, 22,* 639–654.

Hogg, M. A., & Abrams, D. (2001). Intergroup relations: An overview. In M.A. Hogg & D. Abrams (Eds.), *Intergroup relations: Essential readings* (pp. 1–14). Hove, England: Psychology Press.

Hummert, M.L. (2002). Implicit age stereotyping in interpersonal communication. Paper presented at the 8th International Conference on Language and Social Psychology, Hong Kong, July.

Kiger, G. (1997). The structure of attitudes towards persons who are deaf: Emotions, values, and stereotypes. *The Journal of Psychology, 131,* 554–560.

King, K.M., Humen, D.P., Smith, H.L., Phan, C.L., & Teo, K.K. (2001). Psychosocial components of cardiac recovery and rehabilitation attendance. *Heart, 85,* 290–294.

Kubler-Ross, E. (1969). *On death and dying.* New York: Macmillan.

McIntosh, A. (2000). When the Deaf and the hearing interact: Communication features, relationships, and disability issues. In D.O. Braithwaite & T.L. Thompson (Eds.), *Handbook of communication and people with disabilities: Research and application* (pp. 353–368). Mahwah, NJ: Erlbaum.

Merrigan, G. (2000). Negotiating personal identities among people with and without identified disabilities: The role of identity management. In D.O. Braithwaite & T.L. Thompson (Eds.), *Handbook of communication and people with disabilities: Research and application* (pp. 223–238). Mahwah, NJ: Erlbaum.

Newell, C. (2000). The right to live and be different: An exploration of the significance of the DPI Europe Declaration on bioethics and human rights. *Interaction, 13,* 6–9.

Oakes, P.J., Haslam, A., &Turner, J.C. (1994). *Stereotyping and social reality.* Oxford: Blackwell.

Ryan, E.B., Giles, H., Bartolucci, G., & Henwood, K. (1986). Psycholinguistic and social psychological components of communication by and with the elderly. *Language and Communication, 6,* 1–24.

Ryan, E. B., Bajorek, S., Beaman, A., & Anas, A. P. (in press). Intergroup perspectives on communication and disability. In J. Harwood & H. Giles (Eds), *Intergroup communication: Multiple perspectives.* New York: Peter Lang.

Shultz, K. (2000). Deaf activists in the rhetorical transformation of the construct of disability. In D.O. Braithwaite & T.L. Thompson (Eds.), *Handbook of communication and people with disabilities: Research and application* (pp. 257–272). Mahwah, NJ: Erlbaum.

Soule, K.P., & Roloff, M.E. (2000). Help between persons with and without disabilities from a resource theory perspective. In D.O. Braithwaite & T.L. Thompson (Eds.), *Handbook of communication and people with disabilities: Research and application* (pp. 67–85). Mahwah, NJ: Erlbaum.

Spencer, A., & Gallois, C. (2003). Interability interactions: Impact of type and visibility of disability on perceptions. Paper presented at the 32nd Annual Meeting of the Society of Australasian Social Psychologists, Adelaide, April.

Street, R.L., Jr. (2001). Active patients as powerful communicators. In W.P. Robinson & H. Giles (Eds.), *The new handbook of language and social psychology* (pp. 541–560). Chichester, England: Wiley.

Tajfel, H., & Turner, J.C. (1979). An integrative theory of intergroup conflict. In W.G.Austin & S. Worchel (Eds.), *The social psychology of intergroup relations* (pp. 33–47). Monterey, CA: Brooks/Cole.

Thomas, A. (2000). Stability of Tringo's hierarchy of preference towards disability groups: 30 years later. *Psychological Reports, 86,* 1155–1156.

Thompson, T.L. (2000). A history of communication and disability research: The way we were. In D.O. Braithwaite & T.L. Thompson (Eds.), *Handbook of communication and people with disabilities: Research and application* (pp. 1–16). Mahwah, NJ: Erlbaum.

Tringo, J.L. (1970). The hierarchy of preference towards disability groups. *The Journal of Special Education, 4,* 295–306.

15

Will You be My Mentor?
The Intercultural Language
of Initiating
Mentoring Relationships

Pamela J. KALBFLEISCH

Whether referenced in English as *mentor* and *protégé*, in Japanese as *onshi* and *kogai*, or in Hawaiian simply as *kokua ke ohana*, the concept of someone helping another to succeed is part of being human. Mentors and protégés may have different linguistic referents in differing languages and cultures, but the concept of helping is consistent. Kalbfleisch (2002) defines this helping relationship or more specifically a mentoring relationship as:

> A personal relationship between a more sophisticated mentor and a less advanced protégé. The mentor has achieved personal or professional success and is willing and able to share covert and overt practices that have assisted him or her in becoming successful. The protégé has the potential or desire to learn the methods used by the mentor in becoming personally or professionally successful. (p. 63)

Mentoring and guiding a less advanced person to succeed is a laudable goal and mission. Being willing to be mentored and open to another's advice is a key to being a successful protégé. Both participants in these mentoring relationships reap benefits personally and professionally. Protégés can learn valuable skills and build helpful alliances for the future. Mentors can gain satisfaction from helping another to succeed and can gain status as a respected leader.

Success in Finding Mentors

Those who have been mentored achieve more accelerated professional success (Peluchette & Jeanquart, 2000), higher incomes (Whitely, Dougherty, & Dreher, 1991, 1992), and more desirable outcomes (Hill, Bahniuk, & Dobos, 1989; Ragins & Cotton, 1999) than those not mentored. Mentoring relationships are clearly beneficial relationships for protégés, therefore mentors are in great demand. It is the unusual student, new employee, or new professional who is not aware that finding a mentor and establishing a relationship with a mentor will facilitate achieving personal and professional goals. However, finding a willing mentor and establishing a relationship with this mentor is not as easy as a neophyte may believe.

There are a number of formalized mentoring programs designed to help junior members of associations, disadvantaged youth, and members of target populations that are at risk (e.g., Pawson & Gibbes, in press; Renger, in press). However such programs are not always readily available, their success is uncertain, and the characteristics of the mentoring relationships that form as part of these programs are distinct from the mentoring relationships that form independently.

Programmatically formed mentoring relationships are typically formed by an agent who is outside of the relationship; they begin as mentoring relationships without going through stages of relational development as would a naturally occurring relationship. Programmatically formed mentoring relationships are essentially an arranged relationship and as in other arranged relationships the mentorship partners may come to develop a caring personal relationship or they may simply fulfill their assigned roles without developing relational depth. Naturally developing relationships will occur over time and the partners may achieve greater knowledge of one another as individuals with more relational commitment. Programmatic relationships begin with an abrupt start whereas naturally occurring relationships develop over time.

In order to be a part of a programmatic relationship, one must be in the target population of potential protégés for which the program is designed to help. Even if one is selected to be in these programs, one may not actually develop a helpful mentoring relationship with a more advanced other as some mentors and protégés in these programs are functioning simply under the relationship label and are not functioning relationally as a mentors and protégés.

This situation leaves most potential protégés on their own for finding a mentor. Popular press magazines and trade publications encourage people desiring mentors to simply go ask a person to mentor them (Kalbfleisch & Keyton, 1995). However, the experience of getting a person to agree to mentor another is much more complex than it may originally appear.

While mentors may achieve personal satisfaction from helping another achieve, the outcomes of a mentoring relationship are not as tangible as they are for the protégé. Greater professional status and assistance with tasks, two of the tangible outcomes for the mentor (Kalbfleisch & Davies, 1993), while desirable, are less tied to the professional success of the mentor when compared to the more concrete outcomes of the mentoring relationship for the protégé, such as enhanced income and quicker advancement professionally.

The number of potential protégés desiring help also greatly exceeds the number of potential mentors available and willing to help others achieve their goals (Kalbfleisch, 1997). This supply and demand ratio becomes even more skewed when one considers gender (Kalbfleisch 2000) and race (Kalbfleisch & Davies, 1991). Specifically, the problem becomes exacerbated in that there are more male mentors available than female mentors and both male and female mentors have been found to prefer assisting protégés of the same gender (Kalbfleisch, 2000). This preference for similarity between mentors and those they choose for protégés has also been displayed with members of a particular race preferring to mentor others of the same race over those who differ racially from one another (Kalbfleisch & Davies, 1991).

Further, the mentoring relationship is a relationship that can be risky for the mentor (cf. Kalbfleisch, 2002). Mentors may fear losing their job, position, or advantage to their protégé. Mentors may not be willing or able to spend the time helping protégés. Mentors may also be concerned that protégés may share their secrets with others, even sharing the mentor's strategies for success with the mentor's competitors (Kalbfleisch & Davies, 1993).

Furthermore, some mentors fear that others may make sexual innuendos regarding their relationship with a protégé. Other mentors are concerned an actual romantic relationship may develop from having a mentoring relationship with a protégé (Kalbfleisch, 1997, 2000, 2002; Kabfleisch & Keyton, 1995).

Time constraints, perceived or real fears, and supply and demand all work against the formation of a mentoring relationship. Potential protégés are plentiful; mentors are few; yet the rewards of a mentoring relationship are numerous, especially for the protégé.

So how do potential protégés persuade those who are more advanced than they to be their mentors? In her theory of communication in mentoring relationships, Kalbfleisch (2001) posit that potential protégés can be more successful at getting help from potential mentors if they make requests for help with specific tasks rather than requests for mentorship as whole. While a request for mentorship may seem overwhelming to a potential mentor, a request for help seems reasonable. By building on these requests for help, protégés will be more likely to be successful at establishing a mentoring relationship in stages rather than in an abrupt start.

Presentation of the Study

Kalbfleisch examined this proposition of her theory while spending six months as a visiting colleague at the University of Hawai'i on the island of Oahu, in the Hawai'ian archipelago. This was a particularly vibrant location to explore this theory because multicultural data were readily available. This island is the home of 25 distinct Asian American and Pacific Islander cultural groups such as Chinese Americans, Hawai'ians, Japanese Americans, Korean Americans, Philippine Americans, etc, as well as other cultural groups.

In a sample of 119 students enrolled in Speech classes the University of Hawai'i, 61 students or 51 percent of the sample reported having a mentor. To assist respondents in determining whether or not they had a mentor, students were given the Kalbfleisch (2002) definition of a mentoring relationship as provided in the introduction to this chapter. Of the 43 males in the sample, 24 reported having a mentor (56 percent), while 36 of the 69 females reported having a mentor (52 percent). The remaining students did not report their gender.

In examining the cultural differences and similarities of this sample 22 of the 40 Japanese American students or 55 percent reported having mentors, 9 of the 14 Chinese American students or 64 percent reported having mentors, 9 of the 14 Hawai'ian students or 64 percent reported having mentors, 6 of the 12 Korean American students or 50 percent reported having mentors, 4 of the 8 Filipino American students or 50 percent reported having mentors, 2 of the 7 mixed race non-Hawai'ian students or 29 percent reported having mentors, 4 of the 7 Caucasion students or 57 percent reported having mentors, 2 of the 4 Hispanic/Mexican American students or 50 percent reported having a mentor. Additionally, the one African American student reported having a mentor, 2 Vietnamese students reported not having mentors, and the 2 of the 4 remaining students of various cultures reported having mentors. The remaining students did not report on their cultural background.

What is interesting about this sample is that for males and females and for all cultural groups with the exception of the mixed race non-Hawai'ian group and the Vietnamese, over half of those participating in the research had mentors. This is more people reporting mentors than is traditionally found in college samples in the contiguous United States. One should note that this sample is also predominately drawn from Asian and Pacific Islander cultural groups and may also be influenced by these groups rather than the predominately Caucasian samples drawn on the United States mainland. It may be that the more collectivist and less individualist Asian and Pacific Islander cultures may have influenced the experience of these students being helped by others who are more advanced. Also a possibility is that the culture of Hawai'i and its primary university may facilitate mentoring behavior. This author is not aware of any previous research that has studied mentoring choices in Asian and Pacific Islander cultural groups or the mentoring choices in the cultural context of Hawai'i or at the University of Hawai'i.

Across cultural groups, when looking at the communication patterns that these protégés reported using with their mentors to develop their relationships, five percent of the protégés in this sample reported exclusively asking for help with specific tasks to initiate their relationship with a mentor. Eighty-five percent of the sample reported asking for help with specific tasks as a strategy to begin their mentorship relationship. Sixty-seven percent of the sample reported that they had directly asked the person who was helping them to be their mentor. None of the respondents reported simply asking a person to be their mentor as the only method they had used for initiating a relationship with their mentor.[1]

This finding suggests initial support for the idea that asking for help with specific tasks may be an effective method of developing a mentoring relationship rather than asking a person directly to be a mentor. However, clearly this investigation is an initial exploration and a more detailed evaluation is needed.

Obviously the proposition needs to be explored in greater detail with a larger sample. It should also be tested in other locations where previous mentoring research has been conducted for comparison. Additionally the effectiveness of this initiation strategy compared exclusively with direct requests to mentor should be examined, as should the time ordering of initiation strategies such as which strategies are used first and in what sequence, and the band width of types of the tasks and requests for help.

Conclusion

In closing, this author finds it is refreshing to see that there may be a communication strategy that can assist protégés in establishing relationships with mentors. The sample in this study expressed more experiences with having a mentor than in samples taken in the United States mainland. However, if protégés in cultures or locations where people appear to be more predisposed to help each other find success using a variety of relationship initiation strategies, than perhaps those in less willing cultures will also find mentors with a language-based approach to developing mentoring relationships.

Note

1. All averages are rounded up.

References

Hill, S. E. K., Bahniuk, M. H., & Dobos, J. (1989). The impact of mentoring and collegial support on faculty success: An analysis of support behavior, information adequacy, and communication apprehension. *Communication Education, 38*, 13–33.

Kalbfleisch, P. J. (1997). Appeasing the mentor. *Aggressive Behavior, 23*, 389–403.

Kalbfleisch, P. J. (2000). Similarity and attraction in business and academic environments: Same and cross-sex mentoring relationships, *Review of Business, 21*, 58–61.

Kalbfleisch, P. J. (2002). Communication in mentoring relationships: A theory for enactment. *Communication Theory, 12*, 63–69.

Kalbfleisch, P. J., & Davies, A. B.(1991). Minorities and mentoring: Managing the multicultural institution. *Communication Education, 40*, 266–271.

Kalbfleisch, P. J., & Davies A. B. (1993). An interpersonal model for participation in mentoring relationships. *Western Journal of Communication, 57*, 399–415.

Kalbfleisch, P. J., & Keyton, J. (1995). Power and equality in mentoring relationships. In P. J. Kalbfleisch, & M. J. Cody (Eds.). *Gender, power and communication in human relationships.* (pp. 189–212). Mahwah, NJ: Lawrence Erlbaum Associates.

Pawson, C. J., & Gibbes, C. (in press, 2004). Mentoring recidivist youth offenders. In Ng, C. H., Candlin, C. N., & Chiu, C. Y. (Eds.) *Language and Social Psychology.* Hong Kong: City University of Hong Kong Press.

Peluchette, J. V., & Jeanquart, S. (2000). Professionals' use of different mentor sources at various career stages: Implications for career success. *Journal of Social Psychology, 140*, 549–564.

Ragins, B. R., & Cotton, J. L. (1999). Mentor functions and outcomes: A comparison of men and women in formal and informal mentoring relationships. *Journal of Applied Psychology, 84*, 529–550.

Renger, R. (in press, 2004). Improving the Evaluation of mentoring programs: An evaluator's perspective. In Ng, C. H., Candlin, C. N., & Chiu, C. Y. (Eds.) *Language and Social Psychology.* Hong Kong: City University of Hong Kong Press.

Whitely, W., Dougherty, T. W., & Dreher, G. F. (1991). Relationsip of career mentoring and social economic origin to managers and professionals' early career progress, *Academy of Management Journal, 34*, 331–351.

Whitely, W., Dougherty, T. W., & Dreher, G. F. (1992). Correlates of career-oriented mentoring for early career managers and professionals. *Journal of Organizational Behavior, 13*, 141–153.

16

Mentoring
Recidivist Youth Offenders

C. J. PAWSON
C. GIBBES

Mentoring can be loosely defined as a developmental or learning relationship between a more experienced or knowledgeable individual and a less equipped individual. A substantial history of community mentoring specifically for the socially disadvantaged and for those "at risk" has developed over the last 60 years, predominantly in the United States (for a review see Freedman, 1993). The last 10 years have witnessed considerable growth in mentoring in educational and employment developmental contexts (Philip, 2000), but also in providing support and inspiration to individuals whose behavior or circumstances may limit their entry into, or participation in education or the labour market.

Youth Offender Mentoring

While meta-analyses of evaluations of the effects of mentoring programs on youth samples (e.g. Rhodes, 2002) have identified only a modest beneficial impact, the most likely to benefit are shown to be "at risk" youths. Furthermore, these benefits are greatly increased by the implementation of theory- and empirically-based schemes (DuBois, Holloway, Cooper & Valentine, in press). In light of these findings a rationale exists for implementing and evaluating "data-driven" mentoring as a potential intervention for a sample of critically at risk youths, convicted young offenders.

The Rationale

In order to further explain mentoring and its potential as an intervention with youth offenders, it is useful to examine the socio-psychological theory underpinning the implementation of such a scheme. However, beyond any social psychological theory hypothesising the potential benefits of mentoring young offenders; crime statistics, and the economic impact of crime, provide a clear socio-political rationale for its consideration. Figures compiled by the then British government, before the 1997 general election, showed that approximately 70 percent of all crimes that affect ordinary people are committed by a small number of young men, almost all of who began offending in their teenage years. Coupled with this, 72 percent of male young adult offenders discharged in 1997 were reconvicted within two years. With these figures in mind, tackling youth crime, and specifically rates of recidivism, has become a focus of the British government policy on national crime reduction.

While life-course persistent antisocial behavior and offending exist, it is important to recognize the prevalence of adolescent-limited behavior of this nature. The majority of criminal offenders are teenagers, but by the late teenage years and early 20s the number of active offenders decreases by over 50 percent (Moffitt, 1993). The potential social factors responsible for the drop in these figures, and the limiting of some individuals to "adolescent limited" offenders rather than "persistent life offenders", provide clues to reductions in recidivism.

Meta-analyses of interventions aimed at reducing recidivism in juveniles (Lipsey & Wilson, 1998), and the previous research discussed, identify several key social "risk" and "protective" factors in the lives of juveniles (Hoge, Andrews & Leschied, 1996). These factors may exacerbate or ameliorate the risk of juvenile delinquency and criminality and can be broadly conceptualized as relating to the individual, their family, and, socio-economic and social context factors (Loeber, Farrington, Stouthamer-Loeber & van Kammen, 1998; Farrington, Jolliffe, Loeber, Stouthamer-Loeber

& Kalb, 2001). Any intervention aimed at reducing recidivism amongst youth offenders must try to account for most of these risk and protective factors and understand how they contribute to an individual's decision to re-offend.

Individual factors identified as correlates of youth offending behavior include low guilt, drug dependence and substance abuse, low achievement, depressed mood, and anxiety (Stallard, Thomason & Churchyard, 2003). Furthermore, an individual's understanding of social limits afforded through socialization is also central to offending behavior. Significant differences have been found between young offenders and controls on their understanding of behavioral alternatives and inclination to transgress social limits (Grietens, Rink & Hellincks, 2003). Acknowledging these factors, research demonstrates individual protective factors such as empathic understanding; control over amount and frequency of drug and alcohol use; educational achievement, self esteem, and accurate attribution processing (Luthar, 1991; Rae-Grant, Thomas, Offord & Boyle, 1989).

Family risk factors include poor parental supervision, parental rejection, physical punishment, low attachment, poor parent-child communication and unhappy parents (Hoge *et al.*, 1996). Furthermore, studies have revealed criminal convictions within a family to be predictive of youth offending (Farrington, Barnes & Lambert, 1996). Interestingly, paternal and maternal criminal activity is not found to be predictive of youth offending behavior after controlling for family factors such as poor supervision (Sampson & Laub, 1993). Protective factors rooted in the family include parental disapproval of alcohol & substance abuse, authoritative parenting and consistent discipline, and expectations for, and reinforcement of, pro-social and independent values & behavior (Farrington, 1987a; Jang, 1999).

Several socio-economic status (SES) and social context factors have also been shown to be associated with youth offending, such as poor housing, domestic overcrowding, and father's occupation (Ferguson, 1952). Conversely, positive peer associations (Hoge *et al*, 1996) and meaningful, challenging opportunities to contribute to the community (Stouthamer-Loeber, Loeber, Farrington, Zhang, van Kammen & Maguin, 1993) have been identified as social context protective factors, ameliorating the risk of offending.

The complexity and multiplicity of potential factors leading to delinquency and offending behavior is clearly too vast to be satisfactorily covered in this chapter. Many of the factors discussed thus far are clearly co-contributors to a range of developmental sequelae and mechanisms leading to the problem of youth offending. For example, the finding that a history of family offending is positively associated with youth offending can be explained in terms of social modelling of criminal behavior by the youth, or, and more likely, due to continuing intergenerational exposure to several of the family and SES risk factors highlighted above. Hence, risk factors should be viewed as inter-related. Indeed, examination of the criminal records of a sample of convicted young offenders reveals that many of the risk factors discussed above are clearly evident in many of these individual's lives. Two-thirds of the young adult offenders in the case study discussed below had no educational qualifications, and a large number had dropped out or had been excluded from school. Furthermore, 85 percent of the participants in the scheme came from single parent families or had limited contact with either parent. This figure, rather than labelling the single-parent family as detrimental per se, is intended to be viewed in combination with the apparent negative educational experiences of many young offenders, and is thus suggestive of a vacancy for positive adult role models in the lives of these individuals Many young offenders feel let down by their family, peers, and proximal community and need positive role models to challenge their understandably isolated perspective and the negative stereotypes and expectations they face (Gambone, 1993; Jacks, 1994).

It is clear that whether individually predictive, or mediated by other variables, the constellation of predictive factors create a host of pervasive societal problems and repercussions for the offenders and their victims. Therefore, any intervention aimed at reducing offending behavior and recidivism should attempt to address the majority of these risk factors while harnessing and nurturing as many protective factors as possible. In response to this, the specific nature of the risk and protective factors outlined above, and the concerns of the prison service regarding the lack of continuity of interventions through the transition from prison to post-release life, the authors propose a prison and community "through-care" mentoring intervention for consideration.

A New Model

Specifically, the authors suggest that an appropriate mentor may go some way to filling this void left by poor social experiences. Mentors may provide an alternative social relationship beyond those of the family or "street culture" of the peer network (Higgins *et al.*, 1991), and in so doing alter existing and potentially detrimental social networks, thus ameliorating a host of risk factors. An appropriate mentor can enhance the buffering effect of protective factors through providing assistance and support with issues pertaining to education, further training and employment. As a means of illustrating the potential role of the mentor in ameliorating offending risk and nurturing protective factors, the authors suggest a model whereby mentoring can in itself become a protective factor as it actively intervenes to buffer against risk factors, and serves to enhance the protective characteristics of the individual youth, their family, and their wider social context (see Figure 1).

A number of mentoring programmes for "at risk" youth have been evaluated in the United States (Grossman and Tierney, 1998; Royse, 1998; Sterba, 2001); however, there is a dearth of literature examining mentoring for convicted and incarcerated youth. Furthermore, few mentoring evaluations begin at the implementation stages of the scheme, seemingly prioritizing the outcomes analyses with little investigation of the model or process of mentoring (Morzinski & Fisher, 1996). If empirical research and models under-pinning mentoring interventions are to be satisfactorily assessed, the strategies of implementation must be

Figure 1
Social risk and the potential buffering role of a mentor

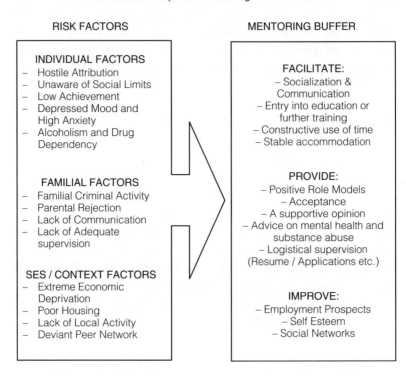

RISK FACTORS   MENTORING BUFFER

INDIVIDUAL FACTORS
– Hostile Attribution
– Unaware of Social Limits
– Low Achievement
– Depressed Mood and
  High Anxiety
– Alcoholism and Drug
  Dependency

FAMILIAL FACTORS
– Familial Criminal Activity
– Parental Rejection
– Lack of Communication
– Lack of Adequate
  supervision

SES / CONTEXT FACTORS
– Extreme Economic
  Deprivation
– Poor Housing
– Lack of Local Activity
– Deviant Peer Network

FACILITATE:
– Socialization &
  Communication
– Entry into education or
  further training
– Constructive use of time
– Stable accommodation

PROVIDE:
– Positive Role Models
– Acceptance
– A supportive opinion
– Advice on mental health and
  substance abuse
– Logistical supervision
(Resume / Applications etc.)

IMPROVE:
– Employment Prospects
– Self Esteem
– Social Networks

assessed prior to any outcomes analyses. One such model based on empirical research has been outlined above and with this in mind, and serving to address the paucity of literature in this area, the following descriptive study documents a YOMI from its inception. The aim of this documentation is threefold: 1) to outline the task of implementing a YOMI, thus providing an understanding of the mentoring process from which, 2) we may examine its convergence with, and divergence from, the proposed model, and in so doing, 3) highlight recommendations for the strategic implementation of a more theoretically adherent intervention in the future.

The Implementation of
a Young Offenders Mentoring Intervention (YOMI):
A Descriptive Study

The Sample and Recruitment

Mentees

A total of 42 male recidivist youth offenders volunteered to take part in the YOMI. Their ages ranged from 17.1 to 22.8 years, with a mean age of 19.8 years. Mentees were from a range of ethnic backgrounds (Afro-Caribbean = 17, Caucasian = 17, Asian = 8) and were all due for release under the supervision of the Inner London Probation Service (ILPS). All were convicted and serving sentences of less than 60 months for a range of violent and non-violent crimes (mean = 24 months). The number of previous convictions for each participant ranged from 2–35, with a mean of 6.23 previous convictions per participant.

The volunteer mentees were recruited through leaflet distribution within a large youth offender prison and any interested offenders received an introductory presentation outlining the aims of the scheme. Those who were interested in being mentored met with a mentee support officer (MSO) based in the prison and completed an application. The MSO screened these forms and potential mentees considered to be serious about addressing their offending behavior with a mentor to steer them in a more positive direction, were interviewed. Potential mentees who displayed a willingness to commit to the demands of the project (e.g. attending interpersonal skills training, improving their basic skills, and honoring appointments with mentors) were selected.

Mentors

The mentor sample consisted of 42 adults (12 males, 30 females) from a range of professional backgrounds and occupations (18 of whom were currently studying). Mentors ranged in age from 19.2 to

57.2 years with a mean age of 30.4 years (20 of whom were under 27 years of age). They were recruited in London employing a range of methods, for example, internal advertisements within academic institutions, a radio and newspaper recruitment campaign, and presentations and leaflet campaigns in high-density business districts. The resulting sample were from a wide range of employment and ethnic backgrounds (Afro-Caribbean = 19, Caucasian = 17, Asian = 5).

Previous schemes have recruited mentors from the retired or elderly community (McCartney, Styles & Morrow, 1994). However, to limit the social distance between mentor and mentee, mentees would be best supported by younger mentors from their local community and preferably from the same ethnic group (Mincy & Wiener, 1990; Wright, 1992). Following initial screening of application forms, the majority of mentor applicants were invited for interview. A ten-point checklist of personal qualities considered necessary for enhancing the protective factors within the mentees environment was employed. Criteria included patience, good communication skills, honesty and the ability to build productive and equitable relationships with young people.

The Intervention

Training

Mentees were provided with a single induction/training session during which they were provided with a background to mentoring and a general introduction to the YOMI. To clarify the role of the mentors a formula for success in building the mentoring relationship and utilising it for post-release success was presented. All mentees had previously received training in career planning, communication and presentation, assertiveness, time management, and organizational skills as part of their prison sentence planning. It was therefore deemed unnecessary to include any further personal development training within the scheme.

Mentors received a series of training sessions on skills for mentoring, dealing with difficult mentoring situations, drugs and health awareness, and interpersonal coaching and counselling. During these sessions mentors were encouraged to explore their understanding of mentoring and similarly to the mentees were provided with a proposed plan of how this type of partnership may be best developed and maintained.

A series of induction sessions familiarized the mentors with the prison system, probation, and youth offending teams. The purpose of these sessions was chiefly to inform mentors of how their role would complement and support the work of the prison and probation services. In addition, the sessions aimed to provide mentors with an understanding of the likely pre-sentencing experience of mentees, the characteristics of young adult offenders, and the barriers that prevent them from leading "law-abiding" lives.

The Matching Process

The MSO reported that on most occasions matches were based on subjective, intuitive consideration rather than any specific criteria. Preliminary interviews with participants elicited background information in order to assist the matching process e.g., interests, reasons for joining the scheme, employment history (mentors), and career / education aims (mentees). Efforts were made to match ethnic background, although 90 percent of mentees reported no preference for the ethnicity of their mentor. Twenty-seven of the forty-two partnerships were ethnically matched. Approximately half of the mentees specified a preference for a female mentor.

The Pre-release Mentoring Relationship

In compliance with the rationale for a "through-care" intervention aimed at providing a continuous supportive relationship across the pre-post release transition, the mentoring relationship was intended to last for a minimum of six-months, beginning three months before mentees were due for release, and continuing for a further three months in the community. The intervention required the mentors to meet with their mentee for an average of two hours per week, thus providing a total contact time of forty-eight hours over six months.

Before the initial introduction, mentors and mentees were not informed of the interests or background of their matched partner. This included withholding any information relating to the mentee's offending behavior. In all but one partnership (the mentee was convicted of a sex offence), mentees convictions were not disclosed. After the introductions each mentor and mentee were interviewed to assess their reaction and deal with any problems. After each subsequent meeting or telephone conversation the mentors completed a weekly report documenting the mentor-mentee contact. These reports included information about any specific assistance planned by the mentor and the thoughts and feelings about time spent and progress with their mentee. The mentors were briefed thoroughly on issues of confidentiality with their mentee.

During the first few meetings mentors were encouraged to introduce the concept of setting goals and identify opportunities to explore the mentee's motivations to enter employment, training or education (ETE). At the earliest opportunity mentors were advised to develop a learning contract serving to formalize the strategy for achieving the ETE goals. Mentees were required to complete a progress form after each interaction with their mentor or the MSO. Information to be recorded included who they met or spoke to, what was discussed, tasks agreed including the rationale and completion date. These forms were intended to encourage adherence to the learning contract.

The Post-release Mentoring Relationship

It was suggested to mentors that maintaining contact with mentees post-release would be a major challenge to the success of the mentoring relationship. Therefore, provision was made for the mentor and MSO to meet the mentee at the prison on the day of release in order to ensure the transition to the community-based relationship. At this time, mentors were instructed to arrange the time and location of the first post-release mentoring meeting.

The intervention code stipulated that post-release meetings should take place in alcohol free venues and most meetings took place in cafés or within the researchers offices. It was intended that these meetings should serve to further discuss the strategy for achieving the goals set out in the learning contract and provide an opportunity for mentors to assist mentees in practical tasks such as completing applications, and attending interviews.

Evaluation and Recommendations

The implementation of the YOMI reveals strengths and limitations, and crystallizes recommendations for future mentoring interventions with young offenders. These are discussed within three emerging phases of the intervention. These phases are evaluated with the previously described model in mind, and include:

- The recruitment, matching, and training processes
- The prison-based mentoring relationship
- The community-based mentoring relationship

Recruitment, Matching, and Training Processes

Recruitment of mentees within the prison proved easier than anticipated with many volunteering from the initial leaflet advertisements. However, the demands of the intervention in terms of time and commitment resulted in a number of potential mentees opting out of the intervention after initial induction. Interviews with the mentee volunteers revealed that the YOMI appeared to attract three types of young adult offenders:

1. those who genuinely wanted to change their behavior and saw the project as an opportunity to do this, for example, by helping them get into ETE, increase confidence and generally help sort themselves out;
2. those with readjustment-specific concerns relating to being released into the community (e.g., immigration, substance

abuse (20 percent), accommodation (35 percent), and employment (78 percent); and,

3. those who perceived the project as an "easy option" or departure from prison routine.

The authors recommend that mentee selection be as inclusive as allowed for by the parameters of the intervention. Many of the individual risk factors identified in Figure 1 are clearly identifiable and are inevitably present to some degree in any sample of incarcerated youth. Frequently, their presence and the consequences of these risk factors result in narrow targeted interventions or even punitive measures which may restrict the individual's participation in a mentoring intervention. The authors believe that, such are the individual protective benefits of mentoring, where necessary a mentoring intervention can be considered complimentary, even catalytic, to the success of many other prison-based interventions.

Internal advertisements within academic institutions proved the most successful mentor recruitment strategy, as reflected in the large number of mentors who were undergraduates. This provided the ethnically diverse sample of mentors required and many were young enough not to be perceived as an authority figure by the mentee. A number of mentors were also recruited from local business communities and media advertisements. Interviews revealed that the motivations of the mentors varied widely but were linked with the method of recruitment. For example many of the mentor applicants from academic institutions were studying criminology or forensic psychology degrees and this was reflected in their motivation (e.g., to gain experience of working with offenders in a criminal justice setting). The majority of non-studying volunteers reported a motivation to "give something back to the community".

Steps should be taken to ensure the suitability of mentors as positive role models and while no potential mentors need be rejected on the basis of previous criminal background, interventions must consider the implications of recruiting mentors with employment experience of the criminal justice system (e.g. social workers, police officers), or those who may be perceived as affiliated to a system with which many offenders may unfortunately have had negative experiences. Beyond the potentially negative experiences of mentees with authority and the justice system it is clear that many offenders may have been let down by a host of individuals. With this in mind, following an interview, successful applicants should agree to attend all induction and training sessions, visit their mentee in prison regularly, and keep project staff informed of any developments or problems with their mentoring relationships.

While the correlates of youth offending have been found in diverse samples, any potential intervention requires an evaluative examination without the presupposition that it will succeed for all. The probability exists that certain interpersonal combinations will evidence greater benefits suggesting some cause for careful consideration of the matching process. As with previous mentoring projects, the matching process in the YOMI was more of an art than a science. However, interactions and the development of a mentoring relationship are recognized as easier if both parties share attitudes and beliefs (Ragins, 1997a). Driven by the rationale that the experiences and beliefs of a mentor from the same ethnic background and community may have more salience to the mentee, few structured criteria were employed other than ethnicity and mentor-mentee proximity. A couple of partnerships were formed on the basis of very specific shared interests and adopting these limited criteria matching was considered successful from the mentor's perspective (80 percent of mentors felt they were matched "well" or "very well").

Conversely, the mentees reported that they were considerably less satisfied with their match (only 36 percent reporting that they were matched "well" or "very well"). Further investigation revealed that many mentees held expectation that their mentor would be specifically involved in the activities or employment that the mentees discussed in their application. For the purposes of enhancing the protective impact of employment and use of leisure time, such matching is preferable, although the sample size was prohibitively small. To assist in implementing a more accurate matching process a large pool of mentors from diverse employment, and ethnic backgrounds is recommended. A cautionary note to be heeded with regard ethnic criteria for matching is the potential need for consideration of specific ethnicity within the unsuitably broad ethnic groupings of Black or Asian (e.g. African, Caribbean, Indian, Pakistani). On the other hand many mentees reported ethnicity was of less importance than proximal age and an understanding of issues pertaining to their ethnicity. The authors suggest the elicitation of any specific mentee preferences at the earliest opportunity.

Training was evaluated through questionnaires and interviews with mentors and mentees immediately after training and at the end of the mentoring relationship. This allowed an insight in to the style and implementation of training and the benefits or shortcomings when put in to practice in the relationship. The initial mentor evaluation indicated that the training procedures were considered to be comprehensive. The only negative feedback was that there was an excess of information to digest and some repetition. A number of the mentors reported that the probation and prison service training sessions were particularly useful for preparing them for the likely experiences of their mentees. It is recommended that mentors gain an insight in to the regime and lifestyle of young adult offenders prior to establishing a relationship with their mentee. This provides an important facilitation of interpersonal connection early in the mentoring relationship resulting in a more immediate assessment of the mentee's needs on the part of the mentor, and an immediate awareness of the potential of the mentoring buffer on the part of the mentee.

Mentee training was limited to an introduction to the theory of mentoring and what mentees could expect from the experience. It was clear from observing their previous training that many of the listening and communication exercises were very difficult to initiate in large groups. To encourage improved attention and motivation, it is recommended that mentee training should occur in small groups (4 or 5 individuals). Furthermore, care must be taken when introducing the potential role of mentoring and mentors to the mentee sample. Any misleading expectations must be avoided lest the relationship begin with dissatisfaction. Instead, mentees should be given a brief introduction to mentoring and encouraged to contemplate their post-release goals, perceived limitations to achievement of these goals, and the potential individual risk factors for recidivism. The authors suggest that formulaic training will be unsuitable for the mentee and that their individual needs should be addressed including training targeted toward empowering the mentee in assisting with the facilitation, provision and improvements integral to the mentoring buffer (see Figure 1). Recommendations include specific briefings relating to education and employment facilitating agencies and advice on the prerequisites of various employment and education options. Ideally mentors should be equipped with the rudimentary means for furthering mentee's training in areas such as self esteem, social skills and organization such that the mentoring buffer may be further augmented.

Reflections on training after the completion of the intervention proved difficult to obtain from mentees as many lay incommunicado and the remaining could not recollect the training sessions. This perhaps further reflects the need for mentee training to take a more mentee-centered approach. Post-mentoring training evaluations from mentors revealed that the listening exercises and advice on detachment were particularly useful, although there was felt to be insufficient preparation for the specific needs of mentees (e.g., advice on housing and benefits) and a lack of advice regarding the maintenance of the relationship in the community post-release. The authors recommend that mentor training include provision of information about resources available for young adult offenders, advice or a presentation from ex-mentors on how to maintain the relationship once mentees are released, and discussion of the specific complexities surrounding the post-release experience e.g., substance abuse and peer pressure.

The Prison-Based Mentoring Relationship

Initial responses from mentors and mentees after the introductory meetings were extremely positive, with most partnerships departing their introduction having organized their next meeting. Mentors and mentees were expected to meet for two hours per week for three months prior to the mentees release. Mentors were clearly briefed on the required time commitment, however, the prison-based mentoring meetings proved difficult for those mentors who were working full-time as prison visits required significant planning and were restricted to standard working hours. As a result one in two partnerships met only once or twice prior to release and no partnership met for the proposed twenty-four pre-release contact hours. The maximum pre-release contact time was twelve hours and this was reached by a number of the student mentors suggesting a clear benefit of including this cohort of the mentoring sample.

Many of the partnerships that did complete pre-release contact hours reported that these meetings were dominated by discussions about interests, family backgrounds and day-to-day work or prison routine. The majority of mentors reported that when contact was mentee-driven the meetings focussed rather more on these issues than discussion of goals and development of the learning contract. All partnerships reported that, as advised, they had discussed the aspirations of the mentee to some extent within the second meeting, however, many of the mentees appeared reticent to discuss specific goals at such an early stage.

It is important to note that all of the mentees had experienced guidance counselling within prison and as such, discussions of this nature may be perceived as part of the prison "system". The underlying philosophy of the mentor as supportive confidante, detached from the prison and authority, is perhaps not best served by discussion of goals and contracts before communication and trust are secured. Considering the crucial role of communication in the initiation and subsequent maintenance of mentoring relationships (Kalbfleisch, 2002), future mentoring interventions should consider the importance of nurturing interpersonal communication without any underlying motive other than initiation and maintenance. With this in mind, a cautionary note regarding meeting report forms is salient. The unusual request for documenting the contact between mentor and mentees for a third party is atypical in most non-professional dyadic relationships, and is likely to arouse suspicion, not least amongst youth offenders whose experience of dyadic relationships with adults will almost always involve the recording of what is said within the justice or prison system.

In practice, few learning contracts were developed. However, there was evidence that aspirations were assessed and plans for facilitating these were formed through negotiation during pre-release meetings.

If such discussions are to benefit the mentee it would seem prudent that mentors receive more theoretical briefing of risk and protective factors and shape goals around these. The authors suggest that the focus on ETE goals is merely a symptom of intended outcomes analyses and fails to acknowledge the individual and unique needs of the mentee. A conceptual awareness of risk and protective factors would allow the mentor to identify and discuss strategies for the amelioration of specific risks while developing their protective role within the relationship. This is echoed by the data from mentees who reported very specific risk factors they anticipated leading to recidivism (e.g. debts, deviant peer pressure, outstanding immigration issues).

Further echoing the need for mentor training in understanding and negotiating the hurdles for newly released young offenders, mentees reported that the most valuable aspect of their mentoring relationship lay in the mentor's ability to obtain information on practical issues (e.g. advice on benefits, education and accommodation) which lessened some of their anxiety about their release. Many also cited the emotional support provided by mentors, as a release from the emotionally barren existence of prison. These are very positive findings from this study and also suggest the need for inclusion of specific mentor training in emotional support and preparation for acting as a socialising agent prior to release. Beyond the individual skills brought to the relationship by the individual mentor, it is clear that even introducing incarcerated youth offenders to an adult entirely removed from the institutions which are so salient in many of their lives, is novel to many and may play a role in changing their belief systems and perception of society and societal functioning.

The Community-Based Mentoring Relationship

Working with a sample of newly released young offenders reveals the transient and often isolated nature of their lives. While this further advocates the role of a mentor in providing continual and stable support, in reality it proved very difficult for mentors to trace and arrange meetings with their mentees. In practice, only two mentees were met on release at the prison by their mentor, with most mentee's immediate post-release priorities, unsurprisingly, involving family, girlfriends, or friends. On reflection, while well intended in terms of ensuring the transition of the mentoring relationship from prison to the community, this strategy was naïve. Unfortunately this trend of sparse post-release meetings was to continue throughout the community-mentoring phase and as a result limits the reporting of any meaningful analysis of the impact of the community-mentoring phase.

While a key obstacle to the continuation of the mentoring partnerships was the difficulty in contacting mentees, perhaps the clearest destructive factor in terms of continuing the intervention is highlighted in the reports from mentors that three-quarters did arrange meetings, but that mentees failed to turn up. Many mentors showed rapidly dwindling commitment in the face of unidirectional attempts to continue and reported that they felt their role had been purely as a prison visitor and their mentoring role was only employed while the mentee was incarcerated. Encouragingly, half of the mentors who never met their mentee in the post-release period did at least manage to make contact with the mentee's family or probation officer for an update on their mentee's progress.

Despite the apparent breakdown in the intervention, those post-release meetings that did occur proved valuable in many respects. Five partnerships met for more than five hours in the community. During these meetings, mentors provided practical advice and support (e.g., help in writing a curriculum vitae, securing a job and accommodation, providing a mentee with a reference, and opening a bank account). Mentees reported that this practical help was invaluable and the important mentor role of providing emotional support continued to be utilized as mentees tried to adapt to life back in the community.

The likelihood exists that the same positive trend of pre-release mentoring contact would extend to post-release mentoring. Indeed, previous literature suggests that mentoring relationships with young people of a year or longer evidence the largest number of benefits (Grossman and Rhodes, 2002). It is therefore imperative to examine the reasons for the breakdown at this phase of the mentoring relationships. Unfortunately, a full explanation is not available as researchers were subject to the same lack of contact with mentees as the mentors. One explanation did arise from interviews with probation services which revealed that many young offenders may wish to disassociate themselves with the prison regime as quickly as possible. Despite the best attempts of mentors to appear independent from the prison system, an unfortunate stigma may exist.

One proposed solution to maintaining the mentoring relationship in the community is that post-release meetings should form part of mentees' statutory supervision (terms of probation). Failure to arrange and attend meetings would thus be seen as a breach of their supervision with grave repercussions for the mentee. While increasing the likelihood of maintaining the mentoring relationship across the prison-community transition, this strategy is likely to have the undesirable effect of blurring the mentoring relationship into a continuation of the prison sentence and as such would threaten its utility. Instead the authors propose the initiation of a persistent multi-contact process throughout the relationship, serving to remind participants of the importance and benefits of maintaining contact. Acknowledging the risk factors associated with the family relationships of offenders, such a process could extend to the mentoring of the family and in so doing serve to extend the post-release relationship, but also further enhance the protection of the mentee.

Conclusion

This chapter has argued that a theoretical research-based approach to the implementation of mentoring interventions must be adopted. On the basis of previous literature concerning youth offending, and current perspectives on mentoring, the authors extended research on mentoring with "at risk" youths by integrating relevant social psychological and criminological evidence with theory to provide a theoretical rationale for the consideration of mentoring with young offenders. Specifically, several risk and protective factors in the lives of young offenders have been identified and a model of risk amelioration and protective enhancement by mentors is proposed.

Any model for intervention and its efficacy must be evaluated, but the traditional prioritization of outcomes analyses over an investigation of the implementation fails to interrogate the underlying rationale and its suitability for application in any meaningful way. Through observing a young offender mentoring intervention in practice and interviewing multiple informants, the authors documented an intervention from inception to its, albeit premature, completion. A descriptive study of this nature provides crucial data for future interventions as it highlights potential impediments and crystallizes strategies for overcoming them.

The authors witnessed clear obstructions to the observed programme at every stage of the mentoring process. Both intra-personal and intra-programme issues require a strategic approach grounded not only in previous experience but sound theoretical understanding. Specifically, and from the outset, recruitment of mentees must be as inclusive as possible, acknowledging that key risk factors such as lack of socialization and awareness of social limits restrict the participation of young offenders in many pre-release interventions and post-release activities. Beyond the limited contact with the offender's family, a mentor is likely to be the only non-institutional adult socialising agent in contact with a young offender during their time in prison. The benefits of socialization and introduction of social limits by the mentor may serve to ameliorate key risk factors and facilitate transferable skills of social behavioral awareness and communication such that a number of post-release protective factors become self-attainable by the mentee. In contrast to the inclusiveness of mentee recruitment, the commitment, motivation and non-judgmental approach required of mentors clearly necessitates more stringent mentor recruitment procedures. Not only must the mentor provide a positive role model capable of facilitating and enhancing the buffer of protective factors, the mentor must also possess a temperament capable of addressing risk factors, withholding judgment in the face of substance abuse or inappropriate social behavior, and facing hostility without being demoralized.

Not only is an awareness of the intrapersonal aspects of a mentor required by intervention teams for appropriate selection, but also a knowledge of the interests and experiences of mentors such that interpersonal communication between mentor and mentee may be fostered. The authors recommend recruitment of a large pool of mentors such that the matching process might include criteria of shared interests and relative experience. Shared interests and experiences will facilitate the nurturing of communication within the mentoring partnership while relevant experience holds the potential to catalyse and facilitate post-release activities of a protective value. Without wishing to ignore the relevance of ethnicity, the appropriately matched temperament, interests, and experiences of the mentor and mentee are likely to contribute to the mentoring buffer significantly more than ethnically- or culturally-driven matching criteria.

In order that the necessary enlightenment of the mentee's individual, familial, or social context risk factors can be reached by the mentor, interpersonal communication and a realistic concept of young offenders must be achieved. Mentor training must encompass a briefing of the likely sentencing experience of offenders and the prison regime that provides their current environment. Without such awareness, unrealistic perceptions and expectations are likely to hamper the necessary communication between participants. Without the means to identify specific risks to the mentee through communication, the facilitation, provision and improvement of protective factors will remain elusive. With this in mind, it is recommended that mentee training should focus on encouraging exploration of pre-sentencing risk factors on an individual basis. Such awareness on the part of the mentee encourages mentee empowerment and is likely to facilitate the early articulation of these risks such that the mentor can act upon them. While familial and socio-economic risk factors may appear impenetrable to the mentor, the mentor is ideally positioned to act as an independent confidante and should aim to cement this position with the mentee through providing supportive opinion and facilitating more extensive social networks and constructive use of time. Contact with the mentee's family as a means of knitting a more extensive support network may be appropriate if requested by the mentee, however care must be taken not to blur the independent "non-authority" based role of the mentor.

Furthermore, the enhancement of many protective factors such as further education, accommodation and substance awareness will facilitate the amelioration of many familial and socio-economic risk factors. This buffering role may be significantly enhanced through mentor and mentee training from other advisory agencies. It is clear that knowledge or easy access to knowledge on post-release practicalities serves to persuade mentees of the benefits of mentoring and further enhances the likelihood of a continuing post-release mentoring relationship.

In summary, the current descriptive study found the implementation strategy in the intervention described, facilitated to some degree the protective role of a mentor in each of the three sources of risk outlined in the model: the individual, the family, and SES and the social context. However, several individual risk factors emanating from these sources were not independently or adequately addressed due to shortcomings in the implementation process. Recommendations are made regarding specific selection, matching, and training strategies, as well as approaches toward the initiation, maintenance and repair of the mentoring relationship itself. It is hoped that such recommendations will benefit future interventions and facilitate their adherence to sound theoretical rationale and a "mentee-centered" approach.

Acknowledgments

Many thanks to the mentors, mentees, and H.M. Prison and Probation services for participating in the Young Offenders Mentoring Intervention project. We are also very grateful to Rachel Tanner, William Pocknell, Gavin Nobes and Brian Clifford for their continued support of this research

References

DuBois, D. L. Holloway, B. E. Cooper H., Valentine, & J. C. "Effectiveness of mentoring programs for youth: A meta-analytic review." *American Journal of Community Psychology* (in press).

Farrington, D.P. (1987a). "Early precursors of frequent offending", in *From Children to Citizens, Volume 3: Families, Schools, and Delinquency Prevention*. J. Q. Wilson & G. C. Loury (Eds.), Springer-Verlag, New York.

Farrington, D. P., Barnes, G. C. & Lambert, S. (1996). The concentration of offending in families. *Leg. Criminol. Psychol.* 1, 47–63;

Farrington D. P., Jolliffe D, Loeber R, Stouthamer-Loeber M, Kalb LM (2001). The concentration of offenders in families, and family criminality in the prediction of boys' delinquency. *Journal of Adolescence* 24 (5): 579–596

Ferguson, J. (1952). *The young delinquent in his social setting*. Oxford: Oxford University Press.

Freedman, M. (1993). *The kindness of strangers: Adult mentors, urban youth, and the new voluntarism*. San Francisco, CA: Jossey-Bass.

Gambone, M. A. (1993). *Strengthening programs for youth: Promoting adolescent development in the JTPA system*. Philadelphia: Public/Private Ventures.

Grietens, H., Rink, J., & Hellincks, W. (2003). Nonbehavioral correlates of juvenile delinquency: Communications of detained and nondetained young people about social limits. *Journal of Adolescent Research*, Vol. 18, No. 1, 68–89.

Grossman, J. B. & Rhodes, J. E. (2002). The test of time: Predictors and effects of duration in youth mentoring programs. *American Journal of Community Psychology*, 30, 199–206.

Grossman , J. B. & Tierney, J. P. (1998). Does mentoring work? An impact study of the big brothers big sister program. *Evaluation Review*, 22, 403–426

Higgins, C. *et al*, *I Have a dream in Washington*, DC: Initial Report, Public/Private Ventures, Philadelphia, 1991.

Hoge, R. D., Andrews, D. A., & Lescheid, A.W. (1996). An investigation of risk and protective factors in a sample of youthful offenders. *Journal of Child Psychology and Psychiatry*, Vol. 37, No. 4, 419–424.

Jang, S. (1999). Age varying effects of family, school and peers on delinquency: A multilevel modelling test of interactional theory. *Criminology*, 37, 643–686.

Kalbfleisch, P. J. (2002). Communication-based theory development: Building theories for communication research. *Communication Theory*. 12 (1, February), 5–7.

Lipsey, M.W. & Wilson, D.B (1998). Effective intervention for serious juvenile offenders. Chapter 13 In Loeber, R. & Farrington D. P. *Serious and violent juvenile offenders; Risk factors and successful interventions.* Thousand Oaks CA, Sage pp. 313–345.

Loeber, R., Farrington, D. P., Stouthamer-Loeber, M. and van Kammen, W. B. (1998). *Antisocial Behaviour and Mental Health Problems: Explanatory Factors in Childhood and Adolescence.* Mahwah, N.J.: Lawrence Erlbaum.

Luthar, S. (1991). Vulnerability and resilience: A study of high-risk adolescents. *Child Development*, 62, 600–616.

Mincy, R.B. & Wiener, S.J.(1990). A Mentor, Peer Group Incentive Model for Helping Underclass Youth. Research Paper.

Moffitt, T.E. (1993). Adolescence-Limited and Life-Course-Persistent Antisocial Behaviour: A Developmental Taxonomy. *Psychological Review*, Vol. 100, No. 4, 674–701.

Morrow, K. V., & Styles, M. B. (1995). Building relationships with youth in program settings: A study of Big Brothers / Big Sisters. Philadelphia: Public/Private Ventures.

Morzinski, J. A., Fisher, J. C., (1996). An evaluation of formal mentoring studies and a model for their improvement. *Evaluation Practice*, 17:43–56.

Pawson, C. J. (2003). *Mentoring and the recidivist youth offender: An evaluation.* Research development and statistics directorate, Home Office, U.K.

Philip, K. (2000) "Mentoring: pitfalls and potential for young people", *Youth and Policy*, 67, 1–15.

Rae Grant, N., Thomas, B. H., Offord, D. R., & Boyle, M. H. (1989). Risk,

Protective Factors, and the Prevalence of Behavioral and Emotional Disorders in Children and Adolescents. *Journal of the American Academy of Child and Adolescent Psychiatry*, 28:, 262–268.

Ragins, B. R. (1997). Diversified mentoring relationships in organizations: A power perspective. *Academy of Management Review*, 22, 482–521.

Rhodes, J. E. (2002). *New Directions for Youth Development, A Critical View of Youth Mentoring*, San Francisco, CA: Jossey-Bass.

Royse D. (1998). Mentoring high-risk minority youth: evaluation of the Brothers Project. *Adolescence*. Vol.33:145–158

Sampson, R., & Laub. J. (1993). *Crime in the Making: Pathways and Turning Points through Life*. Cambridge, MA: Harvard University Press.

Stallard, P., Thomason, J., & Churchyard, S. (2003) The mental health of young people attending a Youth Offending Team: A descriptive study. *Journal of Adolescence*. Vol.26, No.1, 33–43.

Sterba, J. P. (2001). Three challenges to ethics: Environmentalism, feminism, and multiculturalism. New York: Oxford University Press.

Stouthamer-Loeber, M., Loeber, R., Farrington, D. P., Zhang, Q., Van Kammen, W. B., & Maguin, E. (1993). The double edge of protective and risk factors for delinquency: Interrelations and developmental patterns. *Development and Psychopathology*, 5, 683–701.

Wright. W. J. (1992) "The endangered black child", *Educational Leadership*, 49,4:14–17.

17

Improving the Evaluation of Mentoring Programs

Ralph RENGER

As noted by Kalbfleisch (earlier in this volume) there are many types of mentoring relationships. The focus of this chapter is on the evaluation of the effectiveness of mentoring programs targeting at-risk youth. The mentoring movement continues to grow. Evidence for this growth can be found in television, the popular press, website links, and special conferences (Gibb, 1999). It seems reasonable to posit that this growth could be attributed to the fact that mentoring has intuitive appeal, is easy to relate to, and understand. After all, mentoring is really no different than one of our most basic human functions: parenting. Mentoring also appeals to our altruistic side and sense of community (Gibb, 1999). It makes sense to us and makes us feel good to think that we can nurture the development of someone else.

I would argue that the mentoring movement has depended largely on these intuitive and altruistic aspects to grow, appealing to people's emotions and sense of community for financial support. While some funding agencies continue to provide dollars based on a good idea, many more are now requesting evidence that mentoring is indeed effective before providing additional funds. The honeymoon period is rapidly coming to an end.

Evidence for the Effectiveness
of Mentoring is Lacking

There is ample anecdotal evidence to support the effectiveness of mentoring. We all know a story of how a youth has been touched by a mentor. The problem, however, is that anecdotal evidence is no longer sufficient to convince politicians and funding agencies to provide the resources necessary to sustain existing programs and develop new ones to meet the growing demand.

In reviewing the literature several authors have noted a dearth of empirical studies documenting the effectiveness of mentoring (Grossman & Tierney, 1998; Royse, 1998). A few of the studies that have completed an assessment of the effectiveness of their programs are now briefly reviewed.

O'Connor (1995) studied the effectiveness of a mentoring program in reducing high school dropout rates. The study findings were not convincing as O'Connor concluded that participating in a mentoring program *may* improve dropout rates, school attendance, and student self-efficacy.

Johnson (1997) examined the effectiveness of the Sponsor-A-Scholar program, a mentoring program for at-risk youth. Johnson found limited support for mentoring, noting improvements in academic standing among students in the tenth and eleventh grades, but not grade twelve students. She also found mentoring to be ineffective in improving self-esteem.

One of the empirical studies most often cited in support of mentoring is that of the Big Brothers Big Sisters program conducted by Grossman and Tierney (1998). The study concluded that youth involved with mentors who are carefully screened, matched, provided case management, and meet regularly were less likely than controls to skip school, hit someone or use drugs. This study addressed many methodological shortcomings of other studies examining the effectiveness of mentoring by randomization youth to an intervention or control group, using a large sample size and including a structured protocol. One limitation of the study is that 20 percent of the youth randomly assigned to the intervention group did not receive a match. Therefore, it might be argued that the findings are a liberal estimate of the effectiveness of mentoring, as it is known that it is more difficult to find a match for high-risk youth. In other words, the youth who were most likely to produce poor outcomes were excluded from the intervention sample.

Royse (1998) also used a randomized design to study the effects of a mentoring program on improving outcomes in African-American teenagers between the ages of 14 and 16 living in a female-headed household. The study found "no quantitative evidence that mentors had a beneficial impact on mentees" (p.149).

Sterba (2001) studied the impact of a mentoring program at improving the self-esteem of at-risk youth. When compared to a control group, students in the mentorship program did not show any significant improvements in self-esteem. Further, there were no differences between the two groups on measures of attendance, referrals, or days suspended.

More recently, Dubois, Holloway, Valentine and Cooper (2002) completed a meta-analysis of 55 mentoring programs for which evaluations were completed. Dubois *et al.* (2002) concluded, ". . . that it may be most appropriate to expect the typical youth participating in a mentoring program to receive benefits that are quite modest in terms of absolute magnitude" (p.187).

In summary, relative to the large numbers of mentoring programs very few studies have been conducted to examine the effectiveness of mentoring. Further, the findings of the majority of studies that have attempted to provide research support for mentoring can be characterized as equivocal at best. The Grossman and Tierney (1998) was an experimentally sound study, but is likely an overestimate of the effectiveness of mentoring. If additional research evidence is not forthcoming, it is reasonable to conclude that financial support for mentoring programs will dwindle.

Explaining the Shortage of Research Data

One could argue that the limited research support might be attributed to poorly designed studies. Non-experimental designs with small sample sizes and inadequate power may offer some explanation. The difficulty is that real world constraints restrict the ability to incorporate experimental designs. There are also considerable ethical implications in randomizing at-risk youth, essentially withholding the support of a caring adult for the sake of research. The potential to do harm is high. The likelihood that the Grossman and Tierney (1998) or Royse (1998) studies would receive ethical clearance from an Internal Review Board (IRB) is small. Further, the majority of mentoring programs are much smaller than the Nationwide Big Brothers Big Sisters program. Thus, the likelihood of obtaining large sample sizes needed to detect small but significant differences is low.

From an evaluator's perspective, however, the reason for a lack of research support is more basic and occurs well before issues of study design and sampling become salient. The problem is that advocates and mentoring experts have not taken the time to make explicit the underlying rationale by which mentoring is thought to work (Pawson and Gibbes, this volume). In research terms, the theoretical foundation of mentoring is missing.

In evaluation terms, the failure is in the planning process. The implications of this poor planning are shown in Figure 1. In assessing the effectiveness of mentoring programs all the studies reviewed above assess change in dropout rates, referrals, truancy, and so forth. These are all endpoints, or in evaluation terms, outcomes[1]. These endpoints are symptoms. There are a host of antecedent conditions[2], or root causes, of these symptoms.

Sometimes factors that researchers believe to be antecedent conditions are in fact still symptoms. For example, Pawson and Gibbes (this volume) cite low achievement, depressed mood, and drug dependency as individual risk factors. Similarly, Johnson (1997) and Sterba (2001) assessed changes in self-esteem as an indicator of program success. I would argue that these are all symptoms whose antecedent conditions are many and which have not been explicitly identified.

The fact that studies have only identified endpoints as measures of effectiveness for mentoring programs is evidence that they are operating without a theoretical basis for mentoring. As Pawson and Gibbes (earlier in this volume) rightly note, "any model for intervention and its efficacy must be evaluated, but the traditional prioritization of outcomes analyses [i.e., endpoints] over an investigation of the implementation fails to interrogate the underlying rationale [i.e., the antecedent conditions]". Why has the focus remained on outcome evaluation? Experience suggests that the failure to collect more proximal data or in evaluation terms to conduct an impact evaluation, occurs because there is no idea of what should be collected.

Significant consequences arise when focusing on endpoints and not taking the time to understand the antecedent conditions, or underlying rationale, of a problem. First, change in symptoms are often difficult to demonstrate because they are at the end of a sequence of events and as such a) are dependent on changes in antecedent conditions to occur, and b) take longer to change and thus require long-term tracking for which resources are often not available.

A second consequence of not making the antecedent conditions of a problem explicit is that resulting strategies tend to target symptoms. For example, many programs designed to improve self-esteem are founded on the concept of telling youth through direct messages that they are competent individuals. The problem is that messages alone do not provide the opportunity to build skills necessary to achieve the competence needed to meet challenges the youth will face. Thus, when the youth is presented with a challenge the likelihood of succeeding is small. The resulting failure negatively affects self-esteem. Taking the time to understand the foundation upon which self-esteem is built, that is the antecedent conditions of self-esteem, will result in better-grounded programs that have a higher probability of producing intended effects. This point is illustrated again later.

To uncover the antecedent conditions the most important question to ask is: *why* do we have this problem? This is at the heart of the planning process and is missing in studies attempting to evaluate the effectiveness of mentoring. Once the antecedent conditions are identified we can then determine how mentoring is thought to change them and develop appropriate measures to assess impact. The key then to a more comprehensive evaluation plan is better and explicit planning.

Figure 1
The focus of mentoring studies

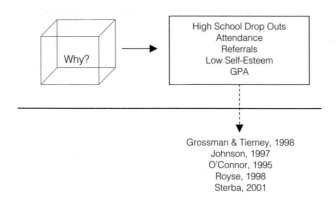

Building the Foundation
for Better Empirical Evidence

My colleague and I have developed a three-step process to help identify more meaningful indicators of effectiveness, called the ATM approach (Renger & Titcomb, 2002). In addition to a brief description I will show how the product of each step can be used to improve studies dedicated to demonstrating the effectiveness of mentoring.

Step 1. Identify the Antecedent Conditions.

The key to uncovering antecedent conditions is to ask "why" the problem exists? Why are high school students dropping out? Why are they not attending classes? Experts, research literature, and existing theories are used to help answer why. As noted earlier one symptom often targeted and evaluated by mentoring programs is low self-esteem (See Figure 1). There is a significant body of literature devoted to the study of self-esteem, which indicates that many at-risk youth have low self-esteem. However, Renger, Kalbfleisch, Smolak, & Crago (1999) argued that self-esteem is in itself a symptom for which there are many root causes. The basic premise of the Renger *et al.* (1999) article was that self-esteem improves when youth experiences mastery in life domains that they value and are valued by a significant adult in their life. These antecedent conditions for self-esteem are shown in Figure 2.

Figure 2
Uncovering the why

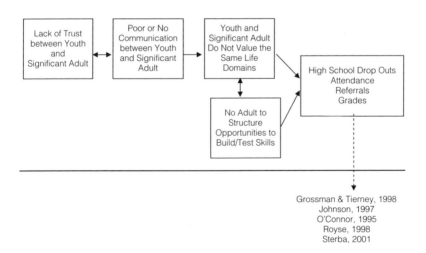

Grossman & Tierney, 1998
Johnson, 1997
O'Connor, 1995
Royse, 1998
Sterba, 2001

It is important to note that I am in no way suggesting that this is the only explanation or theory about how self-esteem is improved or that self-esteem is the only premise upon which mentoring is founded. For example, Gibb (1999) suggested that social exchange theory and communitarianism are other theories that may be useful in understanding the antecedent conditions to successful mentoring relationships. The purpose of presenting this theory is to demonstrate how taking the time to make implicit understandings explicit, can help create a more meaningful evaluation plan that includes better measures of process, impact, and outcome.

Mentoring programs will benefit from taking the time to visually depict the antecedent causes believed to be salient in affecting self-esteem. Renger *et al.* (1999) showed how an understanding of the antecedent conditions shown in Figure 2 could assist programs in recruitment, orientation, screening, training, and monitoring of mentoring programs.

From an evaluation standpoint, taking the time to understand and make explicit the antecedent conditions contributing to a problem also serves another important function. Undoubtedly, a myriad of antecedent conditions will be identified as contributing to any one symptom. For example, Pawson and Gibbes (this volume) noted several familial, socioeconomic, and individual factors that place individuals at risk. Many of these factors, especially those in the familial and socioeconomic domains, are those over which a mentor has no control to change. Two important points can be made with this understanding. First, if changes in endpoints, or outcomes, are dependent on so many factors, many over which a mentoring program has no control, then why would any mentoring program hinge its success on changing these outcomes? Second, in evaluation terms, the depiction of the antecedent conditions underlying a problem will assist in properly focusing the evaluation away from outcomes (i.e., endpoints over which any single program has little influence in changing) and toward impacts (i.e., those antecedent conditions that a program directly targets).

Step 2. Ensure the Activity Targets Antecedent Conditions

The next step is to ensure that the proposed activity targets the antecedent conditions. This may seem intuitive, however it is not uncommon to find many agencies operating "activity traps" (Lynn, 1999). Activity traps are programs that seem like good ideas, but upon close inspection do not target antecedent conditions of the problem. They often have been operating for many years, passed on from director to director. No one is sure anymore why they do them and are often maintained for good public relations. The Girl Power Program sponsored by the U.S. Department of Health and Human Services is an example of a program that targets self-esteem directly. The basic premise of the program is to rely on reinforcing the message that "girls are great". Numerous, resource intensive events, such as rallies, camps, and special days are held across the country that sends this same message. The problem is that the program is targeting self-esteem without understanding its antecedent conditions. Such a program is unlikely to demonstrate effectiveness because it does not target antecedent conditions of self-esteem. Within the context of Figure 2, no matter how many times you tell a young girl she is great, if she fails at a task in a life domain that is important to her, because she does not have the skills, her self-esteem will not improve. Thus, the program, while noble, is inappropriately targeted.

For the sake of illustration assume that the antecedent conditions in Figure 2 are true. If true, then a mentoring program must be able to demonstrate how it will provide the guidance necessary to help mentors understand this process of building self-esteem, including how to identify life domains of importance to the youth, how to build a common value system, and how to structure opportunities for the youth to experience success.

This is a fatal error of many mentoring programs. They do not have a conceptual framework from which they operate. They simply operate from the premise that placing an at-risk youth and an adult together will generate positive outcomes. Thus, it is not surprising that youth matched with mentors who receive no additional guidance as to how to mentor have similar outcomes to those youth placed in control groups (e.g., Royse, 1998). Under these conditions one is simply comparing the impact of the presence of two adults who simply go by different names.

In evaluation terms the lack of a conceptual understanding is evidenced by the type of data that is typically collected, namely the frequency and duration of time spent together (Pawson and Gibbes, [this volume]; Royse, 1998). The reason why more meaningful data about the *quality* of time spent together (e.g., type of activity and purpose) is not collected is because there is no understanding of what this data should be. From Figure 2, one would suggest that data be gathered to assess whether time was spent together developing a common value system and structuring opportunities to build skills in valued domains. Royse (1998) also noted the importance of gathering data on the *quality* of the mentor-youth relationship. Engaging in this step will form the foundation of the process evaluation. The importance of the process evaluation is discussed in greater detail below.

Step 3. Measure Change in Antecedent Conditions

Once one understands why the problem exists and what antecedent conditions will be targeted, the focus can switch to how to measure change in these antecedent conditions. Figure 3 illustrates how a more comprehensive and meaningful evaluation plan can now be developed. Meaningful is defined as data collected for antecedent conditions being targeted for change.

The evaluation plan now includes not only the traditional outcome measures, but also measures of impact as well. The evaluation plan will now include an assessment of the quality of the mentoring relationship itself, something that is lacking in every study devoted to the assessment of effectiveness. Harter (1988) for example has developed instruments used to assess life domains of value and competency in these domains. From Figure 3, it is also evident that trust and communication are necessary before a mentor and youth can begin to meaningfully work together to develop a common value system and structure opportunities to experience mastery. Thus, an evaluation plan should include assessments of the strength of trust and communication between mentor and youth.

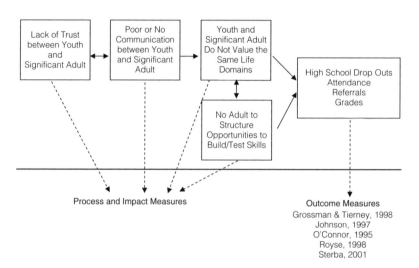

Figure 3
Toward a more comprehensive evaluation

Monitoring this information is important in ensuring the success of the match. Knowing that communication and trust is lacking could serve as a flag for case managers to intervene. Intervening early to ensure that there is strong trust and communication between the youth and mentor will strengthen the likelihood of sustaining a match and realizing positive outcomes. Results from the assessment of more intermediate impacts such as perceptions of competency and valued life domains can also be used to increase the likelihood of achieving positive changes. If the mentor and youth do not share similar values and/or the mentor is not structuring opportunities to build skills in life domains of mutual importance, then improvements in self-esteem are unlikely. Gathering data on these two critical antecedent conditions will again allow for appropriate intervention and in so doing improve the likelihood of demonstrating positive change in long-term outcomes of interest.

An Example of a Study on the Right Track

Despite the number of poorly conceived evaluation plans, there is evidence in the research literature of movement toward higher quality evaluations. The study by Taylor, LoSciuto, Fox, Hilbert, and Sonkowsky (1999) is an example of one such study. The authors describe not only the problem, but the underlying rationale of the program which is ". . . to help children develop the awareness, self-confidence, and life skills they may need to resist drugs and to meet the unique challenges facing today's youth" (p.78). The goals of the program primarily target antecedent conditions such as increasing knowledge, shifting attitudes, increasing problem solving abilities, improving parenting communication, and so forth. Although not couched in the ATM framework, it is clear that these goals are evidence that the authors have identified many precursors, or antecedent conditions, to drug use.

The mentoring program consisted of many components, each thoughtfully linked to the antecedent conditions being targeted. For example, the community service component was designed to develop skills to enhance personal responsibility, a problem-solving curriculum was instituted to improve critical thinking, and so forth. The authors clearly linked the development of strategies to identified antecedent conditions, not the symptoms.

Finally the program included a comprehensive set of measures designed to assess those antecedent conditions being directly targeted. Thus, scales assessing problem solving efficacy, knowledge, attitudes, and so forth were included. It is important to note that the authors also gathered data on outcome measures, but what distinguishes this study from the others reviewed in this chapter is that it included an impact evaluation of the antecedent conditions being targeted by the program.

Another important feature of this study is the inclusion of a process evaluation. A process evaluation is needed to determine whether the program was delivered as intended. In this study, mentor logs, tracking logs, and goal plans were examples of some of the instruments used to determine the extent to which the program happened as planned. Knowing whether the program was implemented as intended is important in interpreting the results of the impact and outcome evaluation. If the impact and outcome evaluation suggest the program was ineffective, then results of the process evaluation are critical in assisting in the decision as to whether to continue the program. For example, if the process evaluation suggests that the program was delivered with fidelity, then significant changes to the program or perhaps discontinuing the program are warranted. However, if the process evaluation suggests that major components of the program protocol were not adhered to, then a more appropriate focus would be to take steps to correct problems with the implementation of the program. It is important to note that a process evaluation must extend past the notion of client satisfaction and tap all aspects of program implementation that can lead to improvements.

The authors were able to demonstrate that the mentoring program was effective in changing several of the antecedent conditions. It is important to note that following the ATM approach does no guarantee that a program will in fact produce expected results. Following the approach does however ensure the greatest likelihood of success and that the data gathered from the evaluation will be useful in assisting program decision-making.

Summary

Mentoring programs are attempting to do good and demonstrate effectiveness. As a mentoring colleague of mine once concluded after a lengthy discussion on evaluation, "We are doing things right, we're just not doing the right things." The focus on endpoints, or outcomes, is prevalent in the evaluation of mentoring programs. Shifting focus away form endpoints to antecedent conditions is paramount to begin doing the right things. An understanding of the antecedent conditions will help better target programs and shift the focus of the evaluation to those factors over which mentoring programs have immediate and direct control to change. In so doing, a fairer test of the effectiveness of mentoring programs can be completed. While this does not guarantee that data demonstrating the effectiveness of mentoring programs will be forthcoming, it does ensure that the data gathered from such evaluations will be meaningful and assist in programmatic decision making.

Results from a well-conducted process and impact evaluation can also help advance the theoretical underpinnings of mentoring programs. If results from the process evaluation provide evidence that the mentoring program was implemented as intended, but results from the impact evaluation indicate that the program was unsuccessful in altering targeted antecedent conditions, then this suggests that the underlying rationale by which mentoring is thought to effect change needs to be revisited. For example, if the process evaluation suggests that a self-esteem component of a mentoring program was successfully implemented, but that the no improvements in self-esteem were observed, then the question of how mentoring is hypothesized to affect self-esteem should be revisited.

Support for mentoring programs is limited. It is tempting to conclude that the evaluations were poorly conducted and that by simply improving the evaluation, support for mentoring programs will be forthcoming. This would of course be erroneous. The antecedent condition of a poor evaluation is poor planning because ". . . everything which follows depends on how well the project is initially conceptualized" (Trochim, 1989, p. 1). Simply put, you get out what you put in.

Notes

1. The term outcome is often used to refer to any result or finding. In the evaluation literature the term outcome has a very specific meaning. Outcomes refer to long term measures of success. These are differentiated from impacts, which refer to more intermediate measures of success.

2. Other terms for antecedent conditions include preconditions, causal factors, risk factors, protective factors, and precursors.

References

DuBois, D. L., Holloway, B. E., Valentine, J. C., & Cooper, H. (2002). Effectiveness of mentoring programs for youth: A meta-analytic review. *American Journal of Community Psychology, 30(2)*, 157–196.

Gibb, S. (1999). The usefulness of theory: A case study in evaluating formal mentoring schemes. *Human Relations, 52 (8)*, 1055–1075.

Grossman, J. B., & Tierney, J. P. 1998. Does mentoring work? An impact study of the Big Brothers Big Sisters Program. *Evaluation Review, 22 (3)*, 403–426.

Johnson, A. W. 1997. Mentoring at-risk youth: A research review and evaluation of the impacts of Sponsor-A-Scholar Program on student performance. *Dissertations Abstracts International Section A: Humanities & Social Sciences, 58 (3-A)*, 0813.

Kalbfleisch. P. J. (2004). Will you be my mentor? The intercultural language of initiating mentoring relationships. In S. H. Ng *et al.* (Eds.), *Language Matters: Communication, Identity, and Culture*, pp. 375–382. Hong Kong: City University of Hong Kong Press.

Lynn, D. (1999). *Personal Communication.*

O'Connor, S. M. (1995). Evaluation of a mentoring program for youth at risk. *Dissertation Abstracts International: Section B: The Sciences & Engineering, 56 (2-B)*, 1130.

Pawson, C.J., & Gibbes, C. (2004). Mentoring recidivist youth offenders. In S.H. Ng *et al.* (Eds.), *Language Matters: Communication, Identity, and Culture*, pp. 383–407. Hong Kong: City University of Hong Kong Press.

Renger, R., & Titcomb, A. A three-step approach to teaching logic models. *American Journal of Evaluation*, 23 (4), 493–503.

Renger, R., Kalbfleisch, P., Smolka, L., & Crago, M. (1999). A self-esteem approach to effective resiliency building: The process of mentoring. *Resiliency in Action, 4 (1)*, 1–3.

Royse, D. (1998). Mentoring high-risk minority youth: Evaluation of the Brothers Project. *Adolescence, 33 (129)*, 145–158.

Sterba, L. M. (2001). An evaluation of the self-esteem of at-risk middle-level youth with intervention of the mentorship program. *Dissertations Abstracts International Section A: Humanities & Social Sciences, 61 (12-A)*, 4728.

Taylor, A.S., LoSciuto, L., Fox, M., Hilbert, S. M., & Sonkowsky, M. (1999). The mentoring factor: Evaluation of the Across Ages' intergenerational approach to drug abuse prevention. *Child and Youth Services, 20 (1/2)*, 77–99.

Trochim, W. M. K. (1989). An introduction to concept mapping for planning and evaluation. *Evaluation and Program Planning, 12*, 1–16.

18

Discursive Construction of Knowledge and Narratives about Gangster Youth: A Critical Discourse Analysis of Social Work Research Interviews

Angel M. Y. LIN
T. Wing LO

And the kinds of revolutions that then try to take place are attempts to reconstruct how it is that things are seen, where the attempt is, in part, for some group to get to enforce a view of themselves by others, that they administer. And a big difference between the categories "teenager" and "hotrodder" is that "teenager" is a category that adults administer. What's known about those things, "teenagers," is enforced by adults. And of course parallel things hold for the Negro. (Sacks, 1966/1992, p. 399)

Many social workers working with youth have now begun to realize that one main focus in dealing with problems of marginalized youth should be the reconstruction of the society's narratives about them. (Wong, 2002, p. 114, original in Chinese).

425

Society's Narratives and
Categories about Youth

Youth as a category attracts media, public, academic and government attention mainly when it occurs in negatively predicated phrases such as "youth problems", "problem youth", "at-risk youth", "gangster youth", or in the recently coined category of "seung-sat ching-nihn" (literally, "double-loss youth") in Hong Kong, referring to youth who have lost both the opportunity to attend school (because no school would admit them) and the opportunity to find employment (because no employer would employ them). Needless to say, all these categories are first created and enforced *by adults* to refer to youth and they reflect mainstream adults' views of what is, and what can be, known about youth.

In an article on youth sexuality in Hong Kong, Erni and Fung (2003) collated youth-related headlines occurring in the *South China Morning Post* in the past few years and pointed out how the media trundles out regular negative news about youth, portraying them as naive, ignorant, gullible, reckless, socially irresponsible, and self-destructive:

- Desire does not equal love (27-5-1997)
  Nowadays, if you ask young people what they understand about virginity and chastity, they probably can't tell you.

- Youth remains in dark over sex (17-6-1997)
  Alarming findings of a study on youth sexuality have prompted the Family Planning Association of Hong Kong to make several recommendations to parents and teachers.

- Materialism at root of teenage rebellion (5-8-1997)
  It is often said that young people are the pillars of future society, but I think today's youth lack proper values, moral judgment and a sense of responsibility.

- Survey reveals on-line lies (8-4-1999)
  As the Internet becomes increasingly popular, young

people should be aware of the dangers of making friends on-line, youth workers say.

- Youth, 16, sentenced for unlawful sex (20-11-1999)
A teenager whose sexual relationship with a girl of 12 was revealed by notes in her diary was sentenced to two years' probation yesterday.

- Mainland drug raves draw young teens (13-6-2000)
Teenagers as young as 14 and 15 have admitted crossing the border at weekends for drugs and sex at rave parties, social workers said yesterday.

- Primary pupils with problems on the increase (24-3-2001)
Co-ordinated and professional efforts must be adopted to stem growing signs of behavioral problems among primary school pupils, a leading social scientist has urged.

- SAR youngsters self-conscious about appearance, survey reveals (11-8-2001)
What do you most desire in life? Happiness? Good grades? Quality time with your parents or something more superficial like beauty?

- Young now know less about sex – but have it more often (24-4-2002)
Young people in Hong Kong are more ignorant about sex but far more sexually active than 10 years ago, according to a survey by the Family Planning Association.

- Girls "lured into vice" by cyber-cafes (6-7-2002)
Female students are being lured into working as prostitutes after being offered summer jobs at Internet cafes in Hong Kong, a charity warned yesterday.

(Erni and Fung, 2003, pp. 40–41)

From Erni and Fung's analysis (2003), we see how the Hong Kong mainstream society has (perhaps largely un- or subconsciously) kept discrediting youth with its dominant narratives and categories about youth. These discrediting narratives and categories have the effect of putting the blame largely on the individual adolescents or their family; e.g., by saying that the root of the problem lies in mainly individual morality, suggesting that they are morally and emotionally underdeveloped, lazy, hedonistic, immature, reckless, and unable to make rational, responsible decisions, for instance. To the mainstream adult society, the world of street gangsters is always a mystery, dramatized (often negatively) in gangster movies and the mainstream narratives and categories about youth have the tendency of further demonizing them. It is in this context that the social work service and the disciplinary welfare rhetoric (Gray, 1994) occupy a highly contested position in the society: what should be the role of social work? Is it merely one of the institutions of social control (disguised as a well-intentioned social service) that the dominant society uses to keep disenfranchised youth under control (e.g., with the police officer playing the bad guy and the social worker playing the good guy) without critically reflecting on and seeking to change the existing social and economic structures (e.g., education policies and schools that construct failure identities, unequal distribution of resources to families in different social classes) which perpetuate social inequalities that have led to the rebellion and criminal actions of some disenfranchised youth in the first place?

The branch of social work service that deals with illegitimate youth groups (e.g., youth gangs) in Hong Kong is outreaching social work (or gang work service). Austin pointed out that the goal of gang work service is one of reaching out for positive communication:

> . . . his service is not initially requested by the group. . . . It is a reaching-out service because the community through the worker takes the first step, *takes the initiative to break through the fear and suspicion and hostility that are blocking positive communication between this group and the community.* (Austin, 1957, p. 45, emphasis added)

Echoing Austin (1957), Lo (1986) elaborated the role of outreach and gang workers as follows:

> Being a group of pioneers, outreaching social workers relinquish all the adult and middle-class prejudices and step into their territories. Serving as a *bridge* between the two parties, we render on behalf of the frightened community our genuine concern to the puzzled teenagers. Of course, they may not believe us right away as they do not trust other adults they have come across. To most of them adults are all of the same kind – control agents who come to "teach" them to obey the authorities. But our initiative, unconditional love and tangible help would break down their stereotypes that adults are hostile to them. Once we succeed in refuting their biases, the door for better communication with the worker and ultimately with the larger society is then opened. (Lo, 1986, pp. 14–15, emphasis original)

It is clear from the above quotes that the outreach worker is conceived in the social work discipline as a bridge between gangster youth and the society. While the gangster is seen as "puzzled" (or confused – a benign but patronizing adjective often used by adults to describe misbehaving adolescents), the larger society (referring actually to middle-class mainstream society) is seen as "frightened" (by the behavior of the gangsters). The outreach worker sees her/himself as an ambassador of good will from the mainstream society (or law-abiding middle-classes), seeking to re-establish a relationship and positive and better communication with the rebellious, alienated youth, who see adults as hostile and control agents merely wanting to teach them to obey the authorities. We can see that the key word here is *communication* – how can the dominant privileged adult groups achieve positive and better communication with the alienated, disenfranchised, underprivileged youth groups and achieve some kind of mutual understanding, e.g., by clearing up the negative conceptions and prejudices that each group holds against the other? About three decades ago, Erikson already warned us to listen:

> We all want to "tell them" but few of us take the time to stop and listen, to see what juvenile delinquency is telling us about youth, and about our times. (Erikson, quoted in Leissner, 1969, p. 3)

Listening to what youth have to tell us (both directly in words and indirectly in their actions), for instance, is perhaps a first step towards achieving better communication and mutual understanding and reconciliation. However, in interactions between social workers and their clients, it is usually the social worker who has discursive control in reinterpreting client behavior, and the power to construct differential roles for their clients and themselves. Hall, Sarangi and Slembrouck (1999) analysed the ways in which social work professionals construct and negotiate deficit roles and identities for their clients in relation to themselves:

> In the first analysis (social worker-client data) we have seen how several client categories are identified and the role of the social worker and other professionals are constructed in relation to client identities. The dangerous father requires surveillance and psychiatric intervention, the vulnerable children require the social worker talking to them and the passive mother requires support. Attempts to alter the identity of the mother as more active or the children as needing "other help" pose challenges to the social worker's role and by extension the professional identity of social work. These are of course quickly rebutted. In the second analysis (the case conference data) our particular interest has been in the complex layering of the client's deficit identity as a good mother but as an inadequate parent. Professional identity is less explicitly developed in the case conference since the type of the intervention is not

discussed, but the chair's control over discourse is a clear demonstration of the role of the professional in re-interpreting the client's behavior in terms of wider versions of parenthood. In both analyses a wide range of discursive mechanisms are used by clients and professionals to state their cases. In particular type-token formulations appear to be the stock in trade of the social worker seeking to establish underlying patterns, backed up by modes of talk (including reported speech and face-related strategies) which are denied to clients. (Hall, Sarangi and Slembrouck, 1999, p. 316)

Their analyses point to the need for social work as a discipline and profession to develop a critical, reflexive practice. There is a need to critically analyse their own practices and interactions with their clients, to critically rethink their role in the society and their involvement in constructing or perpetuating deficit roles and identities for and negative narratives of their clients, especially disadvantaged and marginalized youth in the society.

As social work researchers commissioned to conduct a research study on gangster youth by the Hong Kong Southern District Board, Lee and Lo in 1993 conducted sixteen interviews with gangster youth (defined as those who have had current or past experiences of joining in a gang associated with a triad society). Thirty-three informants in the age range of 13–20 were interviewed by research assistants who were university social work students or experienced outreach social workers. The informants were contacted and recruited through outreach social workers who had worked with and befriended them. In this chapter we attempt a critical reflexive account of what has transpired during the research interviews. Drawing on the fine-grained, sequential analytical methods of conversation analysis (Sacks, 1966/1992, 1972; Jefferson, 1992), we aim at understanding what kinds of knowledge and narratives about gangster youth were being discursively constructed in the research interviews as well as the subsequent research report writing based on the interviews. In the following sections, we shall provide a background of the research interviews and illustrate with some interview excerpts the kind of analysis we conducted. Finally we shall discuss the importance of dialogic communication and the possibility of envisioning social work as a critical practice.

The Research Interview: A Special Speech Event

The research interview is not simply a neutral, transparent means of obtaining information from informants, as is sometimes assumed in the positivist sciences. Being a method of research data collection, it is at the same time constitutive of the data it collects (Mishler, 1986, 1999). The research interviewing process is itself a highly interesting interactional phenomenon worthy of detailed analysis in its own right. Epistemologically, understanding the discourse structure and strategies in the research interview will contribute to our understanding of how interview research data are shaped and constituted in particular ways and in turn how academic disciplinary knowledge is socially and discursively constructed. Ontologically, understanding the interactional process in the research interview will contribute to our understanding of how different subject positions are created or excluded and how particular identities are imposed, resisted or co-constructed in the interviewing process.

The research interview is distinguished from other speech events (e.g., ordinary conversations, debates, lectures) by its typical discourse structure of a series of question-answer pairs. The interviewer occupies the questioner speaking turns and the interviewee the respondent speaking turns most of the time. Conversation analysts have long noted the strength of the question-answer sequence or adjacency pair (Sacks, 1972). The interviewer and interviewee take turns to speak and the interviewer's questioning turn exerts strong interactional pressure on the interviewee both to respond and to respond with material relevant to the question in the immediately preceding questioning turn. No response or irrelevant response will pose high interpersonal pressure on the interviewee. For instance, when the interviewee becomes perceived as un-cooperative/unreasonable, the relationship breaks down and the interview cannot continue. Given this special discourse structure of the speech event of the research interview, the interviewer typically possesses much more power than the interviewee in decisions regarding selection, initiation, continuation or change of topics.

In the following sections, we shall present the results of a discourse analysis of sixteen audio-recorded research interviews of gangster youth in Hong Kong. The interviews were conducted in community youth centers in the interviewees' neighborhood by an experienced social worker and/or a university student majoring in social work. Usually the social worker who had befriended the teenager(s) and who introduced the teenager(s) to the interviewers was also present in the interview. The number of interviewees was usually one or two but there were also two interviews, each of four teenagers, and one interview of six teenagers. The interviews ranged from one hour to one and a half hours long. The interviews were conducted as part of a university social work research project commissioned by the Hong Kong Southern District Board with three major aims:

(1) to understand why adolescents join gangs,
(2) to identify the typical activities of gangsters, and
(3) to identify different kinds of effect on adolescents after joining the gangs.

The interviews were semi-structured with the interviewers following a schedule of basic items to be elicited from the teenagers but the interviewers could be flexible and ask other open-ended questions as well. The list of items reflected the three major aims of the research project mentioned above. Among the 33 teenagers interviewed, 26 were male, 7 female, aged from 13 to 20. Some were studying in secondary schools, some working and some unemployed. Most of them had joined gangs for more than one year and some for as long as seven or eight years. Most of them started joining gangs young, in primary school or secondary one (i.e., grade 7). In the next section, we shall analyse the recurrent discourse format and strategies used by the participants in the research interviews, which will help us understand how certain kinds of knowledge and narratives about gangster youth were discursively constructed (and sometimes contested by the youth).

Discourse Strategies in the Research Interview

A discourse format is a recurrent discourse structure characterized by a patterned sequence of speaker-turns each with specific discourse functions (Heap, 1988). For instance, a typical discourse format in the school classroom is the Initiation-Response-Feedback (IRF) format (Sinclair and Coulthard, 1975; Mehan, 1979). The teacher typically does the initiation by asking a question. The response speaker-turn is typically taken by a student or students and the student response is invariably followed by the teacher's feedback turn in which the teacher typically comments on the student response. Most school lessons are organized by the use of a series of IRF formats. The use of the IFR format enables the teacher to have the power of topic selection, initiation, continuation or change. It also enables the teacher to monitor student attention, understanding and performance. It gives the teacher the opportunity to provide feedback that is tailor-made for a specific student response, and typically it allows the teacher to "have the last word" on a lesson topic. It marks the school lesson as a special speech event in which participants do not have equal power regarding decisions on topic selection and change and on what kind of knowledge being constructed.

The research interviews analysed in this study are characterized by a recurrent discourse format that somewhat resembles the school lesson IRF format. Let us look at an example to see how the format is used in the interviews. The following example is taken from the early part of a research interview of two gangster girls, Candy (C) and Winnie (W)[1], 15 and 16 years old respectively. In this interview, a social work university student was the interviewer (I). The social worker who had introduced Candy and Winnie to the interviewer was not present in the interview.

Excerpt (1):
(From Data Set 261093A)
(Cantonese utterances are transcribed in the Yale system and English translations are given in pointed brackets immediately following the Cantonese utterances)

1. I: Gum Winnie neih ne? Neih gaa-yahp-jo ji-hauh, di friend yauh dim-yeung tai neih aa?
   <Then what about you Winnie? After you had joined the gang, how did your friends look at you?>
2. W: Waaih-jo.. gok dak ngoh!
   <Become bad.. felt that I had!>
3. I: Gok-dak neih waaih-jo, heui-deih gok-dak neih waai-jo, daahn gok-dak neih gok-yeuhng-yeh yauh-mouh bin-dou?
   <Felt that you had become bad, they felt that you had become bad, but did they find changes in the other aspects of you?>
4. W: Yauh!
   <Yes!>
5. I: Dim-yeung?
   <How?>
6. W: Yauh-haih ok-jo! Chyun-jo gum-yeung!
   <Also more violent! And arrogant!>
7. I: Gum heui-deih yauh-mouh beih-hoi neih, dihng yihng-yihn gum jip-juk neih?
   <And did they avoid you, or did they stay in touch with you?>

In the above example, we see that the interviewer asks a *question* about how Winnie's friends saw her after she had joined the gang (1). This question is followed by Winnie's *answer* that her friends felt that she had become bad (2). The interviewer *acknowledges* Winnie's answer by restating it two times and then asks a follow-up question which requires Winnie to further elaborate the changes perceived by her friends (3).

We can schematically represent the discourse format in use in the above example as follows:

1. Interviewer: Question
2. Winnie: Answer
3. Interviewer: Acknowledgment of Answer

This cycle is repeated many times in all the 14 research interviews albeit with some variation in the acknowledgment slot. Sometimes, there is a short acknowledgment particle (e.g., Mh. <Yes.>) or a comment in the place of restatement of the answer. Sometimes the acknowledgment is omitted altogether and a new question is asked immediately.

Since the pre-set list of questions referred to by the interviewers during the interview includes a large section on how different kinds of people (e.g., parents, neighbors, friends, classmates, teachers) see the teenagers after they have joined gangs, the teenagers are in effect led to actively co-construct with the interviewer a corpus of more or less negative evaluative statements which state how other people (mainstream adults) see (or judge) them after they have joined gangs. The interviewer's power to determine/shape the choice of the topic through the use of this discourse format in effect induces the teenagers into active participation in the co-construction of a corpus of negative, evaluative statements about themselves and their image that comes with gang membership. Examples of this abound in all the 16 research interviews analysed. For instance, in the following excerpt taken from the second half of another interview, Aah-Mouh (A-M), a 19-year-old male who has joined a gang since grade six, was led to state in his own words that in the eyes of his neighbors he and his gangster friends were not good guys and would cause fear in his neighbors:

Excerpt (2):
(From Data Set 201193A)

1. I: Di gaai-fong gin-dou neih-deih waahk-je heui-deih
         goh-di yat-kwahn yih-dong yauh di mat-yeh faan-ying
         aa?
         <When the neighbors saw you guys or other
         gangsters, what were their response?>

2. A-M: Sehng daaih baan yahn cho haih-douh, mh-fong
         hou-yahn lo!
         <Such a big group of people squatting there, (and
         they) certainly won't be good people!>

3. I: Wui geng aah?
         <Would be afraid?>

4. A-M: Wui geng ge ngoh lam!
         <Would be afraid I guess!>

In the above excerpt, the discourse format of question-answer
(with the optional acknowledgment slot omitted) is repeated in the
co-construction of statements about the negative, unwelcome image
that their neighbors had of Ah-Mouh and his gangster friends.

In many similar examples, the question-answer
(-acknowledgment)[2] discourse format was used quite skillfully by
the interviewers (perhaps not consciously) to lead the teenagers into
expressing in their own words the negative attitudes and images that
mainstream society (e.g., especially adults in authority such as
parents, school teachers) holds towards and of them when they had
joined gangs, and these negative opinions of mainstream society
towards them were however phrased by the interviewer as an effect
of gang membership: "the effect on you after joining gangs". Thus
the agents (mainstream adults) giving negative opinions on youth
were masked and the prejudices of these agents were re-presented as
the natural outcome of the youth's act of joining gangs: i.e.,
suggesting that they bring it upon themselves.

However, some defiant teenagers might contest or resist
collusion in co-constructing negative, judgmental statements about
themselves and gang membership, especially when the interviewer

does not ask apparently factual questions but uses conspicuously value-laden words in the questions. For instance, in the following excerpt, Aah-Huhng (A-H), a 19-year-old male who had joined a gang since twelve, refused to directly answer the interviewer's questions:

Excerpt (3):
(From Data Set 271093A)

1. I: Gum yauh-mouh gok-dak gan-jo yahn go-di pahng-yauh hou-chih waaih-jo di?
    <Then do you think those friends who have joined gangs seem to have become a bit bad?>

2. A-H: Gong gwaai neih dou mh-seuin laa!
    <If I say they're good, you won't believe it!>

3. I: Mh mh... heui-deih haih dim-yeung waaih faat aa?
    <Yes yes... they are bad in what ways?>

4. A-H: Dim-yeung waaih faat aa?
    <Bad in what ways?>

5. I: Je-haih heui-deih gan-jo yahn ji-hauh wui heui si-haah
    <That is after they have joined a gang they would go to try (drugs)>

6. A-H: Do-jo yi-di yeh cheuit aa-maa, neih pihng-sih bin wuih waah yauh ho-yih hai sau je!
    <More of these (drugs) become available that is; otherwise, usually how can you have them in hand!>

7. I: Mh mh.
    <Yes yes.>

8. A-H: Taam dak-yi, maih si leuhng haah.
    <For fun, might try a couple of times.>

9. I: Mh mh... gum-yeung, je-haih yauh-mouh waah, gan-jo yahn ji-hauh, tuhng uk-kei yahn ge gwaan-haih, wui-mh-wui chaa-jo?
    <Yes yes... in that manner, that is after having joined gangs, would the relationship with family members become bad?>

10. A-H: Go-biht gwaa.
    <It varies (from person to person).>

11. I: Go-biht. Gum neih ji-gei ne? ....
         <It varies. But what about you? .... >

In the above excerpt, we can see that Aah-Hung did not directly answer the interviewer's obviously value-laden, leading question (1: "Then do you think those friends who have joined gangs seem to have become a bit bad?"). Instead of saying "yes" or "no", Aah-Hung exposed the hidden assumption that seemed to be already firmly held by the interviewer by saying that if he said they were good the interviewer would not believe it (2). This statement of Aah-Hung is remarkable because it seems to have achieved the following multiple functions:

(1) It enables him to avoid giving a direct answer of either "yes" or "no" to the interviewer's immediately preceding question. If he says "yes", he's condemning his friends, which most probably he does not feel comfortable doing. If he says "no", he is likely to be pestered further with questions about why and how he thinks these friends have not become bad and probably he knows he cannot gather enough warrants acceptable to this mainstream authority figure (the interviewer from the university).

(2) It exposes the assumption hidden in the interviewer's leading question.

(3) It asserts his observation that the real point of the interviewer's question is not one of obtaining information but one of forcing Aah-Hung to take a stance that aligns with the mainstream societal view that gang membership causes one to become bad.

By subverting the normal question-answer cycle, Aah-Hung seems to have succeeded in resisting participation in co-constructing a negative statement about his gangster friends. In turns 3 to 8, he further subverts the question-answer cycle by changing the question-answer sequence into a question-question sequence. When the interviewer asks in what ways his friends are bad (turn 3),

Aah-Hung simply asks the same question back (turn 4: Bad in what ways?). The interviewer answers by suggesting that after joining gangs they would try drugs (turn 5). Notice that this is no longer formulated as a question but as a statement or a claim. Aah-Hung then offers another statement/claim about how this is facilitated by the greater degree of availability of drugs (turn 6). Notice also that he does not directly link gang membership to drug-taking. In turn 7, the interviewer acknowledges Aah-Hung's statement and in turn 8, Aah-Hung offers another statement claiming that drugs are tried for fun. Turns 6 to 8 are rare instances of utterances that do not fit the question-answer format recurring in the research interviews. These two turns resemble more ordinary conversation between equal interactional partners than research interview conversation.

Aah-Hung's substitution of a question-answer sequence with a question-question sequence (turns 3-4) is quite remarkable as it rarely occurs in research interviews. In fact the interviewer resumes his questioner role soon. In turn 9, she asks another obviously value-laden, leading question about the effect of gang membership on one's relationship with family members. In turn 10, Aah-Hung answers by saying it varies (across people), thereby avoiding giving a definite answer. However, the interviewer zooms in by forcing Aah-Hung to answer the question about his own relationship with his family members. What follows (not shown in Excerpt 3 above) is another lengthy negotiation process between Aah-Hung and the interviewer with Aah-Hung refusing to collude with the interviewer to cast himself and his gangster friends in a negative light.

The kinds of knowledge and narratives that are discursively constructed are ones which confirm and reinforce the society's existing meta-narratives about gangster youth: that they have simply come under bad influences and become bad after joining gangs. The reasons for their joining gangs are reduced to a simple set of advantages, both physical and emotional: e.g., companionship, friendship, sense of security and actual mutual protection. As some interviewees went along with the interviewer's questions and condemned and expressed regrets about their past behaviors, other kinds of knowledge about them are also constructed and established in the research report. These research data have constituted part of the knowledge we have about them: that some of them are now repentant and have learnt the right ways again.

The kind of knowledge and narratives constructed in the research interviews and in the subsequent research report (Lee and Lo, 1994) thus does not seem to add any new perspectives to what we (mainstream adults) already have about gangster youth, except that we now know more factual information about the places they hang around, the activities they engage in, and most importantly to gang workers, the ways gangs exercise group control over their members (Lo, 1984, 1993). This kind of knowledge is important to outreach social workers who seek to *degroup* gangsters (Lo, 1986, 1992), to crack the cohesiveness of gangster groups, for instance. While this knowledge is important, it does not offer us any views on the youth that are alternative to the views that mainstream society already holds about them. In other words, we seek to know only what we want to know, and what we want to know is already constituted by our existing views of gangster youth: that they are victims of bad influences of criminal organizations (e.g., triad or other kinds of gangs recruiting young members) and the good ones have repented their ways and turned to the right way under the guidance of social workers. If this is the main kind of narratives and knowledge that we gain from the research interviews, then we still need to ask questions about the missing pieces of knowledge which have not been given a chance to surface: for instance, what do young people like Aah-Hung think and feel about their own activities, and why they might choose not to "repent their old ways"? Apart from the set of advantages (physical and affective) listed in the research report, what other reasons might they have for choosing a certain life style (e.g., one that is considered illegitimate or bad by mainstream adults)? In short, it is *members'* knowledge, categories and narratives – the *emic* perspective – that we are missing. And it is consistently the *outsider adults'* categories, perspectives and narratives generated by mainstream society about youth that we continue to recruit, enforce, reinforce and administer to youth in our dealing and communication with them.

Ambassador of Good Will or
Agent of Social Control?
Dialogic Communication and Social Work
as a Critical Practice

The above analysis shows that the question-answer discourse format in interviews can be used to induce (or coerce) gangster youth to come face-to-face with the effect of gang membership on the image that mainstream adults have of them as well as the social and personal consequences that come with gang membership. They can be led to express in their own words what happened to them after they have joined gangs. While this strategy might be an effective one in administering corrective counseling to gangster youth to re-subject them to mainstream societal norms, this discourse strategy might be less effective with those gangster youth who somehow choose to adopt and stick to alternative sets of norms and values for various reasons of their own (and since we have not been interested in listening to their own views, we do not have clear knowledge of them). Explicitly adult-value-laden questions that already cast the teenagers and their friends in a negative light can incite resistance and might put the teenagers further on the defensive. Positive communication might be blocked as the interviewer did not seem to be genuinely interested in what the young person had to say, but seemed to be keen on coercing the person to agree with what the interviewer already had in mind. There has not been any genuine dialogic communication between the two groups (or representatives of them). The interviewer thus seems to be more an agent of one-way didactic communication ('teaching' youth about what's right and wrong) rather than an ambassador of good will from the mainstream society to initiate any genuine dialogues and communication.

Moreover, the one-sided questions (e.g., asking questions of how others see them and no questions on how they see others and themselves after they have joined gangs) put the teenagers in a narrow range of subject positions that render them as more or less passive objects of ridicule, evaluation or inspection by mainstream adults. They are positioned as more or less passive victims on the receiving end of the "effects" of gang membership or positioned as contagious objects who can pass on the effects to other teenagers rather than as actors with agency who choose specific life styles and kinds of friends sometimes for reasons other than some concretely formulated advantages, whether physical or affective (e.g., money, companionship, confidence, fear of violence, assurance of protection). A more comprehensive and in-depth picture of the psychological history and journey of the gangster teenagers as seen by themselves (and not only by judgmental adults) might perhaps be gained by asking a wider range of questions that do not prioritize a narrow range of subject positions; for instance, questions such as the following:

- How do you feel about yourself before and after joining gangs? Do you feel more confident (or proud) of yourself, or less confident (or proud) of yourself? Do you feel that you're a different person? If yes, in what ways (give an example)?
- Who is (are) the person(s) you care about most? And who care(s) about you most?
- Who do you admire? Who do you look down upon? Why?
- When are you most happy? When are you most sad?
- Do you have any worries or fears? What are they? What do you do when you have worries or fears? Are there anyone to turn to for help? Who do you (not) trust? Why do you (not) trust her/him/them?
- What do you think of your teachers, parents, or neighbors? What kind of people do you think they are? Do you like them, why, why not? Do you want to become someone like them? Why, why not?
- What do you think of school? What do you think of society? What are your comments on them? Anything good about them? Anything wrong about them?

- Do you like your lifestyle after joining gangs? Are there any changes in your lifestyle that you like or not like before and after joining gangs? What is your ideal way of living? What kind of living do you least desire?
- Do you have any hopes, plans; what do you want to become? Does joining gangs help you achieve some of them or does it not help? In what ways does it help, and/or in what ways does it not help? What are other possible strategies to achieve your goals?
- What kind of person do you think you are (and you were), and what kind of person do you want to become? Have you ever thought about this? When do you usually think about this, if you do?

In contrast to the set of research questions of the research interviewers, questions like the above would provide more active, autonomous subject positions to the interviewee from which to reflect on and express her/his experiences from her/his own perspectives, i.e., not restricted to the perspectives of mainstream, authoritative adults. They will be treated with respect as someone who can take responsibility for their own decisions and someone who can (or have the potential to) rationally evaluate and plan for their own (past, current and future) situation from their own perspectives. They are seen as persons who have their own opinions of themselves as well as things and people in the world. They are seen as capable of having their own knowledge, narratives and categories of who they are and what they want to be, and capable of doing a critical analysis of the school and society (including instances of inequality and unfairness), and are worthy of listening to when they comment on them.

In critically and reflexively examining the kind of talk found in the interviews of the social work research study (reflexively, as the co-author of this chapter was a co-investigator in the interview study), are we just pointing out the inexperience of interviewers who do not know how to ask a wider range of indirect questions? While this might be the case, the interview questions used were however those specified by the investigators for the research assistants (i.e., the interviewers) to follow. The issue is then not merely one of inexperienced interviewers, but also the research design of the social work study. The social work study seems to have been driven by its limited range of research questions and its limited conceptions of ways of eliciting information from the youngsters. The everyday voices (Hall, Sarangi, & Slembrouck, 1999) of the gangster youth have not been taken seriously in the research questions and the design of the study. The study seems to have already formed its conclusion about why young people joined gangs (e.g., that gangster youth joined gangs because they had been under bad influences) and its aim seems to be the straightforward one of finding out more factual details about the process (e.g., what are the bad influences, how did they come into contact with them, what are the "different kinds of effect" on youth after joining gangs, etc).

This critical, reflexive examination is important if the social work researcher's aim is not just to reproduce and reinforce what mainstream adults think they already know about gangster youth, but to genuinely try to imagine and understand the culturally different *Other*, and still see normality in it. Without such attempts at intercultural dialogues and understanding (between mainstream adult culture and marginalized youth cultures, for instance), we might not be able to achieve much genuine communication with teenagers whom mainstream society labels as "deviants", "victims" or "double-loss youth". While some of the "deviants" might re-subscribe to mainstream societal norms that we preach and teach, there are always some others who see that we have deeply misunderstood them, or even if we try to show that we care about them, want to help them, they may still see us as imposing our norms on them without understanding them and listening to their voices. Is dialogic communication possible or even desirable? If we abandon our conception of youth as imperfect, immature copies of adults but see them as autonomous beings having their own views and cultures worthy of our attention, we need to embark on the difficult task of intercultural communication.

Our mainstream norms have often blinded us to the realities of those young people who have been disenfranchised by the social structures that maintain the subordination of marginal social groups. To illustrate, let us look at an outreach social worker's soul-searching reflection on his work with an adolescent, Aah-Leuhng, who wanted to get out of poverty through drug trafficking (Lau, 1993):

> . . . should an outreach social worker just rely on advocating the larger society's social norms and impose them on the so-called 'bad elements' who exhibit deviant behavior? Aah-Leuhng's personal values might be deviant, but that does not mean that the operation of the larger societal norms is reasonable and fair.
>
> Aah-Leuhng immigrated to Hong Kong from mainland China when he was a child. Living in poor slum areas, he has grown up in a relatively under-resourced environment. Being the object of ridicule and discrimination by his classmates in school, he was pushed to rely on some powerful ones to solve his problems and pushed to identify with triad society culture in an attempt to survive and to get a share of the benefits in this so-called prosperous society. This witnesses a resistant voice emerging from behind this prosperous society. Outreach social workers have been called a tool of social control for maintaining society's prosperity and stability. In my experience of helping Aah-Leuhng to deconstruct his dream [that of getting out of poverty through drug traffiking], I cannot help having a dream myself, as an outreach social worker who is concerned for the society: ten years later Aah-Leuhng will become an upright 'social being' with a good career and appropriate ways of doing things, and with sharp critical eyes that can analyse and critique the unjust and unfair phenomena of the society. (Lau, 1993, pp. 63-64, original in Chinese)

Adults in mainstream society need to subject their values, norms and the society's unfair structures to challenge by alternative voices – voices of frustration and anger at social inequalities, discrimination and marginalization. If we fail to do this, the knowledge and narratives we produce about disadvantaged youth in the social work discipline might only serve to reinforce the self-righteousness of *us* and the demonization of *them*. Unless mainstream adults start to see that "youth problems" are in no small proportions also "adult problems" and mainstream societal problems (e.g., unfairness, unequal distribution of resources, labeling and discrimination of the underclasses, a schooling process that constructs failure identities), there cannot be any basis for a dialogue. However, one also has to recognize that critical social theory to date seems to have had little to offer regarding practical programmes, methods and strategies in social work practice (Choi and Lo, 2002). We must work with social workers who are constantly striving to achieve the difficult balance between care and control and develop this very difficult and delicate interactional skill in their social work practice. More and more critically oriented social workers and researchers are also actively exploring ways of working with youth that will contribute to the empowerment of youth (e.g., Chan, 1999, Chiu and Wong, 1999; Chow, 1999). As Wong (2002) pointed out, one important first step would be the reconstruction of the society's narratives about *youth*. This observation might reflexively inform our research design of future social work studies, which should not start with negative narratives and theories about youth.

Acknowledgments

The chapter is based on a study titled "A Discourse Analysis of Social Work Interviews of Gangster Youth", funded by a small-scale research grant awarded to Angel Lin and T. Wing Lo by the City University of Hong Kong.

Notes

1. All personal names are pseudo names.
2. The brackets around "acknowledgment" indicate that this functional part of the format is optional.

References

Austin, D. M. (1957). Goals for gang workers. *Social Work*, 2(4), 43–50.

Chan, Y. M. (1999). The empowerment of adolescent girls. In W. S. Chiu and C. W. Wong (Eds.), *Youth work and empowerment: Theory and practice* (pp. 151–166). Hong Kong: Hong Kong Policy Analysis. [in Chinese]

Chiu, W. S., & Wong, C. W. (Eds.) (1999). *Youth work and empowerment: Theory and practice.* Hong Kong: Hong Kong Policy Analysis. [in Chinese]

Choi, A., & Lo, T. W. (2002). *Fighting youth crime: Success and failure of two little dragons.* Singapore: Times Academic Press.

Chow, S. S. (1999). The empowerment of marginalized youth. In W. S. Chiu and C. W. Wong (Eds.), *Youth work and empowerment: Theory and practice* (pp. 135–150). Hong Kong: Hong Kong Policy Analysis. [in Chinese]

Erni, J. N., & Fung, A. Y. H. (2003). Dislocated intimacies: A social relational perspective on youth, sex, and the popular media. *Perspectives: Working Papers in English & Communication*, 15(1), 30–51.

Gray, P. (1994). *Inside the Hong Kong juvenile court: the decision-making process in action.* Hong Kong: University of Hong Kong, Department of Social Work and Social Administration, Resource Paper Series, No.23.

Hall, C., Sarangi, S., & Slembrouck, S. (1999). The legitimation of the client and the profession: Identities and roles in social work discourse. In S. Sarangi, & C. Roberts (Eds.), *Talk, work and institutional order: Discourse in medical, mediation and management settings* (pp. 292–322). Berlin: Mouton de Gruyter.

Heap, J. L. (1988). On task in classroom discourse. *Linguistics and Education*, 1, 177–198.

Jefferson, G. (Ed.) (1992). *Lectures on conversation: Harvey Sacks*. Oxford: Blackwell.

Lau, W. C. (1993). Dream weaving, dream breaking and dream shattering. In H. T. Cheung, K. H. Mak, F. P. Tam, & W. C. Lau (Eds.), *North Star in street corner* (pp. 56–64). Hong Kong: The Boys' and Girls' Clubs Association of Hong Kong, Kwun Tong Outreach Social Worker Team. [in Chinese]

Lee, W. L. & Lo, T.W. (1994). *Research report on youth problems in the Southern District*. Hong Kong: Southern District Board. [in Chinese]

Leissner, A. (1969). *Street club work in Tel Aviv and New York*. New York: Longmans.

Lo, T. W. (1984). *Gang dynamics: Report of a study of the juvenile gang structure and subculture in Tung Tau*. Hong Kong: Caritas Outreaching Service.

Lo, T. W. (1986). *Outreaching social work in focus*. Hong Kong: Caritas Outreaching Service.

Lo, T. W. (1992). Groupwork with youth gangs in Hong Kong. *Groupwork*, 5(1), 58–71.

Lo, T. W. (1993). Neutralization of group control in youth gangs. *Groupwork*, 6(1), 51–63.

Mehan, H. (1979). *Learning lessons: Social organization in the classroom*. Cambridge, Mass.: Harvard University Press.

Mishler, E. G. (1986). *Research interviewing: Context and narrative*. Cambridge, Mass.: Harvard University Press.

Mishler, E. G. (1999). *Storylines: Craftartists' narratives of identity*. Cambridge, Mass.: Harvard University Press.

Sacks, H. (1972). On the analyzability of stories by children. In Gumperz, J., & Hymes, D. (Eds.), *Directions in sociolinguistics: The ethnography of speaking*. New York: Holt, Rinehart and Winston.

Sacks, H. (1966/1992). 'Hotrodders' as a revolutionary category. In G. Jefferson (Ed.), *Lectures on conversation: Harvey Sacks* (pp. 396–403). Oxford: Blackwell.

Sinclair, J. M., & Coulthard, R. M. (1975). *Towards an analysis of discourse: The English used by teachers and pupils*. London: Oxford University Press.

Wong, C. W. (2002). Postmodernist perspectives on youth problems. In W. L. Lee (Ed.), *Hong Kong youth problems* (pp. 97–118). Hong Kong: Hong Kong University Press. [in Chinese]

19

Rap Lyrics and Their Antisocial Effects on Young People in Hong Kong

Jacky Chau-kiu CHEUNG

The study of Hong Kong Chinese young people's perceptions and attributions about rap songs following terror priming is important for testing the application of terror management theory (Janssen & Dechesne, 1999; Pyszczynski *et al.*, 1999). Such understanding would have important implications for policy and practice dealing with rap music because rap music is notorious for its antisocial characteristics and deleterious effects on the audience (Lynxwiler & Gay, 2000; McLeod & Eveland, 1997). Rap songs, arising from African American culture, tend to be fraught with violent, misogynous, profane, and prurient contents that have aroused public concern, notably that of government officials, educators and parents (Binder, 1993; McLeod & Eveland, 1997). The concern appears to mobilize actions to censor problematic rap songs and protect the young audience from their nefarious influences. As young people form an important part of the audience and are potential victims of rap music, their views should be relevant to formulating policy.

Theoretical and Research Background

The primary concern of the study is the application of terror management theory to explaining young people's perceptions and attributions regarding rap songs. Terror management theory, as a version of psychoanalytic theory, proposes that awareness of mortality would trigger a defense mechanism in the individual to bolster the self (Pyszczynski *et al.*, 1999; Solomon *et al.*, 1991). In line with psychoanalytic theory in general, the theory assumes that the notion of death comprises a salient impulse in the individual that is motivational. One crucial motivational outcome is the defense of one's self. The defense can take a dual process involving a distal and unconscious process and a proximal, conscious process (Pyszczynski *et al.*, 1999). With the unconscious process, the individual would enhance the self without taking note of the impulse of death. One way is to bolster an optimistic view about the self. In the present study, this is denying the deleterious effect of rap music on oneself. Another way is to attach oneself to a culture or subculture, even if it is deviant and antisocial (Janssen & Dechesne, 1999). As such, one may find protection from the group associated with the culture. Religion can be a typical refuge for attachment in response to the death impulse. Alternatively, an antisocial subculture such as that characterized by rap lyrics can act as a refuge for young people alerted by the idea of death. With the conscious process, the individual would deliberately remove anxiety related to death. One way is denigrating the source of the anxiety, that is, rap music. It is likely for social science undergraduates aware of the stigma of rap songs to associate them with anxiety and discontent and disengage oneself from it. Thus, the major hypotheses arising from the application of terror management theory state that awareness of death triggers, on the one hand, a person's unconscious denial of the harm of rap music and adherence to the rap or antisocial subculture, and on the other hand, his or her conscious dislike of rap music.

The present study draws from two streams of research about young people's reaction to terror management and the influence of rap music. One stream is the study of the effect of death awareness on the young person's support for youth culture or subculture (Janssen & Dechesne, 1999). Another stream is the series of studies of the third-person effect in the attribution of effects of rap songs. The third-person effect refers to the over-estimation of the harmful effects of rap songs on others than on self (Eveland *et al.*, 1999; McLeod & Eveland, 1997; McLeod *et al.*, 2001). This effect tends to be a reflection of the fundamental attribution error and unrealistic optimism that are self-serving and ego-enhancing (McLeod *et al.*, 2001).

The past demonstration of the effect of terror management has shown that high school students in the Netherlands (Janssen & Dechesne, 1999) became more supportive of youth culture after writing their ideas about death as required in the experimental study. Their support for youth culture manifested in their endorsement (or disapproval) of arguments favoring (or criticizing) youth culture. Thus, young people who become aware of death would seek reassurance to bolster their self-images by adhering to youth culture.

The other stream of research, pertaining to the third-person effect, has demonstrated repeatedly such an effect of rap music based on attributions by Americans of various ages. Such studies have shown that people base their attributions on the magic bullet theory of media influence, which primarily states that exposure to adversarial media necessarily generates harm to the audience (McLeod & Eveland, 1997; McLeod *et al.*, 2001). Nevertheless, the sources of the attribution and perceived harm or benefit and related attitudes are not yet transparent (Golding & van Snippenburg, 1995). Apparently, dislike of rap songs does not stem from one's interest in protecting one's children because American parents of young children like them more than non-parents (Lynxwiler & Gay, 2000). This finding is contrary to the observation that parents form pressure groups to lobby against rap music (Binder, 1993; Smith & Bryson, 2002). Thus, attitudes and beliefs about rap music may not simply originate from interest or reasoned action. They are also likely to be susceptible to the influence of conscious and unconscious processes of terror management, rooted in psychoanalytic theory.

Hong Kong is a cultural mix of East and West with a youth/pop subculture heavily influenced by the United States, Japan, and South Korea. Localized rap music developing in Hong Kong tends to attract a substantial proportion of young fans. Hong Kong Chinese rap, like its American paragon, is primarily monotonous vocal with little melody but rich in lyrics, which are the major sources of gratification for young fans (Christenson & Roberts, 1998). The Chinese rap lyrics, like those in the United States, are fraught with antisocial, violent, pornographic, and profane messages. Using plenty of foul language, the rap tends to be responsible for generating a vulgar culture of foul or objectionable language in Hong Kong. It is primarily anti-establishment, demeaning the government, family, work and business institutions. For instance, laziness is a value treasured by a rap band that brands itself the Hall of Great Laziness. This and other antisocial themes would form a subculture that attracts young people and helps them construct their identity, for instance, by self-addressed lyrics and repetitive rhythm that would uphold the self-image (Simpson, 1996).

The present study is to examine the effect of death awareness on the Hong Kong undergraduate's self-defense in terms of denying the harm of rap songs on oneself, approving of antisocial rap lyrics, and concealing preference for rap music. Research on the third-person effect suggests that death awareness would accentuate greater attribution of *harm* to peers rather than to oneself. The third-person effect can also plausibly operate in the perception of the *benefit* of rap. To bolster the self, the student would regard rap music as more beneficial to oneself than to others. However, the third-person effect of benefit attribution tends to be weak because it suggests the person's vulnerability to media influence and is detrimental to one's self-esteem (McLeod *et al.*, 2001). On balance, the individual would be reluctant to admit that rap could have too great an influence on oneself.

Approval of rap lyrics would reflect the student's adherence to the antisocial, foul language subculture that can enhance young people's identity. Use of foul language can be an important means to publicize one's identity (Ballard & Dodson, 1999). The use can be an act shared in a subculture which young people resort to under stress (Johansson, 1994). Adhering to a subculture is important because it creates an image of empowerment through reference to a group (Felson *et al.*, 1994). It can generate security to the individual and this effect is consistent with the prediction of terror management theory. Its logic is similar to the effect of strain on one's identification with gangs (Kennedy & Baron, 1993).

Apparently dislike of rap music would project a public image superior to a socially undesirable subculture. In the study of social science, the student should be aware of the cultural war or moral crusade against rap in the West (Lynxwiler & Gay, 2000). As such, declaring one's dislike of rap would enhance the publicly desirable self.

The above discussion would be the basis for the following hypotheses concerning the effects of drawing students' attention to death through questionnaire items. Students primed with death in this way, when compared to those who are not, will:

(1)   Perceive less harm (or more benefit) from rap songs;
(1.1) Perceive less harm (or more benefit) from rap songs to self than to peers;
(2)   Show more approval of antisocial rap lyrics; and
(3)   Like rap songs less.

The study assumes that priming with death will trigger an awareness of death. The priming occurs when the student had responded to eight questions measuring death anxiety before responding to questions about attribution, approval, and liking of rap songs and lyrics. It is necessary to distinguish the concept of death awareness from that of death anxiety because awareness does not necessarily mean anxiety. Nevertheless, the effects of death anxiety may be similar to those of death awareness. To explore this point, it is useful to refer to the literature on delinquent behavior and strain theory in particular, which suggests that anxiety tends to be a precursor to delinquent behavior (Seeman *et al.*, 1988; Helzer & Canino, 1992). Thus, the young person would opt to behave deviantly in order to reduce tension. Addiction to drugs appears to be an outcome of anxiety (Amaro *et al.*, 2001) and the addiction may be similar to adherence to rap songs whereas the denial of the harmful effect of drugs may be akin to the denial of the harmful effect of rap. However, reasons underlying effects of death awareness and death anxiety may be different. Whereas the effect of death awareness stems from self-defense, the effect of death anxiety serves the function of tension reduction. In the former case, one is not motivated to relieve death anxiety by consuming and enjoying rap songs.

Method

The study prepared two survey conditions to collect responses and other data from 54 first-year social science students at the City University of Hong Kong. The sample size was comparable to that ($N = 53$) of a similar study (Janssen & Dechesne, 1999). One condition ($n = 29$) required respondents to respond to questions about death anxiety in the beginning whereas another condition ($n = 25$) put the questions at the end of the survey. The former condition served to induce awareness of death and primed the student's responses to subsequent questions about attribution, approval, and liking about rap songs and lyrics. No priming effect would be possible in the second survey condition that placed questions of death anxiety at the end.

Students participating in the study responded to the computerized survey questionnaire independently. The study assigned students to either one of the two different survey conditions based on alternate seats. This arrangement could maximize the matching of students responding to the two conditions because students with similar characteristics and orientations would like to sit close to each other. Thus, it was one way to minimize extraneous effects due to different students being assigned to the two conditions. Besides, the computerized survey minimized errors due to data entry and question order because it restricted the ordering of questions showing up on the screen. The study took place in three sessions in early 2002.

The respondents were mostly born in Hong Kong, with 9.4

percent having migrated from Mainland China and other places (see Table 1). Two-thirds were female. Over half (57.4 percent) had religious faith and this proportion tended to be greater than that among the general population. Apparently, young people with religious faith were more likely to enroll in the program of social science, which included a stream of social work that seemed attractive to religious students.

Table 1
Means and percentages of background characteristics by terror priming

Variable	Terror priming	No terror priming	Total
Years living in Hong Kong	19.1	18.8	19.0
Living with the father (%)	75.9	76.0	75.9
Living with the mother (%)	96.6	92.0	94.4
Income (HK$)	2012	2257	2120
Having religious faith	68.9	44.0	57.4
Age (years)	20.1	19.6	19.9
Female (%)	55.2	80.0	66.7
Born in Hong Kong (%)	89.7	91.7	90.6
Father being an ownership-class member (%)	17.9	40.0	28.3
Mother being an ownership-class member (%)	10.7	12.0	11.3
Father education (1-5)	1.93	1.79	1.87
Mother education (1-5)	2.00	1.88	1.94

Measurement

A five-point rating scale was the common format for capturing responses from students to questions about death anxiety, perceived harm and benefit from rap songs to self and peers, liking of rap songs, antisocial orientation or approval of rap lyrics, and social desirability orientation. Each of the concepts involved multiple items to obtain a composite score that demonstrated satisfactory internal consistency (see Table 2). To minimize the order effect, the survey questionnaire presented the items, except those measuring death anxiety, in a random order. The five points on the scale, ranging from "very little" to "very much," were later scored 0, 25, 50, 75, 100, respectively.

Table 2
Internal reliability of composite scores

Composite score	Number of items	alpha
Approval of rap lyrics (antisocial orientation)	15	.738
Perceived harm of rap songs on self	10	.917
Perceived benefit of rap songs to self	5	.864
Perceived harm of rap songs on age peers	10	.897
Perceived benefit of rap songs to age peers	5	.813
Liking of rap songs	4	.735
Death anxiety	8	.700
Social desirability orientation	10	.587

Death anxiety. The eight questions measuring death anxiety served to induce awareness of death. They were an abridged version of a scale with proven reliability and factorial validity (Chung *et al.*, 2000). The version kept items that were simple and short for easy understanding by students. It measured death anxiety experienced in the recent month. Two sample items were: "The thought of death bothers you." "You are not at all afraid to die (reverse scoring)."

Liking of rap. The composite measure of liking of rap combined scores of four items, about liking of rap culture and rap bands and dislike of rap music and vulgar culture, which was another term to represent rap culture in Hong Kong.

Approval of rap lyrics. Fifteen items comprised the measure of approval of rap lyrics or antisocial orientation. The item statements were rap lyrics for respondents to make their endorsement. There was no mention that the statements were rap lyrics. Sample items were: "It is the best ideal of no working," "Cunning merchants cheat again," "The one you trust is really the incarnation of a devil," "Care for nothing but to wait for the pay day."

Perceived harm of rap songs. Ten statements measured the perceived harm of rap songs to oneself and the same ten items measured the perceived harm of rap songs to peers with only the object changed from "oneself" to "peers." The items pertained to the harm of violence, misogyny, alienation, and others mentioned in the literature (Christenson & Roberts, 1998; Lynxwiler & Gay, 2000; McLeod & Eveland, 1997; Rudman & Lee, 2002). Sample items for measuring perceived harm to self were: "Makes you distrust others," "Makes you speak foul language," "Makes you dissatisfied with the family," and "Makes you act on impulse."

Perceived benefit of rap songs. The measures of the perceived benefit of rap songs to oneself and the perceived benefit of rap songs to peers relied on the same five items, with objects referring to the self and peers respectively. Benefit from rap songs could arise from rap artists' defense that the functions of rap music are to relieve stress and convey information about reality, particularly grievances, in society (Binder, 1993). Sample items for measuring perceived benefit to self were: "Makes you relieved," "Increases you self-confidence," and "Increases your knowledge."

Third-person effect. The third-person effect was the differential of the perception of harm or benefit to self from that to peers. Higher scores indicated greater harm or benefit to others than to self.

Social desirability orientation. Ten items, adapted from previous works (Paulhus, 1991), measured the social desirability orientation. Although the social desirability orientation was not a hypothesized outcome, it was an essential control variable to filter the part of outcomes not due to social desirability.

Acquiescence. The measure of acquiescence referred to the mean score of all rating items, before any reversal of scoring, in the questionnaire (Zagorski, 1999). It was another control variable to identify the unique part of outcomes.

Overview of Statistical Analysis

Statistical analysis involved two essential predictors, death awareness and death anxiety, and eight outcomes, including liking of rap songs, approval of rap lyrics, perceived harm and benefit of rap songs to self and age peers, and third person effects of the harm and benefit. It relied on regression analysis to estimate and test the effects of death awareness and death anxiety on the outcomes, concerning the hypotheses. The analysis of the effects of death anxiety would show whether the hypotheses formulated for death awareness apply to death anxiety as well. Besides, all background characteristics, social desirability orientation, and acquiescence were potential control variables screened by the stepwise selection procedure built in the regression analysis algorithm. Accordingly, the analysis retained control variables that were significant at .05 level in the regression equation before estimating the effects of death awareness and death anxiety. Consequently, results reported in the following reflected the net effects of death awareness and death anxiety, free of contamination by the host of background characteristics, social desirability, and acquiescence. In addition, the regression analysis held death awareness and death anxiety as controls for each other.

Results

Research participants showed a rather low level of liking for rap songs ($M = 35.7$). Nevertheless, their liking was not too low to deny their acceptance of rap music. The students, on average, showed a modest level of approval of rap lyrics or antisocial orientation ($M = 40.1$). Such a level does not appear to be low and it reveals that even social science students showed an antisocial tendency. Hence, even though rap music is not in the mainstream of pop culture, it is likely to gain substantial support from the young population in Hong Kong.

Table 3
Means and percentages of attitudinal variables by terror priming

Variable	Terror priming	No terror priming	Total
Liking of rap songs	33.0	38.7	35.7
Approval of rap lyrics (antisocial orientation)	41.1	39.0	40.1
Perceived harm of rap songs on self	14.5	16.8	15.6
Perceived benefit of rap songs to self	15.5	11.9	13.8
Perceived harm of rap songs on age peers	29.7	25.7	27.8
Perceived benefit of rap songs to age peers	15.5	14.3	14.9
Third-person effect regarding the harm of rap songs	15.2	8.9	12.2
Third-person effect regarding the benefit of rap songs	3.1	2.5	2.8
Death anxiety	35.3	40.5	37.7
Social desirability orientation	60.0	55.1	57.7
Acquiescence	31.9	30.3	31.1

Perceptions of harm and benefit of rap songs on self and peers were unanimously low. Thus, university students tended to find themselves immune to the detrimental and salutary influences of rap music. Furthermore, their unrealistic optimism was apparent with the affirmative findings on the third-person effects. As expected (McLeod *et al.*, 2001), the third-person effect (i.e., benefit/harm to others minus benefit/harm to self) about the harm of rap songs was greater than that about the benefit (M = 12.2 vs. 2.8). The third-person effect, however low, was close to the perceived harm to the self (M = 15.6). Essentially, perceived harm to peers was nearly two times of that to self (M = 27.8 vs. 15.6). The third-person effects were both significant in terms of the paired *t*-test (*t*'s = 5.12 & 2.07). In all, the simple descriptive results reveal social science students' acceptance and tolerance of rap music even though they learn about the harm of rap songs in their lessons. They may be an indication of the rebellious tendency of university students (Li & Song, 1992; Rest *et al.*, 1999).

Effects of Death Awareness

Results of regression analysis show tendencies in line with the hypotheses, albeit not in a statistically significant way. In support of Hypothesis 1, death awareness induced by questions about death anxiety yielded a significant negative effect on the student's perceived harm of rap songs to self. The regression coefficient that showed the raw difference due to terror priming was a reduction of 6.56 points on perceived harm (see Table 4). It had a rather large effect of .326 (metric effect divided by the standard deviation of the outcome variable, [Cohen, 1988]). Furthermore, Hypothesis 1.1 about the effect of death awareness on the third-person effect concerning harm due to rap songs is likely to be sustainable even though the effect was not significant. In this case, the effect size was .442, which was rather large. That is, terror priming tended to provoke one's self-defense by holding oneself invulnerable especially in comparison with peers. In contrast, terror priming appeared to have little effect on the third-person effect regarding the benefit of rap songs (*effect size* = −.031). Nevertheless, the reduced third-person effect is consistent with terror management theory in that it shows the self-serving purpose of taking relatively more benefit from rap songs. That is, terror priming tended to prime one to maintain more advantage for oneself.

Table 4
Metric and standardized effects of death awareness

Outcome	Metric	Standard-ized	Effect size
Liking of rap songs	−3.79	−.088	−0.175
Approval of rap lyrics (antisocial orientation)	2.32	.082	0.163
Perceived harm of rap songs to self	−6.56	−.164*	−0.326
Perceived benefit of rap songs to self	2.01	.045	0.088
Perceived harm of rap songs to age peers	1.06	.022	0.043
Perceived benefit of rap songs to age peers	−1.44	−.038	−0.076
Third person effect regarding the harm of rap songs	7.58	.223	0.442
Third person effect regarding the benefit of rap songs	−0.30	−.015	−0.031

*: $p < .05$

Results show some support for Hypothesis 2 about the effect of death awareness on antisocial orientation. The student having received terror priming was 2.32 points, as estimated, higher on antisocial orientation than was the student not yet receiving the priming. The effect size was .163. It was, nevertheless, not large enough to be statistically significant.

In line with Hypothesis 3, death awareness showed a negative effect on liking of rap songs. The metric difference was 3.79, which meant an effect size of .175. This effect, albeit not significant, indicates a tendency for terror priming to encourage young people to defend their public selves by dissociating themselves from rap songs.

Effects of Death Anxiety

Death anxiety was another predictor that would affect beliefs and attitudes about rap independent of effects of death awareness, thanks to the experimental design and regression analysis technique. The anxiety showed a significant positive effect on the third-person effect regarding the harm of rap songs (β = .286, see Table 5).

Table 5
Metric and standardized effects of death anxiety

Outcome	Metric	Standard-ized	Effect size
Liking of rap songs	21.8	.163	1.009
Approval of rap lyrics (antisocial orientation)	1.32	.015	0.093
Perceived harm of rap songs to self	−10.0	−.080	−0.498
Perceived benefit of rap songs to self	−12.4	−.086	−0.547
Perceived harm of rap songs to age peers	18.8	.128	0.781
Perceived benefit of rap songs to age peers	12.8	.110	0.677
Third person effect regarding the harm of rap songs	30.6	.286*	1.786
Third person effect regarding the benefit of rap songs	10.9	.179	1.115

*: $p < .05$

However, its effects on perceived harm to oneself and to peers were weaker. Thus, death anxiety primarily invoked one's downward comparison with others by claiming more harm to peers than to oneself.

Death anxiety had minimal effect (β = .015) on approval of rap lyrics or antisocial orientation. Thus, death anxiety was unlikely to encourage adherence to an antisocial subculture. However, death anxiety showed a greater effect on liking of rap songs (β = .163). Apparently, death anxiety instigated one to seek relief in listening to rap songs, thus generating one's liking of them. Adherence to the antisocial subculture is therefore different from liking of rap songs, which can have a direct euphoric function of tension reduction. These patterns of effects are in sharp contrast with those of death awareness.

Discussion

Terror management theory appears to be useful for predicting Hong Kong university students' attribution and attitudes about rap songs. In line with its predictions, the student tends to enhance the self by an unconscious process of denying the harm of rap songs but adhering to its antisocial subculture. Moreover, the student tends to enhance the self by a conscious process of distancing oneself from rap songs or denying one's liking of them. The condition triggering the ego-enhancement motivation is death awareness induced by exposure to questions about death anxiety. Death awareness so induced is a situational impulse that can prime subsequent thoughts. This terror management effect tends to be different from the tension reduction effect generated by death anxiety. The differential effects stem from the difference in nature between death awareness and death anxiety. In the first place, death awareness is a momentary product induced by terror priming in the study whereas death anxiety may be a trait that stabilizes over time. Secondly, death awareness and death anxiety were two different predictors subject to regression analysis. There is no reason that the effects of the two concepts should be the same.

The most conspicuous difference in the effects of death awareness and death anxiety occurs in liking of rap songs. Whereas death awareness reduces the liking, death anxiety raises it. The former accords with the self-serving prediction of terror management theory in that it would present a more socially desirable public self. This explanation is plausible in view of university students' rather low liking of rap songs. That is, realizing that rap songs are socially undesirable, students would defend their self by showing their dislike of rap songs. By contrast, students with greater death anxiety like rap songs more, probably because they expect rap songs to relieve their death anxiety. Their motivation to reduce tension may override that for self-defense triggered by death awareness, a precondition for death anxiety.

On the other hand, downward comparison appears to be a significant response to death anxiety. Downward comparison is apparent in the third-person effect regarding the greater harm of rap songs to peers and oneself. It can be a means for both self-defense and tension reduction (Wills, 1987). For one, it may be a particularly important means for seeking gratification in music listening (Christenson & Roberts, 1998). It therefore accords with the significant effect of death anxiety on the third-person effect.

Death anxiety only shows little effect on approval of rap lyrics or antisocial orientation. This effect may partly reflect the negative effect of anxiety on delinquent involvement (Vitaro & Ladouceur, 1996). Accordingly, anxious people may not be daring enough to be deviant and antisocial. Nevertheless, the motivation of tension reduction would spur the anxious person's delinquent involvement (Cappell & Greeley, 1987). On balance, anxiety would not show a sizable positive effect on antisocial orientation. On the contrary, death awareness would have a greater effect on antisocial orientation, a finding supporting that in past research (Janssen & Dechesne, 1999). Apparently, people motivated to self-defend would have no emotional barrier to their adherence to the antisocial subculture.

Adherence to the antisocial subculture as a way of self-defense among Hong Kong university students tends to rest on conditions favoring acceptance of the subculture. In the first place, the students show a considerable orientation to antisocial subculture, reflecting the rebellious tendency common in university students (Li & Song, 1992; Rest *et al.*, 1999). Nevertheless, particularly in Hong Kong is the absence of the racial barrier to young people's acceptance of local Chinese rap culture. Whereas rap culture in the United States is appealing more to African Americans than to Caucasians (Christenson & Roberts, 1998; Wester *et al.*, 1997), indigenous rap music in Hong Kong pervades all young people because they are ethnically homogeneous. Besides, adverse economic conditions and the inability of the government to ameliorate them would lead to reverberating social grievances. The situation would precipitate students' discontent and adherence to the antisocial culture (Mesch, 1996). As such, if contextual conditions were favorable and people were conformist, endorsement to the antisocial subculture would not be likely as a self-defensive response to terror priming.

The effects of death awareness appear to be more salient for the harm than for the benefit of rap lyrics. These findings are consistent with findings about the weaker third-person effect for socially desirable messages (Eveland & McLeod, 1999). They probably reflect the case that the perception of harm is more germane to self-defense than that of benefit. Obviously, self-defense is a likely response to devaluation, frustration, irritation, and other negative experiences rather than to positive ones (Heaven, 1994). Acquiring benefit is not always desirable because it would introduce a sense of indebtedness (Midlarsky & Kahana, 1994). The defensive individual would rather minimize the harm than accentuate the benefit.

Limitations

Obviously, the small sample size inhibits drawing statistically significant inference for many of the effects examined in the study. Even though effect sizes are remarkable in many cases, they are not significant due to the small sample size. Therefore, the study at best illustrates tendencies that are consistent with theoretical predictions but not yet adequate to make conclusive generalization. Even if the findings can be generalizable, they can only hold for Hong Kong Chinese social science students because the sample is a very homogeneous one. The homogeneity can offer both strengths and weaknesses. Its strengths lie in the minimization of extraneous effects due to the heterogeneity of variables. With many characteristics kept constant, the homogeneity can highlight the effects of death awareness induced in the study. Nevertheless, homogeneity has the weakness of limiting the variance of all variables and this poses a difficulty to statistical testing. It obviously limits the generalization of the findings necessitating a caveat for accepting the findings.

Whereas the study illustrates that death awareness and death anxiety can have different effects on the student's attribution and attitude about rap songs, it does not assess a pure effect of death awareness independent of awareness of death anxiety. Priming of death awareness is likely to make death anxiety subjectively salient. The difficult task of disentangling awareness of death from awareness of death anxiety should be a challenge for future research.

Implications

The study identifies an alternative path to liking and adhering to rap culture based on terror management theory. Impulse for self-defense rather than reasoned action contributes to attitudes toward rap. The importance of the study is in affirming the generality of using terror management theory to predict human reactions. It thus gives more credence to using the theory to predict a diversity of human behaviors, among which terrorism may be a case. In this connection, terrorism and other antisocial and criminal practice may be rooted in the impulse of death, among other more rational causes. Accordingly, the prediction of terror management theory can incorporate the effect of "nothing to lose" on criminal offense

(Harris *et al.*, 2002). The notion of nothing to lose states that when a person is aware of death, the person is eager to take risk, including various criminal offenses and suicidal terrorism. While the original logic of the effect of "nothing to lose" may reflect a rational response to life being short, terror management theory would emphasize it as an impulsive response of self-defense, suggesting that death priming can spur people's to adherence to subcultures, including those conceivably advocating terrorism. Furthermore, priming can boost the individual's need to create a dignified public self, such as being a martyr for a terrorist cause. At any rate, terror priming may be an adversarial device of radicalism and at the same time create an illusion of invulnerability in the person. These effects may be responsible for instanteous escalation of terrorist acts. The terrorists' mentality of "nothing to lose" reflects their awareness of terror or death and their terrorist activities are manifestations of terror management.

Rap lyrics can serve as indicators of both antisocial subculture and terror. For instance, there is no shortage of description of bloodshed, murder, and simply death in rap lyrics (Lynxwiler & Gay, 2000; Mcleod *et al.*, 1997). Whereas the study examines rap lyrics as an indicator of antisocial subculture, future research can evaluate how rap lyrics induce terror and terror management. In light of the "nothing to lose" argument and terror management theory, the terror-provoking rap lyrics would be considered responsible for instigating deviant behavior. The theory would therefore be an explanation for the antisocial effects of rap and its affiliated subculture. Testing the potency of the explanation can be a fruitful focus in future research on language and social psychology.

References

Amaro, H., Blake, S.M., Schwartz, P.M., & Flinchbaugh, L.J. (2001). Developing theory-based substance abuse prevention programs for young adolescent girls. *Journal of Early Adolescence, 21,* 256–293.

Ballard, M.E., &. Dodson, A.R. (1999). Genre of music and lyrical content: Expectation effects. *Journal of Genetic Psychology, 160,* 476–487.

Binder, A. (1993). Constructing racial rhetoric: Media depiction of harm in heavy metal and rap music. *American Sociological Review, 58,* 553–767.

Cappell, H., & Greeley, J. (1987). Alcohol tension reduction: An update on research and theory. In H.T. Blane & K.E. Leonard (Eds.), *Psychological theories of drinking and alcoholism* (pp. 15–54). New York: Guilford.

Christenson, P.G., & Roberts, D.F. (1998). *It's not only rock & roll: Popular music in the lives of adolescents.* Cresskill, NJ: Hampton.

Chung, M.C., Chung, C., & Easthope, Y. (2000). Traumatic stress and death anxiety among community residents exposed to an aircraft crash. *Death Studies, 24,* 689–704.

Cohen, J. (1988). *Statistical power analysis for the behavioral sciences* (2nd ed.). Hillsdale, NJ: Lawrence Erlbaum.

Eveland, W.P., & McLeod, D.M. (1999). The effect of social desirability on perceived media impact: Implications for third-person perceptions. *International Journal of Public Opinion Research, 11,* 315–333.

Eveland, W.P., Jr., Nathanson, A.I., Detenber, B.H., & McLeod, D.M. (1999). Rethinking the social distance corollary: Perceived likelihood of exposure and the third-person perception. *Communication Research, 26,* 275–302.

Felson, R.B., Liska, A.E., South, S.J., & McNulty, T.L. (1994). The subculture of violence and delinquency: Individual vs. school context effects. *Social Forces, 73,* 153–173.

Golding, P., & van Snippenburg, L. (1995). Government, communications, and the media. In O. Borre & E. Scarbrough (Eds.), *The scope of government* (pp.283–312). Oxford: Oxford University Press.

Harris, K.Mullan, Duncan, G.J., & Boisjoly, J. (2002). Evaluating the role of nothing to lose attitudes on risky behavior in adolescence. *Social Forces, 80,* 1005–1039.

Heaven, P.C.L. (1994). Family of origin, personality, and self-reported delinquency. *Journal of Adolescence, 17,* 445–459.

Helzer, J.E., & Canino, G.J. (1992). *Alcoholism in North America, Europe, and Asia.* New York: Oxford University Press.

Janssen, J., & Dechesne, M. (1999). The psychological importance of youth culture. *Youth & Society, 31*, 152–167.

Kennedy, L.W., & Baron, S.W. (1993). Routine activities and a subculture of violence: A study of violence on the street. *Journal of Research in Crime and Delinquency, 30*, 88–112.

Li, J., & Song, D. (1992). *Political consciousness and political behavior of contemporary China's youth.* Beijing, China: China's People Public Order University.

Lynxwiler, J., & Gay, D. (2000). Moral boundaries and deviant music: Public attitudes toward heavy metal and rap. *Deviant Behavior, 21*, 63–85.

McLeod, D.M., & Eveland, W.P., Jr. (1997). Support for censorship of violent and misogynic rap lyrics. *Communication Research, 24*, 153–174.

McLeod, D.M., Detenber, B.H., & Eveland, W.P., Jr. (2001). Behind the third-person effect: Differing perceptual processes for self and other. *Journal of Communication, 51*, 678–695.

Mesch, G.S. (1996). The effect of environmental concerns and governmental incentives on organized action in local areas. *Urban Affairs Review, 31*, 346–366.

Midlarsky, E., & Kahana, E. (1994). *Altruism in Late Life.* Thousand Oaks, CA: Sage.

Paulhus, D.L. (1991). Measurement and control of response bias. In J.P. Robinson, P.R. Shaver & L.S. Wrightsman (Eds.), *Measures of personality and social psychological attitudes, Vol.1: Measures of social psychological attitudes* (pp. 17–60). San Diego, CA: Academic Press.

Pyszczynski, T., Greenberg, J., & Solomon, S. (1999). A dual-process model of defense against conscious and unconscious death-related thoughts: An extension of terror management theory. *Psychological Review, 106*, 835–835.

Rest, J., Narvaez, D., Bebeau, M.J., & Thoma, S.J. (1999). *Postconventional moral thinking: A neo-Kohlbergian approach.* Mahwah, NJ: Lawrence Erlbaum.

Rudman, L., & Lee, M.R. (2002). Implicit and explicit consequences of exposure to violent and misogynous rap music. *Group Process & Intergroup Relations, 5*, 133–150.

Wester, S.R., Crown, C.L., Quartman, G.L., & Heesacker, M. (1997). The influence of sexually violent rap music on attitudes of men with little prior exposure. *Psychology of Women Quarterly, 21*, 497–508.

Seeman, M., Seeman, A.Z., & Burdos, A. (1988). Powerlessness, work, and community: A longitudinal study of alienation and alcohol use. *Journal of Health and Social Behavior, 29*, 185–198.

Simpson, T.A. (1996). Constructions of self and other in the experience of rap music. In D. Grodin & T.R. Lindlof (Ed.), *Constructing the self in a mediated world* (pp. 107–123). Thousand Oaks, CA: Sage.

Smith, S.L., & Bryson, A.R. (2002). Violence in music videos: Examining the prevalence and content of physical aggression. *Journal of Communication, 52,* 61–83.

Solomon, S., Greenberg, J., & Pyszczynski, T. (1991). A terror management theory of social behavior: The psychological functions of self-esteem and cultural worldviews. *Advances in Experimental Social Psychology, 24,* 93–159.

Vitaro, F., & Ladouceur, R. (1996). Predictive and concurrent correlates of gambling in early adolescent boys. *Journal of Early Adolescence, 16,* 211–228.

Wills, T.A. (1987). Help-seeking as a coping mechanism. In C.R. Snyder & C.E. Ford (Eds.), *Coping with negative life events: Clinical and Social Psychology perspectives* (pp. 19–50). New York: Plenum Press.

Zagorski, K. (1999). Egalitarianism, perception of conflicts, and support for transformation in Poland. In S. Svallfors & P. Taylor-Gooby (Eds.), *The end of the welfare state? Responses to state retrenchment* (pp. 190–217). London: Routledge.

20

Conflict in Families with Adolescents: How Family Relationships Affect Each Other

Patricia NOLLER
Judith A. FEENEY

The goals of this chapter are to provide an integrative review of our research on families with adolescents, to demonstrate the links between different family relationships (marital, parent-child and sibling), and to describe the ways in which these different family relationships affect each other. The studies we describe generally focus on conflict in these families, and involve a range of different methodologies including questionnaires, interviews, behavioral observation of videotaped interaction, and content analysis.

One principle of Family Systems Theory (developed from the General Systems Theory of von Bertalanffy, 1962) is circular causality. This principle assumes that each dyadic relationship affects other relationships in the family, and that change in one member affects other members and the family system as a whole. Similarly, Parke and Tinsley (1987) have commented on the interdependence among various roles and relationships in the family. As Stafford and Dainton (1995) note, in systems models,

> "parenting is not seen as unidirectional, or even
> bi-directional. Instead, family processes and patterns are

seen as influencing and being influenced by, parent-child interaction" (p. 3).

Belsky (1981) has also emphasized the importance of recognizing the links between various family relationships. He noted that:

> "Parenting affects and is affected by the infant, who both influences and is influenced by the marital relationship, which in turn both affects and is affected by parenting" (p. 3).

In this chapter, we report on links between the marital and parent-child relationships, between the parent-child and sibling relationships, and between the marital and sibling relationships, and also explore the effects of siblings on one another. It is important to keep in mind that, from a family systems perspective, it is inappropriate to assume that a particular relationship consistently affects another; rather, various relationships affect each other in reciprocal, or even circular, ways.

Linking Marital, Parent-Child and Sibling Conflict Patterns: A Questionnaire Study

The first study to be discussed (Noller, Feeney, Peterson & Sheehan, 1995) focused on a number of research questions, such as: If parents are destructive in how they deal with conflict in their couple relationship, will they also use destructive conflict patterns in handling conflicts with their children? Similarly, if marital and parent-child conflict is destructive in nature, is conflict between the siblings also destructive? The study involved obtaining parents' self-reports of behaviors employed when dealing with conflicts with the spouse and with one of their adolescent children, and adolescents' reports on their conflict with their parents and with their siblings.

The measure of conflict behavior used in this study was the Communication Patterns Questionnaire (CPQ; Christensen, 1988; Christensen & Sullaway, 1984). The original CPQ was designed for couples, and thus the questions were modified to apply to parent-child and sibling relationships. The factors common to all versions of the CPQ included mutuality (mutual problem-solving), coercion, demand-withdraw and post-conflict distress. These are similar to the factors found by Noller and White (1990) using the original marital version of the scale. There were moderate to high levels of agreement between husbands and wives, mothers and adolescents, and fathers and adolescents, in terms of their reports of conflict behavior. In general, the family members reported moderate to high levels of mutuality (means around 6 on a 9-point scale), moderate levels of demand-withdraw and post-conflict distress (means between 3.5 and 4.5), and low levels of coercion (means below 2). The mean age of the 154 adolescent participants was 17.5 years, and the mean age of the sibling on which they reported was 18.1 years.

We correlated parents' reports of marital and parent-child conflict in two ways, in order to deal (at least to some extent) with the problem of common-method variance. For example, when exploring the link between marital and mother-daughter conflict, we first correlated mothers' reports of conflict in the marital relationship with mothers' reports of conflict in the parent-child relationship. We then correlated fathers' reports of conflict in the mother-child relationship with mothers' reports of conflict in relationships with their daughters, thus using the perspectives of two different reporters.

As can be seen from Table 1, correlations between marital and parent-child conflict were generally moderate to strong when the same reporter was used; however, the correlations were somewhat weaker when different reporters were used (the latter correlations are not tabulated here). For the same-reporter data set, some correlations were particularly strong. For example, the correlation between coercion in the marital and mother-son relationship suggests that sons may tend to learn their coercive behaviors from interactions with their mothers. Also of interest are the correlations between demand/withdraw in the marital relationship and in the parent-adolescent relationship: These links were particularly strong for males, who seem to learn the demand-withdraw pattern in interaction with both of their parents. This finding fits with a large amount of data showing that in marriage, the male is more likely to withdraw in conflict interactions (e.g., Christensen, 1988), although there is also evidence that this pattern is strongest when wives' issues are being discussed (Christensen & Heavey, 1990).

Table 1
Correlations between marital and parent-child conflict patterns

	Mother/ daughter	Mother/ son	Father/ daughter	Father/ son
Mutual	.48**	.24	.54**	.49**
Coercion	.34*	.58**	.34*	.36*
Demand/withdraw	.47**	.55**	.41**	.54**
Post-conflict distress	.50**	.39**	.51**	.57**

Note: *p*<.05 *; *p*<.01 **

We also correlated reports of conflict patterns in the parent-child relationship with reports of conflict patterns in the sibling relationship. There were moderate to high correlations between conflict patterns in these different relationships, when the same reporter was used to evaluate both relationships. Correlations between demand/withdraw in the parent-child and sibling relationships were particularly strong for sons, as was the correlation between coercion in the mother-child and sibling relationships. Findings were again generally weaker when different reporters were used.

We also correlated perceptions of marital conflict with perceptions of conflict in the sibling relationship, but no significant links were found. This finding suggests that adolescents do not model their conflict behavior with one another directly on their parents' reactions in the marital relationship. Rather, it seems to us that adolescents may learn their ways of dealing with conflict directly in interaction with their parents. In other words, parents behave rather similarly in conflict with their children to the way they behave in conflict with their spouse. Adolescents may then learn their conflict patterns in interaction with their parents, and implement these in sibling conflicts. Although we must caution against assuming causal relationships from correlational data, it seems logical that parents' conflict patterns are well established long before children come along. Hence, the influence from parent to child is likely to be stronger than that from child to parent, but children's behavior will also influence the development of some patterns. The parent who says of her interactions with her son, "He gets me so frustrated I could scream", certainly believes that the child's behavior affects her own communication.

Several authors (e.g., Boer, Goedhart & Treffers, 1992; Hetherington, 1988) have suggested that sibling relationships may also be affected by parents showing favouritism to one child. Thus we would expect more destructive conflicts in sibling relationships characterized by parental favouritism. Modified versions of the subscales from the Sibling Inventory of Differential Treatment (SIDE; Daniels & Plomin, 1985; maternal affection, maternal control, paternal affection, paternal control) were administered to test this hypothesis. The SIDE can be scored to assess absolute differential treatment (that is, the absolute difference in treatment between the two siblings) or relative differential treatment (taking into account who is favored and who is disfavored).

Correlations between absolute differential treatment and conflict patterns in the sibling relationship indicated significant links between children's reports of a lack of mutuality between siblings and mothers' differential control and affection and fathers' differential control ($r = -.33$, $-.22$ and $-.34$, respectively). There were also links between children's reports of coercion between siblings and mothers' differential control and affection ($r = .22$ in both cases). These findings, although not strong, suggest that differential treatment by mothers, in particular, is related to destructive conflict patterns between siblings.

Marital and Parent-Child Conflict
and Family Members' Perceptions of One Another

As we have already suggested, an important aspect of the family environment is the frequency and nature of marital conflict. A lot of evidence suggests that marital conflict is linked to children's behavior problems and adjustment difficulties (Dadds & Powell, 1991; Mann & McKenzie, 1996; Osborne & Fincham, 1996). There are several limitations to previous studies, however, including the difficulty in establishing causal relations, the failure to distinguish between different types of conflict, and the focus on predicting child adjustment, rather than the quality of family relationships.

As we did in the earlier study using the CPQ, we explored the links between conflict patterns in the marital relationship and parents' perceptions of their children, and between conflict patterns in the parent-child relationship and siblings' perceptions of one another (Noller, Feeney, Sheehan, & Peterson, 2000). We wanted to know whether parents who reported negative conflict patterns in their marital relationship would have negative perceptions of their adolescents, and whether, in families where parents reported negative conflict patterns with their adolescents, those offspring would have negative perceptions of one another.

The participants were 68 two-parent families with adolescent twins from Anglo-Australian backgrounds. There were 25 pairs of monozygotic twins, nine of which were male and 16 female; there were also 43 dizygotic pairs (9 male-male dyads, 14 female-female dyads and 20 male-female dyads). The twins' ages ranged from 12 to 17 years, with a mean age of 14.1.

As noted already, we again used CPQ to assess conflict patterns in the marital and parent-child relationships. Correlations between the reports of husbands and wives indicated a high level of agreement between spouses about their conflict patterns. It was also clear from the mean scores on the scales of the CPQ that these were not, overall, highly conflicted families: Scores tended to be high for mutuality, moderate for both demand/withdraw and post-conflict distress, and low for coercion.

Following completion of the questionnaire measures, all four family members engaged in an interaction task where they were asked to plan a 2-week vacation and to reach an agreement about where they wanted to go, how they would get there, and the kinds of activities that they would engage in. On conclusion of the interaction, the middle three-minute segment of the five-minute videotape was replayed, and participants were asked to make participants global ratings of each family member using the following 6-point scales: calm-anxious, involved-uninvolved, friendly-unfriendly, loving-rejecting and controlling-democratic. Levels of agreement between family members in their ratings were generally low to moderate, suggesting that the global ratings were affected not only by how family members behaved in the interaction, but also by preconceived ideas about the likely behavior and attitudes of parents and siblings.

The first set of analyses relevant to this discussion focused on the link between parents' reports of their marital conflict patterns and their perceptions of their adolescent children in the family interaction. Canonical correlation analysis was used to explore the links between the four factors of the CPQ and the five sets of ratings of the adolescents, separately for each parent's reports and for first- and second-born twins. Links were restricted to fathers' reports. Fathers who saw their marital conflict as low on mutuality and high on coercion tended to perceive their adolescent twins negatively, although the patterns were slightly different depending on which twin was the focus.

The second set of analyses followed a similar pattern, except that we examined the link between parents' perceptions of their conflict with their adolescents and the adolescent twins' perceptions of each other. Again, results were significant only for fathers. Fathers' reports of destructive parent-child conflict were associated with siblings' negative perceptions of one another for both first and second-born twins, although once again, the specific pattern of variables differed for each twin.

Together, these findings support the link between family members' reports of conflict behavior and their perceptions of one another in the course of specific interactions. Men who reported negative patterns of conflict with their wives also tended to see their adolescents in a negative light. Thus fathers' perceptions of couple communication seem to affect their views of their children, although it is also possible that difficult or oppositional adolescents contribute to fathers' perceptions of negative interaction between spouses. Further, in families where fathers perceived their conflict with their adolescents negatively, the adolescents had more negative perceptions of one another. Hence, it seems that in some families, fathers and offspring become caught up in a pattern of negative attitudes and behaviors. It is also possible that fathers project aspects of their marital relationship onto their children, and that children project aspects of their relationship with their father onto one another. In either case, these data support the congruence hypothesis (Boer *et al.*, 1992), that proposes a positive association between the quality of different family relationships.

Linking Differential Parenting with Sibling Communication

In the first study reported here we have already seen evidence that differential parenting is related to siblings displaying less mutuality and more coercion in their conflict interactions. Whereas that study relied on questionnaire data, the study to be reported next assessed sibling conflict using both questionnaire and observational methods (Sheehan, 2000; Sheehan, Feeney, Noller, & Peterson, 1998). The aim of this study was to examine the relations between twins' perceptions of differential treatment and twins' experiences of communication in their sibling relationship.

Sixty-seven pairs of adolescent twins (aged 12 to 17 years) completed the SIDE and the Conflict Resolution Style Questionnaire (CRS; Rands, Levinger & Mellinger, 1981; Peterson, 1990), and took part in an interaction task. Four scales were obtained from a factor analysis of the CRS: avoidance, problem-solving, attack and post-conflict distress. Canonical correlation analysis was again used to explore the links between differential parenting and the factors of the CRS.

Links were found between twins' reports of differential treatment (absolute) and destructive communication patterns used during conflict interactions with one another (see Sheehan, 2000; Sheehan *et al.*, 1998). Specifically, twins who reported experiencing more differential treatment also reported more avoidance, more attack, more post-conflict distress and less problem-solving. No relation was found, however, between perceived differential parenting and *differences between twins* in their reports of destructive conflict patterns. That is, both the favored and the disfavored twin seemed to experience their conflict interactions as equally negative.

Twins' behavior in the interaction task was rated both by the twins themselves and by an outside coder, using the same five global dimensions used in the study reported previously. Based on factor analysis, twins' ratings of themselves and their twin were aggregated into a composite (positivity), involving all scales except democratic-controlling. Correlations were calculated between perceived differential parenting and twins' ratings of the positivity of their own and their twins' relational behavior. Twins who reported experiencing differential parenting rated their own and their twins' relational behavior less positively (see Table 2). Correlations were also calculated between twins' reports of differential parenting and *differences between twins* in their reports of their own and their twins' relational behavior, but no significant correlations were found, again suggesting that both the favored and the disfavored twin experience their conflict equally negatively.

To assess whether outsiders' ratings would yield similar results, we correlated their reports of the twins' interaction behavior with the twins' reports of differential parenting. Outsider ratings were combined to form scales of positivity (friendly and loving), and arousal (anxious and involved); democratic-controlling ratings were analysed separately. First-born twins' reports of differential parenting were generally related to outsider ratings of first-born twins as more unfriendly and rejecting in their interaction with their twin. As with the results using twins' reports, these findings suggest clear links between differential parenting and negative interactions between twins. However, it is not clear whether the negative behavior of offspring is a reaction to differential parenting, or differential parenting is a reaction to the negative behavior of offspring.

Table 2
Correlations between Differential Parenting and Twins' Ratings of
the Positivity-Negativity of Their Own and Their Twins' Relational Behavior

	Ratings of Self		Ratings of Twin	
	First born	Second born	First born	Second born
Mother control	−.30**	−.40***	−.29**	−.36**
Mother affection	−.27*	−.35*	−.27*	−.26*
Father control	−.24*	−.39***	−.24*	−.18
Father affection	−.23*	−.38***	−.33**	−.29**

Note: $p<.05$ *; $p<.01$ **

Linking Differential Parenting
with Sibling Attachment and Adjustment

In a recent study (Sheehan & Noller, 2002), we assessed the relations between adolescent twins' perceptions of differential parenting and adolescent attachment and adjustment. Again, differential parenting was assessed using the modified SIDE (mentioned earlier); in this study we focused on relative differential treatment, taking account of which twin was favored and which was disfavored. Attachment was assessed using the Attachment Style Questionnaire (ASQ; Feeney, Noller & Hanrahan, 1994), which assesses five factors of attachment security: Confidence in self and others, Discomfort with closeness, Preoccupation with relationships, Need for approval and Relationships as secondary. These factors show systematic relations with working models of self and other, as discussed by Bartholomew (1990; Bartholomew & Horowitz, 1991). Adolescent adjustment was assessed using the Coopersmith Self Esteem Inventory (SEI; Coopersmith, 1975), and the trait measure of the State-Trait Anxiety Scales (Spielberger, Gorsuch & Lushene, 1968).

Using regression analyses, we found an association between twins' reports of differential parental treatment and their reported attachment style. Twins who reported receiving less maternal affection than their co-twin reported less confidence in self and others than those receiving equal or favored treatment, and those who reported receiving less paternal affection reported more discomfort with closeness (Sheehan & Noller, 2002). As attachment theory would predict, it seems that experiencing differential affection from mother *or* father is likely to impact on the attachment security of adolescents, albeit in rather different ways.

We also found an association between twins' reports of differential treatment and their psychological adjustment. Twins who reported receiving less maternal affection also reported higher levels of trait anxiety, and those who reported receiving higher levels of maternal control tended to report lower personal self-esteem and higher anxiety. On the other hand, receiving higher levels of paternal control was associated with higher self-esteem. Thus perceptions of differential treatment, particularly from the mother, seem to have negative effects on adolescents' psychological adjustment.

Finally, we used regression analyses to explore the possibility that attachment security mediates the relation between differential parenting and psychological adjustment. We found evidence that the confidence factor of the ASQ mediated the association between differential maternal affection and trait anxiety. In addition, discomfort with closeness mediated the relation between differential paternal affection and personal self-esteem. It would seem that differential parenting, particularly in terms of differential affection, affects security of attachment which, in turn, affects psychological adjustment.

In summary, our findings showed that differential parenting is linked to the psychological adjustment of the disfavored child. Disfavored adolescents were more likely to be insecure in attachment style, and to report lower self-esteem and higher anxiety than their favored siblings. These findings fit with earlier research on the associations between differential parental treatment and the poor adjustment of the disfavored child (Baker & Daniels, 1990; Daniels, Dunn, Furstenberg & Plomin, 1985; Dunn, Stocker & Beardsall, 1989). We also found evidence that attachment mediated the association between differential parenting and adolescent adjustment, suggesting that differences in affection from parents may be particularly salient for insecure adolescents, and are likely to contribute to ongoing problems in adjustment. Differences in parental control were also problematic, but had direct (rather than mediated) relations with adolescent adjustment.

Parent-Adolescent Relationships and Adolescent Adjustment

It is also important to understand the links between parent-adolescent relationships and the psychological adjustment of adolescents. The next study involved the content analysis of adolescents' responses to open-ended questions about their relationships with their parents (Hurd, Wooding & Noller, 1999). Three groups of adolescents were involved in the study: a group who had recently engaged in self-harming behavior, a group who were similarly depressed to those in the self-harming group but had not engaged in self-harming behavior, and a control group of non-clinical, non-depressed adolescents.

Adolescents were asked to audiotape their responses to five questions, including the only one discussed here: how they got along with their parents. They were left alone to make their responses, in order to optimise the openness and spontaneity of their answers. These responses were later transcribed and content-analysed, and a set of scales were derived for rating the adolescents' perceptions of their relationship with mother, relationship with father, frequency of communication with mother, frequency of communication with father, conflict with mother, and conflict with father.

As would be expected, adolescents in the control group reported better relationships, more frequent communication and lower levels of conflict with both parents, than either of the clinical groups (see Hurd *et al.*, 1999). The main differences between the two clinical groups were that the self-harmers reported less positive relationships with their fathers and higher levels of conflict with their mothers than did adolescents who were depressed but had not engaged in self-harming behavior. These findings suggest that distant and conflicted relationships with parents may have particularly negative effects on adolescents who are already depressed.

In summary, this study provides further evidence of links between parent-adolescent relationships and adolescent adjustment. These findings suggest that relationships with parents are critical for the mental health of adolescents, although it is important to acknowledge that both parents and adolescents contribute actively to the quality of these relationships. Moody and depressed adolescents are likely to be very difficult for parents to manage, and their consequent frustration may lead to higher levels of conflict with their adolescents.

Comparison and Competition in Sibling Relationships: How Siblings Affect Each Other

The overall family environment is likely to be affected not only by the marital relationship and parent-child relationships, but also by the relationships between siblings. In this section, we explore the effects of comparison and competition on sibling relationships.

According to the Self-Evaluation Maintenance model (Tesser, 1980; 1988), a person's reaction to comparison and competition is likely to depend on three important variables that affect appraisals of the self: the closeness of the relationship with the comparison person, relative performance (better or worse than that person), and the relevance of the activity to the self-concept. In the next study (Noller, Conway, Blakeley-Smith & Beach, 2001), we used a sample of young adult siblings (18 –25 years old) to evaluate this model. All sibling pairs were same sex, as we expected that comparison and competition would be more salient in same-sex pairs.

Siblings were asked to describe eight situations in which they had competed with or been compared with a sibling or a friend (four situations involved siblings, and four involved friends). Two situations in each set of four were required to be situations where the respondent had performed better than the sibling or friend, and two were to involve situations where they had performed worse. In addition, one of each of these pairs of situations was to involve an activity of high relevance to the self and low relevance to the sibling or friend, and one was to involve low relevance to the self but high relevance to the sibling or friend. The situations described by the respondents involved a wide range of areas of comparison and competition, including sporting activities, academic achievement, artistic pursuits, and performances in music and drama, as well as more personal comparisons involving personality and attractiveness.

After they had described each situation, participants were asked to rate the positivity and negativity of their emotional reactions in that situation, the likelihood that they would 'play down' the significance of their performance, and the likelihood that they would continue engaging in that particular activity. These ratings were the dependent variables for the study.

Participants' negative reactions to these situations were related to all three independent variables: relevance, performance and closeness (see Noller *et al.*, 2001). Participants reported feeling more negative when they competed on high-relevance than on low-relevance activities, and when they performed worse than their competitor (rather than better). They also reported more negativity towards their sibling than towards their friend, irrespective of performance. As anticipated, participants felt particularly negative when they performed worse on a high-relevance activity, and were more likely to play down the importance of their success or failure if the activity was of low relevance. The negativity engendered by situations of comparison and competition between siblings is likely to have ramifications for other interactions, and for the overall family environment.

Participants were particularly likely to report that they would continue the activity when they performed better on an activity of high relevance. Older males were more likely to continue an activity if they performed better than their friend than if they performed worse. When they competed against their sibling, however, their likelihood of continuing the activity was unaffected by their performance.

Attachment security also affected participants' reactions in situations of comparison and competition. Participants were categorised according to the four attachment styles proposed by Bartholomew (Bartholomew, 1990; Bartholomew & Horowitz, 1991). Overall, secure individuals were significantly more positive in situations of comparison and competition than were fearful individuals, and significantly less negative than preoccupied individuals.

Further analyses were carried out separately for younger and older siblings. These analyses showed that, when outperformed, dismissing and fearful participants felt significantly more negative when they competed against a younger sibling than when they competed against a friend (presumably of similar age). In addition, secure older siblings were significantly less negative than dismissing or fearful older siblings when outperformed by their younger sibling, and preoccupied individuals were more negative than others when outperformed by their friends. Clearly, attachment style has an impact on reactions to being outperformed for dismissing or fearful individuals competing against their younger sibling. In short, avoidant individuals seem to be especially vulnerable in these situations.

In addition, older siblings who were preoccupied in attachment were more likely to downplay the importance of poor performance against their sibling than against their friend. They were also more likely to downplay the importance of poor performance against their sibling than were secure individuals. Although attachment insecurity was clearly associated with downplaying the significance of poor performance against younger siblings, it did not affect the decision to continue with the activity in these situations.

We also correlated emotional reactions to comparison and competition with the quality of the sibling relationship, using the Sibling Relationships Questionnaire (SRQ; Furman & Buhrmester, 1985) to assess levels of sibling warmth and hostility. These correlations consistently showed that respondents felt more positive towards their sibling when their relationship was high in warmth and low in conflict, irrespective of their performance. Thus, it seems that the quality of the relationship between siblings can help minimize the negative effects of comparison and competition.

Finally, reactions to comparison and competition were also associated with psychological adjustment. Those with higher self-esteem tended to have more positive and less negative reactions to competition than those with low self-esteem, irrespective of performance (see Table 3). Conversely, those who were depressed reported responding more negatively and less positively, irrespective of performance. In contrast, there was some evidence that the effects of trait anxiety depended on performance. Those who were more anxious reacted more negatively to being *outperformed* by their sibling than did those who were less anxious, whereas negative reactions to outperforming the sibling were unaffected by anxiety. (However, those who were more anxious had less positive reactions to competition, irrespective of relative performance).

In summary, although participants generally reported reacting negatively in situations of comparison and competition against their siblings, a complex set of factors are related to these reactions. Those who are vulnerable because of attachment insecurity or poor psychological adjustment are likely to react more negatively in these situations, with implications for sibling relationships and the overall family environment. It is also interesting to note that reactions were more strongly related to the quality of the sibling relationship than to relative performance.

Table 3
Correlations of Adjustment Variables with
Reactions to Comparison and Competition

Emotional reactions	Self-esteem	Depression	Trait anxiety
Positive when do better	.26**	−.28**	−.26**
Negative when do better	−.16*	.19*	.10
Positive when do worse	.27**	−.28**	−.25**
Negative when do worse	.25**	.27**	.22*

Note: p<.05 *; p<.01 **

Divorce and Sibling Relationships

Much has been written about the effects of parental divorce on young people's lives (Amato, 2001; Amato & Keith, 1991; Buchanan, Maccoby, & Dornbusch, 1996), but little is known about the effects of parental divorce on sibling relationships. The next study involved collecting both quantitative and qualitative data about adolescents' perceptions of their sibling relationships during this difficult time (Sheehan, Darlington, Noller, & Feeney, 2003). We again used the Sibling Relationship Questionnaire (SRQ) to assess the quality of the sibling relationship. Following from a study by McGuire, McHale and Updegraff (1996), we performed a cluster analysis using sibling conflict and sibling warmth as the dependent variables, and found four clusters similar to those found by McGuire and colleagues: harmonious (high on warmth and low on conflict), hostile (low on warmth and high in conflict), affect-intense (high on both warmth and conflict) and uninvolved (low on both warmth and conflict). The most interesting finding from this study was that adolescents in the divorcing families were about twice as likely as those in intact families to report affect-intense relationships with their siblings. (Sibling relationships in intact families were evenly spread across the four types.)

When we examined scores on the other scales of the SRQ, we found that those in affect-intense relationships reported equally high levels of nurturance (of and by the sibling) as those in harmonious relationships (Sheehan *et al.*, 2003). Further, they reported equally high dominance (of and by the sibling) as those in hostile relationships. In other words, these affect-intense relationships were as positive as the harmonious relationships and as negative as the hostile relationships.

The comments that the adolescents made about their sibling relationships during semi-structured interviews further our understanding of how these relationships can be simultaneously high on positivity and high on negativity. Older siblings tended to feel responsible for their younger siblings and to "watch out for [them] and stuff". They also acknowledged that their younger siblings were not always grateful for this kind of attention, and saw these protective behaviors as "sometimes good and sometimes bad". On the other hand, younger siblings often expressed gratitude for the support that they received, especially when parents were arguing. As one younger sibling explained, "She comes to my room and talks to me and makes me feel better".

In summary, although there is considerable variability in sibling relationships in divorcing families, they are more likely than those from intact families to be affect-intense. On the one hand, these relationships are highly nurturant, with siblings working to resolve disagreements constructively and to support one another; on the other hand, they are also negative in tone, with high levels of dominance and hostility. Interestingly, the interview data suggest that the dominance and hostility tend to be related to the nurturance and support: Older siblings are somewhat overprotective of their younger siblings, who sometimes resent this behavior. While these older siblings may "mean well", they are not always sensitive to the feelings of their younger siblings, and may be coercive or intrusive in their attempts to provide support. Hence, when older children take on the role of protecting their younger siblings, they need to recognize that although younger siblings are likely to appreciate the support, they may resist perceived attempts to control their behavior.

Integrating the Findings

The studies presented here suggest a number of conclusions about how different family relationships affect each other, particularly with regard to conflict. In the remainder of this chapter, we integrate these findings by asking which groups of the primarily middle-class young people studied here seem to be most disadvantaged in terms of relational and personal adjustment. We argue that those where there is high conflict (or actual breakdown) between the parents, and those in families where there is pervasive differential parenting, are likely to have more problems in their present and future relationships, and with their psychological adjustment.

Because marital communication and parent-child communication are moderately highly correlated, young people in families with destructive marital conflict are likely to learn negative ways of dealing with conflict themselves. According to recent research by Lindsey, MacKinnon-Lewis, Campbell, Frabutt and Lamb (2002), who studied the effect of marital conflict on pre-adolescent boys, marital conflict affected these boys' peer relationships through its effect on the emotional tone of the mother-son relationship. Lindsey *et al.* argue that "marital conflict interferes with the emotional tenor of the mother-son relationship, creating patterns of emotional expressiveness between mother and son that are problematic for the establishment of positive peer relationships" (p. 472).

This proposition certainly fits with our findings linking marital and parent-child conflict patterns (Noller *et al.*, 1995), and with our suggestion that children learn their negative conflict patterns in interaction with their parents.

Lindsey *et al.* see their results as supporting the emotional security hypothesis of Davies and Cummings (1994, 1998); that is, children's attachment security is likely to be adversely affected by marital conflict, because of the stress and negative emotional arousal experienced by young people in this context. Further support for this hypothesis is found in a diary study by Cummings, Goeke-Morey, Papp, and Dukewich (2002). These researchers found that children's insecure emotional and behavioral responses were associated with parents' negative emotionality and destructive conflict patterns, whereas children's secure emotional responding was associated with parents' positive emotional expression and constructive responses to conflict.

Our findings linking marital conflict and fathers' perceptions of their children suggest that marital conflict also affects the relationship between fathers and their sons and daughters, and indirectly affects the relationship between the siblings. In the study by Lindsey *et al.* (2002) mentioned earlier, the researchers focused primarily on mothers and their relationships with sons, but they did have fathers complete questionnaires, including the Conflict Tactics Scale (Straus, 1979), with regard to their own conflict behaviors. They found an association between fathers' displays of verbal and physical aggression towards their wives and sons' tendency to reciprocate their mothers' negative emotions, providing further evidence for links between marital and parent-child conflict.

Evidence that the sibling relationship is also disrupted by marital conflict comes from the study which showed that adolescents in families with destructive marital conflict tend to have negative views of each other (Noller *et al.*, 2000). These negative perceptions are likely to increase the potential for conflict and rivalry between siblings. The sibling relationship is likely to be further affected in families disrupted by parental separation or divorce, if older siblings take on inappropriate parenting roles (at least as seen by the younger sibling), and provide unwanted or excessive help (Sheehan *et al.*, 2003). It is important to remember, however, that these sibling relationships also provide necessary support, as young people try to deal with the breakdown of the relationship between their parents.

Another relevant factor is differential parenting. Where differential parenting is seen to occur (especially on the part of mothers), young people are more likely to have conflicted relationships with each other, and to use negative conflict behaviors in their interactions. These findings were robust, regardless of whether adolescents' conflict behavior was assessed using questionnaires, ratings by family members or ratings by an outside coder. These findings underline the pervasive effects of differential treatment in families, particularly in terms of relationships between siblings.

Disfavored children are also at risk of being insecure in attachment, low in self-esteem and high in anxiety. Given that insecurity seems to affect reactions to comparison and competition between siblings, a vicious cycle is likely to develop, particularly for the disfavored child, with insecurity and perceptions of "missing out" on parental resources reinforcing each other. Attachment insecurity is also likely to result in increasingly negative reactions to situations involving the sibling, with these reactions exacerbating problems in relationships with both the sibling and the parents.

Adolescents dealing both with disrupted relationships between their parents and with differential parental treatment are likely to be doubly disadvantaged in terms of relational and personal adjustment. Problems may even extend to relationships with peers, leaving adolescents with little real support, except perhaps for that from an older sibling (support that may be associated with some resentment and hostility).

Overall, the findings from the studies presented here support a systems view of the family. Specifically we have shown that each dyadic relationship affects other relationships and the family as a whole, and that patterns of influence are likely to include bi-directional and circular effects. We have explored links between the marital and parent-child relationships, and shown that highly conflicted or disrupted marital relationships tend to create a negative emotional climate in the family and impact on the ways in which parents treat their children. These difficult marital relationships can further affect the sibling relationship both directly and indirectly, and may even interfere with the development and maintenance of peer relationships. We have also seen how difficulties in the parent-child relationship, particularly in terms of differential treatment, affect adolescents' psychological adjustment and interactions with siblings. In addition, we have explored the effects that siblings have on each other's relational adjustment and emotional health, particularly in situations involving comparison and competition. Much more work is needed before the dynamics of family relationships are completely understood, but the studies presented in this chapter help to clarify some of these associations.

References

Amato, P. R., (2001). Children of divorce: An update of the Amato and Keith (1991) meta-analysis. *Journal of Family Psychology, 15*, 355–370.

Amato, P. R., & Keith, B. (1991). Parental divorce and the well-being of children: A meta-analysis. *Psychological Bulletin, 110*, 26–46.

Baker, L. A., & Daniels, D. (1990). Non-shared environmental influences and personality differences in adult twins. *Journal of Personality and Social Psychology, 58*, 103–110.

Bartholomew, K. (1990). Avoidance of intimacy: An attachment perspective. *Journal of Social and Personal Relationships, 7*, 147–178.

Bartholomew, K., & Horowitz, L. M. (1991). Attachment styles among young adults: A test of the four-category model. *Journal of Personality and Social Psychology, 61*, 226–244.

Belsky, J. (1981). Early human experience: A developmental perspective. *Developmental Psychology, 17*, 3–23.

Boer, F., Goedhart, A. W., & Treffers, P. D. A. (1992). Siblings and their parents. In F. Boer & J. Dunn (Eds.), *Children's sibling relationships: Developmental and Clinical issues* (pp. 41–54). Hillsdale, NJ: Lawrence Erlbaum Associates.

Buchanan, C. M., Maccoby, E. E., & Dornbusch, S. M. (1996). *Adolescents after divorce*. Cambridge, MA: Harvard University Press.

Coopersmith, S. (1975). Building self esteem in the classroom. In S. Coopersmith (Ed.) *Developing motivation in young children*. San Francisco: Allan.

Christensen, A. (1988). Dysfunctional interaction patterns in couples. In P. Noller & M. A. Fitzpatrick (Eds.), *Perspectives on marital interaction* (pp. 31–52). Avon: Multilingual Matters.

Christensen, A., & Sullaway, M. (1984). *Communication Patterns Questionnaire.* Unpublished questionnaire, University of California, Los Angeles, CA.

Christensen, A., & Heavey, C. L. (1990). Gender, power and marital conflict. *Journal of Personality and Social Psychology, 59,* 73–85.

Cummings, E. M., Goeke-Morey, M. C., Papp, L. M., & Dukewich, T. L. (2002). Children's responses to mothers' and fathers' emotionality and tactics in marital conflict in the home. *Journal of Family Psychology, 16,* 478–492.

Dadds, M. R., & Powell, M. B. (1991). The relationship of interparental conflict and global marital adjustment to aggression, anxiety and immaturity in aggressive and nonclinic children. *Journal of Abnormal Child Psychology, 19,* 553–567.

Daniels, D., Dunn, J., Furstenberg, F. F., & Plomin, R. (1985). Environmental differences within the family and adjustment differences within pairs of adolescent siblings. *Child Development, 56,* 764–774.

Daniels, D., & Plomin, R. (1985). Differential experience of siblings in the same family. *Developmental Psychology, 21,* 747–760.

Davies, P. T., & Cummings, E. M. (1994). Marital conflict and child adjustment: An emotional security hypothesis. *Psychological Bulletin, 116,* 387–411.

Davies, P. T., & Cummings, E. M. (1998). Exploring children's emotional security as a mediator of the link between marital relations and child adjustment. *Child Development, 69,* 124–139.

Dunn, J., Stocker, C., & Beardsall, L. (1989). *Sibling differences in self-esteem.* Paper presented at the Biennial Meeting of the Society for Research in Child Development, Kansas City, Kansas.

Feeney, J. A., Noller, P., & Hanrahan, M. (1994). Assessing adult attachment: Developments in the conceptualisation of security and insecurity. In M. B. Sperling & W. H. Berman (Eds.), *Attachment in adults: Theory, assessment and treatment* (pp. 128–152). New York: Guilford.

Furman, W., & Buhrmester, D. (1985). Children's perceptions of the personal relationships in their social networks. *Developmental Psychology, 21,* 1016–1024.

Hetherington, E. M. (1988). Parents, children and siblings: Six years after divorce. In R. Hinde & J. Stevenson-Hinde (Eds.), *Relationships within families: Mutual influences* (pp. 311–331). Oxford: Oxford University Press.

Hurd, K., Wooding, S., & Noller, P. (1999). Parent-adolescent relationships in families with depressed and self-harming adolescents. *Journal of Family Studies, 5*, 47–68.

Lindsey, E. W., MacKinnon-Lewis, C., Campbell, J., Frabutt, J. M., & Lamb, M. E. (2002). Marital conflict and boys' peer relationships: the mediating role of mother-son emotional reciprocity. Journal of Family Psychology, 16, 466–477.

Mann, B. J., & McKenzie, E. P. (1996). Pathways among marital functioning, parental behaviours and child behaviour problems in school-age boys. *Journal of Clinical Child Psychology, 25*, 183–191.

McGuire, S., McHale, S. M., & Updegraff, K. (1996). Children's perceptions of the sibling relationship in middle childhood: connections within and between family relationships. *Personal Relationships, 3*, 229–240.

Noller, P., Conway, S., Blakeley-Smith, A. & Beach (2001, July). *Comparison and competition in sibling relationships: a Self-Evaluation Maintenance perspective*. Paper presented at the International Conference on Personal Relationships, Prescott, Arizona.

Noller, P., Feeney, J. A., Peterson, G., & Sheehan, G. (1995). Learning conflict patterns in the family: Links between marital, parent-child and sibling relationships. In T. Socha, & G. Stamp (Eds.), *Parents, children and communication: Frontiers of theory and research* (pp. 273–298). Hillsdale, NJ: Erlbaum.

Noller, P., Feeney, J. A., Sheehan, & Peterson, C. (2000). Marital conflict patterns: Links with family conflict and family members' perceptions of one another. *Personal Relationships, 7*, 79–94.

Noller, P., & White, A. (1990). The validity of the Communication Patterns Questionnaire. *Psychological Assessment: A Journal of Consulting and Clinical Psychology, 2*, 478–482.

Osborne, L. N., & Fincham, F. D. (1996). Marital conflict, parent-child relationships and child adjustment: Does gender matter? *Merrill-Palmer Quarterly, 42*, 48–75.

Parke, R. D., & Tinsley, B. J. (1987). Family interaction in infancy. In J. D. Osofsky (Ed.) *Handbook of infant development* (pp. 579–641). New York: John Wiley & Sons Inc.

Peterson, C. (1990). Disagreement, negotiation and conflict resolution in families with adolescents. In P. Heaven & V. J. Callan (Eds.), *Adolescence: An Australian perspective* (pp. 66–79). Sydney, Australia: Harcourt Brace Jovanovich.

Rands, M., Levinger, G., & Mellinger, G. (1981). Patterns of conflict resolution and marital satisfaction. *Journal of Family Issues, 2*, 297–321.

Sheehan, G. (2000). *Parental favouritism: Implications for adolescents' family relationships*. Unpublished Ph.D. thesis, University of Queensland.

Sheehan, G., Darlington, Y., Noller, P., & Feeney, J. A. (2003, February). *Children's experiences of their sibling relationship during parental separation and divorce.* Paper presented at the Australian Institute of Family Studies Conference, Melbourne.

Sheehan, G., Feeney, J. A., Noller, P., & Peterson, C. (1999). *Sibling differences in communication: The influence of parental favouritism.* Unpublished manuscript, University of Queensland.

Sheehan, G., & Noller, P. (2002). Adolescents' perceptions of differential parenting: Links with attachment style and adolescent adjustment. *Personal Relationships, 9,* 173–190.

Spielberger, C., Gorsuch, R,, & Lushene (1968). *The State-Trait Anxiety Scale.* Palo Alto, CA. Consulting Psychologists' Press.

Stafford, L., & Dainton, M. (1995). Parent-child communication within the family system. In T. Socha, & G. Stamp (Eds.), *Parents, children and communication: Frontiers of theory and research* (pp. 273–298). Hillsdale, NJ: Erlbaum.

Straus, M. A. (1979). Measuring intrafamily conflict and violence: The Conflicts Tactics (CT) Scales. *Journal of Marriage and Family, 41,* 75–86.

Tesser, A. (1980). Self-esteem maintenance in family dynamics. *Journal of Personality and Social Psychology, 39,* 77–91.

Tesser, A. (1988). Toward a self-evaluation maintenance model of social behaviour. In L. Berkowitz (Ed.), *Advances in Experimental Social Psychology Vol. 21: Social psychological studies of the self: Perspectives and programs* (pp. 181–227) . San Diego, CA: Academic Press.

von Bertalanffy, L. (1962). General systems theory: A critical review. *General Systems Yearbook of the Society for General Systems Research, 7,* 1–20.

About the Editors and Contributors

Editors

Sik Hung NG, *Department of Applied Social Studies, City University of Hong Kong, Hong Kong SAR.* Sik-hung received his PhD from the University of Bristol. He was appointed to a Chair in Psychology at Victoria University of Wellington (1992), and now holds a Chair in Social Psychology at the City University of Hong Kong. His long-term research has been on power and language use; in recent years, he has begun work on positive ageing, intergenerational relations and the bicultural self. Books include *The Social Psychology of Power; Power in Language* (with James Bradac); and *Ages Ahead: Promoting Intergenerational Relationships* (with A. Weatherall, J. H. Liu, and C. S. F. Loong). He is a Fellow of the Royal Society of New Zealand.

Christopher N. CANDLIN, *Department of Linguistics, Division of Linguistics & Psychology, Macquarie University, Australia.* Chris is Senior Research Professor in the Department of Linguistics at Macquarie University, and Professor of Applied Linguistics in the Centre for Language and Communication at the UK Open University. Currently, he also holds a Leverhulme Visiting Professorship at the Centre for Health Communication Research at Cardiff University. His recent research includes adolescent discourse, stereotyping in educational materials in Hong Kong schools, quality of life and risk issues in healthcare in Hong Kong, and professional-client interaction in the delivery of healthcare to HIV+ persons in the Australian context. Books include *Writing: Texts, Processes and Practices (with K. Hyland); Legal Discourse in Multilingual and Multicultural Contexts* (with V.K. Bhatia and M. Gotti); and *Sociolinguistics and Social Theory* (with N. Coupland and S. Sarangi). He is a Fellow of the Royal Society of Arts, and has an honorary doctorate from Jyvaskyla University in Finland.

Chi Yue CHIU, *Department of Psychology, University of Illinois at Urbana-Champaign, USA.* Chi-yue received his PhD from Columbia University (New York) in 1994. He had taught in the Department of Psychology of the University of Hong Kong for several years, before he took up an Associate Professorship at the University of Illinois at Urbana-Champaign in 2002. His current research projects focus on the social psychology of culture, personality process, and language and cognition. Publications include: "Multicultural minds: A dynamic constructivist approach to culture and cognition" (with Y. Hong, M. Morris and V. Benet) in the *American Psychologist;* "Culture and psychology" (with D. Lehman and M. Schaller) in the *Annual Review of Psychology;* and a forthcoming chapter on "Cultural competence: Dynamic processes" (with Y. Hong) in the *Handbook of Motivation and Competence* edited by A. Elliot and C. S. Dweck.

Contributors

Jessica R. ABRAMS, *Department of Speech Communication, California Polytechnic University, USA.* Jessica studies intergroup communication, and has a particularly strong interest in the role of mass media in shaping perceptions of social group memberships, the relationship between communication and identity, and intergenerational communication. She recently published an article in *Communication Yearbook* and the *Handbook of International and Intercultural Communication.*

Terry Kit-fong AU, *Department of Psychology, University of Hong Kong, Hong Kong SAR.* Terry received her A.B. in Psychology & Social Relations from Harvard University in 1982 and her Ph.D. in Psychology from Stanford University in 1987. She was an Associate Professor at Brown University and a Professor at UCLA, and is currently a Chair Professor at the University of Hong Kong.

James J. BRADAC, *Department of Communication, University of California, Santa Barbara, USA.* James is Professor of

Communication at the University of California, Santa Barbara. He wrote *Language and Social Knowledge* (with Charles Berger) and *Power in Language* (with Sik Hung Ng), and edited *Message Effects in Communication Science*. He is past editor of *Human Communication Research* and is currently co-editor of the *Journal of Language and Social Psychology* (with Howard Giles). He is a Fellow of the International Communication Association and a recipient of the Outstanding Scholar Award from the Language and Social Interaction Division of the ICA (1994).

Jing CHEN, *Department of Psychology, University of Illinois at Urbana-Champaign, USA.* Jing received her bachelor's degree from Peking University, and is now a PhD student in the Social-Personality-Organizational Program of the Department of Psychology, University of Illinois at Urbana-Champaign. Her research interests include interpersonal dynamics within and between cultural groups, and the emotional attachment of immigrants in the process of acculturation.

Jacky Chau-kiu CHEUNG, *Department of Social Work, The Chinese University of Hong Kong, Hong Kong SAR.* Jacky has published articles on moral values, civic consciousness, political participation, delinquency, academic achievement, underachievement, work commitment, and quality of life. In his research, which is based on both students and the general population, he has attempted to investigate various causal factors such as gender, postmodernization, social class, fields of study, educational stratification, media exposure, lay theorizing, idol worship, and use of social services.

Richard CLÉMENT, *School of Psychology, University of Ottawa, Canada.* Richard is Professor of Psychology. His current research interests include issues related to bilingualism, second language acquisition and identity change in the acculturative process. He is particularly interested in the role of interethnic communication in the social and psychological adjustment of minority group members and immigrants. In 2001 he was awarded the Otto Klineberg Intercultural & International Relations Prize by the Society for the Psychological Study of Social Issues and in 2002, he received the Robert C. Gardner Award from the International Association of Language & Social Psychology.

Judith A. FEENEY, *School of Psychology, University of Queensland, Australia.* Judith received her PhD in 1991 from University of Queensland, where she is now an Associate Professor of Psychology. She has previously worked in teaching and counselling positions with a variety of client groups. She has published widely in the areas of marital and family relationships, interpersonal communication, and the link between personal relationships and health.

Cindy GALLOIS, *Centre for Social Research in Communication, The University of Queensland, Australia.* Cindy is Professor of Psychology and Director of the Centre for Social Research in Communication at the University of Queensland. Her research focuses on intergroup communication, social identity and communication accommodation, including identity and blaming in HIV prevention, communication between health professionals and patients, and identity and communication accommodation and their influence on hospital staff members' adjustment to major organisational change. A former President of the International Communication Association (2001–2002) and editor of *Human Communication Research* (1995–1998), she is currently the President of the International Association of Language and Social Psychology (2002–2004).

Peter GARRETT, *Centre for Language and Communication Research, Cardiff University, UK.* Peter's primary research interests are evaluational aspects of language and communication, intergroup and lifespan communication. He teaches language attitudes, persuasive communication, and communication research methods. His books include *Investigating Language Attitudes: Social*

Meanings of Dialect, Ethnicity and Performance (co-authored with Nikolas Coupland and Angie Williams), and *Approaches to Media Discourse* (co-edited with Allan Bell). He is editor of the journal *Language Awareness*.

Sophie GAUDET, *School of Psychology, University of Ottawa, Canada.* Sophie is a PhD candidate at the University of Ottawa. Her research interests include language and communication, ethnic identity, psychological adjustment, and inter-group processes.

Carla GIBBES, *School of Psychology, University of East London, UK.* Carla is a Visiting Lecturer at Birkbeck College, London, and a member of the teaching staff at the University of East London. She is currently conducting research into police work and psychological distress for her doctoral thesis.

Howard GILES, *Department of Communication, University of California, USA.* Howard has had a longstanding interest in matters intergroup as well as a commitment to the development of the social psychology of language and communication. Most recently, these interests and commitments have been accomplished by studying intergenerational communication and law enforcement-civilian interactions, both cross-culturally.

Michael A. HOGG, *School of Psychology, University of Queensland, Australia.* Michael received his PhD from Bristol University, and has held teaching and research positions at Bristol University, Macquarie University, the University of Melbourne, and Princeton University. He has also been a Visiting Professor at UCLA, UCSC, and UCSB. He is currently Professor of Social Psychology at the University of Queensland, and a Fellow of the Academy of the Social Sciences in Australia. Michael has been centrally involved in the development of the social identity perspective in social psychology, and has published 200 scientific books, chapters and articles in this area.

Mary Lee HUMMERT, *Communication Studies Department, University of Kansas, USA.* Mary Lee is a Professor at the University of Kansas, and studies the social cognitive processes linking age stereotypes and communication funded by the U.S. National Institute on Aging/National Institutes of Health. She has published extensively in communication, psychology, and gerontology journals, and is the co-editor of two books: *Interpersonal Communication in Older Adulthood: Interdisciplinary Research* (1994), and *Aging, Communication, and Health: Linking Research and Practice for Successful Aging* (2001). She is a Fellow of the Gerontological Society of America and a Giles-Nussbaum Distinguished Scholar in Communication and Aging.

Adam JAWORSKI, *Centre for Language and Communication Research, Cardiff University, UK.* Adam is Reader in Language and Communication and co-editor of book series *Oxford Studies in Sociolinguistics* (OUP, with Nikolas Coupland). He is Reviews Editor for the *Journal of Sociolinguistics,* and a member of the editorial boards of five other journals. His latest book is *Metalanguage: Social and Ideological Perspectives* (with Nikolas Coupland and Dariusz Galasiński). His current research interests include media language, non-verbal communication, visual communication, and the sociolinguistics of tourism and art criticism.

Pamela J. KALBFLEISCH, *School of Communication, University of North Dakota, USA.* Pamela received her doctorate in 1985 from Michigan State University. She is Professor and Director of the School of Communication at the University of North Dakota in Grand Forks. Her research interests include communication in mentoring relationships, deceptive communication, and gender and communication. She is the editor of several scholarly works including *Communication Yearbook 27, Communication Yearbook 28,* and *Interpersonal Communication: Evolving Interpersonal Communication,* and co-editor with Michael Cody of *Gender, Power, and Communication in Human Relationships.*

Amanda Lee KUNDRAT, (July 10, 1977 – January 21, 2003), *Department of Communication Arts and Sciences, The Pennsylvania State University, USA.* Amanda received her MA in Speech Communication from Penn State in 2001. Her thesis investigating invisible illness, identity, and contextual age across the lifespan received the 2002 NCA/ICA thesis of the year award in Health Communication and is published in Health Communication, 15, 2003. Amanda (co)authored over 15 competitively selected papers, two of which received top paper recognition within the NCA and the ICLASP. Amanda expected to complete her doctoral dissertation on communicating about organ donation during the summer of 2004.

Angel M.Y. LIN, *Department of English and Communication, City University of Hong Kong, Hong Kong SAR.* Angel received her PhD from the Ontario Institute for Studies in Education, University of Toronto, Canada. Her research and teaching have been centred on connections between face-to-face interactions and the larger sociocultural, historical, socioeconomic, institutional and political contexts in which they are situated. She works in the areas of youth cultural studies, feminist media studies, critical discourse analysis, school ethnography and classroom interaction studies. She is currently an Associate Professor at the City University of Hong Kong.

T. Wing LO, *Department of Applied Social Studies, City University of Hong Kong, Hong Kong SAR.* Wing is an Associate Professor of Social Work at the City University of Hong Kong and is the founding director of its Youth Studies Net. He received his PhD from the Institute of Criminology, Cambridge, and had worked as a social worker for seventeen years, helping young triad gangsters on the street. Since joining the City University of Hong Kong in 1990, he has led several large-scale reviews of services for young people and juvenile offenders and drawn up blueprints for the development of those services in Hong Kong and Macau.

Kimberly A. NOELS, *Department of Psychology, University of Alberta, Canada.* Kimberley is an Associate Professor. Her research concerns the social psychology of language and communication processes, with a focus on intercultural communication. Her publications include articles on motivation for language learning, the role of communication in the process of cross-cultural adaptation, and intergenerational communication from a cross-cultural perspective. Her research has been recognized through awards from the Modern Language Association, the International Association of Language and Social Psychology, and the Society for the Psychological Study of Social Issues.

Patricia NOLLER, *School of Psychology, University of Queensland, Australia.* Patricia is an Emeritus Professor at the University of Queensland. She is a Fellow of the Academy of the Social Sciences in Australia and of the National Council of Family Relations, USA. She is the founding editor of *Personal Relationships,* and former President, International Society for the study of Personal Relationships (1998-2000). She has published over 100 journal articles and book chapters, including *Nonverbal communication and marital interaction; Marriage and the family; The adolescent in the family; Communication in family relationships; Personal relationships across the lifespan; Becoming parents; Perspectives on marital interaction;* and *Understanding marriage.*

Hiroshi OTA, *Faculty of Studies on Contemporary Society, Aichi Shukutoku University, Japan.* Hiroshi received his PhD from the University of California Santa Barbara, and is an Associate Professor at Aichi Shukutoku University. His major research interests include communication between people in different age groups, communication between Japanese and people from other countries, and second language learning.

Nicholas A. PALOMARES, *Department of Communication, University of California, Santa Barbara, USA.* Nicholas is a doctoral student in the Department of Communication at UCSB. He is interested in language and conversational behavior in face-to-face and computer-mediated social interactions, such as strategic communication and goal pursuit, message production and comprehension, and language and gender.

Chris J. PAWSON, *School of Psychology, University of East London, UK.* Chris is a research psychologist affiliated to H.M. Government Home Office, U.K. He is a Visiting Lecturer at the University of London (Birkbeck College) and serves on the teaching staff at the University of East London. His research interests include peer relations, mentoring, and the development of pro-social and antisocial behavior. He is a founder member of the Commission for Children, Youth and Childhood (International Union of Anthropological and Ethnographic Studies).

Margaret Jane PITTS, *Department of Communication Arts and Sciences, The Pennsylvania State University, USA.* Maggie's research interests are in the area of intergroup communication, specifically identity transitions across the lifespan. She conducts naturalistic research among identity groups across contexts and borders. Her doctoral dissertation is the continuation of her earlier research on social identity and social support among student sojourners, for which she was awarded the 2002 outstanding thesis award from the International and Intercultural Division of the National Communication Association.

Scott A. REID, *Department of Communication, University of California, Santa Barbara, USA.* Scott is an Assistant Professor. His research interests are in social identity and self-categorization, with particular reference to power and language use in intergroup relations.

Ralph RENGER, *College of Public Health, University of Arizona, USA.* Ralph is an Associate Professor at the University of Arizona, the Director of Planning and Evaluation for the Arizona Area Health Education Centers (AHEC), and Chair of the National

AHEC Committee on Research and Evaluation. He teaches planning and evaluation in the graduate program at the University of Arizona College of Public Health. His evaluation experiences are diverse ranging from the evaluation of $28 million dollar neighborhood revitalization projects to assessing the effectiveness of mentoring programs for smaller non-profit organisations.

Marie Y. SAVUNDRANAYAGAM, *Gerontology Center, University of Kansas, USA.* Marie is currently in the doctoral program in gerontology and working on a concentration in Health Care Outcomes Management and Research at the University of Kansas. Her research interests include communication problems associated with dementia, caregiver burden, and health care policies associated with home care and long-term care.

Rosalind TENNANT, *National Centre for Social Research, UK.* Rosalind is a researcher at the National Centre for Social Research, Britain's largest independent social research organization. She has worked in the field of research for several years, first in quantitative consumer market research, and is now a dedicated qualitative social researcher. Rosalind gained a BA Communication and MA Research in Language and Communication from the University of Wales, Cardiff.

Crispin THURLOW, *Department of Communication, University of Washington, USA.* Crispin is an Assistant Professor at the University of Washington. He moved to Seattle in 2003 after three years lecturing in the Centre for Language & Communication Research at Cardiff University. His main research interests are in communication and new technologies, lifespan communication and adolescence, transcultural communication and global tourism. Work in these areas has been published in places such as the *Journal of Language and Social Psychology, Discourse Analysis Online, Language Awareness and the Journal of Sociolinguistics.* Crispin is Associate Editor of *Language & Intercultural Communication.*

Bernadette WATSON, *UQ Business School, University of Queensland, Australia.* Bernadette received her PhD from the University of Queensland, and is a Lecturer in the UQ Business School in Brisbane, Australia. Her research interests centre on health communication and organizational change in the workplace. Currently, she is carrying research into the impact of communication on nurses' job satisfaction, stress and willingness to stay in the field; on effective interactions between health professionals and patients; and on organisational changes and IT implementation in government organisations. Bernadette is a member of the Centre for Social Research in Communication at UQ.

Angie WILLIAMS, *Centre for Language and Communication Research, Cardiff University, UK.* Angie's main research interest is in intergroup communication particularly as it relates to culture, age, lifespan and health issues. She has published extensively on these topics in outlets such as the *Journal of Language and Social Psychology, Human Communication Research,* and *Communication Research.* Her recently published books include *Intergenerational Communication Across the Lifespan* (with Jon Nussbaum) and *Investigating Language Attitudes: Social Meanings of Dialect, Ethnicity and Performance* (with Peter Garrett & Nik Coupland).

Rong ZHOU, *South China Normal University, Guangzhou, People's Republic of China.* Rong is a Professor of English at South China Normal University. She received her MA in TESOL from the Institute of Education, London University and her PhD in education from Southwest China Normal University. Her research interests include applied linguistics, psycholinguistics and sociolinguistics.

Index

511